CIMA

STUDY TEXT

Foundation Paper 3b

Business Law

IN THIS JULY 2002 EDITION:

- Targeted to the **syllabus** and **learning outcomes**
- **Quizzes and questions** to check your understanding
- Clear layout and style designed to save you time
- Plenty of **exam-style** questions
- **Chapter Roundups** and summaries to help revision
- **Mind Maps** to integrate the key points

NEW IN THIS JULY 2002 EDITION

- Two exam style question banks reflecting the two formats of the paper

BPP's **MCQ cards** and **i-Pass** also support this paper.

BPP Publishing
July 2002

First edition 2000
Third edition July 2002

ISBN 0 7517 3752 6 (Previous edition 0 7517 3159 5)

British Library Cataloguing-in-Publication Data
A catalogue record for this book
is available from the British Library

Published by

BPP Publishing Ltd
Aldine House, Aldine Place
London W12 8AW

www.bpp.com

Printed in Great Britain by WM Print
45-47 Frederick Street
Walsall
West Midlands
WS2 9NE

All our rights reserved. No part of this publication may be reproduced, stored in a retrieval system or transmitted, in any form or by any means, electronic, mechanical, photocopying, recording or otherwise, without the prior written permission of BPP Publishing Limited.

We are grateful to the Chartered Institute of Management Accountants for permission to reproduce past examination questions and questions from the pilot paper. We are also grateful to the Association of Chartered Certified Accountants for permission to reproduce past examination questions. The suggested solutions to the illustrative questions have been prepared by BPP Publishing Limited.

©
BPP Publishing Limited
2002

BPP
PUBLISHING

MULTIPLE CHOICE QUESTION CARDS

Multiple choice questions form a large part of the exam. To give you further practice in this style of question, we have produced a bank of 150 **multiple choice question cards**, covering the syllabus. This bank contains exam style questions in a format to help you revise on the move.

COMPUTER-BASED LEARNING PRODUCTS FROM BPP

For **self-testing**, try **i-Pass,** which offers a large number of objective test questions, particularly useful where **objective test questions** form part of the exam.

See the order form at the back of this text for details of these innovative learning tools.

VIRTUAL CAMPUS

The Virtual Campus uses BPP's wealth of teaching experience to produce a fully **interactive** e-learning resource **delivered via the Internet**. The site offers comprehensive **tutor support** and features areas such as **study**, **practice**, **email service**, **revision** and **useful resources**.

Visit our website www.bpp.com/virtualcampus/cima to sample aspects of the campus free of charge.

LEARNING TO LEARN ACCOUNTANCY

BPP's ground-breaking **Learning to learn accountancy** book is designed to be used both at the outset of your CIMA studies and throughout the process of learning accountancy. It challenges you to consider how you study and gives you helpful hints about how to approach the various types of paper which you will encounter. It can help you **get your studies both subject and exam focused**, enabling you to **acquire knowledge, practice and revise efficiently and effectively**.

THE BPP STUDY TEXT

Aims of this Study Text

To provide you with the knowledge and understanding, skills and application techniques that you need if you are to be successful in your exams

This Study Text has been written around the **Business Law** syllabus.

- It is **comprehensive**. It covers the syllabus content. No more, no less.
- It is written at the **right level**. Each chapter is written with CIMA's precise learning outcomes in mind.
- It is targeted to the **exam**. We have taken account of the pilot paper, questions put to the examiners at the recent CIMA conference and the assessment methodology.

To allow you to study in the way that best suits your learning style and the time you have available, by following your personal Study Plan (see page (viii))

You may be studying at home on your own until the date of the exam, or you may be attending a full-time course. You may like to (and have time to) read every word, or you may prefer to (or only have time to) skim-read and devote the remainder of your time to question practice. Wherever you fall in the spectrum, you will find the BPP Study Text meets your needs in designing and following your personal Study Plan.

To tie in with the other components of the BPP Effective Study Package to ensure you have the best possible chance of passing the exam (see page (vi))

BPP STUDY TEXTS AND THE CIMA CERTIFICATE IN BUSINESS ACCOUNTING

In supporting your Foundation level studies, this text is your passport to success in the **CIMA Certificate in Business Accounting**, awarded from May 2002 to students who complete their Foundation level exams.

Recommended period of use	Elements of the BPP Effective Study Package
From the outset and throughout	**Learning to learn accountancy** Read this invaluable book as you begin your studies and refer to it as you work through the various elements of the BPP Effective Study Package. It will help you to acquire knowledge, practice and revise, both efficiently and effectively.
Three to twelve months before the exam	**Study Text** Use the Study Text to acquire knowledge, understanding, skills and the ability to use application techniques.
Throughout	**Virtual Campus** Study, practice, revise and take advantage of other useful resources with BPP's fully interactive e-learning site with comprehensive tutor support.
Throughout	**MCQ cards and i-Pass** Revise your knowledge and ability to use application techniques, as well as practising this key exam question format, with 150 multiple choice questions. **i-Pass**, our computer-based testing package, provides objective test questions in a variety of formats and is ideal for self-assessment.
One to six months before the exam	**Practice & Revision Kit** Try the multiple choice questions and objective test questions for your chosen assessment format. Then attempt the mock paper-based exam or the mock computer based assessment.
From three months before the exam until the last minute	**Passcards** Work through these short, memorable notes which are focused on what is most likely to come up in the exam you will be sitting.
One to six months before the exam	**Success Tapes** These audio tapes cover the vital elements of your syllabus in less than 90 minutes per subject. Each tape also contains exam hints to help you fine tune your strategy.
Three to twelve months before the exam	**Breakthrough Videos** Use a Breakthrough Video to supplement your Study Text. They give you clear tuition on key exam subjects and allow you the luxury of being able to pause or repeat sections until you have fully grasped the topic.

HELP YOURSELF STUDY FOR YOUR CIMA EXAMS

Exams for professional bodies such as CIMA are very different from those you have taken at college or university. You will be under **greater time pressure before** the exam - as you may be combining your study with work. There are many different ways of learning and so the BPP Study Text offers you a number of different tools to help you through. Here are some hints and tips: they are not plucked out of the air, but **based on research and experience**. (You don't need to know that long-term memory is in the same part of the brain as emotions and feelings - but it's a fact anyway.)

The right approach

1 **The right attitude**

Believe in yourself	Yes, there is a lot to learn. Yes, it is a challenge. But thousands have succeeded before and you can too.
Remember why you're doing it	Studying might seem a grind at times, but you are doing it for a reason: to advance your career.

2 **The right focus**

Read through the Syllabus and learning outcomes	These tell you what you are expected to know and are supplemented by Exam Focus Points in the text.
Study the Exam Paper section	Past papers are a reasonable guide of what you should expect in the exam.

3 **The right method**

The big picture	You need to grasp the detail - but keeping in mind how everything fits into the big picture will help you understand better. • The **Introduction** of each chapter puts the material in context. • The **Syllabus content, learning outcomes** and **Exam focus points** show you what you need to **grasp.** • **Mind Maps** show the links and key issues in key topics.
In your own words	To absorb the information (and to practise your written communication skills), it helps to **put it into your own words.** • **Take notes.** • Answer the **questions** in each chapter. As well as helping you absorb the information, you will practise the assessment formats used in the exam and your written communication skills, which become increasingly important as you progress through your CIMA exams. • Draw **mind maps**. We have some examples. • Try 'teaching' a subject to a colleague or friend.

Give yourself cues to jog your memory	The BPP Study Text uses **bold** to **highlight key points** and **icons** to identify key features, such as **Exam focus points** and **Key terms.** • Try **colour coding** with a highlighter pen. • Write **key points** on cards.

4 **The right review**

Review, review, review	It is a **fact** that regularly reviewing a topic in summary form can **fix it in your memory**. Because **review** is so important, the BPP Study Text helps you to do so in many ways. • **Chapter roundups** summarise the key points in each chapter. Use them to recap each study session. • The **Quick quiz** is another review technique to ensure that you have grasped the essentials. • Go through the **Examples** in each chapter a second or third time.

Developing your personal Study Plan

One thing that the BPP Learning to learn accountancy book emphasises is the need to prepare a study plan (and to use it!). Planning and sticking to the plan are key elements of learning success.

There are four steps you should work through.

Step 1. How do you learn?

First you need to be aware of your style of learning. The BPP Learning to learn accountancy book commits a chapter to this **self-discovery** at the outset. What types of intelligence do you display when learning? You might be advised to brush up on certain study skills before launching into this Study Text.

BPP's **Learning to learn accountancy** book helps you to identify what intelligences you show more strongly and then identifies how you can tailor your study process through your preferences. It also includes handy hints on how to develop intelligences you exhibit less strongly, which might be needed as you study accountancy.

Are you a **theorist** or more **practical**? If you would rather get to grips with a theory before trying to apply it in practice, you should follow the study sequence below. If the reverse is true (you like to know learning theory before you do so), you might be advised to flick through your Study Text chapter and look at questions, case studies and examples (Steps 7, 8 and 9 in the **Suggested Study sequence** below) before reading through the detail of theory.

Step 2. How much time do you have?

Work out the time you have available per week, given the following.

- The standard you have set yourself
- The time you need to set aside later for work on the Practice & Revision Kit and Passcards
- The other exam(s) you are sitting
- Very importantly, practical matters such as work, travel, exercise, sleep and social life

		Hours
Note your time available in box A.	A	

Step 3. Allocate your time

• Take the time you have available per week for this Study Text shown in box A, multiply it by the number of weeks available and insert the result in box B.	B	
• Divide the figure in Box B by the number of chapters in this text and insert the result in box C.	C	

Remember that this is only a rough guide. Some of the chapters in this book are longer and more complicated than others, and you will find some subjects easier to understand than others.

Step 4. Implement

Set about studying each chapter in the time shown in box C, following the key study steps in the order suggested by your particular learning style.

This is your personal **Study Plan**. You should try and combine it with the study sequence outlines below. You may want to modify the sequence a little (as has been suggested above) to adapt it to your **personal style.**

Suggested study sequence

It is likely that the best way to approach this Study Text is to tackle the chapters in the order in which you find them. Taking into account your individual learning style, you could follow this sequence.

Key study steps	Activity
Step 1 **Topic list**	Each numbered topic is a numbered section in the chapter.
Step 2 **Introduction**	This gives you the **big picture** in terms of the **context** of the chapter, the **content** you will cover, and the **learning outcomes** the chapter assesses - in other words, it sets your **objectives for study.**
Step 3 **Knowledge brought forward boxes**	In these we highlight information and techniques that it is assumed you have 'brought forward' with you from your earlier studies. If there are topics which have changed recently due to legislation for example, these topics are explained in more detail.
Step 4 **Explanations**	Proceed methodically through the chapter, reading each section thoroughly and making sure you understand.

Key study steps	Activity
Step 5 **Key terms and Exam focus points**	• **Key terms** can often earn you *easy marks* if you state them clearly and correctly in an appropriate exam answer (and they are highlighted in the index at the back of the text). • **Exam focus points** give you a good idea of how we think the examiner intends to examine certain topics.
Step 6 **Note taking**	Take brief notes, if you wish. Avoid the temptation to copy out too much. Remember that being able to put something into your own words is a sign of being able to understand it. If you find you cannot explain something you have read, read it again before you make the notes.
Step 7 **Examples**	Follow each through to its solution very carefully.
Step 8 **Case examples**	Study each one, and try to add flesh to them from your own experience – they are designed to show how the topics you are studying come alive (and often come unstuck) in the real world.
Step 9 **Questions**	Make a very good attempt at each one.
Step 10 **Answers**	Check yours against ours, and make sure you understand any discrepancies.
Step 11 **Chapter roundup**	Work through it very carefully, to make sure you have grasped the major points it is highlighting.
Step 12 **Quick quiz**	When you are happy that you have covered the chapter, use the **Quick quiz** to check how much you have remembered of the topics covered and to practise questions in a variety of formats.
Step 13 **Question(s) in the Exam question bank**	Either at this point, or later when you are thinking about revising, make a full attempt at the **Question(s)** suggested at the very end of the chapter. You can find these at the end of the Study Text, along with the **Answers** so you can see how you did. If you have purchased the **MCQ cards** or **i-Pass**, use these too.

Short of time: Skim study technique?

You may find you simply do not have the time available to follow all the key study steps for each chapter, however you adapt them for your particular learning style. If this is the case, follow the **skim study** technique below (the icons in the Study Text will help you to do this).

- Study the chapters in the order you find them in the Study Text.
- For each chapter, follow the key study steps 1-3, and then skim-read through step 4. Jump to step 11, and then go back to step 5. Follow through steps 7 and 8, and prepare outline answers to questions (steps 9/10). Try the Quick quiz (step 12), following up any items you can't answer, then do a plan for the Question (step 13), comparing it against our answers. You should probably still follow step 6 (note taking), although you may decide simply to rely on the BPP Passcards for this.

Moving on...

However you study, when you are ready to embark on the practice and revision phase of the BPP Effective Study Package, you should still refer back to this Study Text, both as a source of **reference** (you should find the index particularly helpful for this) and as a way to **review** (the Chapter roundups and Quick quizzes help you here).

And remember to keep careful hold of this Study Text – you will find it invaluable in your work.

SYLLABUS AND LEARNING OUTCOMES

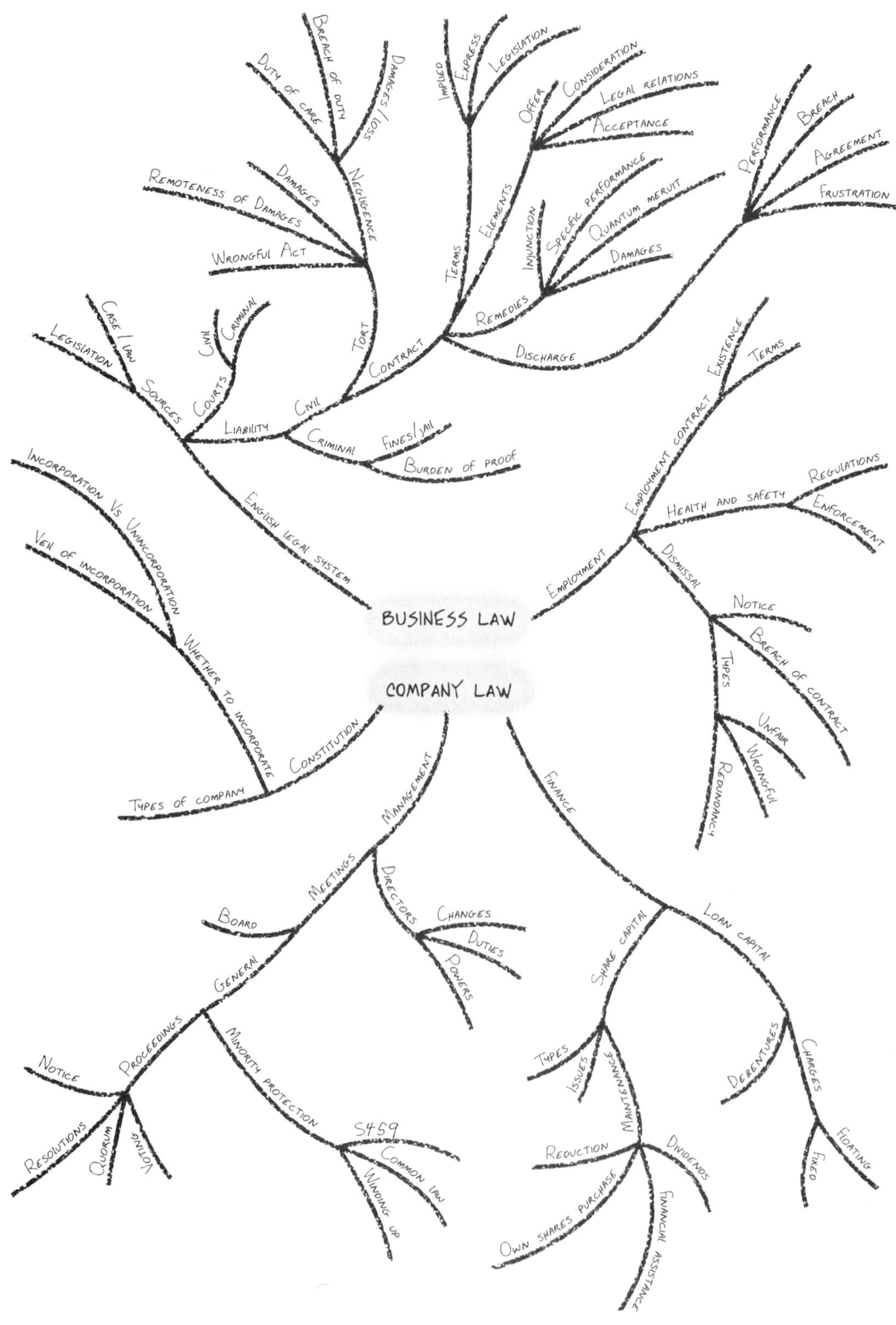

Syllabus overview

The Business Law syllabus deals with those aspects of law which affect businesses and which contribute towards establishing the competence of the Management Accountant. By way of introduction, it covers fundamental elements of the English legal system, and uses professional negligence as the vehicle for demonstrating the system of judicial precedent. The syllabus then proceeds to look at the essentials of establishing and performing simple contracts and the remedies available in the event of a breach.

As an introduction to company law, the syllabus then proceeds to look at the essential characteristics of the various forms of business organisation. Following this introduction the emphasis is placed upon the company limited by shares and the rules relating to company formation, finance and management. Candidates may be required to present their explanations in the form of a letter or memorandum.

Aims

This syllabus aims to test the candidate's ability to:

- Explain fundamental aspects of the organisation and operation of the English legal system
- Explain the elements of the tort of negligence and the manner in which the tort impacts upon professional advisers
- Identify and explain the essential elements of a single contract, what is regarded as adequate performance of the simple contract, and the remedies available to the innocent party in the event of a breach
- Explain the essential differences between sole traderships, partnerships, and companies limited by shares
- Explain the way in which companies are administered, financed and managed
- Apply legal knowledge to business problems and communicate the explanations in an appropriate form

Assessment

There will be a written paper of 2 hours. Initially, objective testing will form a minimum of 50% of the marks awarded on the paper.

Learning outcomes and syllabus content

(i) The English legal system 10%

Learning outcomes

On completion of their studies students should be able to:

- Explain the manner in which behaviour within society is regulated by civil and criminal law
- Identify and explain the sources of English law
- Explain and illustrate the operation of the doctrine of precedent by reference to the elements of the tort of negligence, ie duty, breach and damage/loss/injury
- Explain the application of the tort to professional advisers

Syllabus content	**Covered in chapter**
• The sources of English law	1
• The system of judicial precedent	1
• The essential elements of the tort of negligence, including duty, breach and damage / loss / injury	2
• The liability of professionals in respect of negligent advice	2

(ii) Establishing contractual obligations 10%

Learning outcomes

On completion of their studies students should be able to:

- Identify the essential elements of a valid simple contract and situations where the law requires the contract to be in a particular form
- Explain how the law determines whether negotiating parties have reached agreement
- Explain what the law regards as consideration sufficient to make the agreement enforceable
- Explain when the parties will be regarded as intending the agreement to be legally binding
- Explain when an apparently valid agreement may be avoided because of misrepresentations

Syllabus content	**Covered in chapter**
• The essential elements of a valid simple contract	3
• The legal status of the various types of statements which may be made by negotiating parties. Enforceable offers and acceptances, and the application of the rules to standard form contracts and modern forms of communication	3
• The meaning and importance of consideration	3
• The principles for establishing that the parties intend their agreement to have contractual force	3
• How a contract is affected by a misrepresentation	3

(iii) Performing the contract-10%

Learning outcomes

On completion of their studies students should be able to:

- Explain how the contents of a contract are established
- Explain the status of contractual terms and the possible repercussions of non-performance
- Explain how the law controls the use of unfair terms in respect of both consumer and non-consumer business agreements
- Explain what the law regards as performance of the contract, and valid and invalid reasons for non-performance

Syllabus content	**Covered in chapter**
• Incorporation of express and implied terms	4
• Conditions and warranties and the nature and effect of both types of term	4
• The main provisions of sale of goods and supply of services legislation	4
• The manner in which the law controls the use of exclusion clauses and unfair terms in consumer and non-consumer transactions	4
• The level of performance sufficient to discharge contractual obligations	5
• Valid reasons for non-performance by way of agreement, breach by the other party and frustration	5

(iv) Contractual breakdown-10%

Learning outcomes

On completion of their studies students should be able to:

- Explain the type of breach necessary to cause contractual breakdown
- Describe the remedies which are available for serious and minor breaches of contract

Syllabus content	**Covered in chapter**
• The remedies of specific performance, injunction, recission, and requiring a contract party to pay the agreed price	5
• Causation and remoteness of damage	5
• The quantification of damages	5

(v) The law of employment-10%

Learning outcomes

On completion of their studies students should be able to:

- Distinguish between employees and independent contractors and explain the importance of the distinction
- Explain how the contents of a contract of employment are established
- Explain the distinction between unfair and wrongful dismissal
- Demonstrate an awareness of how employers and employees are affected by health and safety legislation, including the consequences of a failure to comply

Syllabus content	**Covered in chapter**
• The tests used to distinguish an employee from an independent contractor	6
• The express and implied terms of a contract of employment	6
• Unfair and wrongful dismissal	7
• An outline of the main rules relating to health and safety at work, sanctions on employers for non-compliance and remedies for employees	7

(vi) Company formation-15%

Learning outcomes

On completion of their studies students should be able to:

- Explain the essential characteristics of the different forms of business organisations
- Explain the concept and practical effect of corporate personality
- Explain the difference between public and private companies
- Explain the distinction between establishing a company by registration and purchasing 'off the shelf'
- Explain the purpose and legal status of the memorandum and articles of association
- Explain the ability of a company to contract
- Explain the main advantages and disadvantages of carrying on business through the medium of a company limited by shares

Syllabus content	**Covered in chapter**
• The essential characteristic of sole traderships / practitionerships, partnerships and companies limited by shares	8
• Corporate personality and its legal consequences	8
• 'Lifting the corporate veil' both at common law and by statute	8
• The distinction between public and private companies	8
• The procedure for registering a company, the advantages of purchasing a company 'off the shelf', and the purpose and contents of the memorandum and articles of association	9
• Corporate capacity to contract	9

(vii) Corporate administration-10%

Learning outcomes

On completion of their studies students should be able to:

- Explain the use and procedure of board meetings and general meetings of shareholders
- Explain the voting rights of directors and shareholders
- Identify the various types of shareholder resolutions

Syllabus content	**Covered in chapter**
• Board meetings: when used and the procedure at the meeting	10
• Annual and Extraordinary General Meetings: when used and the procedure at the meeting	10
• Company resolutions and the uses of each type of resolution	10

(viii) Corporate finance-10%

Learning outcomes

On completion of their studies students should be able to:

- Explain the nature of a share and the essential characteristics of the different types of share
- Explain the procedure for the issue of shares, and the acceptable forms of payment
- Explain the legal repercussions of issuing shares for an improper purpose
- Explain the maintenance of capital principle and the exceptions to the principle
- Explain the procedure to increase and reduce share capital
- Explain the ability of a company to take secured and unsecured loans, the different types of security and the registration procedure

Syllabus content	**Covered in chapter**
• The rights attaching to the different types of shares issued by companies	14
• The procedure for issuing shares	14
• The purposes for which shares may be issued	14
• The maintenance of capital principle and the ability of a company to redeem, purchase and provide financial assistance for the purchase of its own shares, and the situations in which such powers are useful	14
• The rules for the reduction and increase of share capital	15
• The ability of a company to borrow money and the procedure to be followed	15
• Unsecured loans, and the nature and effect of fixed and floating charges	15

(ix) Corporate management- 15%

Learning outcomes

On completion of their studies students should be able to:

- Explain the procedure for the appointment, retirement, disqualification and removal of directors
- Identify the power and duties owed by directors to the company, shareholders, creditors and employees
- Explain the rules dealing with the possible imposition of personal liability upon the directors of insolvent companies
- Identify and contrast the rights of shareholders with the Board of a company
- Explain the qualifications, powers and duties of the company secretary

Syllabus content	**Covered in chapter(s)**
• The appointment, retirement and removal of directors	12
• Directors' powers and duties	12
• Fraudulent and wrongful trading, preferences and transactions at an undervalue	12, 15
• The division of powers between the board and the shareholders	12
• The rights of majority and minority shareholders	13
• The qualifications, powers and duties of the company secretary	11

THE EXAM PAPER

Format of the paper

November 2001		*Number of marks*
Section A:	objective test questions	50
Section B:	two questions from three	50
		100

Time allowed: 2 hours

Analysis of papers

May 2002

Section A

1.1 Criminal/civil law
1.2 Sources of law
1.3 Negligence
1.4 Offer
1.5 Offer and acceptance
1.6 Consideration
1.7 Terms
1.8 Warranties and conditions
1.9 Specific performance
1.10 Damages
1.11 Employee/independent contractor
1.12 Terms of a contract
1.13 Business organisation
1.14 Plcs
1.15 Shelf companies
1.16 Object clause
1.17 Memorandum of association
1.18 Elective resolutions
1.19 Pre-emption
1.20 Authorised share capital
1.21 Removal of a director
1.22 Directors' remuneration
1.23 Company management
1.24 Fiduciary duties
1.25 Wrongful trading

Section B

2 Company incorporation
3 Misrepresentation
4 Shares, voting rights, debentures

November 2001

Section A

1.1 Common law and equity
1.2 Court system: criminal law
1.3 Negligence
1.4 Employment particulars

1.5 Employment implied contract terms
1.6 Simple contracts
1.7 Offer and acceptance
1.8 Terms of a contract
1.9 Consideration
1.10 Remedies for breach
1.11 Performance/frustration
1.12 Damages/specific performance
1.13 Company liability
1.14 Partnership formation
1.15 Company registration
1.16 Share capital
1.17 Articles of association
1.18 Resolutions
1.19 Shares
1.20 Elective resolutions
1.21 Public/private companies
1.22 Preferences
1.23 Wrongful trading
1.24 Breach of fiduciary duty
1.25 Directors' interests in contracts

Section B

2 Contract: agreement, exclusion clauses
3 Employee status, dismissal
4 Directors' powers, borrowing, articles of association

May 2001

Section A

1.1 Court structure
1.2 Judicial precedent
1.3 Damages for negligence
1.4 Vicarious liability
1.5 Employment contract
1.6 Unfair dismissal
1.7 Employer's duties
1.8 Intention
1.9 Misrepresentation
1.10 Discharge of contract
1.11 Remedies for breach
1.12 Consideration
1.13 Exclusion clauses
1.14 Companies
1.15 Partnership
1.16 Share capital/memorandum
1.17 Share capital/pre-emption
1.18 Public and private companies
1.19 Articles/resolutions
1.20 Directors
1.21 Financial assistance
1.22 Resolutions
1.23 Articles
1.24 Charges

1.25 Elective resolutions

Section B

2 Sources of law, professional negligence
3 Terms of a contract, exclusion clauses
4 Directors, shareholders' powers

Analysis of pilot paper

Section A

1.1 English and EU law
1.2 Negligence
1.3 Liability for employees
1.4 Employer's implied duties
1.5 Legal relations
1.6 Fraudulent misrepresentation
1.7 Specific performance
1.8 Frustration
1.9 Breach of contract
1.10 Liability of company and partnership
1.11 Partnerships
1.12 Company's capacity to contract
1.13 Directors and shareholders
1.14 Short notice
1.15 Board of directors
1.16 Maintenance of capital
1.17 Issue of shares
1.18 Removal of director
1.19 Company secretary
1.20 Directors' fiduciary duties

Section B

2 Elements of contract; form of contract; partial performance
3 Documents on registration; off-the-shelf companies; separate legal personality
4 Characteristics of shares; issue of shares; appointment of director

WHAT THE EXAMINER MEANS

The table below has been prepared by CIMA to help you interpret exam questions.

Learning objective	Verbs used	Definition
1 Knowledge What you are expected to know	• List • State • Define	• Make a list of • Express, fully or clearly, the details of/facts of • Give the exact meaning of
2 Comprehension What you are expected to understand	• Describe • Distinguish • Explain • Identify • Illustrate	• Communicate the key features of • Highlight the differences between • Make clear or intelligible/state the meaning of • Recognise, establish or select after consideration • Use an example to describe or explain something
3 Application Can you apply your knowledge?	• Apply • Calculate/compute • Demonstrate • Prepare • Reconcile • Solve • Tabulate	• To put to practical use • To ascertain or reckon mathematically • To prove with certainty or to exhibit by practical means • To make or get ready for use • To make or prove consistent/compatible • Find an answer to • Arrange in a table
4 Analysis Can you analyse the detail of what you have learned?	• Analyse • Categorise • Compare and contrast • Construct • Discuss • Interpret • Produce	• Examine in detail the structure of • Place into a defined class or division • Show the similarities and/or differences between • To build up or compile • To examine in detail by argument • To translate into intelligible or familiar terms • To create or bring into existence
5 Evaluation Can you use your learning to evaluate, make decisions or recommendations?	• Advise • Evaluate • Recommend	• To counsel, inform or notify • To appraise or assess the value of • To advise on a course of action

TACKLING MULTIPLE CHOICE QUESTIONS

The MCQs in your exam contain four possible answers. You have to **choose the option that best answers the question**. The three incorrect options are called distracters. There is a skill in answering MCQs quickly and correctly. By practising MCQs you can develop this skill, giving you a better chance of passing the exam.

You may wish to follow the approach outlined below, or you may prefer to adapt it.

Step 1. **Skim read** all the MCQs and **identify** what appear to be the **easier** questions.

Step 2. Attempt each question - **starting with the easier questions** identified in Step 1. Read the question thoroughly. You may prefer to work out the answer before looking at the options, or you may prefer to look at the options at the beginning. Adopt the method that works best for you.

Step 3. Read the four options and see if one matches your own answer. **Be careful with numerical** questions, as the distracters are designed to match answers that incorporate common errors. Check that your calculation is correct. Have you followed the requirement exactly? Have you included every stage of the calculation?

Step 4. You may **find that none of the options matches your answer**.

- Re-read the question to ensure that you understand it and are answering the requirement
- Eliminate any obviously wrong answers
- Consider which of the remaining answers is the most likely to be correct and select the option

Step 5. If you are still **unsure** make a note **and continue to the next question**.

Step 6. **Revisit unanswered** questions. When you come back to a question after a break you often find you are able to answer it correctly straight away. If you are still unsure have a guess. You are not penalised for incorrect answers, so **never leave a question unanswered!**

After extensive practice and revision of OTs, you may find that you recognise a question when you sit the exam. Be aware that the detail and/or requirement may be different. If the question seems familiar read the requirement and options carefully - do not assume that it is identical.

TACKLING OBJECTIVE TEST QUESTIONS IN THE PAPER-BASED EXAM

What is an objective test question?

An objective test (**OT**) question is made up of some form of **stimulus**, usually a question, and a **requirement** to do something.

(a) **Filling in a blank or blanks in a sentence**

(b) **Listing items in rank order**

(c) **Stating a definition**

(d) **Identifying a key issue, term or figure**

(e) **Calculating a specific figure**

(f) **Completing gaps in a set of data where the relevant numbers can be calculated from the information given**

(g) **Identifying points/zones/ranges/areas on graphs or diagrams**

(h) **Matching items or statements**

(i) **Stating whether statements are true or false**

(j) **Writing brief (in a specified number of words) explanations to the data given**

Multiple choice questions (MCQs) – selecting the most appropriate option from a number of options provided – are the most common form of OT questions. We looked at them in detail on page (xxiii).

OT questions in the paper-based exam

Section A of the paper will consist of 25 MCQs worth 50 marks.

In Section B of the paper, which will be worth **50 marks**, you will be provided with two or more **scenarios** and will be asked **several OT questions** about each scenario.

There will be **no optional questions**, you will have to attempt all the questions in both sections.

CIMA has offered the following **guidance** about OT questions in the exam.

- **Only your answers will be marked,** not workings or any justifications.
- If you **exceed a specified limit on the number of words** you can use in an answer, you will **not be awarded any marks**.
- If you make **more than one attempt** at a question, clearly **cross through** any answers that you do not want to submit. If you don't do this, only your first answer will be marked.

We strongly suggest therefore, that you **take note of the guidance given above when answering OT questions in the paper-based exam.**

November 2002 is the last sitting of the paper in this format. Candidates sitting this format of the paper in November should ensure they work through the Quick Quizzes in this book, which reflect some of the formats discussed above, and the May 2002 exam paper, in the Exam Question Bank (Paper-Based Format).

Part A

The English legal system

Chapter 1

INTRODUCTION TO ENGLISH LAW

Topic list		Syllabus reference	Ability required
1	Criminal and civil liability	(i)	Comprehension
2	Features and sources of English law	(i)	Comprehension
3	Case law and judicial precedent	(i)	Comprehension
4	Legislation	(i)	Comprehension
5	European Community law	(i)	Comprehension

Introduction

The **English legal system** consists of practical and down-to-earth sets of procedures and rules designed to provide resolutions to ordinary problems. Publicity tends to focus on the higher courts, such as the Court of Appeal and the House of Lords. However the vast majority of cases are heard in the magistrates' courts or the county courts.

Many people, when they think of the law, have an image in their minds of judge and jury, or 'cops and robbers'. These are manifestations of **criminal** law. Business conduct is generally regulated by **civil** law. The distinction between criminal and civil law is fundamental to the English legal system. In order to understand the English legal system, it is necessary to understand the differences between criminal and civil cases.

There are four **current** (legal) sources of law. These are the means by which the law is currently brought into existence.

The two **historical** sources of law are **equity** and the **common law**. The development of historical sources has led to one of the main legal sources of law, **case law** and **judicial precedent** (section 3), and informs much of the other main source, **legislation** (section 4). An understanding of judicial precedent is vital for your exam.

Judicial precedent is specifically linked in the syllabus to the study of **negligence**. The law relating to the negligence of **professional advisers** has developed as more cases come to court and judges refine their decisions based upon each new set of circumstances. This is covered in Chapter 2.

The impact of the **EC** is increasing (section 5). It is therefore very important for you to understand the effect EC law has on English law.

Learning outcomes covered in this chapter

- **Explain** the manner in which behaviour within society is regulated by the civil and the criminal law
- **Identify** and **explain** the sources of English law
- **Explain** and **illustrate** the operation of the doctrine of judicial precedent by reference to the essential elements of the tort of negligence, ie duty, breach and damage/loss/injury

Syllabus content covered in this chapter

- The sources of English law
- The system of judicial precedent

1 CRIMINAL AND CIVIL LIABILITY 5/02

1.1 The distinction between criminal and civil liability is central to the legal system and to the way the court system is structured.

Criminal law

KEY TERM

A **crime** is conduct prohibited by the law. Criminal law exists to regulate behaviour in society.

1.2 In a criminal case the State is the prosecutor (in rare cases it may be a private person) because it is the community as a whole which suffers as a result of the law being broken. **Persons guilty of crime are punished by fines payable to the State or imprisonment.**

1.3 The **police** or the **Director of Public Prosecutions** take the initial decision to prosecute, but this is then reviewed by the Crown Prosecution Service.

1.4 In a criminal trial, the burden of proof to convict the **accused** rests with the **prosecution,** which must prove its case **beyond reasonable doubt**.

1.5 A criminal case might be referred to as *R v Smith*. The prosecution is brought in the name of the Crown (R signifying *Regina,* the Queen).

Civil proceedings

KEY TERM

Civil law exists to regulate disputes over the rights and obligations of persons dealing with each other.

1.6 In civil proceedings, the case must be proven on the **balance of probability,** to convince the court that it is more probable than not that the assertions are true. Terminology is different from that in criminal cases. The **claimant** sues the **defendant**. A civil case would therefore be referred to as, for example, *Smith v Megacorp plc.*

1.7 One of the most important areas of civil liability for business, and accountants in particular, is the law of **contract**.

KEY TERM

A **contract** is a relationship between two parties. It is a legally binding agreement, breach of which infringes one person's legal right given by the contract to have it performed.

Distinction between criminal and civil cases

1.8 It is **not an act** or **event** which **creates the distinction**, but the **legal consequences**. A single event might give rise to criminal and civil proceedings.

1.9 EXAMPLE

A broken leg caused to a pedestrian by a drunken driver is a single event which may give rise to:

- A criminal case (prosecution by the State for the offence of driving with excess alcohol), and
- A civil case (the pedestrian sues for compensation for pain and suffering).

1.10 The two sorts of proceedings are usually easily distinguished by the fact that the **courts**, the **procedures** and the **terminology** are **different**. In criminal cases the rules of evidence are very strict. For example, a confession will be carefully examined to see if any pressure was brought to bear upon the accused, but an admission in a civil case will not be subjected to such scrutiny.

1.11 An alternative to taking civil proceedings to court is to take them to **arbitration**. The advantages of arbitration are that it is usually cheaper and quicker and an expert can be chosen to be arbitrator. There is also a system of **tribunals** in the UK, the most key being the Employment Tribunal, where employment matters are heard, and the Employment Appeal Tribunal which is a court of equal standing with the High Court.

Question 1

The criminal law aims

A To compensate injured parties

B To recover property which has been taken from the true owner
C To enforce obligations
D To penalise wrongdoers

Answer

D

2 FEATURES AND SOURCES OF ENGLISH LAW 5/01

2.1 There are four current (legal) **sources of law**. These are the means by which the law is brought into existence.

- **Case law and precedent**
- **Legislation**
- **Custom**
- **EC law**

2.2 There are a number of important characteristics of English law which together distinguish the English legal system from most other systems.

Continuity

2.3 **Principles** of English law **do not become inoperative** through the **lapse of time**. Thus in *R v Casement 1916*, the Treason Act 1351 was consulted. This does not just apply to Acts of Parliament, but also to case law. The outcome of *Pinnel's case 1602* is still important today when examining the law of contract.

Judicial precedent

2.4 The doctrine of **judicial precedent** means that a judge is bound to apply a decision from an earlier case to the facts of the case before him, provided, among other conditions, that there is no material difference between the cases.

KEY TERM

A **precedent** is a previous court decision which another court is bound to follow by deciding a subsequent case in the same way.

Common law and equity 11/01

2.5 The earliest element of the legal system to develop was the **common law**, a harsh system incorporating rigid rules applied by royal courts. Equity was developed, several hundred years later, as a system of law applied by the Chancellor where justice did not appear to be done under common law principles.

KEY TERMS

Common law is the body of legal rules common to the whole country which is embodied in judicial decisions.

Equity is a term which applies to a specific set of legal principles which were developed by the Court of Chancery to supplement (but not replace) the common law. It is based on fair dealings between the parties. It added to and improved on the common law by introducing the concept of fairness.

2.6 The interaction of equity and common law produced three major changes.

(a) **New rights**. Equity recognised and protected rights for which the common law gave no safeguards.

(b) **Better procedure**. Equity could be more effective than common law in bringing a disputed matter to a decision.

(c) **Better remedies**. The standard common law remedy for the successful claimant was the award of damages for his loss. The Chancellor developed remedies not available in other courts. Equity was able to order the defendant to do the following.

- What he had agreed to do (**specific performance**)
- Abstain from wrongdoing (**injunction**)
- Alter a document to reflect the parties' true intentions (**rectification**)
- Restore the pre-contract status quo (**rescission**)

Question 2

While on a sales trip, one of your employees is involved in a car accident. The other vehicle involved is damaged and it is alleged that your employee is to blame. What legal proceedings may arise as a result of this incident?

Answer

Your employee may be guilty of a driving offence such as careless driving. The police, to whom the incident should be reported, will investigate, and if the facts indicate a driving offence, will prosecute him, probably in the local magistrates' court. The owner of the damaged vehicle (or his insurers) may sue the driver at fault in civil proceedings to recover damages. A claim would probably be brought in the county court.

3 CASE LAW AND JUDICIAL PRECEDENT 5/01

3.1 A court's decision is expected to be **consistent with previous decisions** and to provide an opinion which can be used to direct future relationships. This is the basis of the system of **judicial precedent**.

KEY TERM

In any later case to which that principle is relevant the same principle should (subject to certain exceptions) be applied. This doctrine of consistency, following precedent, is expressed in the maxim **stare decisis** which means 'to stand by a decision'.

3.2 Judicial precedent is based on three elements.

Reports	There must be adequate and reliable reports of earlier decisions.
Rules	There must be rules for extracting a legal principle from a previous set of facts and applying it to current facts.
Classification	Precedents must be classified into those that are **binding** and those which are merely **persuasive**.

3.3 There are major series of law reports on general law bound as annual volumes.

Question 3

What do you think are the advantages of case law as a source of law?

Answer

The law is decided fairly and **predictably**, so that businessmen and individuals can regulate their conduct by reference to the law. The **risk** of mistakes in individual cases is reduced by the use of precedents. Case law can **adapt** to changing circumstances in society, since it arises directly out of the actions of society. Case law, having been developed in **practical** situations, is suitable for use in other practical situations.

KEY TERM

The **doctrine of judicial precedent** is based on the view that the function of a judge is to decide cases in accordance with existing rules.

3.4 The doctrine of judicial precedent is designed to provide **consistency** in the law. Four things must be considered when examining a precedent before it can be applied to a case.

A decision must be based on a **proposition of law** before it can be considered as a precedent. It may **not** be a decision on a **question of fact.**
It must form part of the **ratio decidendi** of the case.
The **material facts** of each case must be the same.
The preceding court must have had a **superior (or in some cases, equal) status** to the later court, such that its decisions are binding on the later court.

Ratio decidendi

3.5 A judgement will start with a description of the facts of the case and probably a review of earlier precedents. The judge will then make statements of law applicable to the legal problems raised by the material facts which, if the basis for the decision, are known as the *ratio decidendi* of the case, which is the vital element which binds future judges.

KEY TERM

'The **ratio decidendi** of a case is any rule of law expressly or impliedly treated by the judge as a necessary step in reaching his conclusion, having regard to the line of reasoning adopted by him, or a necessary part of his direction to the jury.'

(Cross: *Precedent in English Law.*)

3.6 Statements made by a judge are *ratio decidendi* or *obiter dicta*. There are two types of *obiter dicta*, something said 'by the way'.

- A judge's statements of legal principle might not form the basis of the decision.
- A judge's statements might not be based on the existing material facts but on hypothetical facts.

KEY TERM

Obiter dicta are words in a judgement which are said 'by the way'. They do not form part of the **ratio decidendi** and are not binding on future cases but merely persuasive.

3.7 It is not always easy to identify the *ratio decidendi*. In decisions of appeal courts, where there are three or even five separate judgements, the members of the court may reach the same conclusion but give different reasons. Many judges indicate in their speeches which comments are *ratio* and which *obiter*.

Distinguishing the facts

3.8 Although there may arguably be a finite number of legal principles to consider when deciding a case, there is an infinite variety of facts which may be presented. It is necessary to consider how far the facts of the previous and the latest case are similar. If the differences appear significant the court may **distinguish** the earlier case on the facts and thereby avoid following it as a precedent.

Status of the court 11/01

3.9 Not every decision made in every court is binding as a judicial precedent. The court's status has a significant effect on whether its decisions are binding, persuasive or disregarded.

The civil courts

3.10 The diagram below sets out the English civil court structure. The key civil court is the county court, where the majority of civil courts are heard. Claims up to a value of £50,000 are heard here, others start in the High Court. Small claims (up to £5,000) can be heard informally in the small claims court. After the Woolf Reforms to civil justice, claims up to £15,000 will be 'fast-tracked' and heard within a day. Claims in the County Court include: contract, tort, partnership matters, probate, some land matters, undefended matrimonial claims, some bankruptcy claims and mortgage matters.

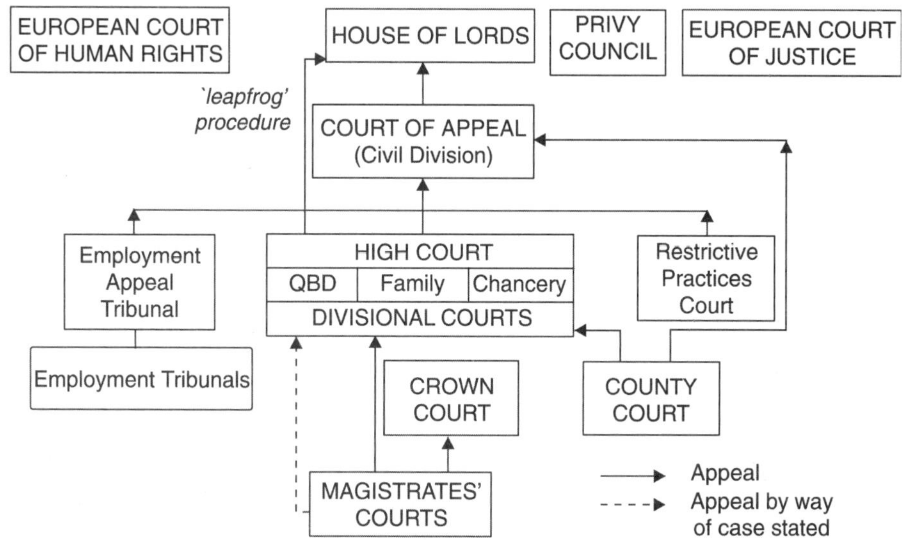

The criminal court structure

3.11 The diagram below sets out the English criminal court structure. The two key courts in the original system are the crown court and the magistrates' court.

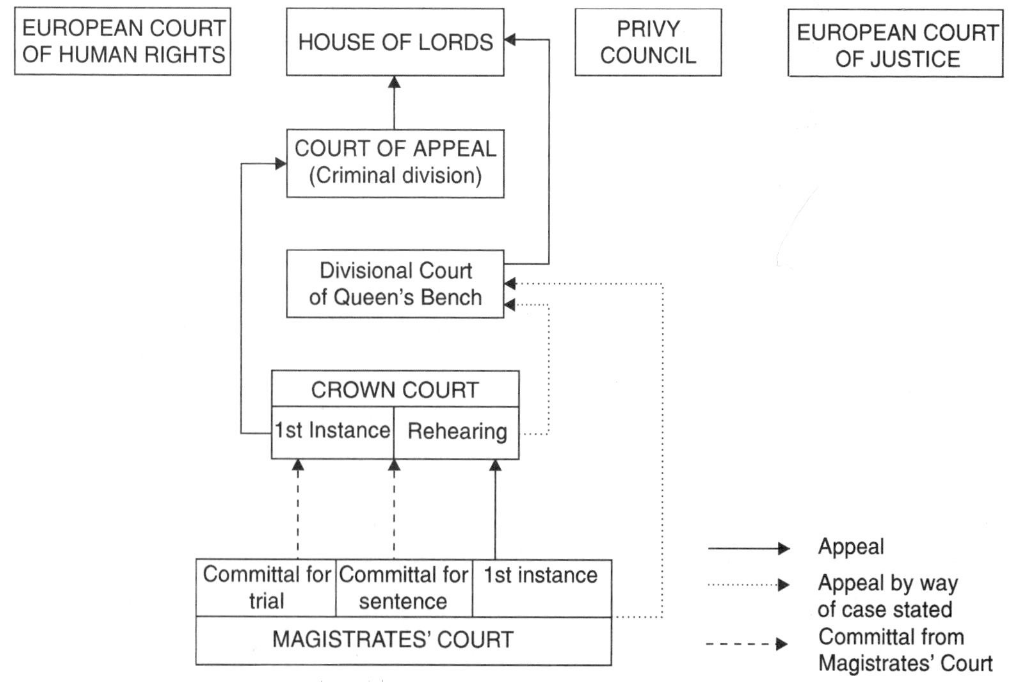

Court	Bound by	Decisions binding
Magistrates Court	• High Court • The Court of Appeal • House of Lords • European Court of Justice	• No one • Not even itself
County Court	• High Court • The Court of Appeal • House of Lords • European Court of Justice	• No one • Not even itself
Crown Court	• High Court (QBD) • Court of Appeal • House of Lords • European Court of Justice	• No one • However, its decisions are reported more widely and are more authoritative
The High Court consists of divisions: • Queen's bench • Chancery • Family	(a) Judge sitting alone • The divisional court • Court of Appeal • House of Lords • European Court of Justice (b) Judges sitting together • Any divisional court • Court of Appeal • House of Lords • European Court of Justice	(a) Judge sitting alone • Magistrates Court • County Court • Crown Court (b) Judges sitting together • Magistrates Court • County Court • Crown Court • Divisional Courts
The Court of Appeal	• Own decisions • House of Lords (subject to an exception below) • European Court of Justice	• All inferior English courts • Itself (subject to the exception)
The House of Lords	• Itself (except in exceptional cases) • European Court of Justice	• All English Courts • Itself (except in exceptional cases)
The European Court of Justice	• No one • Not even itself	• All English Courts

3.12 *Court of Appeal exception*

In *Young v Bristol Aeroplane Co 1944,* it was decided that the civil division of the Court of Appeal is usually bound by its own decisions and the House of Lords, unless:

- Two of its previous decisions conflict, when it must decide which to follow
- The previous decision conflicts with a subsequent House of Lords decision
- The previous decision was made with a lack of care (per incuriam)

Exam focus point

It is particularly important that you know the position of the Court of Appeal and the House of Lords in this hierarchy.

Question 4

Before a High Court judge is required to apply a previous decision to the case actually before him, he must

1 Decide whether the decision is binding or merely persuasive

2 Distinguish the *obiter dicta* from the *ratio decidendi* and apply the former in his reasoning

3 Determine that the material facts of the two cases are similar

4 Be convinced that the decision was made by a court of higher status than the county court or magistrate's court

A 1 and 3 only
B 2 and 4 only
C 1, 2 and 3 only
D 1, 3 and 4 only

Answer

A. A High Court judge sitting alone is only compelled to follow a previous decision if it is binding on him and if the material facts are similar.

Persuasive precedents

3.13 Apart from binding precedents, reported decisions of any court may be treated as **persuasive precedents**. Persuasive precedents may be, but need not be, followed in a later case.

KEY TERMS

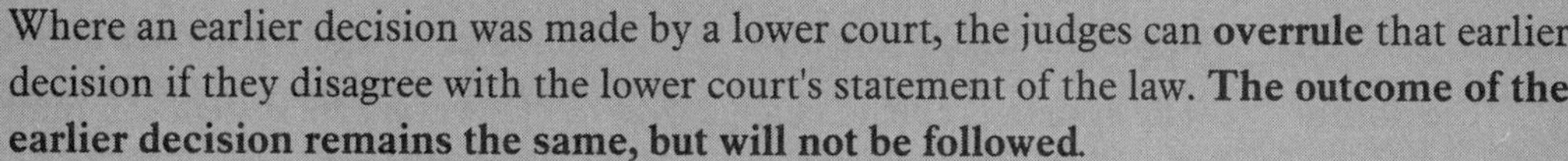

Where an earlier decision was made by a lower court, the judges can **overrule** that earlier decision if they disagree with the lower court's statement of the law. **The outcome of the earlier decision remains the same, but will not be followed.**

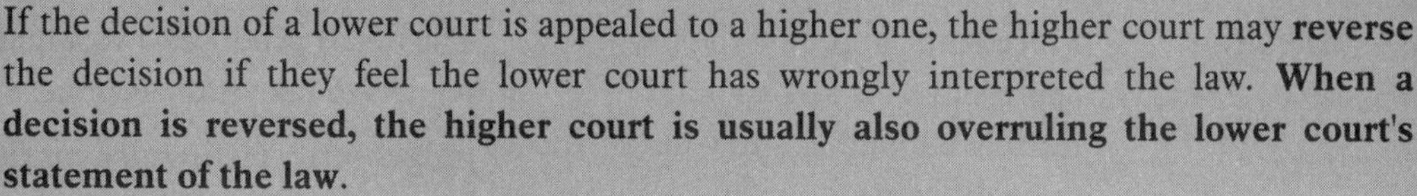

If the decision of a lower court is appealed to a higher one, the higher court may **reverse** the decision if they feel the lower court has wrongly interpreted the law. **When a decision is reversed, the higher court is usually also overruling the lower court's statement of the law.**

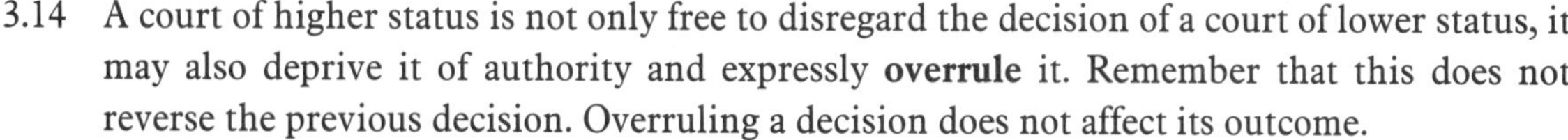

3.14 A court of higher status is not only free to disregard the decision of a court of lower status, it may also deprive it of authority and expressly **overrule** it. Remember that this does not reverse the previous decision. Overruling a decision does not affect its outcome.

3.15 If, in a case before the House of Lords, there is a dispute about a point of European Community law it must be referred to the European Court for a ruling. The European court does not create or follow precedents as such, and the provisions of EC directives should not be used to interpret UK legislation.

3.16 A case in the High Court may be taken on appeal to the Court of Appeal. If the latter reverses the former decision, that first decision cannot be a precedent. If the original decision had been reached by following precedent, then reversing that decision overrules the precedent.

Avoidance of a binding precedent

3.17 Even if a precedent appears to be binding, there are a number of grounds on which a court may decline to follow it.

(a) It may be able to **distinguish the facts**.

(b) It may declare the ratio decidendi **obscure**, particularly when a Court of Appeal decision by three or five judges gives as many *rationes*.

(c) It may declare the previous decision made **per incuriam**: without taking account of some essential point of law, such as an important precedent.

(d) It may declare it to be in conflict with a fundamental principle of law

(e) It may declare an earlier precedent to be **too wide.**

The advantages and disadvantages of precedent

3.18 Many of the strengths of judicial precedent as the cornerstone of English law also indicate some of its weaknesses.

Factor	Advantage	Disadvantage
Certainty	The law is decided fairly and predictably Guidance given to judges and risk of mistake reduced.	Judges may sometimes be forced to make illogical distinctions to avoid an unfair result.
Clarity	Following the reasoning of *ratio decidendi* should lead to statements of general legal principles	Sometimes, judgements may appear to be inconsistent with each other or legal principles followed.
Flexibility	The system is able to change with changing circumstances	However, the system can limit judges' discretion.
Detail	Precedent states how the law applies to facts and should be flexible enough to allow for details to be different.	The detail produces a vast body of reports to take into account. Judges often distinguish on the facts to avoid a precedent.
Practicality	Case law is based on experience of actual cases brought before the courts. This is an advantage over legislation which can be found wanting when tested.	

4 LEGISLATION

4.1 Statute law is made by Parliament (or in exercise of law-making powers delegated by Parliament). Until the United Kingdom entered the European Community in 1973 the UK Parliament was completely **sovereign**.

4.2 In recent years however, UK membership of the European Community has restricted the previously unfettered power of Parliament. There is an obligation, imposed by the Treaty of Rome, to bring UK law into line with the Treaty itself and with directives. Regulations, having the force of law in every member state, may be made under provisions of the Treaty of Rome.

Parliamentary sovereignty

4.3 Parliamentary sovereignty gives rise to a number of consequences. Parliament may **repeal** earlier statutes, **overrule** case law developed in the courts or **make new law** on subjects which have not been regulated by law before.

4.4 No Parliament can legislate so as to prevent a future Parliament changing the law.

4.5 The judges have to **interpret** statute law and they may find a meaning in a statutory rule which those Members of Parliament who promoted the statute did not intend.

4.6 The **validity** of an Act of Parliament cannot be questioned.

4.7 In addition to making new law and altering existing law, Parliament may make the law clearer by passing a **codifying** statute (such as the Sale of Goods Act 1979) to put case law on a statutory basis, or a **consolidating** statute to incorporate an original statute and its successive amendments into a single statute (such as the Employment Rights Act 1996 or the Companies Act 1985).

Parliamentary procedure

4.8 A proposal for legislation is originally aired in public in a **Government Green Paper**. After comments are received a **White Paper** is produced, which sets out the intended aim of the legislation. It is then put forward in draft form as a **Bill**, and may be introduced into either the House of Commons or the House of Lords. When the Bill has passed through one House it must then go through the same stages in the other House.

4.9 In each House the successive stages of dealing with the Bill are as follows.

Stage 1. **First reading**. Publication and introduction into the agenda. No debate.

Stage 2. **Second reading**. Debate on the general merits of the Bill. No amendments at this stage.

Stage 3. **Committee stage**. The Bill is examined by a Standing Committee of about 20 members, representing the main parties and including some members at least who specialise in the relevant subject. If the Bill is very important all or part of the Committee Stage may be taken by the House as a whole sitting as a committee.

Stage 4. **Report stage.** The Bill as amended in committee is reported to the full House for approval.

Stage 5. **Third reading.** This is the final approval stage.

4.10 When it has passed through both Houses it is submitted for the **Royal Assent** which is given on the Queen's behalf by a committee of the Lord Chancellor and two other peers. It then becomes an Act of Parliament (or statute) but it does not come into operation until a commencement date is notified by statutory instrument.

Statutory interpretation

4.11 There are a series of rules concerning how a judge should interpret statute. In general, he is required to consider the purpose of the statute and interpret the statute so that it achieves its purpose. After the incorporation of the European Convention on Human Rights and Fundamental Freedoms into UK law in the form of the Human Rights Act 1998, the UK is required to interpret statute in a way that is compatible with the convention, as far as is possible.

4.12 There are a number of historic rules, summarised here:

- **The literal rule**. Words should be given their plain, ordinary or literary meaning.
- **The golden rule**. A statute should be construed to avoid a manifest absurdity or contradiction within itself.
- **The mischief rule**. The court will adopt the meaning which allows the purpose of the statute to be given effect.
- **The contextual rule**. A word should be construed in its context.
- **The eiusdem generis rule.** Lists of general words are limited in their meaning to other things of the same kind as the specific items which precede them.

4.13 There are also a number of presumptions of statutory interpretation:

- **A statute does not alter the existing common law.**
- **If a statue deprives a person of his property**, say by nationalism, he is to be compensated for its value.
- **A statute is not intended to deprive a person of his liberty.**
- **A statute does not have retrospective effect** to date earlier than its becoming law.
- **A statute does not bind the crown.**
- **A statute has effect only in the UK.**
- **A statute cannot impose criminal liability** without proof of guilty intention.
- **A statute does repeal other statutes.**

Delegated legislation

4.13 To save time in Parliament, Acts usually contain a section by which power is given to a minister, or public body such as a local authority, to make **subordinate or delegated legislation**.

KEY TERM

Delegated legislation means rules of law, often of a detailed nature, made by subordinate bodies to whom the power to do so has been given by statute.

4.14 Delegated legislation appears in various forms.

- Ministerial powers are exercised by **statutory instruments.** Statutory instruments are the most common form of delegated legislation.
- **Local authorities** are given statutory powers to make **bye-laws**.
- Parliament gives power to certain **professional bodies** to regulate their members' conduct.
- **Rules of Court** may be made by the judiciary to control court procedure.
- Emergency powers of the Crown are contained in **Orders in Council**

Control over delegated legislation

4.15 Parliament does exercise some control over delegated legislation by keeping the making of new delegated legislation under review.

Question 5

Fill in the following table, then check your answer.

Name of court	*Binds*	*Bound by*
Magistrates' court		
County court		
Crown court		
High Court (single judge)		
High Court (Divisional court)		
Court of Appeal		
House of Lords		
European Court of Justice		

5 EUROPEAN COMMUNITY LAW — Pilot Paper, 5/02

5.1 The sources of Community Law may be described as primary or secondary. The **primary sources of law** are the foundation treaties themselves.

- The **Treaty of Paris 1951**, which established the **ECSC**.
- The **First Treaty of Rome 1957**, which established the **EEC**
- The **Second Treaty of Rome 1957**, which established **EURATOM**.

5.2 **Secondary legislation** takes three forms, with the Council and Commission being empowered to do the following:

- Make regulations
- Issue directives
- Take decisions

They may also make recommendations and deliver opinions although these are only persuasive in authority.

Direct applicability and direct effect

5.3 To understand the importance of regulations, directives and decisions, it is necessary to appreciate the distinction between **direct applicability** and **direct effect**.

5.4 Community law which is directly applicable in member states comes into force without any act of implementation by member states. Law has direct effect if it confers rights and imposes obligations directly on individuals.

Regulations

5.5 Regulations may be issued. They have the force of law in every EU state without need of national legislation. In this sense regulations are described as **directly applicable**. Their objective is to obtain uniformity of law throughout the EU.

KEY TERM

Regulations apply throughout the Community and they become part of the law of each member nation as soon as they come into force without the need for each country to make its own legislation.

5.6 Direct law-making of this type is generally restricted to matters within the basic aims of Treaty of Rome, such as the establishment of a single unrestricted market in the EC territory in manufactured goods.

5.7 Acts of implementation are actually prohibited, in case a member state alters the scope of the regulation in question.

Directives

KEY TERM

Directives are issued to the governments of the EU member states requiring them within a specified period (usually two years) to alter the national laws of the state so that they conform to the directive.

5.8 Thus the Financial Services Act 1986 embodied certain directives on company securities and the Companies Act 1989 gives force to the Eighth Directive.

5.9 Until a directive is given effect by a UK statute it does not usually affect legal rights and obligations of individuals. The wording of a directive may be cited in legal proceedings, but generally **statutory interpretation has been a matter for the UK courts**. However, as noted above, under the Human Rights Act 1998, the courts are now required to interpret UK legislation in a way which is compatible with the European Convention on Human Rights.

POINT TO NOTE

Directives are the most significant and important means of importing continental law into the UK legal system.

Decisions

5.10 Decisions of an administrative nature are made by the European Commission in Brussels.

KEY TERM

A **decision** may be addressed to a state, person or a company and is immediately binding, but only on the recipient.

Legislative procedure

5.11 Proposals for EC legislation are drafted by the Commission. These drafts are referred to member states for comments. The directives are also debated in the preparatory stage by the European Parliament. The final stage is the consideration of a directive by the Council of Ministers. The Council authorises the issue of the directive and the member states must then alter their law accordingly.

Question 6

Describe the three types of secondary legislation.

Answer

A **regulation** is a rule of law designed to obtain uniformity throughout the member states. It is directly applicable without the need for national legislation. A **directive** is issued to member states requiring them to make such changes to their own law as prescribed by the directive. A **decision** is binding in its entirety upon those to whom it is addressed, whether they be member states or corporate bodies. In the case of member states, a decision has direct effect.

Exam focus point

EC law is an increasingly important topic, so do not neglect it.

Chapter roundup

- The distinction between **criminal liability** and **civil liability** is central to the English legal system.
- There are a number of sources of law.
- **Common law** (legal rights) is applied **automatically** and comprises a **complete system** of law.
  - **Rights** are enforceable against anyone and everyone, regardless of their knowledge that the rights exist.
  - **Remedies**, for example damages, are given against property.
- **Equity** (equitable rights) is applied **at the court's discretion** and does **not** comprise a **complete system** of law.
  - **Rights** are enforceable only against those persons who know or ought to know of their existence and must be exercised without undue delay.
  - **Remedies**, for example an injunction, are given against the person.
- **Legal sources** are the means by which the law is currently brought into existence. There are four legal sources: judicial precedent, UK legislation, EC legislation and custom.
- Decisions made in the courts are **case law**, which is judge-made law based on the underlying principle of consistency. Once a legal or equitable principle is decided by an appropriate court it is a **judicial precedent**.
- In order that judicial precedent provides consistency in law, the **ratio decidendi** must be identified. The material facts must be the same. The status of the court which set the precedent must be such as to bind the present court. Rationes decidendi are the reasons for the decision being made - they alone are binding. **Obiter dicta** are comments made by the deciding judge in passing and are persuasive only.
- Judicial precedent is illustrated by reference to the tort of **negligence** in the next chapter.

- The House of Lords binds itself (but may depart from its own decisions) and all lower courts. The Court of Appeal binds itself and all lower courts. A Divisional Court of the High Court (two or more judges) binds itself and all lower courts. The High Court (single judge) binds all lower courts. Crown Court decisions may be of persuasive authority. The county court and magistrates' courts do not make binding precedent.
- One of the major legal sources of law is **legislation**. UK statute law may take the form of Acts of Parliament, or delegated legislation under the Acts, for example statutory instruments or bye-laws.
- There are three individual European Communities. The European Coal and Steel Community was established by the Treaty of Paris 1951, the European Economic Community by the First Treaty of Rome 1957 and the European Atomic Energy Community by the Second Treaty of Rome 1957.
- The European Commission is the executive and legislative body of the Community. The Council of Ministers is the Community's decision-making body. The European Parliament has a consultative role. The European Court of Justice is the judicial body of the Community.
- The sources of EC law may be described as primary or secondary. The primary sources of law are the Foundation treaties themselves. The secondary sources of law are legislation, which takes three forms. Regulations are self-executing. Directives require national legislation to be effective, usually within two years. Decisions are immediately binding on the person to whom they are addressed.

Quick quiz

1 **Fill in the blanks** in the statements below, using the words in the box.

- The distinction between (1) .... and (2) .... liability is central to the English legal system.
- (3) .... allows parties to bring their dispute before a non-legal independent expert so that he may decide the case.
- The sources of English law can be divided into two categories.
  - The historical sources are (4) .... and (5) ....
  - Legal sources are (6) .... (7) .... and (8) ....

• case law	• common law
• equity	• civil
• arbitration	• EC law

2 The Employment Appeal Tribunal is a court of equal status with the High Court.

☐ True

☐ False

3 Which of the following is true of a criminal case?

A A convicted person must pay compensation to his victim
B The case must be proven beyond reasonable doubt
C The Crown Prosecution Service is the claimant
D Law reports of criminal cases are confidential

4 **Fill in the blanks** in the statements below, using the words in the box.

- In order that (1) .... provides (2) .... in the law, a precedent must be carefully examined before it can be applied to a particular (3) .... It must be a proposition of (4) .... The (5) .... must be identified. The (6) .... must be the same.
- The (7) .... of the court which set the precedent must be such as to (8) .... the present court.

• bind	• judicial precedent
• case	• status
• ratio decidendi	• law
• material facts	• consistency

5 The primary sources of EC law are

A Regulations
B Foundation treaties
C Directives
D Decisions

6 *Obiter dicta* form part of the *ratio decidendi.*

☐ True

☐ False

7 Which of these decisions binds the Crown Court?

Decisions of the County Court	☐
Decisions of the High Court	☐
Decisions of the Court of Appeal	☐
Decisions of the House of Lords	☐

8 In 1989, Mr Justice Jeffries, a High Court judge sitting alone, is deciding a case which has similar material facts to one decided by the Court of Appeal in 1889. He can decline to be bound by this decision by showing that

A The status of the previous court is not such as can bind him
B The decision was taken too long ago to be of any relevance
C The decision does not accord with the rules of a statute passed in 1890
D The obiter dicta are obscure

9 What type of EC legislation is directly applicable?

10 The rule that a statute should be construed to avoid a manifest absurdity or contradiction within itself is known as the

literal rule	mischief rule
golden rule	contextual rule

11

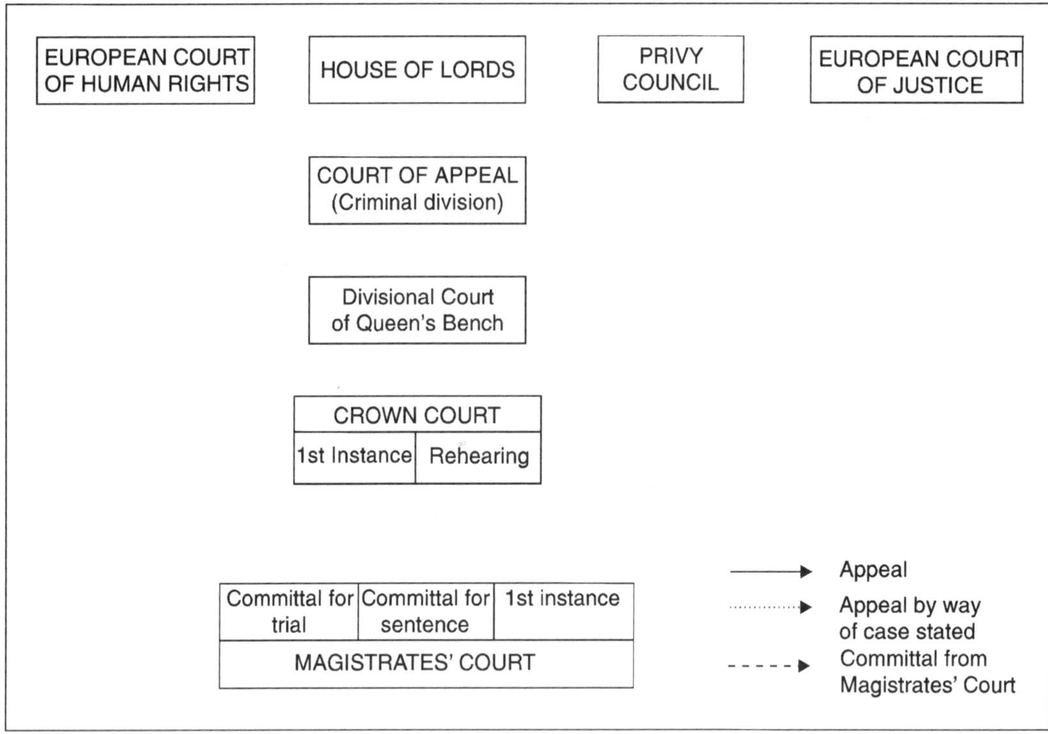

Complete the diagram by filling in arrows to show the lines of appeal in the UK.

12 Delete as applicable.

- In a criminal trial, the burden of proof to convict the accused rests with the prosecution/the defence.
- In civil proceedings the case must be proven beyond reasonable doubt/on the balance of probabilities.
- The Woolf reforms aimed to promote speed and flexibility in civil justice/criminal justice.
- The court that deals with the majority of the country's civil litigation is the county court/crown court/magistrates' court.

13 Judicial precedent is based on the three elements. Which three?

- Reports of previous decisions
- The same judge being involved in the decision
- Facts of cases being classified
- Rules for extracting the legal principle from one set of facts to apply to a different set of facts
- Precedents being classified into those which are binding and those which are not.

14 Complete the table, showing which courts the decisions of each of the courts are binding on.

Court	Bound by	Decisions binding
Magistrates Court	• High Court • The Court of Appeal • House of Lords • European Court of Justice	
County Court	• High Court • The Court of Appeal • House of Lords • European Court of Justice	
Crown Court	• High Court (QBD) • Court of Appeal • House of Lords • European Court of Justice	

Court	Bound by	Decisions binding
The High Court consists of divisions: • Queen's bench • Chancery • Family	(a) Judge sitting alone • The divisional court • Court of Appeal • House of Lords • European Court of Justice (b) Judges sitting together • Any divisional court • Court of Appeal • House of Lords • European Court of Justice	(a) Judge sitting alone (b) Judges sitting together
The Court of Appeal	• Own decisions • House of Lords (subject to an exception) • European Court of Justice	
The House of Lords	• Itself (except in exceptional cases) • European Court of Justice	
The European Court of Justice	• No one • Not even itself	

15 Complete the table using the factors given below.

Statute law	
Advantages	*Disadvantages*

- The House of Commons is elected at intervals of not more than five years. Hence the law making process is theoretically responsive to public opinion.
- Parliament often lacks time to consider draft legislation in sufficient detail.
- Statute law can in theory deal with any problem.
- A substantial statute can take up a lot of Parliamentary time.
- Statute law is a statement of general rules. Those who draft it cannot anticipate every individual case which may arise.
- A new problem in society or some unwelcome development in case law can be dealt with by passing an Act of Parliament.
- Statutes are carefully constructed codes of law.
- Statutes are bulky (about 70 public statutes are passed each year and the complete set of statutes runs to more than 40 volumes of several hundred pages each).

16 Name the five stages of parliamentary procedure with regard to statutes.

Stage 1. .... Publication and introduction into the agenda. No debate.

Stage 2. .... Debate on the general merits of the Bill. No amendments at this stage.

Stage 3. .... The Bill is examined by a Standing Committee of about 20 members, representing the main parties and including some members at least who specialise in the relevant subject. If the Bill is very important all or part of the Committee Stage may be taken by the House as a whole sitting as a committee.

Stage 4. .... The Bill as amended in committee is reported to the full House for approval.

Stage 5. .... This is the final approval stage.

Answers to quick quiz

1 (1) criminal (2) civil (3) arbitration (4) common law (5) equity (6) case law (7) legislation (8) EC law

2 True

3 B

4 (1) judicial precedent (2) consistency (3) case (4) law (5) ratio decidendi (6) material facts (7) status (8) bind

5 B

6 False

7 Decisions of the High Court, Court of Appeal and House of Lords

8 C. A High Court judge is bound by decisions of the Court of Appeal

9 Regulations

10 Golden rule

11

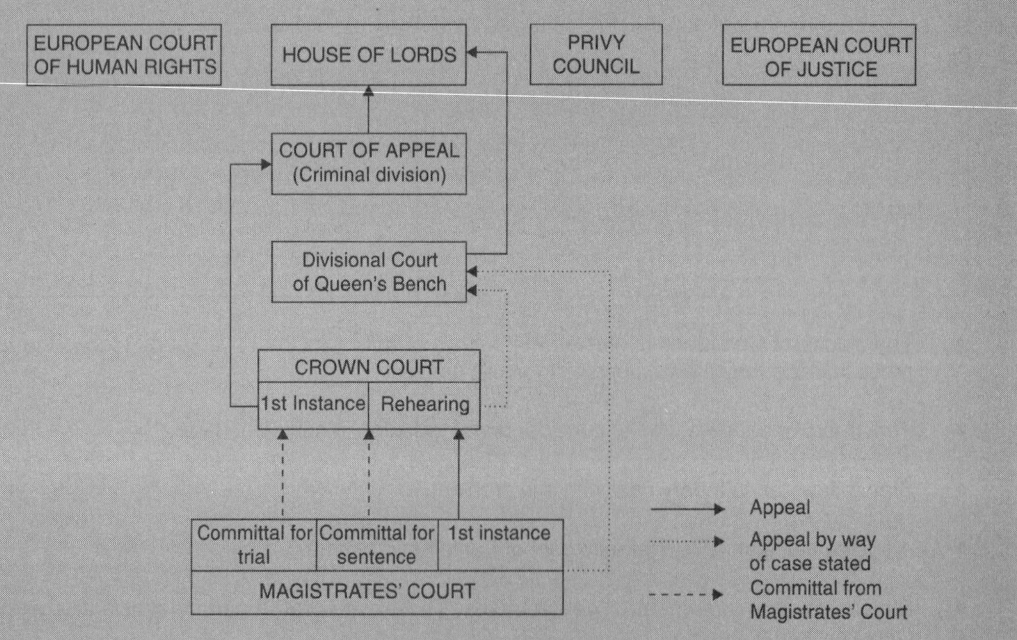

12
- In a criminal trial, the burden of proof to convict the accused rests with **the prosecution**.
- In civil proceedings the cases must be proved on **the balance of probabilities**.
- The Woolf reforms aimed to promote speed and flexibility in **civil justice**.
- The courts that deal with the majority of the country's civil litigation is the **county court**.

13
- Reports **of previous decisions**
- **Rules** for extracting the legal principle from one set of facts to apply to a different set of facts.
- Precedents being **classified** into those which are binding and those which are not.

14

Court	Bound by	Decisions binding
Magistrates Court	• High Court • The Court of Appeal • House of Lords • European Court of Justice	• No one • Not even itself
County Court	• High Court • The Court of Appeal • House of Lords • European Court of Justice	• No one • Not even itself
Crown Court	• High Court (QBD) • Court of Appeal • House of Lords • European Court of Justice	• No one
The High Court consists of divisions: • Queen's bench • Chancery • Family	(a) Judge sitting alone • The divisional court • Court of Appeal • House of Lords • European Court of Justice (b) Judges sitting together • Any divisional court • Court of Appeal • House of Lords • European Court of Justice	(a) Judge sitting alone • Magistrates Court • County Court • Crown Court (b) Judges sitting together • Magistrates Court • County Court • Crown Court • Divisional Courts
The Court of Appeal	• Own decisions • House of Lords (subject to an exception) • European Court of Justice	• All inferior English courts • Itself (subject to the exception)
The House of Lords	• Itself (except in exceptional cases) • European Court of Justice	• All English Courts • Itself (except in exceptional cases)
The European Court of Justice	• No one • Not even itself	• All English Courts

15

Statute law	
Advantages	*Disadvantages*
• The House of Commons is elected at intervals of not more than five years. Hence the law making process is theoretically responsive to public opinion.	• Statutes are bulky (about 70 public statutes are passed each year and the complete set of statutes runs to more than 40 volumes of several hundred pages each).
• Statute law can in theory deal with any problem.	• Parliament often lacks time to consider draft legislation in sufficient detail.
• Statutes are carefully constructed codes of law.	• A substantial statute can take up a lot of Parliamentary time.
• A new problem in society or some unwelcome development in case law can be dealt with by passing an Act of Parliament.	• Statute law is a statement of general rules. Those who draft it cannot anticipate every individual case which may arise.

16 ***Stage 1.*** **First reading**. Publication and introduction into the agenda. No debate.

Stage 2. **Second reading**. Debate on the general merits of the Bill. No amendments at this stage.

Stage 3. **Committee stage**. The Bill is examined by a Standing Committee of about 20 members, representing the main parties and including some members at least who specialise in the relevant subject. If the Bill is very important all or part of the Committee Stage may be taken by the House as a whole sitting as a committee.

Stage 4. **Report stage**. The Bill as amended in committee is reported to the full House for approval.

Stage 5. **Third reading**. This is the final approval stage.

The following relevant questions are included in the Exam Question Banks

You can attempt these now. However, we would advise you to attempt these as mock exams at the end of your initial stage of study

Exam Question Bank	Numbers
Paper based format	1, 2
Computer based assessment	3, 16, 19

Chapter 2

NEGLIGENCE

	Topic list	Syllabus reference	Ability required
1	Tort and other wrongs	(i)	Comprehension
2	The tort of negligence	(i)	Comprehension
3	Duty of care	(i)	Comprehension
4	Breach of duty of care	(i)	Comprehension
5	Consequential harm	(i)	Comprehension
6	Professional advice	(i)	Comprehension

Introduction

This chapter describes the tort of **negligence**, the most significant **tort** of modern times. Tort is an important branch of the law regulating business conduct, so this chapter begins with an introduction to the concept of tort, distinguishing it from criminal liability and liability in contract.

The **three essential elements** of a negligence claim are analysed by reference to the main cases establishing their importance, and a consideration of **negligent professional advice** appears at the end of the chapter. This is linked to the material in the previous chapter on judicial precedent to underline how the **doctrine of precedent** operates.

Learning outcomes covered in this chapter

- **Explain** and **illustrate** the operation of the doctrine of precedent by reference to the essential elements of the tort of negligence, ie duty, breach and damage/loss/injury
- **Explain** the application of the tort to professional advisers

Syllabus content covered in this chapter

- The essential elements of the tort of negligence, including duty, breach and damage/loss/injury
- The liability of professionals in respect of negligent advice

1 TORT AND OTHER WRONGS

1.1 Tort is distinguished from other legal wrongs.

> **KEY TERM**
>
> A **tort** is a civil wrong and the person wronged sues in a civil court for compensation or an injunction. The claimant's claim generally is that he has suffered a loss such as personal injury at the hands of the defendant and the defendant should pay damages.
>
> **In tort no previous transaction or contractual relationship need exist**: the parties may be complete strangers as when a motorist knocks down a pedestrian in the street. The claim in tort is based on the general law of duties and rights.

1.2 The **same event can easily give rise to more than one legal liability**.

1.3 EXAMPLE

A road accident may lead to proceedings for both crime and tort and even in contract if, say, the driver is a hired chauffeur.

1.4 Bad professional advice may give rise to liability both in tort and in contract. We discuss the law of tort in relation to professional advisers in section 6.

Wrong and damage

1.5 The necessary basis of a claim for damages claim is that the claimant has **suffered a wrong**. In some torts it is necessary to establish both wrong and loss resulting from it (the damage). This is the rule in the tort of **negligence**.

Cause and effect

1.6 When the claimant claims damages for the loss caused by the defendant's wrongful act or omission, two main issues of cause and effect may have to be considered.

(a) Was the loss **caused by a wrongful act** or omission of the defendant himself? It may be a case of **inevitable accident** or there may be **contributory negligence** on the part of the claimant.

(b) How far down the **chain of consequences** should the court go in identifying the loss for which the claimant is entitled to recover damages? It is necessary to have rules on **remoteness of damage**.

2 THE TORT OF NEGLIGENCE — Pilot Paper

> **KEY TERM**
>
> The term **negligence** 'may refer to the way in which an act is carried out, that is carelessly, or to the tort which arises when a person breaks a legal duty of care that is owed to another, thereby causing loss to that other.'

2.1 There is a **distinct tort of negligence** which is causing loss by a failure to take reasonable care when there is a duty to do so. This is the most important and far reaching modern tort.

2.2 To succeed in an action for negligence the claimant must prove three things:

- The defendant owed the claimant a **duty of care** to avoid causing injury to persons or property.
- There was a **breach of that duty** by the defendant.
- **In consequence** the claimant suffered **injury, damage** or **loss.**

Exam focus point

You must be aware of the academic requirements for negligence to be proved. The criteria for a successful negligence action are fundamental and should be learnt by all students.

3 DUTY OF CARE

3.1 The question of whether or not a duty of care exists in any situation is generally decided by the courts on a case by case basis, with each new case setting a precedent based on its own particular facts. The argument is built up from case to case, and in that way the development of the law is controlled.

3.2 In the case described below, the House of Lords was attempting to establish a general duty that could be applied to all subsequent cases and situations.

> *Donoghue v Stevenson 1932*
> *The facts:* A purchased a bottle of ginger beer for consumption by B. B drank part of the contents, which contained the remains of a decomposed snail, and became ill. The manufacturer argued that as there was no contract between himself and B he owed her no duty of care and so was not liable.
>
> *Decision:* The House of Lords laid down the general principle that every person owes a duty of care to his 'neighbour', to 'persons so closely and directly affected by my act that I ought reasonably to have them in contemplation as being so affected'.

Development of the doctrine

3.3 This narrow doctrine has been much refined in the seventy-odd years since the snail made its celebrated appearance. For any duty of care to exist, it was stated in *Anns v Merton London Borough Council 1977* that two stages must be tested:

- Is there sufficient **proximity** between the parties, such that the harm suffered was **reasonably foreseeable**?
- Should the duty be **restricted** or **limited** for reasons of economic, social or public policy?

3.4 An example of the duty of care being restricted is *Alcock v Chief Constable of South Yorkshire police 1991*. This was a case brought after the Hillsborough football disaster. It was ruled that the police did not owe a duty of care to people who witnessed their relatives being killed on live television and suffered nervous shock as a result.

3.5 Case law has tended to restrict the width of duty of care owned by professional advisers. This is discussed in Section 6.

Exam focus point

Once we have looked at the second and third elements of an action for negligence, we will look at the specific application of the tort to professional advisers in section 6. It is useful to analyse the duty of care along the lines of proximity and reasonable forseeability and then to see how the courts have recently amended these principles. This treatment will help to link it in your mind to the operation of the doctrine of precedent by providing a practical example.

Question 1

Which of the following elements must be present for a duty of care to exist?

1 There must be a sufficient relationship of proximity between defendant and claimant

2 It must be reasonable that the defendant should foresee that damage might arise from his carelessness

3 The claimant must have acted in good faith and without carelessness

4 It must be just and reasonable for the law to impose liability

A 1 and 2 only
B 3 and 4 only
C 1, 2 and 3 only
D 1, 2 and 4 only

Answer

D. The elements in options 1, 2 and 4 are the formulation of the tort of negligence as in *Anns* and *Caparo* (see section 6). If these are present then there is a right of action for the tort of negligence.

4 BREACH OF DUTY OF CARE

4.1 This is the second issue to be considered in a negligence claim. The standard of reasonable care requires that the person concerned should do what a **reasonable man** would do. This will also mean the reasonable **employer**, or the reasonable **adviser**.

4.2 The rule has been developed as follows.

(a) The test is one of **knowledge and general practice existing at the time**, not hindsight or subsequent change of practice.

(b) In broad terms, a claim against a professional person will fail if he or she can point to a **body of opinion that supports the approach taken**.

(c) In deciding what is reasonable care the **balance must be struck** between advantage and risk. The driver of a fire engine may exceed the normal speed on his way to the fire but not on the way back.

(d) If A owes a duty of care to B and A knows that B is **unusually vulnerable**, a higher standard of care is expected.

Paris v Stepney Borough Council 1951
The facts: P was employed by K on vehicle maintenance. P had already lost the sight of one eye. It was not the normal practice to issue protective goggles since the risk of eye injury was small. A chip of metal flew into P's eye and blinded him.

Decision: There was a higher standard of care owed to P because an injury to his remaining good eye would blind him.

In *Glasgow Corporation v Taylor 1992* the local authority were held to be negligent when children ate poisonous berries in a park. A warning notice was not considered to be sufficient to protect children.

Res ipsa loquitur

4.3 In some circumstances the claimant may argue that the facts speak for themselves (*res ipsa loquitur*) - want of care being the only possible explanation for what happened, negligence on the part of the defendant must be presumed.

KEY TERMS

Res ipsa loquitur can be defined as follows: 'The thing speaks for itself. Where an accident happens of which the most likely cause is negligence, the court may apply this maxim and infer negligence from mere proof of the facts. The burden of proof is reversed and the defendant must prove that s/he was not negligent.'

4.4 What the claimant must first show to rely on this principle:

(a) The thing which caused the injury was under the **management and control** of the defendant.

(b) The accident was such as would not occur if those in control used **proper care**. Therefore in *Richley v Fould 1965* the fact that a car skidded to the wrong side of the road was enough to indicate careless driving.

4.5 EXAMPLE

In *Mahon v Osborne 1939* a surgeon was required to prove that leaving a swab inside a patient after an operation was not negligent.

5 CONSEQUENTIAL HARM 5/01, 11/01

5.1 This is the third element of a negligence claim. A claim for compensation for negligence will not succeed if **damage** or **loss** is not proved.

5.2 A person will only be compensated if he has suffered actual loss, injury, damage or harm **as a consequence** of another's actions. Examples of such loss may include:

- Personal injury
- Damage to property
- Financial loss which is directly connected to personal injury, for example, loss of earnings
- Pure financial loss is rarely recoverable (see below)

5.3 The claim will not be proved under the following circumstances.

- The claimant followed a course of action **regardless of the acts of the defendant**.
- A **third party** is the actual cause of harm.
- A **complicated series of events** takes place such that no one act was the cause of all the harm.

- An intervening act by the claimant or a third party breaks the '**chain of causation**' (*novus actus interveniens*).

5.4 The court will look at whether the harm which occurred was reasonably foreseeable. This is the question of **remoteness of damage**.

Remoteness of damage

5.5 When a person commits a tort with the **intention of causing loss** or harm which in fact results from the wrongful act, that loss can never be too remote.

5.6 Where any intervening act is that of a third party who could be expected to behave as he did in the situation arising from the defendant's original wrongful act, the intervening act does not break the chain.

Reasonable foresight

5.7 When there is a sequence of physical cause and effect without human intervention, the ultimate loss is too remote unless it could have been foreseen that some loss of that kind might occur.

> *The Wagon Mound 1961*
> *The facts:* A ship was taking on oil in Sydney harbour. By negligence oil was spilled onto the water and it drifted to a wharf 200 yards away where welding equipment was in use. The owner of the wharf carried on working because he was advised that the sparks were unlikely to set fire to furnace oil. Safety precautions were taken. A spark fell onto a piece of cotton waste floating in the oil, thereby starting a fire which damaged the wharf. The owners of the wharf sued the charterers of the Wagon Mound.
>
> *Decision:* The claim must fail. Pollution was the foreseeable risk: fire was not.

Financial loss

5.8 Pure financial loss is only recoverable in exceptional circumstances. One example is when professional advisers owe a duty of care to a specific person. Professional liability is discussed in Section 6.

Contributory negligence

5.9 The courts may reduce the amount of damages paid if a person had contributed to the loss suffered. This was the case in *Sayers v Harlow UDC 1958*, where a lady was injured while trying to climb out of a public toilet cubicle which had a defective lock. The court held that she had contributed to her injuries by the method by which she had tried to climb out.

6 PROFESSIONAL ADVICE 5/01, 5/02

6.1 This section seeks to demonstrate how the law relating to negligent professional advice, and in particular **auditors**, has been developed through the operation of precedent, being refined and explained with each successive case that comes to court. It illustrates the often step-by-step development of English law, which has gradually refined the principles laid down in *Donoghue v Stevenson* and *Anns* to cover **negligent misstatements** which cause financial loss.

6.2 Before 1963, it was held that any liability for careless statements was limited in scope and depended upon the existence of a **contractual** or **fiduciary relationship** between the parties. Lord Denning's tests of a further (later termed 'special') relationship were laid down in the Court of Appeal in his dissenting judgement on *Candler v Crane, Christmas & Co 1951.*

KEY TERM

According to Lord Denning, to establish a **special relationship** the person who made the statement must have done so in some professional or expert capacity which made it likely that others would rely on what he said. This is the position of an adviser such as an accountant, banker, solicitor or surveyor.

6.3 It follows that a duty could not be owed to complete strangers, but Lord Denning also stated at the time: 'Accountants owe a duty of care not only to their own clients, but also to **all those whom they know will rely on their accounts** in the transactions for which those accounts are prepared.' This was to prove a significant consideration in later cases.

6.4 However, Lord Denning's view was a dissenting voice in 1951 in the *Candler* case, where the Court of Appeal held that the defendants were not liable (for a bad investment based upon a set of negligently prepared accounts) because there was no direct contractual or fiduciary relationship with the claimant investor.

6.5 It was twelve years later that the **special relationship** was accepted as a valid test. Our starting point is the **leading case** on negligent misstatement, outlined below, which was the start of a **new judicial approach** to cases involving negligent misstatement. You must make sure that you are familiar with it.

Hedley Byrne & Co Ltd v Heller and Partners Ltd 1963
The facts: HB were advertising agents acting for a new client, Easipower Ltd. HB requested information from Easipower's bank (HP) on its financial position. HP returned non-committal replies, which expressly disclaimed legal responsibility, and which were held to be negligent misstatement of Easipower's financial resources.

Decision: While HP were able to avoid liability by virtue of their disclaimer, the House of Lords went on to consider whether there ever could be a duty of care to avoid causing financial loss by negligent misstatement where there was no contractual or fiduciary relationship. It decided (as *obiter dicta*) that HP were guilty of negligence having breached the duty of care, because a special relationship did exist. Had it not been for the disclaimer, a claim for negligence would have succeeded.

6.6 In reaching the decision in *Hedley Byrne*, Lord Morris said the following:

'If someone possessed of a special skill undertakes....to apply that skill for the assistance of another person who **relies** on that skill, a duty of care will arise....If, in a sphere in which a person is so placed that others could reasonably rely on his skill....a person takes it on himself to give information or advice to....another person who, as he **knows or should know**, will place reliance on it, then a duty of care will arise.'

Point to note

As you already know from your study of Chapter 2, section 4, *obiter dicta* such as those made in 1963 do not form part of the *ratio decidendi*, and are not binding on future cases. They will, however, be **persuasive**.

6.7 Note that at the time liability did not extend to those who the advisor might merely **foresee as a possible user** of the statement.

6.8 However in a subsequent case, the courts extended potential liability, and started to take account of third parties not known to the adviser. The following case echoed the principles laid down in *Anns* (section 3.3) and addressed the question of **reasonable foresight** being present to create a duty of care.

JEB Fasteners Ltd v Marks, Bloom & Co 1982
The facts: The defendants, a firm of accountants, prepared an audited set of accounts showing overvalued stock and hence inflated profit. The auditors knew there were liquidity problems and that the company was seeking outside finance. The claimants were shown the accounts; they took over the company for a nominal amount, since by that means they could obtain the services of the company's two directors. At no time did MB tell JEB that the stock value was inflated. With the investment's failure, JEB sued MB, with the following claims.

(a) The accounts had been prepared negligently.

(b) They had relied on those accounts.

(c) They would not have invested had they been aware of the company's true position.

(d) MB owed a duty of care to **all persons whom they could reasonably foresee** would rely on the accounts.

Decision: Even though JEB had relied on the accounts (b), they would not have acted differently if the true position had been known (c), since they had really wanted the directors and not the company. Hence the accountants were not the cause of the consequential harm and were not liable. Significantly (although this did not affect the decision as to liability) it was the judge's view that MB did indeed owe a **duty of care through foresight** (d) and had been negligent in preparing the accounts (a).

6.9 Decisions since *JEB Fasteners* have, however, shied away from the foresight test and gone back to looking at whether the adviser has **knowledge of the user** and the **use to which the statement will be put**.

The Caparo decision

Exam focus point

The Caparo case is fundamental to an understanding of this area.

6.10 This important and controversial case made considerable changes to the tort of negligence as a whole, and the negligence of professionals in particular, and set a precedent which now forms the basis for courts when considering the liability of professional advisers.

Caparo Industries plc v Dickman and Others 1990
The facts: Caparo, which already held shares in Fidelity plc, bought more shares and later made a takeover bid, after seeing accounts prepared by the defendants that showed a profit of £1.3m. Caparo claimed against the directors (the brothers Dickman) and the auditors for the fact that the accounts should have shown a loss of £400,000. The claimants argued that the auditors owed a duty of care to investors and potential investors in respect of the audit. They should have been aware that a press release

stating that profits would fall significantly had made Fidelity vulnerable to a takeover bid and that bidders might well rely upon the accounts.

Decision: The auditor's duty did not extend to potential investors nor to existing shareholders increasing their stakes. It was a duty owed to the body of shareholders as whole.

6.11 In the *Caparo* case the House of Lords decided that there were two very different situations facing a person giving professional advice.

(a) Preparing information in the knowledge that a **particular person** was contemplating a transaction and would rely on the information in deciding whether or not to proceed with the transaction (the 'special relationship').

(b) Preparing a statement for **general circulation**, which could forseeably be relied upon by persons unknown to the professional for a variety of different purposes.

6.12 It was held therefore that a public company's auditors owed **no duty of care to the public at large** who relied on the audit report in deciding to invest - and, in purchasing additional shares, an existing shareholder was in no different position to the public at large.

6.13 In *MacNaughton (James) Papers Group Ltd v Hicks Anderson & Co 1991*, it was stated that it was necessary to examine each case in the light of the following.

- Foreseeability
- Proximity
- Fairness

6.14 This is because there could be **no single overriding principle** that could be applied to the individual complexities of every case. Lord Justice Neill set out the matters to be taken into account in considering this.

- The purpose for which the statement was **made**
- The purpose for which the statement was **communicated**
- The **relationship** between the maker of the statement, the recipient and any relevant third party
- The **size** of any class to which the recipient belonged
- The **state of knowledge** of the maker
- Any **reliance** by the recipient

6.15 The duty of care of accountants is held to be higher when advising on takeovers than when auditing. The directors and financial advisors of the target company in a contested takeover bid were held to owe a duty of care to a **known** take-over bidder in respect of financial statements prepared for the purpose of contesting the bid: *Morgan Crucible Co plc v Hill Samuel Bank Ltd and others 1990.*

6.16 A more recent case highlighted the need for a cautious approach and careful evaluation of the circumstances when giving financial advice, possibly with the need to issue a disclaimer.

ADT Ltd v BDO Binder Hamlyn 1995
The facts: Binder Hamlyn was the joint auditor of BSG. In October 1989, BSG's audited accounts for the year to 30 June 1989 were published. Binder Hamlyn signed off the audit as showing a true and fair view of BSG's position. ADT was thinking of buying

BSG and, as a potential buyer, sought Binder Hamlyn's confirmation of the audited results. On 5 January 1990, the Binder Hamlyn audit partner attended a meeting with John Jermine, a director of ADT. This meeting was described by the judge as the 'final hurdle' before ADT finalised its bid for BSG. At the meeting, Mr Bishop specifically confirmed that he 'stood by' the audit of October 1989. ADT proceeded to purchase BSG for £105m. It was subsequently alleged that BSG's true value was only £40m. ADT therefore sued Binder Hamlyn for the difference, £65m plus interest.

Decision: Binder Hamlyn assumed a responsibility for the statement that the audited accounts showed a true and fair view of BSG which ADT relied on to its detriment. Since the underlying audit work had been carried out negligently, Binder Hamlyn was held liable for £65m. The courts expect a higher standard of care from accountants when giving advice on company acquisitions since the losses can be so much greater.

6.17 This situation was different from *Caparo* since the court was specifically concerned with the **purpose of the statement made at the meeting**. Did Binder Hamlyn **assume any responsibility** as a result of Mr Bishop's comments? The court decided that it did. The court did not need to consider the question of duty to individual shareholders, because *Caparo* had already decided that there was none.

6.18 Following the *ADT* case, another case tested the court's interpretation.

NRG v Bacon and Woodrow and Ernst & Young 1996
The facts: NRG alleged that the defendants had failed to suggest the possibility that certain companies it was targeting might suffer huge reinsurance losses. They had also failed to assess properly whether these losses could be protected against, because defective actuarial methods had been used. As a result, it overpaid for these companies by £255m.
Decision: The judge observed that accountants owe a higher standard of care when advising on company purchases, because the potential losses are so much greater, following *ADT*. However, applying this higher standard of care to the facts, it was decided that NRG had received the advice that any competent professional would have given, because the complex nature of the losses that the companies were exposed to were not fully understood at the time. In addition, the use of defective actuarial methods had not led directly to the losses, because NRG would have bought the companies anyway.

6.19 There have been some other important clarifications of the law affecting accountants' liability in the area of responsibility towards non-clients. The following two cases both concerned auditors' liability to part of a group for losses incurred elsewhere in the group.

Barings plc v Coopers & Lybrand 1997
The facts: Barings collapsed in 1995 after loss-making trading by the general manager of its Singapore subsidiary, BFS. BFS was audited by the defendant's Singapore firm, which provided Barings directors with consolidation schedules and a copy of the BFS audit report. The defendant tried to argue that there was no duty of care owed to Barings, only to BFS.

Decision: A duty of care was owed to Barings, as the defendants must have known that their audit report and consolidation schedules would be relied upon at group level.

BCCI (Overseas) Ltd v Ernst & Whinney 1997

The facts: In this case, the defendants audited the group holding company's accounts, but not those of the claimant subsidiary. The claimant tried to claim that the defendants had a duty of care to them.

Decision: No duty of care was owed to the subsidiary because no specific information is normally channelled down by a holding company's auditor to its subsidiaries.

6.20 UK accountancy firms have been investigating ways of limiting liability in the face of increasing litigation. KPMG, for example, incorporated its audit practice in 1995.

6.21 In 2000, the Limited Liability Partnerships Act 2000 was passed, and limited liability partnerships have been permitted under law from 6 April 2001.

6.22 The Law Commission have also undertaken a review of partnership law.

6.23 The following points highlight the key proposals of the consultation document. The full text of the consultation document can be found at www.lawcom.gov.uk.

- Introduction of separate legal personality
- Legal personality without registration
- Legal personality dependent on registration
- Partners to be agents of the firm rather than each other
- Ownership of property by the entity
- Liability of the entity rather than the partners
- Statutory duty of good faith between partners

6.24 Most of the above proposals stem from the proposal of introducing separate legal personality into all partnerships (as opposed to limited liability partnerships which have already been established). This would clearly have far-reaching effects on partnership law.

6.25 At the time of writing, the Law commission were considering responses to the consultation document.

Exam focus point

Liability in tort for negligent professional advice is a very topical subject, specifically highlighted in the syllabus, and is still developing through case law. It is of particular relevance for accountants and likely to be examined regularly.

Question 2

In order to show that there exists a duty of care not to cause financial loss by negligent misstatement, the claimant must show that

1 The person making the statement did so in an expert capacity of which the claimant was aware

2 The context in which the statement was made was such as to make it likely that the claimant would rely on it

3 In making the statement the defendant foresaw that it would be relied upon by the claimant

4 The claimant had actually relied on the statement

A 1 and 2 only
B 1, 2 and 3 only
C 2, 3 and 4 only
D 1, 2, 3 and 4

Answer

D

Chapter roundup

- The law gives various rights to persons. When such a right is infringed the wrongdoer is liable in **tort**.
- **Negligence** is the most important modern tort. To succeed in an action for negligence the claimant must prove that:
  - The defendant had **a duty of care** to avoid causing injury, damage or loss
  - There was **a breach of that duty** by the defendant
  - *In consequence* the claimant suffered **injury, damage or loss**
- In the landmark case of *Donoghue v Stevenson 1932* the House of Lords ruled that a person might **owe a duty of care to another with whom he had no contractual relationship** at all. The doctrine has been refined in subsequent rulings, but the principle is unchanged.
- The law on **negligent professional advice** is currently influenced strongly by the *Caparo* case. In this case, it was held that the auditors of a public limited company did not owe a duty of care to the public at large who relied upon the audit report in making an investment decision.
- However, when giving advice professionals must be careful what they say. Statements may be relied on and the firm successfully sued as in *ADT v Binder Hamlyn 1995.*
- The development of the law on negligent professional advice is strongly influenced by the facts in each particular case, and it is unlikely that a single set of criteria could be set up to suit every business situation.

Quick quiz

1 In tort no previous transaction or contractual relationship need exist.

☐ True

☐ False

2 The 'neighbour' principle was established by the landmark case

A Caparo v Dickman 1990
B Anns v Merton London Borough Council 1977
C Donogue v Stevenson 1932
D The Wagon Mound 1961

3 **Fill in the blanks** in the statements below, using the words in the box.

- The law gives various rights to persons. When such a right is infringed the wrongdoer is liable in (1) ………………..
- (2) ……………….. is the most important modern tort
- The law on negligent (3) ……………….. advice is currently influenced strongly by the (4) ……………….. case
- To succeed in a claim for negligent misstatement and resultant economic loss, it must be shown that there was a (5) ……………….. of proximity and (6) ……………….. on advice

• Caparo	• reliance	• relationship
• negligence	• tort	• professional

4 In no more than 40 words, why the decision in *Binder Hamlyn v ADT* was different from *Caparo.*

5 There are two/three/six essential elements for a negligence claim to be successful. They are

....	....	....
....	....	....

6 When the court applies the maxim *res ipsa loquitur*, it is held that the facts speak for themselves and the defendant does not have to prove anything, since the burden of proof is on the claimant.

☐ True

☐ False

7 Give the most common example of economic loss.

8 What is the effect of a *novus actus interveniens* when an action is brought for tort?

A It will terminate the defendant's liability in all cases
B It will terminate the defendant's liability unless the *novus actus* was reasonably foreseeable
C It shifts the burden of proving negligence onto the claimant
D It has no effect on the defendant's liability but will reduce the amount of damages

9 In no more than 30 words, explain how a 'special relationship' is defined in the context of professional advice.

10 What is the leading case on negligent misstatement?

11 What three things must a claimant prove to succeed in an action for negligence?

- The defendant owed the claimant a ....
- These was a .... of the .... by the defendant
- In .... the claimant suffered ...., ... or ....

12 Which of the following would prevent a claim for negligence from being successful?

(a) The claimant followed a course of action regardless of the acts of the defendant.
(b) The defendant caused the harm to the claimant.
(c) A third party is the actual cause of harm.
(d) The parties were proximate and the harm suffered was reasonably foreseeable.
(e) An intervening act broke the 'chain of causation'.
(f) The duty of care was restricted by public policy.

13 'A public company's auditors owe no duty of care to the public at large who rely on the audit report in deciding to invest.'

This is the decision from *Caparo.*

True ☐
False ☐

14 In no more than 30 words, explain the factors that must exist for a negligence claim to be successful.

Answers to quick quiz

1 True

2 C

3 (1) tort (2) negligence (3) professional (4) Caparo (5) relationship (6) reliance

4 Binder Hamlyn was held to have specifically assumed responsibility for its statements at a meeting held to discuss the audited results, which made it liable outside the usual sphere laid down by Caparo.

5 Three: Duty of care
Breach of that duty
Consequential damage, injury or loss

6 False

7 When a person who has suffered physical damage makes a claim for loss of profits while the damage is put right.

8 B

9 The person who makes the statement makes it in some professional or expert capacity which makes it likely that another will rely on what he says.

10 *Hedley Byrne v Heller 1963*

11
- Duty of care
- Breach, duty
- Consequence, injury, loss, damage

12 (a), (c), (e), (f)

13 True

14
- The defendant must owe the claimant a duty of care
- There was a breach of duty by the claimant
- In consequence, the claimant suffered injury, damage or loss

The following relevant questions are included in the Exam Question Banks

You can attempt these now. However, we would advise you to attempt these as mock exams at the end of your initial stage of study

Exam Question Bank	Numbers
Paper based format	3
Computer based assessment	5, 11

Part B
Contract

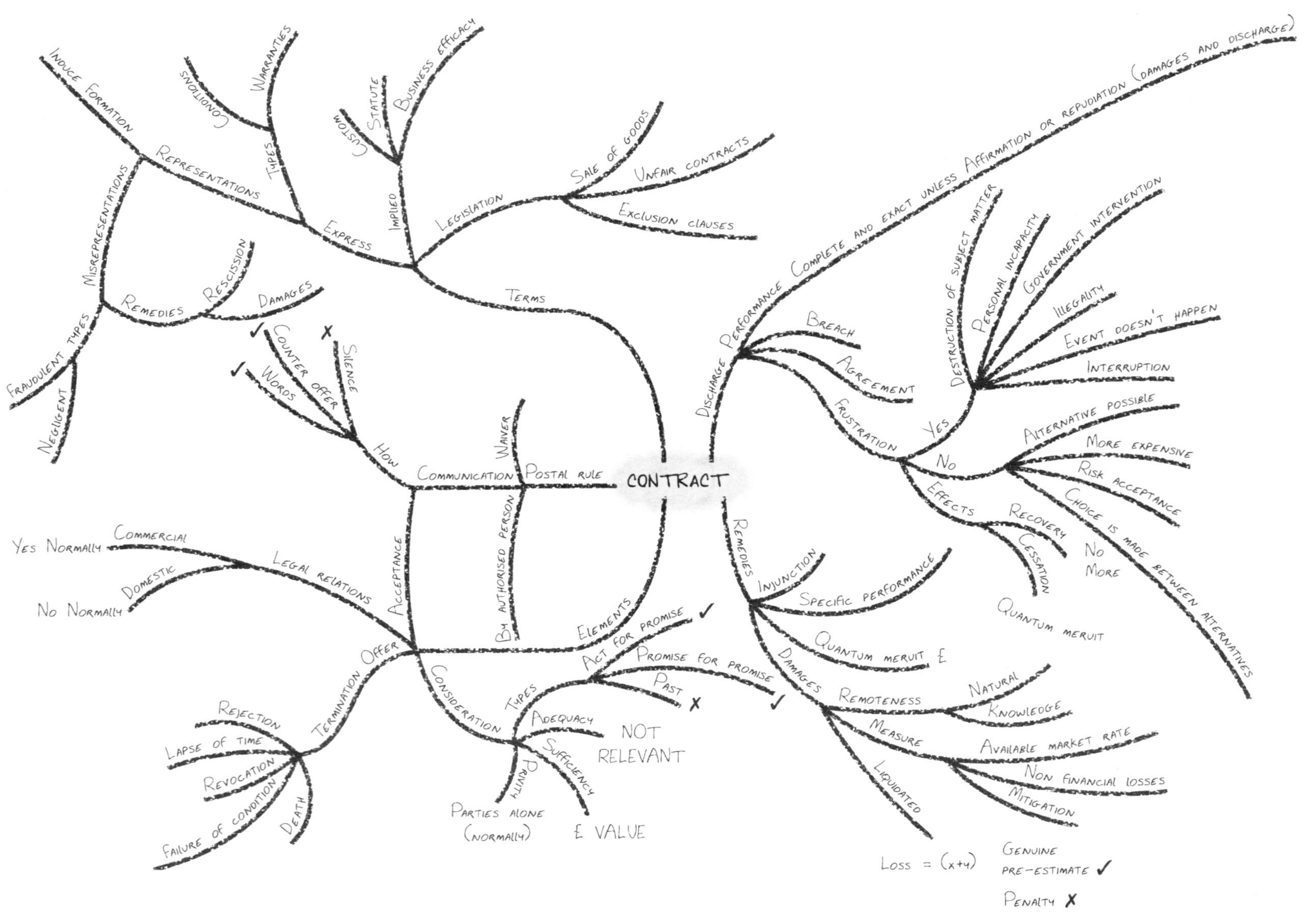

CONTRACT
Discharge
Performance
Complete and exact unless Affirmation or Repudiation (Damages and discharge)
Breach
Agreement
Frustration
Yes
No
Effects
Destruction of subject matter
Personal incapacity
Government intervention
Illegality
Event doesn't happen
Interruption
Alternative possible
More expensive
Risk acceptance
Choice is made between alternatives
Recovery
No More
Cessation
Quantum meruit
Remedies
Injunction
Specific performance
Quantum meruit £
Damages
Remoteness
Natural
Knowledge
Measure
Available market rate
Non financial losses
Mitigation
Liquidated
Loss = (x+y)
Genuine pre-estimate ✓
Penalty ✗
Elements
Act for promise ✓
Promise for promise ✓
Past ✗
NOT RELEVANT
Types
Adequacy
Sufficiency
£ VALUE
Privity
Parties alone (normally)
Consideration
Offer
Acceptance
Communication
Postal rule
Waiver
By authorised person
How
Silence ✗
Counter offer ✓
Words ✓
Termination
Death
Rejection
Lapse of time
Revocation
Failure of condition
Legal relations
Commercial
Yes Normally
Domestic
No Normally
Terms
Legislation
Sale of goods
Unfair contracts
Exclusion clauses
Implied
Business efficacy
Statute
Custom
Express
Types
Warranties
Conditions
Representations
Induce formation
Misrepresentations
Remedies
Rescission
Damages
Types
Fraudulent
Negligent

Chapter 3

ESSENTIALS OF A VALID SIMPLE CONTRACT

	Topic list	Syllabus reference	Ability required
1	Contract basics	(ii)	Comprehension
2	Agreement	(ii)	Comprehension
3	Intention	(ii)	Comprehension
4	Consideration	(ii)	Comprehension
5	Other factors affecting validity	(ii)	Comprehension

Introduction

The first essential element of a binding contract is **agreement**. To determine whether or not an agreement has been reached, the courts will consider whether one party has made a firm **offer** which the other party has **accepted**.

In most contracts, offer and acceptance may be made orally or in writing, or they may be implied by the conduct of the parties. The person making an offer is the offeror and the person to whom an offer is made is the offeree.

An agreement is not a binding contract unless the parties **intend to create legal relations**. What matters is not what the parties have in their minds, but the inferences that reasonable people would draw from their words or conduct.

The third of the three essential elements of a contract is **consideration**. The promise which a claimant seeks to enforce must be shown to be part of a bargain to which the claimant has himself contributed. Related to consideration are the doctrines of **promissory estoppel** and **privity of contract**.

The chapter concludes with a discussion other factors which may affect the validity of a contract. Particularly it focuses on **misrepresentation** and its effect upon a contract, but a person's capacity to contract and the form of the contract may also affect validity.

Learning outcomes covered in this chapter

- **Identify** the essential elements of a valid simple contract and situations where the law requires the contract to be in a particular form
- **Explain** how the law determines whether negotiating parties have reached agreement
- **Explain** when the parties will be regarded as intending the agreement to be legally binding
- **Explain** what the law regards as consideration sufficient to make the agreement enforceable
- **Explain** when an apparently valid agreement may be avoided because of misrepresentation

Syllabus content covered in this chapter

- The essential elements of a valid simple contract

- The legal status of the various types of statements which may be made by negotiating parties. Enforceable offers and acceptances, and the application of the rules to standard form contracts and modern forms of communication
- The principles for establishing that the parties intend their agreement to have contractual force
- The meaning and importance of consideration
- How a contract is affected by a misrepresentation

1 CONTRACT BASICS 11/01

KEY TERM

A **contract** may be defined as an **agreement which legally binds the parties.** The underlying theory is that a contract is the outcome of 'consenting minds'. Parties are judged by what they have said, written or done.

'An agreement which the law will recognise and enforce which, apart from other important applications, forms the basis of most business relationships and transactions.'

The essentials of a contract

1.1 There are **three essential elements** in any contract.

- **Agreement**. This is made by offer and acceptance.
- **Intention**. The parties must have an intention to create legal relations between themselves.
- **Consideration**. There must be a bargain by which the obligations assumed by one party are supported by value given by the other.

1.2 These are the vital elements of a contract. They are looked at in more detail later in the chapter.

Exam focus point

The fact that a contract cannot exist unless these three essential elements are present is the most important thing for you to learn in relation to contract law.

1.3 Even if the essential elements can be shown, a contract may not necessarily be valid. The validity of a contract may also be affected by the following factors.

VALIDITY FACTORS
Capacity. Some persons have only restricted capacity to enter into contracts. (See section 5)
Form. Some contracts must be made in a particular form. (See section 5)
Consent. A misrepresentation made by one party may affect the validity of a contract. (See section 5)

VALIDITY FACTORS
Content. In general the parties may enter into a contract on whatever terms they choose. However, terms must be incorporated properly into the contract. Some terms are also implied by statute. This is discussed in more detail in Chapter 4.
Legality. The courts will not enforce a contract which is deemed to be illegal or contrary to public policy.

1.4 A contract which is not valid may be either **void, voidable** or **unenforceable**.

KEY TERMS

A **void contract** is not a contract at all. The parties are not bound by it and if they transfer property under it they can sometimes recover their goods even from a third party.

A **voidable contract** is a contract which one party may avoid. Property transferred before avoidance is usually irrecoverable from a third party.

An **unenforceable contract** is a valid contract and property transferred under it cannot be recovered even from the other party to the contract. But if either party refuses to perform or to complete his part of the performance of the contract, the other party cannot compel him to do so. A contract is usually unenforceable when the required evidence of its terms, for example, written evidence of a contract relating to land, is not available.

1.5 Once a valid contract has been formed, it remains in existence until discharged. For your studies, the most important means of discharge is **breach of contract**. This is covered in Chapter 5.

Question 1

What are the essential elements of a binding contract?

Answer

There must be an intention to create legal relations. There must be an agreement made by offer and acceptance. There must be consideration.

Question 2

An agreement between Nigel and Rupert was brought before a court. The court found that neither Rupert nor Nigel should feel himself bound by the agreement and that property transferred from one party to the other, but subsequently transferred to Charles, should be recovered. The agreement was

A Void
B Voidable
C Unenforceable
D Illegal

Answer

A. The parties are restored to their pre-contract position.

Factors affecting the modern contract

Inequality of bargaining power

1.6 It is almost invariably the case that the two parties to a contract bring with them differing levels of **bargaining power**. Many contracts are made between experts and ordinary consumers. The law will intervene only where the former takes unfair advantage of his position. **Freedom of contract** is a term sometimes used and can be defined as follows.

> 'The principle that parties are completely unrestricted in deciding whether or not to enter into an agreement and, if they do so, upon the terms governing that relationship. In practice, this is not always the case because one may be in a much stronger economic position, and legislation has been introduced in order to redress the balance.'
>
> (CIMA, *Terminology of Business and Company Law*)

The standard form contract

1.7 Mass production and nationalisation have led to the **standard form contract**.

KEY TERM

The **standard form contract** is a document prepared by many large organisations setting out the terms on which they contract with their customers. The individual must usually take it or leave it.

1.8 EXAMPLE

A customer has to accept his supply of electricity on the electricity board's terms - he is not likely to succeed in negotiating special terms, unless he represents a large consumer such as a factory.

Consumer protection

1.9 In the second half of the twentieth century, there has been a surge of interest in consumer matters. The development of a mass market for often complex goods has meant that the consumer can no longer rely on his own judgement when buying sophisticated goods or services. Consumer interests are now served by two main areas.

- **Consumer protection agencies,** which include government departments (the Office of Fair Trading) and independent bodies (the Consumers' Association).
- **Legislation,** for example, Consumer Credit Act 1974 and Unfair Contracts Terms Act 1977. This is discussed in Chapter 7.

2 AGREEMENT 5/02

Offer

KEY TERM

An offer is a **definite promise to be bound on specific terms**. An offer may be defined as follows.

'An express or implied statement of the terms on which the maker is prepared to be contractually bound if it is accepted unconditionally. The offer may be made to one person, to a class of persons or to the world at large, and only the person or one of the persons to whom it is made may accept it.'

2.1 A definite offer does not have to be made to a particular person. It may be made to a class of persons or to the world at large.

Exam focus point

The case below is very important in the law of contract. Learn it before you learn any others.

Carlill v Carbolic Smoke Ball Co 1893

The facts: The manufacturers of a patent medicine published an advertisement by which they undertook to pay '£100 reward .... to any person who contracts .... influenza .... after having used the smoke ball three times daily for two weeks'. The advertisement added that £1,000 had been deposited at a bank 'showing our sincerity in this matter'. The claimant read the advertisement, purchased the smoke ball and used it as directed. She contracted influenza and claimed her £100 reward. In their defence the manufacturers argued against this.

(a) The offer was so vague that it could not form the basis of a contract, as no time limit was specified.

(b) It was not an offer which could be accepted since it was offered to the whole world.

Decision: The court disagreed.

(a) The smoke ball must protect the user during the period of use - the offer was not vague.

(b) Such an offer was possible, as it could be compared to reward cases.

2.2 An offer must be **distinguished** from other similar things.

Distinguishing an offer

2.3 Only an offer in the proper sense may be accepted so as to form a binding contract.

Item	Distinguishing features
Supply of information	*Harvey v Facey 1893* *The facts:* The claimant telegraphed to the defendant 'Will you sell us Bumper Hall Pen? Telegraph lowest cash price'. The defendant telegraphed in reply 'Lowest price for Bumper Hall Pen, £900'. The claimant telegraphed to accept what he regarded as an offer; the defendant made no further reply. *Decision:* The defendant's telegram was merely a statement of his minimum price if a sale were to be agreed. It was not an offer which the claimant could accept. However, if in the course of negotiations for a sale, the vendor states the price at which he will sell, that statement may be an offer which can be accepted.
Statement of intention	Advertising that an event such as an auction will take place is not an offer to sell. Potential buyers may not sue the auctioneer if the auction does not take place: *Harris v Nickerson 1873*
Invitation to treat (see below)	Where a party is initiating negotiations he is said to have made an invitation to treat. An **invitation to treat** cannot be accepted to form a binding contract. There are four types of invitation to treat. • **Auction** sales • **Advertisements** (eg, price lists or newspaper advertisements) • **Exhibition** of goods for sale • An **invitation** for tenders

An invitation to treat

KEY TERM

An **invitation to treat** can be defined as follows.

'An indication that a person is prepared to receive offers with a view to entering into a binding contract, for example, an advertisement of goods for sale or a company prospectus inviting offers for shares. It must be distinguished from an offer which requires only acceptance to conclude the contract.'

Auction sales

2.4 The bid itself is the offer, which the auctioneer is free to accept or reject: *Payne v Cave 1789.*

Advertisements

2.5 An advertisement of goods for sale is an attempt to induce offers.

Exhibition of goods for sale

2.6 Displaying goods in a shop window or on the open shelves of a self service shop or advertising goods for sale, is an invitation to treat.

Pharmaceutical Society of Great Britain v Boots Cash Chemists (Southern) 1952
The facts: Certain drugs could only be sold under the supervision of a registered pharmacist. The claimant claimed this rule had been broken by Boots who displayed these drugs in a self-service shop. Boots contended that there was no sale until a customer brought the goods to the cash desk and offered to buy them. A registered pharmacist was stationed at this point.

Decision: The court found for Boots and commented that if it were true that a customer accepted an offer to sell by removing goods from the shelf, he could not then change his mind and put them back as this would constitute breach of contract.

Invitation for tenders

2.7 A **tender** is an estimate submitted in response to a prior request.

Question 3

Maud goes into a shop and sees a price label for £20 on an ironing board. She takes the board to the checkout but the till operator tells her that the label is misprinted and should read £30. Maud maintains that she only has to pay £20. How would you describe the price on the price label in terms of contract law?

A An offer
B A tender
C An invitation to treat
D An acceptance

Answer

C

Termination of offer

2.8 An offer is **terminated** in any of the following circumstances.

- Rejection
- Lapse of time
- Revocation by the offeror
- Failure of a condition to which the offer was subject
- Death of one of the parties

Rejection

2.9 Rejection terminates an offer. A counter-offer amounts to rejection (see below).

Lapse of time

2.10 An offer may be expressed to last for a **specified time**. If, however, there is no express time limit set, it expires after a **reasonable time**.

Ramsgate Victoria Hotel Co v Montefiore
The facts: The defendant applied to the company in June for shares and paid a deposit. At the end of November the company sent him an acceptance by issue of a letter of allotment and requested payment of the balance due. The defendant contended that his offer had expired and could no longer be accepted.

Decision: The offer was for a reasonable time only and five months was much more than that. The offer had lapsed.

Revocation of an offer

2.11 The offeror may **revoke** his offer at any time before acceptance: *Payne v Cave 1789.* If he undertakes that his offer shall remain open for acceptance for a specified time he may nonetheless revoke it within that time, unless by a separate contract he has bound himself to keep it open.

Routledge v Grant 1828
The facts: The defendant offered to buy the claimant's house for a fixed sum, requiring acceptance within six weeks. Within the six weeks specified, he withdrew his offer.

Decision: The defendant could revoke his offer at any time before acceptance, even though the time limit had not expired.

2.12 Revocation may be an express statement or may be an act of the offeror. His revocation does not take effect until the revocation is communicated to the offeree. This raises two important points.

(a) The first point is that **posting a letter is not a sufficient act of revocation**.

(b) The second point is that **revocation of offer may be communicated by any third party who is a sufficiently reliable informant**.

Dickinson v Dodds 1876
The facts: The defendant, on 10 June, wrote to the claimant to offer property for sale at £800, adding 'this offer to be left open until Friday 12 June, 9.00 am.' On 11 June the defendant sold the property to another buyer, A. B, who had been an intermediary between Dickinson and Dodds, informed Dickinson that the defendant had sold to someone else. On Friday 12 June, before 9.00 am, the claimant handed to the defendant a formal letter of acceptance.

Decision: The defendant was free to revoke his offer and had done so by sale to a third party; the claimant could not accept the offer after he had learnt from a reliable informant of the revocation of the offer to him.

Failure of a condition

2.13 An offer may be conditional. If the condition is not satisfied, the offer is not capable of acceptance.

Financings Ltd v Stimson 1962
The facts: The defendant wished to purchase a car, and on 16 March signed a hire-purchase form. The form, issued by the claimants, stated that the agreement would be binding only upon signature by them. On 20 March the defendant, not satisfied with the car, returned it. On 24 March the car was stolen from the premises of the dealer, and was recovered badly damaged. On 25 March the claimants signed the form. They sued the defendant for breach of contract.

Decision: The defendant was not bound to take the car. His signing of the agreement was actually an offer to contract with the claimant. There was an implied condition in this offer that the car would be in a reasonable condition.

Termination by death

2.14 The death of the offeree terminates the offer. The offeror's death terminates the offer, unless the offeree accepts the offer in ignorance of the death, and the offer is not of a personal nature.

Acceptance

> **KEY TERM**
>
> **Acceptance** may be defined as follows.
>
> 'A positive act by a person to whom an offer has been made which, if unconditional, brings a binding contract into effect.'

2.15 Acceptance '**subject to contract**' means that the offeree is agreeable to the terms of the offer but proposes that the parties should negotiate a formal contract. Neither party is bound until the formal contract is signed. Agreements for the sale of land in England are usually made 'subject to contract'.

2.16 Acceptance of an offer may only be made by a person authorised to do so. This will usually be the offeree or his authorised agents.

Powell v Lee 1908
The facts: The claimant was appointed to a post as a headmaster. Without authorisation, he was informed of the appointment by one of the managers. Later, it was decided to give the post to someone else. The claimant sued for breach of contract.

Decision: Since communication of acceptance was unauthorised, there was no valid agreement and hence no contract.

2.17 Acceptance may be by **express words**, by **action** or **inferred from conduct** but there must be some **act** on the part of the offeree to indicate his acceptance.

Felthouse v Bindley 1862
The facts: The claimant wrote to his nephew offering to buy the nephew's horse, adding 'If I hear no more about him, I consider the horse mine'. The nephew intended to accept his uncle's offer but did not reply. He instructed the defendant, an auctioneer, not to sell the horse. Owing to a misunderstanding the horse was sold to someone else. The uncle sued the auctioneer.

Decision: The action failed. The claimant had no title to the horse.

2.18 Goods which are sent or services which are rendered to a person who did not request them are not 'accepted' merely because he does not return them to the sender: Unsolicited Goods and Services Act 1971. The recipient may treat them as an unsolicited gift.

2.19 Genuine acceptance must also be **distinguished** from other things.

Distinguishing acceptance

Counter-offer

2.20 Acceptance must be unqualified agreement to the terms of the offer. Acceptance which introduces any new terms is a counter-offer.

KEY TERM

A **counter-offer** is a final rejection of the original offer. If a counter-offer is made, the original offeror may accept it, but if he rejects it his original offer is no longer available for acceptance.

Hyde v Wrench 1840
The facts: The defendant offered to sell property to the claimant for £1,000 on 6 June. Two days later, the claimant made a counter-offer of £950 which the defendant rejected on 27 June. The claimant then informed the defendant on 29 June that he accepted the original offer of £1,000.

Decision: The original offer of £1,000 had been terminated by the counter-offer of £950.

Request for information

2.21 It is possible to respond to an offer by making a **request for information**. Such a request may be a request as to whether or not other terms would be acceptable. This does not constitute rejection of the offer.

Question 4

Nicholas offers to sell his car to Derek for £700 on 1 June, but in reply Derek merely asks how old the car is, what its mileage is and how many owners it has had. Nicholas provides this information on 3 June and on that date states that the offer will be kept open only until 10 June. On 7 June Derek says he will take the car for £600. On 8 June Hughie buys the car from Nicholas for £700. On 10 June Derek agrees to buy the car for £700, and is told it has been sold. On 10 June, what is the state of the relations between Nicholas and Derek?

A There is a contract to sell at £600 so Derek may recover the car from Hughie as his property

B There is a contract to sell at £700 which has been terminated by Nicholas's breach when he sold the car to Hughie

C There is an offer from Nicholas to sell for £700 which is still open for Derek to accept

D There is an offer from Derek to buy at £700 which Nicholas cannot accept

Answer

D

Communication of acceptance

2.22 The general rule is that acceptance **must be communicated** to the offeror and is not effective until this has been done. There are two exceptions.

Waiver of communication

2.23 The offeror may dispense with the need for communication of acceptance. Such a waiver may be express or may be inferred from the circumstances.

The postal rule

2.24 The offeror may expressly or by implication indicate that he expects acceptance by means of a letter sent through the post.

KEY TERM

The **postal rule** states that, where the use of the post is within the contemplation of both the parties, the acceptance is complete and effective as soon as a letter is posted, even though it may be delayed or even lost altogether in the post.

Adams v Lindsell 1818

The facts: The defendants made an offer by letter to the claimant on 2 September 1817 requiring an answer 'in course of post'. It reached the claimants on 5 September; they immediately posted a letter of acceptance, which reached the defendants on 9 September. The defendants could have expected a reply by 7 September, and they assumed that the absence of a reply within the expected period indicated non-acceptance and sold the goods to another buyer on 8 September.

Decision: The acceptance was made 'in course of post' (no time limit was imposed) and was effective when posted on 5 September.

2.25 The intention to use the post for communication of acceptance may be deduced from the circumstances, for example if the negotiations have all been undertaken by letter. If the offeror expressly requires 'notice in writing', the postal rule does not apply.

Question 6

Under the postal rule, acceptance made by letter is complete and effective as soon as the letter is posted. Do you think that the offeree can subsequent withdraw his acceptance before the letter reaches the offeror?

Answer

Any such attempt should fail, as a binding contract is formed when the letter is posted.

2.26 If there is no mode of communication prescribed in negotiations, the offeree must ensure that his acceptance is understood. This applies to any instantaneous method of communication.

Entores v Miles Far Eastern Corporation 1955

The facts: The claimants sent an offer by telex to the defendants' agent in Amsterdam and the latter sent an acceptance by telex. The claimants alleged breach of contract and wished to serve a writ.

Decision: The acceptance took effect (and the contract was made) when the telex message was printed out on the claimants' terminal in London. A writ could therefore be issued.

3 INTENTION

Pilot Paper, 5/01

3.1 Where there is no express statement as to whether or not legal relations are intended, the courts apply one of two **rebuttable presumptions** to a case.

- **Social, domestic and family arrangements** are not usually intended to be binding.
- **Commercial agreements** are usually intended by the parties involved to be legally binding.

KEY TERM

Intention to create legal relations can be defined as follows.

'An agreement will only become a legally binding contract if the parties intend this to be so. This will be strongly presumed in the case of business agreements but presumed otherwise if the agreement is of a friendly, social or domestic nature.'

Domestic arrangements

Husband and wife

3.2 The fact that the parties are husband and wife does not mean that they cannot enter into a binding contract with one another. However the court will assume that they have not, and this presumption must be disproved if they have contracted. The courts are more inclined to consider that legal relations exist if property is involved.

> *Balfour v Balfour 1919*
> *The facts:* The defendant was employed in Ceylon. He and his wife returned to the UK on leave but it was agreed that for health reasons she would not return to Ceylon with him. He promised to pay her £30 a month as maintenance. Later the marriage ended in divorce and the wife sued for the monthly allowance which the husband no longer paid.
>
> *Decision:* An informal agreement of indefinite duration made between husband and wife whose marriage had not at the time broken up was not intended to be legally binding.
>
> *Merritt v Merritt 1970*
> *The facts:* The husband had left the matrimonial home, which was owned in the joint names of husband and wife, to live with another woman. The spouses met and held a discussion, in the course of which he agreed to pay her £40 a month out of which she agreed to keep up the mortgage payments. The wife made the husband sign a note of these terms and an undertaking to transfer the house into her name when the mortgage had been paid off. The wife paid off the mortgage but the husband refused to transfer the house to her.
>
> *Decision:* In the circumstances, an intention to create legal relations was to be inferred and the wife could sue for breach of contract.

3.3 Agreements between other family members may also be examined by the courts. Domestic arrangements also extend to those between people who are not related but who have a close relationship of some form. The nature of the agreement itself may lead to the conclusion that legal relations were intended.

Commercial agreements

3.4 When business people enter into commercial agreements it is presumed that there is an intention to enter into legal relations unless this is expressly disclaimed or the circumstances indicate otherwise.

Rose and Frank v Crompton 1923
The facts: A commercial agreement by which the defendants appointed the claimant to be its distributor in the USA contained a clause described as 'the Honourable Pledge Clause' which expressly stated that the arrangement was 'not subject to legal jurisdiction' in either country. The defendants terminated the agreement without giving notice as required, and refused to deliver goods ordered by the claimants although they had accepted these orders when placed.

Decision: The general agreement was not legally binding as there was no obligation to stand by any clause in it. However the orders for goods were separate and binding contracts. The claim for damages for breach of the agreement failed, but the claim for damages for non-delivery of goods ordered succeeded.

3.5 The words relied on by a party to a commercial agreement to show that legal relations are not intended are not always clear. In such cases, the burden of proof is on the party seeking to escape liability.

4 CONSIDERATION 11/01, 5/02

KEY TERM

Consideration has been defined as:

'A valuable consideration in the sense of the law may consist either in some right, interest, profit or benefit accruing to one party, or some forbearance, detriment, loss or responsibility given, suffered or undertaken by the other.' *From Currie v Misa 1875*

Valid consideration

4.1 There are two broad types of valid consideration - **executed** and **executory**. If consideration is **past** then it is not enforceable.

4.2 **Executed consideration is an act in return for a promise**. The consideration for the promise is a performed, or executed, act.

4.3 EXAMPLE

If A offers a reward for the return of lost property, his promise becomes binding when B performs the act of returning A's property to him. A is not bound to pay anything to anyone until the prescribed act is done. C's act in Carlill's case in response to the smoke ball company's promise of reward was thus executed consideration.

4.4 **Executory consideration is a promise given for a promise**. The consideration in support of each promise is the other promise, not a performed act.

4.5 EXAMPLE

If a customer orders goods which a shopkeeper undertakes to obtain from the manufacturer, the shopkeeper promises to supply the goods and the customer promises to accept and pay for them. Neither has yet done anything but each has given a promise to obtain the promise of the other. It would be breach of contract if either withdrew without the consent of the other.

4.6 **Anything which has already been done before a promise in return is given is past consideration** which, as a general rule, is not sufficient to make the promise binding.

KEY TERM

Past consideration can be defined as follows.

'... something which has already been done at the time the promise is made. An example would be a promise to pay for work already carried out, unless there was an implied promise to pay a reasonable sum before the work began.'

Re McArdle 1951
The facts: Under a will the testator's children were entitled to a house after their mother's death. In the mother's lifetime one of the children and his wife lived in the house with the mother. The wife made improvements to the house. The children later agreed in writing to repay the wife 'in consideration of your carrying out certain alterations and improvements'. But at the mother's death they refused to do so.

Decision: The work on the house had all been completed before the documents were signed. At the time of the promise the improvements were past consideration and so the promise was not binding.

4.7 If there is an existing contract and one party makes a further promise no contract will arise. Even if such a promise is directly related to the previous bargain, it will be held to have been made upon past consideration.

Roscorla v Thomas 1842
The facts: The claimant agreed to buy a horse from the defendant at a given price. When negotiations were over and the contract was formed, the defendant told the claimant that the horse was 'sound and free from vice'. The horse turned out to be vicious and the claimant brought an action on the warranty.

Decision: The express promise was made after the sale was over and was unsupported by fresh consideration.

Question 7

Consideration

1 Must be of adequate and sufficient value
2 Must move from the promisee
3 Must never be past
4 Must be given in every binding agreement
5 May be performance of an existing obligation

A 1 only
B 2 only
C 2, 3 and 4 only
D 3, 4 and 5 only

Answer

B

Adequacy and sufficiency of consideration 5/01

4.8 The court will also seek to ensure that a particular act or promise can actually be deemed to be consideration. Learn these rules:

Consideration need not be adequate (that is, equal in value to the consideration received in return). There is no remedy at law for someone who simply makes a poor bargain.
Consideration must be sufficient. It must be capable in law of being regarded as consideration.

Adequacy

4.9 It is presumed that each party is capable of serving his own interests, and the courts will not seek to **weigh up** the **comparative value** of the promises or acts exchanged.

Thomas v Thomas 1842
The facts: By his will the claimant's husband expressed the wish that his widow should have the use of his house during her life. The defendants, his executors, allowed the widow to occupy the house (a) in accordance with her husband's wishes and (b) in return for her undertaking to pay a rent of £1 per annum. They later said that their promise to let her occupy the house was not supported by consideration.

Decision: Compliance with the husband's wishes was not valuable consideration (no economic value attached to it), but the nominal rent was sufficient consideration.

Sufficiency

4.10 Consideration is sufficient if it has some identifiable value. The law only requires an element of bargain, not necessarily that it should be a good bargain.

Chappell & Co v Nestle Co 1960
The facts: As a sales promotion scheme, the defendant offered to supply a record to anyone who sent in a postal order for 1s.6d and three wrappers from 6d bars of chocolate made by them. The claimants owned the copyright of the tune. They sued for infringement of copyright. In the ensuing dispute over royalties the issue was whether the wrappers, which were thrown away when received, were part of the consideration for the promise to supply the record. The defendants offered to pay a royalty based on the price of 1s.6d per record, but the claimants rejected this, claiming that the wrappers also represented part of the consideration.

Decision: The wrappers were part of the consideration as they had commercial value to the defendants.

4.11 As stated earlier, forbearance or the promise of it may be sufficient consideration if it has some value, or amounts to giving up something of value.

Performance of existing contractual duties

4.12 Performance of an **existing obligation imposed by statute** is no consideration for a promise of reward.

> *Collins v Godefroy 1831*
> *The facts:* The claimant had been subpoenaed to give evidence on behalf of the defendant in another case. He alleged that the defendant had promised to pay him six guineas for appearing.
>
> *Decision:* There was no consideration for this promise.

4.13 But if some **extra service** is given that is sufficient consideration.

> *Glasbrook Bros v Glamorgan CC 1925*
> *The facts:* At a time of industrial unrest, colliery owners, rejecting the view of the police that a mobile force was enough, agreed to pay for a special guard on the mine. Later they repudiated liability saying that the police had done no more than perform their public duty of maintaining order, and that no consideration was given.
>
> *Decision:* The police had done more than perform their general duties. The extra services given, beyond what the police in their discretion deemed necessary, were consideration for the promise to pay.

Promise of additional reward

4.14 If there is already a contract between A and B, and B promises **additional reward** to A if he (A) will perform his existing duties, there is no consideration from A to make that promise binding. If a claimant does **more than perform an existing contractual duty**, this may amount to consideration.

4.15 The courts now appear to be taking a slightly different line on the payment of additional consideration. The principles of consideration may not be applied if the dispute can be dealt with on an alternative basis.

> *Williams v Roffey Bros & Nicholls (Contractors) Ltd 1990*
> *The facts:* The claimants agreed to do carpentry work for the defendants, who were engaged as contractors to refurbish a block of flats, at a fixed price of £20,000. The work ran late and so the defendants, concerned that the job might not be finished on time and that they would have to pay money under a penalty clause, agreed to pay the claimants an extra £10,300 to ensure the work was completed on time. They later refused to pay the extra amount.
>
> *Decision:* The fact that there was no apparent consideration for the promise to pay the extra was not held to be important, as in the court's view both parties derived benefit from the promise. The telling point was that the defendants' promise had not been extracted by duress or fraud: it was therefore binding.

Exam focus point

The examiner has said that the case of *Williams v Roffey Bros* is important because it is a newer case than the bulk of contract cases, most of which were decided in the nineteenth century.

Re Selectmove 1994
The facts: A company which was the subject of a winding up order offered to settle its outstanding debts by instalment. An Inland Revenue inspector agreed to the proposal. The company tried to enforce it.

Decision: Despite the verdict in *Williams v Roffey Brothers* the court followed *Foakes v Beer* (see below) in holding that an agreement to pay in instalments in unenforceable. Even though the creditor may obtain some practical benefit this is not adequate consideration to render the agreement legally binding.

Performance of existing contractual duty to a third party

4.16 If A promises B a reward if B will perform his **existing contract** with C, there is consideration for A's promise since he obtains a benefit to which he previously had no right, and B assumes new obligations.

Waiver of existing rights

4.17 EXAMPLE

If X owes Y £100 but Y agrees to accept a lesser sum, say £80, in full settlement of Y's claim, that is a promise by Y to waive his entitlement to the balance of £20. The promise, like any other, should be supported by consideration.

4.18 The case below is important.

Foakes v Beer 1884
The facts: The defendant had obtained judgement against the claimant. Judgement debts bear interest from the date of the judgement. By a written agreement the defendant agreed to accept payment by instalments, no mention being made of the interest. Once the claimant had paid the amount of the debt in full, the defendant claimed interest, claiming that the agreement was not supported by consideration.

Decision: She was entitled to the debt with interest. No consideration had been given by the claimant for waiver of any part of her rights against him.

4.19 There are, however, exceptions to the rule that the debtor (denoted by 'X' in the following paragraphs) must give consideration if the waiver is to be binding.

EXCEPTIONS	
Alternative consideration	If X offers and Y accepts anything to which Y is not already entitled, the extra thing is sufficient consideration for the waiver.
Anon 1495 *Pinnel's Case 1602*	• Goods instead of cash • Early payment
Bargain between the creditors	If X arranges with creditors that they will each accept part payment in full entitlement, that is bargain between the creditors
Woods v Robarts 1818	X has given no consideration but he can hold the creditors individually to the agreed terms
Third party part payment *Welby v Drake 1825*	If a third party (Z) offers part payment and Y agrees to release X from Y's claim to the balance, Y has received consideration from Z against whom he had no previous claim

EXCEPTIONS	
Promissory estoppel	The principle of promissory estoppel may prevent Y from retracting his promise with retrospective effect. (see below)

Promissory estoppel

KEY TERM

The doctrine of **promissory estoppel** works as follows.

If a creditor (Y) makes a promise (unsupported by consideration) to the debtor (X) that Y will not insist on the full discharge of the debt, and the promise is made with the intention that X should act on it and he does so, Y is **estopped** from retracting his promise, unless X can be restored to his original position.

Central London Property Trust v High Trees House 1947
The facts: In September 1939, the claimants let a block of flats to the defendants at an annual rent of £2,500 p.a. It was difficult to let the individual flats in wartime, so in January 1940 the claimants agreed in writing to accept a reduced rent of £1,250 p.a. No time limit was set on the arrangement but it was clearly related to wartime conditions. The reduced rent was paid from 1940 to 1945 and the defendants sublet flats during the period on the basis of their expected liability to pay rent under the head lease at £1,250 only. In 1945 the flats were fully let. The claimants demanded a full rent of £2,500 p.a., both retrospectively and for the future. They tested this claim by suing for rent at the full rate for the last two quarters of 1945.

Decision: The agreement of January 1940 ceased to operate early in 1945. The claim was upheld. However, had the claimants sued for arrears for the period 1940-1945, the 1940 agreement would have served to defeat the claim.

4.20 If the defendants in the *High Trees* case had sued on the promise, they would have failed for want of consideration. The principle is '**a shield not a sword.**'

4.21 Promissory estoppel only applies to a promise of waiver which is **entirely voluntary**.

D and C Builders v Rees 1966
The facts: The defendants owed £482 to the claimants who were in acute financial difficulties. The claimants reluctantly agreed to accept £300 in full settlement. They later claimed the balance.

Decision: The debt must be paid in full. Promissory estoppel only applies to a promise voluntarily given. The defendants had been aware of and had exploited the claimants' difficulties.

Privity of contract

4.22 There is a maxim in contract law which states that **consideration must move from the promisee**. As consideration is the price of a promise, the price must be paid by the person who seeks to enforce the promise.

4.23 EXAMPLE

If A promises B that (for a consideration provided by B) A will confer a benefit on C, then C cannot as a general rule enforce A's promise since C has given no consideration for it.

> *Tweddle v Atkinson 1861*
> *The facts:* The claimant married the daughter of G. On the occasion of the marriage, the claimant's father and G exchanged promises that they would each pay a sum of money to the claimant. G died without making the promised payment and the claimant sued G's executor for the specified amount.
>
> *Decision:* The claimant had provided no consideration for G's promise.

4.24 In *Tweddle's* case each father could have sued the other but the claimant could not sue. The rule that consideration must move from the promisee overlaps with the rule that **only a party to a contract can enforce it**. No-one may be entitled to or bound by the terms of a contract to which he is not an original party: *Price v Easton 1833*.

KEY TERM

Privity of contract can be defined as follows.

As a general rule, only a person who is a party to a contract has enforceable rights or obligations under it. Third parties have no right of action save in certain exceptional instances.

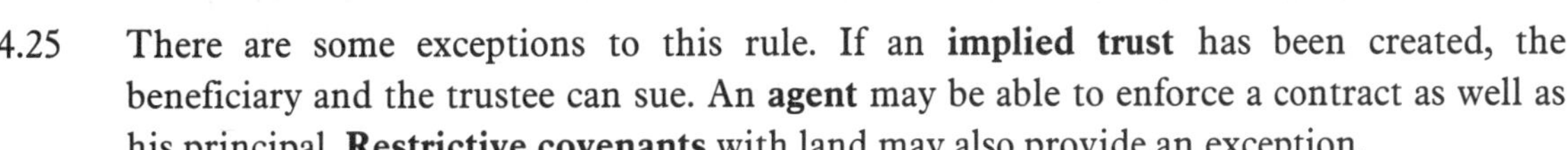

4.25 There are some exceptions to this rule. If an **implied trust** has been created, the beneficiary and the trustee can sue. An **agent** may be able to enforce a contract as well as his principal. **Restrictive covenants** with land may also provide an exception.

4.26 There are also **statutory exceptions**, particularly under the Contract (Rights of Third Parties) Act 1999. This provides a two-limbed test whereby a third party can have enforceable rights under a contract.

- If the contract so provides
- Where a term confers a benefit on a third party (unless it is clear that the parties did not intend that he should enforce it)

5 OTHER FACTORS AFFECTING VALIDITY

Consent 5/02

5.1 A contract will not be valid if either of the two parties did not genuinely consent to the contract. An example of one of the parties not genuinely consenting is where the one party has made a **misrepresentation** to the other in the course of negotiations.

KEY TERM

A **misrepresentation** is:

- A representation of **fact** which is **untrue**
- Made by one party to the other **before the contract is made**
- Which is an **inducement** to the party misled actually to enter into the contract

Representation of fact

5.2 In order to analyse whether a statement may be a misrepresentation, it is first of all necessary to decide whether it could have been a representation at all.

- A statement of fact is a representation.
- A statement of law, intention, opinion or mere 'sales talk' is not a representation.
- Silence does not usually constitute a representation.

5.3 In deciding whether a statement is a statement of fact or of opinion, the extent of the speaker's knowledge determines the category to which the statement belongs.

Bisset v Wilkinson 1927
The facts: A vendor of land which both parties knew had not previously been grazed by sheep stated that it would support about 2,000 sheep. This proved to be untrue.

Decision: In the circumstances this was an honest statement of opinion as to the capacity of the farm, not a statement of fact.

Smith v Land and House Property Corporation 1884
The facts: A vendor of property described it as 'let to Mr Frederick Fleck (a most desirable tenant) at a rental of £400 per annum for 27½ years, thus offering a first-class investment'. In fact F had only paid part of the rent due in the previous six months by instalments after the due date and he had failed altogether to pay the most recent quarter's rent.

Decision: The description of F as a 'desirable tenant' was not a mere opinion but an implied assertion that nothing had occurred which could make F an undesirable tenant. As a statement of fact this was untrue.

5.4 A statement of intention, or a statement as to future conduct, is not actionable. If a person enters into a contract or takes steps relying on a representation, the fact that the representation is false entitles him to remedies at law. If he sues on a statement of intention he must show that the promise forms part of a valid contract if he is to gain any remedy.

Silence

5.5 As a general rule neither party is under any duty to disclose what he knows. But there is a **duty to disclose** information in the following cases.

(a) What is said must be **complete enough** to **avoid** giving a **misleading impression**.

(b) There is a **duty to correct an earlier statement** which was true when made but **which becomes untrue** before the contract is completed.

With v O'Flanagan 1936
The facts: At the start of negotiations in January a doctor, who wished to sell his practice, stated that it was worth £2,000 per year. Shortly afterwards he fell ill and as a result the practice was almost worthless by the time the sale was completed in May.

Decision: His illness and inability to sustain the practice's value falsified the January representation; his silence when he should have corrected the earlier impression constituted misrepresentation. The sale was set aside.

(c) In contracts of **extreme good faith** (*uberrimae fidei*) there is a duty to disclose the material facts which one knows. Non-disclosure can lead to the contract being voidable for misrepresentation. Three types of contract carry a duty of *uberrimae fidei*.

- Contracts of **insurance** (hence failure to disclose, say, a speeding conviction may invalidate motor insurance cover)
- Contracts preliminary to **family arrangements**, such as land settlements
- Contracts where there is a **fiduciary relationship**, such as exists between solicitor and client

5.6 The person to whom a representation is made is entitled to rely on it without investigation.

Statement made by one party to another

5.7 Although in general a misrepresentation must have been made by the misrepresentor to the misrepresentee there are two exceptions to the rule.

- A misrepresentation can be made to the **public in general**, as where an advertisement contains a misleading representation.
- It is sufficient that the misrepresentor knows that the misrepresentation would be **passed on** to the relevant person.

Inducement to enter into the contract

5.8 A representation must have induced the person to enter into the contract.

- He knew of its existence.
- He allowed it to affect his judgement.
- He was unaware of its untruth.

Types of misrepresentation

5.9 Misrepresentation is classified for the purpose of determining what remedies are available.

- **Fraudulent** - a statement made with knowledge that it is untrue, or without believing it to be true or careless whether it is true or false.
- **Negligent** - a statement made in the belief that it is true but without reasonable grounds for that belief.
- **Innocent** - a statement made in the belief that it is true and with reasonable grounds for that belief. It is a misrepresentation made without fault.

5.10 S 21 of the Misrepresentation Act 1967 provides the same remedy (damages) for a victim of non-fraudulent (ie negligent or innocent) representation as for a victim of fraudulent misrepresentation. The representor will escape liability if he can prove that he has reasonable grounds to believe that the facts represented were true.

5.11 This suggests that it may be more advantageous for a claimant to bring a claim under the Act than at common law.

> *Howard Marine and Dredging Co Ltd v A Ogden & Sons (Excavations) Ltd 1978*
> *The facts:* The defendants required two barges for use in an excavation contract. During negotiations with the claimants, the claimant's marine manager stated that the payload of two suitable barges was 1,600 tonnes. This was based on figures given by Lloyds Register, which turned out to be in error. The payload was only 1,055 tonnes. The defendants stopped paying the hire charges and were sued. They counterclaimed for damages at common law and under the Misrepresentation Act 1967.

Decision: The court was unable to decide on whether there was a duty of care (in the common law action), but the claimants had not discharged the burden of proof under the Act, as shipping documents in their possession disclosed the real capacity.

Remedies for misrepresentation — Pilot Paper, 5/01

5.12 There is a fundamental principle that the effect of a misrepresentation is to make a contract **voidable** and not void. The contract remains valid unless set aside by the representee. This means that the representee may choose either to **affirm** the contract or to **rescind** it.

KEY TERM

Rescission can be defined as the act of repudiating or avoiding a contract which, for example, has been induced by misrepresentation or undue influence. It is not available if there has been undue delay, if the innocent party has affirmed the contract, or if the parties cannot be restored to their original positions.

Rescission entails setting the contract aside as if it had never been made.

Rescission

5.13 A contract is rescinded if the representee makes it clear that he refuses to be bound by its provisions; it is then terminated from the beginning (*'ab initio'*). The representee may alternatively **affirm** the contract.

- Declare his intention to proceed with it
- Perform some act from which such an intention may reasonably be inferred

5.14 The general rule is that he must communicate his decision to the misrepresentor, but there are two exceptions to this.

- If property has been delivered to the misrepresentor as a result of the misrepresentation, it is enough simply to take the property back again.
- If the misrepresentor disappears, the representee may announce his intention to rescind by some act that is reasonable in the circumstances.

Car & Universal Finance Co Ltd v Caldwell 1965
The facts: A car was purchased from the defendant by a rogue with a fraudulent cheque. The seller was unable to communicate with the rogue, but informed the police and the AA of the fraud. The rogue had resold the car. (The rogue had fraudulently misrepresented that the cheque would be honoured.)

Decision: The seller had rescinded the contract by taking all reasonable steps and the rogue did not transfer good title to the claimants in a subsequent sale.

Question 8

In many cases, rescission is simply effected when the misrepresentee makes it clear that he refuses to be bound by the contract. When may it be advantageous to bring legal proceedings for an order for rescission?

Answer

Legal action may be desirable if the fraudulent party ignores the cancellation of the contract and fails to return what he has obtained under it. It may be necessary for a formal document, such as a lease, to be set aside by court order. There might also be a possibility that innocent third parties may act on the assumption that the contract still exists.

Damages

5.15 In some instances, there may be a right to damages, either instead of, or in addition to, the remedy of rescission. The available remedies vary depending on the type of misrepresentation.

5.16 The right to damages depends on showing that the statement made by the representor is either fraudulent or negligent.

5.17 In a case of fraudulent misrepresentation the party misled may in addition to, or instead of, rescinding the contract, recover damages for any loss by a common law action for the **tort of deceit.**

5.18 Under the Misrepresentation Act 1967 s 2(2) the court may, in the case of non-fraudulent misrepresentation, award damages instead of rescission.

5.19 The injured party may (under the 1967 Act) claim damages for any actual loss caused by negligent misrepresentation. It is then up to the party who made the statement to prove, if he can, that he had reasonable grounds for making it and that it was not in fact negligent.

5.20 An action at common law is also possible. Damages in this context are intended to put the injured party in the position he would have been in if he had never entered the contract.

5.21 In the case of innocent misrepresentation the remedy of damages is discretionary. An indemnity may be awarded, indemnifying the misrepresentee against any obligations necessarily created by the contract. The misrepresentee may of course choose instead to rescind the contract and refuse to perform his or her obligations.

Capacity

5.22 A contract will not be valid if either of the parties does not have the appropriate legal capacity to enter into the contract.

Companies

5.23 Companies and other artificial legal persons, such as local authorities, do not have the same unlimited capacity as a healthy human being. Often they are limited in what they can do by their constitutions, which only give them certain powers. Actions done outside those powers are said to be *ultra vires* - literally, '**beyond the powers**'. *Ultra vires* contracts are void, so neither party can enforce their terms. *Ultra vires* is discussed in more detail in Chapter 9.

Minors

5.24 Minors are people under the age of 18. Generally they are held not to be bound by contracts they enter into, but two sorts of contract are valid and binding on a minor: a contract for the supply of goods or services which are **necessaries**, and a **service contract** for the minor's benefit.

Mental incapacity

5.25 If a person who is temporarily insane, under the influence of drugs, or drunk, enters into a contract it is binding, with exceptions.

- If he is at the time incapable of understanding the nature of the contract
- If the other party knows or ought to know of his disability

5.26 When goods are supplied to a person under such disability, he must pay a reasonable price for them in any event (s 3 Sale of Goods Act 1979).

Form of a contract

5.27 As a general rule, **a contract may be made in any form**. It may be written, or oral, or inferred from the conduct of the parties.

5.28 EXAMPLE

A customer in a self-service shop may take his selected goods to the cash desk, pay for them and walk out without saying a word.

5.29 However, there will be circumstances in which a contract is not valid if the correct form is not followed.

Writing

5.30 Writing is not usually necessary except in the following circumstances.

- Some contracts must be by **deed.**
- Some contracts must be in **writing.**
- Some contracts must be **evidenced in writing.**

Contracts by deed

5.31 A contract by deed must be in **writing** and it must be **signed**. Delivery must take place. Delivery is conduct indicating that the person executing the deed intends to be bound by it.

5.32 These contracts must be by deed.

- **Leases** for three years or more
- A **conveyance** or transfer of a legal estate in land (including a mortgage)
- A promise not supported by consideration (such as a **covenant**)

5.33 Some types of contract are required to be in the form of a written document, usually signed by at least one of the parties.

5.34 These contracts must be in writing.

- A **transfer of shares** in a limited company
- The sale or disposition of an **interest in land**
- **Bills of exchange** and **cheques**
- **Consumer credit** contracts

5.35 A contract for the sale or disposition of land promises to transfer title at a future date and must be in writing. The conveyance or transfer must be by deed and will therefore also be in writing.

5.36 In the case of consumer credit transactions, the effect of failure to make the agreement in the prescribed form is to make the agreement unenforceable against the debtor unless the creditor obtains a court order.

5.37 Certain contracts may be made orally, but are not enforceable in a court of law unless there is written evidence of their terms. The most important contract of this type is the contract of **guarantee**.

Chapter roundup

- A **valid contract is a legally binding agreement**, formed by the mutual consent of two parties.
- The law seeks to protect the idea of 'freedom of contract', although **contractual terms** may be regulated by **statute**, particularly where the parties are of unequal bargaining strength.
- The **three essential elements** of a contract are **offer and acceptance**, **consideration** and **intention to enter into legal relations**.
- The first essential element of a binding contract is **agreement**. This is usually evidenced by **offer and acceptance**. An offer is a definite promise to be bound on specific terms, and must be distinguished from the mere **supply of information** and from an **invitation to treat**. Acceptance must be unqualified agreement to all the terms of the offer. A **counter-offer** is a rejection of the original offer.
- **Acceptance** is generally not effective until **communicated** to the offeror, the principal exception being where the '**postal rule**' applies, in which case acceptance is complete and effective as soon as notice of it is posted.
- In certain circumstances, the courts may infer the existence of a contract without the formalities of offer and acceptance. This type of contract is a **collateral contract**.
- Both parties to a contract must **intend** the agreement to give rise to legal obligations. Their intentions as to this point may be express - 'this agreement is not subject to legal jurisdiction' - or may be inferred from the circumstances. **Social, domestic and family** arrangements are assumed not to be legally binding unless the contrary is clearly shown. **Commercial** agreements are assumed to be legally binding unless the contrary is clearly demonstrated.
- 'A valuable consideration in the sense of the law may consist either in some right, interest, profit or benefit accruing to one party, or some forbearance, detriment, loss or responsibility given, suffered or undertaken by the other'. This definition of **consideration**, the third essential element of a binding contract, was given in Currie v Misa 1875.
- Consideration need not be **adequate**, but it must be **sufficient**. This means that what is tendered as consideration must be capable in law of being regarded as consideration, but need not necessarily be equal in value to the consideration received in return.
- The principle of **promissory estoppel** was developed in *Central London Property Trust v High Trees House 1947.*
- As a general rule, only a person who is a party to a contract has enforceable rights or obligations under it. This is the doctrine of **privity of contract**, as demonstrated in *Dunlop v Selfridge 1915.*
- There are a number of factors which may affect the **validity** of a contract. For a contract to be binding it must also satisfy various tests relating to **legality**, the **form** of the agreement, **content** of the agreement, **genuineness of consent** and the **capacity** of the parties to contract.
- A **representation** is a statement made in pre-contract negotiations, intended to induce the other party to enter into the agreement; it may or may not subsequently become a contract term.
- A contract entered into following a **misrepresentation** is **voidable** by the person to whom the misrepresentation was made. A misrepresentation is a statement of fact which is **untrue**, made by one party to the other in order to **induce** the latter to enter into the agreement, and a matter of some importance actually **relied upon** by the person misled.

- **Fraudulent misrepresentation** is a statement made knowing it to be untrue, not believing it to be true or recklessly, careless whether it be true or false. **Negligent misrepresentation** is a statement made in the belief that it is true but without reasonable grounds for that belief. **Innocent misrepresentation**, the residual category, is any statement made in the belief that it is true and with reasonable grounds for that belief.
- Although most contracts may be made **in any form**, some must be made in a particular form. A number of commercial contracts must be made in writing, for example.

Quick quiz

1 A valid contract is a legally binding agreement. The three essential elements of a contract are (1) ……………….., (2) ……………….. and (3) ……………….. .

2 A voidable contract is not a contract at all.

☐ True

☐ False

3 Which one of the following is *not* a means by which an offer to enter into legal relations is terminated?

A The period over which the offer is expressed to be kept open expires without acceptance by the offeree

B The offeror tells the offeree before the latter's acceptance that the offer is withdrawn

C The offer is accepted by the offeree

D The offeree responds to the offer by requesting further information

4 **Fill in the blanks** in the statements below, using the words in the box.

- As a general rule, acceptance must be (1) ……………….. to the (2) ……………….. and is not effective until this has been done.
- An (3) ……………….. is a definite promise to be bound on specific terms, and must be distinguished from a supply of (4) ……………….. and from an (5) ………………..
- A counter-offer counts as (6) ……………….. of the original offer

• information	• offer	• invitation to treat
• rejection	• communicated	• offeror

5 As a general rule, silence cannot constitute acceptance.

☐ True

☐ False

6 If two offers, identical in terms, cross in the post

A Either party may accept, to form a contract
B The postal rule applies
C The first offer to arrive is the basis for the contract
D There is no contract as there is no acceptance

7 A misrepresentation is

1 A statement of fact which proves to be untrue

2 A statement of law which proves to be untrue

3 Made by one party to the other before the contract is formed in order to induce the latter to enter into the contract

4 Made by one party before the contract though the other was not aware of it

5 A statement which affects the claimant's judgement

A 2 and 4 only
B 1, 3 and 5 only
C 1, 2, 3 and 5 only
D 1, 2, 3, 4 and 5

8 Past consideration, as a general rule, is not sufficient to make a promise binding.

☐ True

☐ False

9 Consideration need not be (1) .... but it must be (2) ....

10 If Alice promises Ben that (for a consideration provided by Ben) Alice will confer a benefit on Charlotte, then .... cannot as a general rule enforce Alice's promise. This is the doctrine of

privity of contract
frustration

11 Which of the following types of contract are valid and binding on a minor?

- Service contract
- Contract for land
- Contract to purchase shares
- Contract for necessaries
- Partnership agreement

12 The rebuttable presumptions the courts will make with regard to parties' intention to create legal relations are:

- Social, domestic and family arrangement are .... binding.
- Commercial agreements are .... by the parties to be binding.

13 Delete where applicable

- Agreement is made by offer/consideration/privity, and capacity/acceptance/representation.
- An offer is a definite promise to be bound on any terms/specific terms/general terms.
- An advertisement of an auction is an offer/invitation to treat.
- Silence can/can never constitute acceptance.
- Acceptance must/does not have to be communicated to the offeror.
- A letter of revocation of an offer must be posted/received by the offeree to be effective.

14 Delete where applicable

- A representation is a statement of fact/intention/opinion
- Silence may/may not constitute a representation
- A wrong statement made in the reasonable belief that it is true is a negligent/fraudulent/innocent misrepresentation
- Damages may be/are never awarded for misrepresentation

15 Simon offered to sell John his bike for £30. John said, 'The blue one? I'll think about it and let you know on Friday.'

In less than 30 words, explain whether a contract has been formed.

Answers to quick quiz

1 Offer and acceptance, consideration, intention to create legal relations

2 False

3 D

4 (1) communicated (2) offeror (3) offer (4) information (5) invitation to treat (6) rejection

5 True

6 D

7 B

8 True

9 (1) adequate, (2) sufficient

10 Charlotte Privity of contract

11
- Service contracts
- Contract for necessaries

12
- Social, domestic and family arrangement are **not generally intended** to be binding
- Commercial agreements are **generally intended** by the parties to be binding.

13
- Agreement is made by **offer** and **acceptance**
- An offer is a definite promise to be bound on **specific terms**
- An advertisement of an auction is an **invitation to treat**
- Silence **can never** constitute acceptance
- Acceptance **must** be communicated to the offeror
- A letter of revocation of an offer must be **received by the offeree** to be effective

14
- **A** representation is a statement **of fact**
- Silence **may not** constitute a representation
- A wrong statement made in the reasonable belief that it is true is **an innocent** misrepresentation
- Damages **may be** awarded for misrepresentation

15 No contract has been formed to sell the bike as they have not come to agreement (offer and acceptance). Neither have they contracted to keep the offer open.

The following relevant questions are included in the Exam Question Banks

You can attempt these now. However, we would advise you to attempt these as mock exams at the end of your initial stage of study

Exam Question Bank	Numbers
Paper based format	4, 5, 6, 27
Computer based assessment	6, 22, 27, 33

Chapter 4

TERMS OF A CONTRACT

Introduction

In Chapter 3 we considered offer and acceptance. In this chapter we consider how **terms may be incorporated** into a contract other than by offer and acceptance. We will also consider how one party to a contract may seek to exclude his liability under a contract by the use of a specific type of contract term: the **exclusion** (or exemption) clause.

As a general principle the parties may by their offer and acceptance include in their contract whatever terms they prefer. But the law may modify these express terms in various ways.

(a) The terms must be sufficiently **complete and precise** to produce an agreement which can be binding. If they are vague there may be no contract. Statements made in the pre-contract negotiations may become **terms** of the contract or remain as **representations**, to which different rules attach. Express terms are considered in Section 1 of this chapter.

(b) The terms of the contract are usually classified as **conditions** or as **warranties** according to their importance. This classification is described in Section 2.

(c) In addition to the express terms of the agreement, additional terms may be implied by law. In Section 3 we consider **implied terms**.

(d) To be enforceable, terms must be **validly incorporated** into the contract. Because most court decisions about valid incorporation of contract terms are made in respect of exclusion clauses, we will look at this topic in the context of exclusion clauses, in Section 4.

(e) Terms which exclude or restrict liability for breach of contract may be restricted in their effect or be overridden by common law or statute: the law in this area is explained in Section 5.

Learning outcomes covered in this chapter

- **Explain** how the contents of a contract are established
- **Explain** the status of contractual terms and the possible repercussions of non-performance
- **Explain** how the law controls the use of unfair terms in respect of both consumer and non-consumer business agreements

Syllabus content covered in this chapter

- Incorporation of express and implied terms
- Conditions and warranties and the nature and effect of both types of terms
- The main provisions of sale of goods and supply of services legislation

- The manner in which the law controls the use of exclusion clauses and unfair terms in consumer and non-consumer transactions

1 EXPRESS TERMS

1.1 A legally binding agreement must be **complete in its terms**. However, it is always possible for the parties to leave an essential term to be **settled by other means**.

1.2 EXAMPLE

It may be agreed to sell at the open market price on the day of delivery, or to invite an arbitrator to determine a fair price. The price may be determined by the course of dealing between the parties.

> *Hillas & Co Ltd v Arcos Ltd 1932*
> *The facts:* The claimants agreed to purchase from the defendants '22,000 standards of softwood goods of fair specification over the season 1930'. The agreement contained an option to buy a further 100,000 standards in 1931, without terms as to the kind or size of timber being specified. The 1930 transaction took place but the sellers refused to supply any wood in 1931, saying that the agreement was too vague to bind the parties.
>
> *Decision:* The language used, when interpreted by reference to the previous course of dealings between the parties, showed an intention to be bound.

1.3 The courts will seek to uphold agreements by looking at the **intention of the parties**. In business, to save later confusion, contracts are often written in great detail.

Terms and representations

1.4 Once it has been established what the parties to a contract have said or written, it is necessary to decide whether their words actually amount to contract terms. Statements may be classified as terms or as representations.

KEY TERM

A **representation** is something which induces the formation of a contract but which does not become a **term** of the contract. The importance of the distinction is that different remedies are available depending on whether a term is broken or a representation turns out to be untrue.

1.5 If something said in negotiations proves to be untrue, the party misled can claim for breach of contract if the statement became a term of the contract. Otherwise his remedy is for **misrepresentation**, (discussed in Chapter 3).

1.6 The court will consider when the representation was made to assess whether it was designed as a contract term or merely as an incidental statement. If the statement is made with special knowledge it is more likely to be treated as a contract term.

2 CONDITIONS AND WARRANTIES — Pilot Paper, 5/01, 5/02

Exam focus point

The examiner has said that it is fundamental that students can distinguish between conditions and warranties. The effects of their breach are different. He also wrote an article on this issue in CIMA Insider, October 2001.

2.1 The terms of the contract are usually classified by their relative importance as **conditions** or **warranties**.

(a) **A condition is a vital term,** going to the root of the contract, breach of which entitles the injured party to treat the contract as **discharged** and to claim damages.

KEY TERM

A **condition** can be defined as follows.

'An important term which is vital to a contract so that its breach will destroy the basis of the agreement. It may arise from an express agreement between the parties or may be implied by law; for example, the condition that goods shall be of satisfactory quality in the Sale of Goods Act.

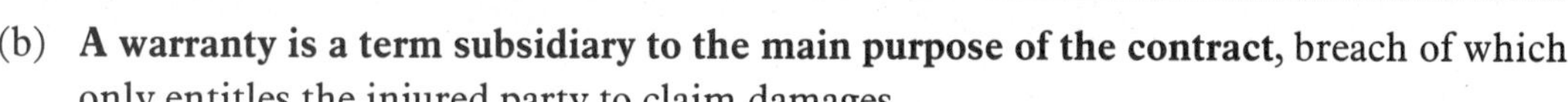

(b) **A warranty is a term subsidiary to the main purpose of the contract,** breach of which only entitles the injured party to claim damages.

KEY TERM

A **warranty** can be defined as follows.

'A minor term in a contract. If broken, the injured party must continue performance but may claim damages for the loss suffered.'

Poussard v Spiers 1876
The facts: Mme Poussard agreed to sing in an opera throughout a series of performances. Owing to illness she was unable to appear on the opening night and the next few days. The producer engaged a substitute who insisted that she should be engaged for the whole run. When Mme Poussard recovered, the producer declined to accept her services for the remaining performances.

Decision: Failure to sing on the opening night was a breach of condition which entitled the producer to treat the contract for the remaining performances as discharged.

Bettini v Gye 1876
The facts: An opera singer was engaged for a series of performances under a contract by which he had to be in London for rehearsals six days before the opening performance. Owing to illness he did not arrive until the third day before the opening. The defendant refused to accept his services, treating the contract as discharged.

Decision: The rehearsal clause was subsidiary to the main purpose of the contract.

2.2 Classification may depend on the following issues.

(a) **Statute** often identifies implied terms specifically as conditions or warranties. An example is the Sale of Goods Act 1979.

(b) **Case law** may also define particular types of clauses as conditions.

(c) The court may construe what was the intention of the parties at the time the contract was made as to whether a broken term was to be a condition or a warranty.

Innominate terms

2.3 The court will only construe a broken term as a condition or warranty if the parties' intentions when the contract was formed are very clear.

2.4 Where it is not clear what the effect of breach of the term was intended to be, it will be classified by the court as **innominate, intermediate** or **indeterminate** (the three are synonymous).

KEY TERM

The consequence of a term being classified as **innominate** is that the court must decide what is the actual effect of its breach. If the nature and effect of the breach is such as to deprive the injured party of most of his benefit from the contract then it will be treated as a breached condition.

2.5 The injured party may terminate the contract and claim damages.

Hong Kong Fir Shipping Co Ltd v Kawasaki Kisa Kaisha Ltd 1962
The facts: The defendants chartered a ship from the claimants for a period of 24 months. A term in the contract stated that the claimants would provide a ship which was 'in every way fitted for ordinary cargo service'. Because of the engine's age and the crew's lack of competence the ship's first voyage, from Liverpool to Osaka, was delayed for 5 weeks and further repairs were required at the end of it. The defendants purported to terminate the contract, so the claimants sued for breach of contract; the defendants claimed that the claimants were in breach of a contractual condition.

Decision: The term was innominate and could not automatically be construed as either a condition or a warranty. The obligation of 'seaworthiness' embodied in many charterparty agreements was too complex to be fitted into one of the two categories. The ship was still available for 17 out of 24 months. The consequences of the breach were not so serious that the defendants could be justified in terminating the contract as a result.

Question 1

Which of the following statements concerning contractual terms are untrue?

1 Terms are usually classified as either conditions or warranties, but some terms may be unclassifiable in this way

2 If a condition in a contract is not fulfilled the whole contract is said to be discharged by breach

3 If a warranty in a contract is not fulfilled the whole contract is said to be discharged by breach, but either party may elect to continue with his performance

4 Terms which are implied into a contract by law are always contractual conditions

A 1 and 2 only
B 3 and 4 only
C 1, 2 and 4 only
D 1, 2, 3 and 4 only

Answer

B

Exam focus point

Do not over emphasise innominate terms. Conditions and warranties are the key items to understand.

Question 2

To what is the injured party to a contract entitled in the event of breach of:

(a) A condition by the other party?
(b) A warranty by the other party?

Answer

(a) He may treat the contract as discharged and rescind or terminate the contract, or alternatively he may go on with it and sue for damages.

(b) He may claim damages only.

3 IMPLIED TERMS 5/02

3.1 There are occasions where certain terms are not expressly adopted by the parties, but may be imported from the context of the contract. Additional terms of a contract may be implied by law: by custom, statute or the courts.

KEY TERM

An **implied term** can be defined as follows.

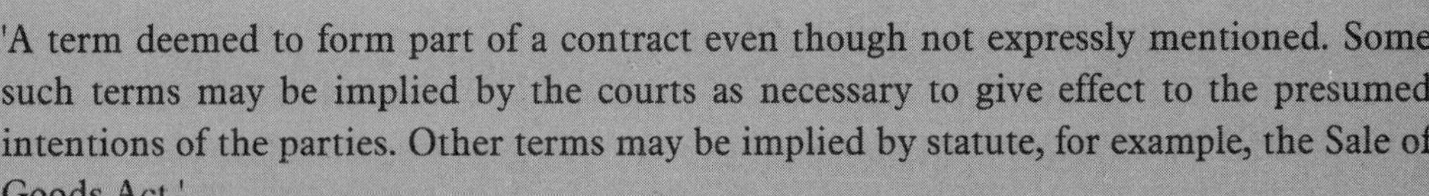

'A term deemed to form part of a contract even though not expressly mentioned. Some such terms may be implied by the courts as necessary to give effect to the presumed intentions of the parties. Other terms may be implied by statute, for example, the Sale of Goods Act.'

Terms implied by custom

3.2 The parties may enter into a contract subject to customs of their trade. Any express term overrides a term which might be implied by custom.

Terms implied by statute

3.3 Terms may be implied by statute. In some cases the statute permits the parties to contract out of the statutory terms. In other cases the statutory terms are obligatory: the protection

given by the Sale of Goods Act 1979 to a consumer who buys goods from a trader cannot be taken away from him.

Sale of Goods Act 1979

3.4 The terms implied by the Sale of Goods Act 1979 have largely evolved from case law. Much depends on some important definitions.

- Whether an implied term is a **condition or a warranty**
- Whether one party to the contract is dealing as a **consumer**

You will be familiar with the distinction between conditions and warranties from earlier in this chapter.

Consumer

3.5 A definition of a consumer sale is contained in s 12, Unfair Contract Terms Act 1977.

KEY TERM

'A party to a contract deals as **consumer** in relation to another party if:

(a) He neither makes the contract in the course of a business nor holds himself out as doing so and

(b) The other party does make the contract in the course of a business, and

(c) In the case of a contract governed by the law of sale of goods ..... the goods are of a type ordinarily supplied for private use or consumption.'

Terms implied by the Sale of Goods Act

3.6 A sale of goods may be subject to statutory rules on the following.

- **Title,** or the seller's right to sell the goods: s 12
- **Description** of the goods: s 13
- **Quality** of the goods: s 14(2)
- **Fitness of the goods** for the purpose for which they are supplied: s 14(3)
- **Sale by sample**: s 15

Exam focus point

Of all the terms implied by the Sale of Goods Act the terms as to quality and fitness for purpose are the most important. Concentrate your reading on S 14 SGA 1979.

Title

3.7 Section 12(1) implies into contracts for the sale of goods an undertaking as to **title,** confirming that the seller has a right to sell. S 12(2) implies undertakings as to freedom from other claims, and quiet possession.

3.8 The condition as to title is broken if the seller can be stopped by a third party from selling the goods. If the seller delivers goods to the buyer without having the right to sell, there is a total failure of consideration. If the buyer has to give up the goods to the real owner he may recover the entire price from the seller.

Description

3.9 Section 13 applies to all sales. Sections 13(1) and (2) provide that where there is a contract for the sale of goods by description, there is an implied condition that the goods correspond with the description.

3.10 If a description is applied to the goods by the contract, it is a sale by description.

Beale v Taylor 1967
The facts: The defendant advertised a Triumph as a 'Herald convertible, white, 1961'. The claimant came to inspect the car and subsequently bought it. After buying the car he found that the back half had been welded to a front half which was part of an earlier model. The defendant relied on the buyer's inspection and argued that it was not a sale by description.

Decision: The advertisement described the car as a 1961 Herald, and this formed part of the contract description.

3.11 It is not the case that all descriptive words used form part of the contract terms. However, Description is interpreted to include ingredients, age, date of shipment, packing, quantity, etc.

Satisfactory quality (s 14 (2))

3.12 There is an implied condition that goods supplied under a contract are of **satisfactory quality**. This condition applies only to goods sold in the course of a business. Thus private sales are excluded.

3.13 The condition applies to **all goods supplied under the contract**: not only to the goods themselves but also to any packaging and instructions.

3.14 The Act (s 14(2B)) identifies factors which may in appropriate cases be aspects of the quality of goods.

- **Fitness for all the purposes for which goods of the kind in question are commonly supplied**
- **Appearance and finish**
- **Freedom from minor defects**
- **Safety**
- **Durability,** suggesting that goods will have to remain of satisfactory quality for a reasonable period.

3.15 The condition that the goods supplied under the contract are of satisfactory quality is excluded if the buyer's attention is drawn to defects before the contract is made or the buyer examines the goods before the contract is made, and that examination ought to reveal the defects. Similarly, if goods are bought second-hand, or very cheaply, it is not reasonable to expect the highest standards of quality: *Bartlett v Sidney Marcus 1965*. Conversely, if the product is of a high price, minor defects may make the quality unsatisfactory: *Rogers v Parish Ltd 1987*.

Fitness for purpose

3.16 Section 14(3) implies a condition that the goods be fit for any particular purpose which the buyer expressly or by implication makes known to the seller. In *Grant v Australian Knitting Mills 1936*, a pair of pants were found not to be satisfactory quality for the purpose of wearing when the buyer contracted dermatitis from a chemical contained in them.

3.17 Usually, a buyer must make known the particular purpose for which he wants the goods. If the goods have only one obvious purpose (as in the *Grant* case above), the buyer by implication makes known his purpose merely by asking for the goods.

3.18 Where goods are required for a particular purpose which is not obvious to the seller or where there is some peculiarity about that purpose, the buyer must make these clear to the seller. However, a buyer may specify the 'particular purpose' quite broadly. Thus where a substance is commonly used as animal feedstuff it is sufficient to specify the latter without naming each kind of animal to which it might be fed: *Ashington Piggeries v Christopher Hill Ltd 1972*

Sale by sample

3.19 Under s 15 of the Act there are requirements in a sale by sample. In the case of a contract for sale by sample there is an implied condition.

(a) That the bulk will correspond with the sample in **quality**

(b) That the buyer will have a reasonable **opportunity of comparing** the bulk with the sample

(c) That the goods shall be free from any **defect** rendering their quality unsatisfactory which would not be apparent on reasonable examination of the sample.

Acceptance of goods by the buyer

3.20 Acceptance of goods deprives the buyer of his right to treat the contract as discharged by breach of condition on the part of the seller. But he may claim damages.

3.21 The buyer is not deemed to have accepted the goods until he has had a reasonable opportunity of examining them. The buyer is deemed to have accepted the goods in the following circumstances.

(a) When he intimates to the seller that he has accepted them.

(b) When the goods have been delivered to the buyer and he does any act in relation to them which is consistent with ownership, such as using or reselling them.

(c) When after the lapse of a reasonable time he retains the goods without intimating to the seller that he has rejected them.

The Supply of Goods and Services Act 1982

3.22 The Sale of Goods Act 1979, including its provisions relating to implied terms under ss 12-15, applies only to contracts where goods are sold for money consideration. Other methods of obtaining goods (eg by hire purchase or barter), and the provision of services, are not protected. These areas are covered by the **Supply of Goods and Services Act 1982**. Part I of the Act affords the protection of statutory implied terms to all contracts for the supply of goods. Part II of the Act covers implied terms in contracts for services.

3.23 Hence the Supply of Goods and Services Act 1982 covers the provision of accountancy services by accountants to their clients, which are covered by the wide statutory term that 'the supplier will carry out the service with reasonable care and skill'.

Terms implied by the courts

3.24 Terms may be implied if the court concludes that the parties intended those terms to apply.

The Moorcock 1889
The facts: The owners of a wharf agreed that a ship should be moored alongside to unload its cargo. It was well known that at low water the ship would ground on the mud at the bottom. At ebb tide the ship settled on a ridge concealed beneath the mud and suffered damage.

Decision: It was an implied term, though not expressed, that the ground alongside the wharf was safe at low tide since both parties knew that the ship must rest on it.

3.25 A term of a contract which is left to be implied and is not expressed is often something that goes without saying; so that, if while the parties were making their bargain an officious bystander were to suggest some express provision for it, they would say "why should we put that in? That's obvious" : This was put forward in *Shirlaw v Southern Foundries 1940.* This is sometimes described as terms being implied on the grounds of business efficacy.

3.26 The court may also imply terms to maintain a standard of behaviour.

Liverpool City Council v Irwin 1977
The facts: The defendants were tenants in a tower block owned by the claimants. There was no formal tenancy agreement. The defendants withheld rent, alleging that the claimants had breached implied terms because *inter alia* the lifts did not work and the stairs were unlit.

Decision: Tenants could only occupy the building with access to stairs and/or lifts, so terms needed to be implied on these matters.

Question 3

During negotiations before entering into a contract for the sale of a car Howard says to Robbie 'the car will be ready for collection on the day you require it'. This statement is described as

A A representation
B A term
C A warranty
D An advertiser's puff

Answer

A

4 EXCLUSION CLAUSES 11/01

KEY TERM

An **exclusion clause** can be defined as follows.

'A clause in a contract which purports to exclude liability altogether or to restrict it by limiting damages or by imposing other onerous conditions. They are sometimes referred to as **exemption clauses**.

4.1 There has been strong criticism of the use of exclusion clauses in contracts made between manufacturers or sellers of goods or services and private citizens as consumers. The seller puts forward standard conditions of sale which the buyer may not understand, but which he must accept if he wishes to buy. With these so-called **standard form contracts**, the presence of exclusion clauses becomes an important consideration.

4.2 For many years the courts demonstrated the hostility of the common law to exclusion clauses by developing various rules of case law designed to restrain their effect. To these must now be added the considerable statutory safeguards provided by the **Unfair Contract Terms Act 1977** (UCTA). This is covered in detail in Section 5. But the statutory rules do permit exclusion clauses to continue in some circumstances. Hence it is necessary to consider both the **older case law** and the **newer statutory rules**.

4.3 The **courts** have generally sought to protect consumers from the harsher effects of exclusion clauses in two ways.

- An exclusion clause must be properly **incorporated** into a contract before it has any legal effect.
- Exclusion clauses are **interpreted** strictly. This may prevent the application of the clause.

4.4 If an exclusion clause is made **void by statute** it is unnecessary to consider how other legal rules might affect it.

Exam focus point

Exclusion clauses may overlap in the exam paper with negligence.

Incorporation of exclusion clauses

4.5 Uncertainty often arises over which terms have actually been **incorporated** into a contract.

- The document containing notice of the clause must be an **integral part** of the contract.
- If the document is an integral part of the contract, a term may not usually be disputed if it is included in a document which a party has **signed**.
- The term must be put forward **before** the contract is made.
- It is not a binding term unless the person whose rights it restricts was made **sufficiently aware** of it at the time of agreeing to it.
- **Onerous terms** must be sufficiently highlighted.

Contractual documents

4.6 The term must be put forward in a document which gives reasonable notice that conditions are proposed by it. It must be shown that this document is an integral part of the contract and is one which could be expected to contain terms.

Chapelton v Barry UDC 1940
The facts: There was a pile of deck chairs and a notice stating 'Hire of chairs 2d per session of three hours'. The claimant took two chairs, paid for them and received two tickets which he put in his pocket. One of the chairs collapsed and he was injured. The defendant council relied on a notice on the back of the tickets by which it disclaimed liability for injury.

Decision: The notice advertising chairs for hire gave no warning of limiting conditions and it was not reasonable to communicate them on a receipt. The disclaimer of liability was not binding on the claimant.

Thompson v LMS Railway 1930
The facts: An elderly lady who could not read asked her niece to buy her a railway excursion ticket on which was printed 'Excursion: for conditions see back'. On the back it was stated that the ticket was issued subject to conditions contained in the company's timetables. These conditions excluded liability for injury.

Decision: The conditions had been adequately communicated and therefore had been accepted.

Signed contracts

4.7 If a person signs a document containing a term he is held to have agreed to the term even if he had not read the document. But this is not so if the party who puts forward the document for signature gives a misleading explanation of the term's legal effect.

L'Estrange v Graucob 1934
The facts: The defendant sold to the claimant, a shopkeeper, a slot machine under conditions which excluded the claimant's normal rights under the Sale of Goods Act 1893. The claimant signed the document described as a 'Sales Agreement' and including clauses in 'legible, but regrettably small print'.

Decision: The conditions were binding on the claimant since she had signed them. It was not material that the defendant had given her no information of their terms nor called her attention to them.

Curtis v Chemical Cleaning Co 1951
The facts: The claimant took her wedding dress to be cleaned. She was asked to sign a receipt on which there were conditions which she was told restricted the cleaner's liability and in particular placed on the claimant the risk of damage to beads and sequins on the dress. The document in fact contained a clause 'that the company is not liable for any damage however caused'. The dress was badly stained in the course of cleaning.

Decision: The cleaners could not rely on their disclaimer since they had misled the claimant. She was entitled to assume that she was running the risk of damage to beads and sequins only.

Prior information on terms

4.8 Each party must be aware of the contract's terms **at the time of entering into the agreement** if they are to be binding.

Olley v Marlborough Court 1949
The facts: A husband and wife arrived at a hotel and paid for a room in advance. On reaching their bedroom they saw a notice on the wall by which the hotel disclaimed liability for loss of valuables unless handed to the management for safe keeping. The wife locked the room and handed the key in at the reception desk. A thief obtained the key and stole the wife's furs from the bedroom.

Decision: The hotel could not rely on the notice disclaiming liability since the contract had been made previously and the disclaimer was too late.

4.9 Complications can arise when it is difficult to determine at exactly **what point in time** the contract is formed so as to determine whether or not a term is validly included.

Thornton v Shoe Lane Parking Ltd 1971
The facts: The claimant wished to park his car in the defendant's automatic car park. He had seen a sign saying 'All cars parked at owner's risk' outside the car park and when he received his ticket he saw that it contained words which he did not read. In fact these made the contract subject to conditions displayed obscurely on the premises. These not only disclaimed liability for damage but also excluded liability for injury. When he returned to collect his car there was an accident in which he was badly injured.

Decision: The reference on the ticket to conditions was received too late for the conditions to be included as contractual terms. At any rate, it was unreasonable for a term disclaiming liability for personal injury to be presented so obscurely. Note that since the Unfair Contracts Terms Act 1977 the personal injury clause would be unenforceable anyway.

4.10 An exception to the rule that there should be prior notice of the terms is where the parties have had **consistent dealings** with each other in the past, and the documents used then contained similar terms.

J Spurling Ltd v Bradshaw 1956
The facts: Having dealt with a company of warehousemen for many years, the defendant gave it eight barrels of orange juice for storage. A document he received a few days later acknowledged receipt and contained a clause excluding liability for damage caused by negligence. When he collected the barrels they were empty and he refused to pay.

Decision: It was a valid clause as it had also been present in the course of previous dealings, even though he had never read it.

4.11 If the parties have had previous dealings (not on a consistent basis) then the person to be bound by the term must be **sufficiently aware** of it at the time of making the latest contract.

Hollier v Rambler Motors 1972
The facts: On three or four occasions over a period of five years the claimant had had repairs done at a garage. On each occasion he had signed a form by which the garage disclaimed liability for damage caused by fire to customers' cars. The car was damaged by fire caused by negligence of garage employees. The garage contended that the

disclaimer had by course of dealing become an established term of any contract made between them and the claimant.

Decision: The garage was liable. There was no evidence to show that the claimant knew of and agreed to the condition as a continuing term of his contracts with the garage.

4.12 Where a term is particularly unusual and onerous it should be highlighted. Failure to do so may mean that it does not become incorporated into the contract.

Interpretation of exclusion clauses

4.13 In deciding what an exclusion clause means, the courts interpret any ambiguity against the person at fault who relies on the exclusion. This is known as the **contra proferentem rule**. Liability can only be excluded or restricted by clear words.

4.14 In the *Hollier* case above, the court decided that as a matter of interpretation the disclaimer of liability could be interpreted to apply (a) only to accidental fire damage or (b) to fire damage caused in any way including negligence. It should therefore be interpreted against the garage in the narrower sense of (a) so that it did not give exemption from fire damage due to negligence. If a person wishes successfully to exclude or limit liability for loss caused by negligence the courts require that the word 'negligence', or an accepted synonym for it, should be included in the clause.

Alderslade v Hendon Laundry 1945
The facts: The conditions of contracts made by a laundry with its customers excluded liability for loss of or damage to customers' clothing in the possession of the laundry. By its negligence the laundry lost the claimant's handkerchief.

Decision: The exclusion clause would have no meaning unless it covered loss or damage due to negligence. It did therefore cover loss by negligence.

The 'main purpose' rule

4.15 When construing an exclusion clause the court will also consider the **main purpose rule**. By this, the court presumes that the clause was not intended to defeat the main purpose of the contract.

Fundamental breach

4.16 For more than twenty years there were conflicting judicial *dicta* on how far an exclusion clause can exclude liability in a case where the breach of contract was a failure to perform the contract altogether - that is, a **fundamental breach.**

Photo Productions v Securicor Transport 1980
The facts: The defendants agreed to guard the claimants' factory under a contract by which the defendants were excluded from liability for damage caused by any of their employees. One of the guards deliberately started a small fire which destroyed the factory and contents. It was contended that Securicor had entirely failed to perform their contract and so they could not rely on any exclusion clause in the contract.

Decision: There is no principle that total failure to perform a contract deprives the party at fault of any exclusion from liability provided by the contract. In this case the exclusion clause was drawn widely enough to cover the damage which had happened. As the fire occurred before the UCTA was in force, the Act could not apply here. But if it had done it would have been necessary to consider whether the exclusion clause was reasonable.

Exam focus point

The reliance on the exclusion clause is an everyday occurrence in business dealings and therefore is of great practical relevance.

5 UNFAIR TERMS REGULATIONS

The Unfair Contract Terms Act 1977

5.1 When considering the **validity** of exclusion clauses the courts have had to strike a balance between:

- The principle that parties should have complete **freedom to contract** on whatever terms they wish, and
- The need to **protect the public** from unfair exclusion clauses

5.2 Exclusion clauses do have a proper place in business. They can be used to allocate contractual risk, and thus to determine in advance who is to insure against that risk. Between businessmen with similar bargaining power exclusion clauses are a legitimate device. The main limitations are now contained in the Unfair Contract Terms Act 1977.

5.3 Before we consider the specific terms of UCTA, it is necessary to describe how its scope is restricted.

(a) In general the Act only applies to clauses inserted into agreements by **commercial concerns or businesses**. In principle private persons may restrict liability as much as they wish.

(b) The Act does not apply to some contracts.

- Contracts relating to the creation or transfer of patents
- Contracts of insurance
- Contracts relating to the creation or transfer of an interest in land
- Contracts relating to company formation or dissolution

5.4 The Act uses two techniques for controlling exclusion clauses - some types of clauses are **void**, whereas others are subject to a **test of reasonableness**. The main provisions of the Act are contained in Sections 2, 3, 6 and 7.

Exclusion of liability for negligence (s 2)

5.5 A person acting in the course of a business cannot, by reference to any contract term, restrict his liability for **death or personal injury** resulting from negligence. In the case of other loss or damage, a person cannot restrict his liability for negligence unless the term is **reasonable**.

Standard term contracts and consumer contracts (s 3)

5.6 The person who imposes the standard term, or who deals with the consumer, cannot (unless the term is reasonable) restrict liability for his own breach or fundamental breach or claim to be entitled to render substantially different performance or no performance at all.

Sale and supply of goods (ss 6-7)

5.7 No contract (consumer or non-consumer) for the sale or hire purchase of goods can exclude the implied condition that the seller has a **right to sell** the goods.

5.8 A consumer contract for the sale of goods, hire purchase, supply of work or materials or exchange of goods cannot exclude or restrict liability for breach of the conditions relating to description, quality, fitness and sample implied by the Sale of Goods Act 1979 and the Supply of Goods and Services Act 1982. For a non-consumer contract, such exclusions are subject to a reasonableness test. The rules are set out in the table below.

Exemption clauses in contracts for the supply of goods

		Sale, HP, exchange and work + materials		Hire	
		Consumer transaction	*Non-consumer transaction*	*Consumer transaction*	*Non-consumer transaction*
Implied terms	Title	Void	Void	Subject to reasonableness test	Subject to reasonableness test
	Description	Void	Subject to reasonableness test	Void	Subject to reasonableness test
	Quality and suitability	Void	Subject to reasonableness test	Void	Subject to reasonableness test
	Sample	Void	Subject to reasonableness test	Void	Subject to reasonableness test

The statutory test of reasonableness (s 11)

5.9 The term must be fair and reasonable having regard to all the circumstances which were, or which ought to have been, known to the parties when the contract was made. The burden of proving reasonableness lies on the person seeking to rely on the clause. Statutory guidelines have been included in the Act to assist the determination of reasonableness. For instance, the court will consider the following.

(a) The relative **strength** of the parties' bargaining positions.

(b) Whether any **inducement** (eg a reduced price) was offered to the customer to persuade him to accept limitation of his rights.

(c) Whether the customer **knew or ought to have known** of the existence and extent of the exclusion clause.

(d) If failure to comply with a condition (eg failure to give notice of a defect within a short period) excludes or restricts the customer's rights, whether it was reasonable to expect when the contract was made that compliance with the condition would be practicable.

(e) Whether the goods were made, processed or adapted to the **special order** of the customer (UCTA Sch 2).

St Albans City and District Council v International Computers Ltd 1994
The facts: The defendants had been hired to assess population figures on which to base community charges (local government taxation). Their standard contract contained a clause restricting liability to £100,000. The database which they supplied to the claimants was seriously inaccurate and the latter sustained a loss of £1.3 million.

Decision: The clause was unreasonable. The defendants could not justify this limitation, which was very low in relation to the potential loss. In addition, they had aggregate insurance of £50 million. The defendants had to pay full damages.

Question 4

The Unfair Contract Terms Act 1977 limits the extent to which it is possible to exclude or restrict *business liability.* What do you understand by the phrase business liability?

Answer

Business liability is liability, in tort or contract, which arises from things done or to be done in the course of a business or from the occupation of premises used for business purposes of the occupier. Business includes a profession and the activities of any government department or public or local authority.

Exam focus point

A good way to look at UCTA is to write down which terms are void under UCTA and which are subject to a reasonableness test. It is vital you understand which contracts UCTA applies to.

The unfair terms in consumer contracts regulations 1999

5.10 These regulations implemented an EC directive on unfair contract terms. UCTA 1977 continues to apply. There are now three layers of relevant law.

(a) The **common law**, which applies to all contracts, regardless of whether or not one party is a consumer

(b) **UCTA 1977**, which applies to all contracts and which has specific provisions for consumer contracts

(c) **The Regulations** (**UTCCR 1999**), which only apply to consumer contracts and to terms which have not been individually negotiated

5.11 The new regulations apply to contracts for the supply of goods or services.

(a) They apply to terms in consumer contracts.

KEY TERM

A **consumer** is defined as 'a natural person who, in making a contract to which these regulations apply, is acting for purposes which are outside his trade, business or profession.'

(b) They apply to contractual terms which have not been individually negotiated.

5.12 A key aspect of the regulations is the definition of an unfair term.

KEY TERM

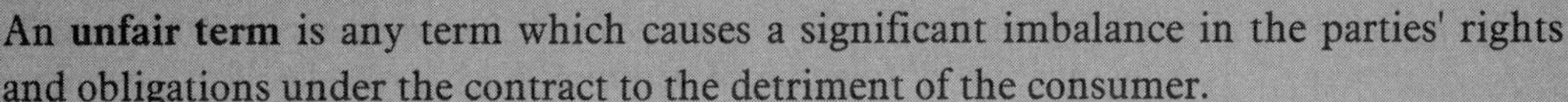

An **unfair term** is any term which causes a significant imbalance in the parties' rights and obligations under the contract to the detriment of the consumer.

5.13 In making an assessment of good faith, the courts will have regard to the following.

(a) The strength of the bargaining positions of the parties

(b) Whether the consumer had an inducement to agree to the term

(c) Whether the goods or services were sold or supplied to the special order of the consumer

(d) The extent to which the seller or supplier has dealt fairly and equitably with the consumer

5.14 The effect of the regulations is to render certain terms in consumer contracts unfair.

(a) Excluding or limiting liability of the seller when the consumer dies or is injured, where this results from an act or omission of the seller

(b) Excluding or limiting liability where there is partial or incomplete performance of a contract by the seller

(c) Making a contract binding on the consumer where the seller can still avoid performing the contract

5.15 Two forms of redress are available.

(a) A consumer who has concluded a contract containing an unfair term can ask the court to find that the unfair term should not be binding.

(b) A complaint, for example by an individual, a consumer group or a trading standards department can be made to the Director General of Fair Trading.

Other statutory protection

5.16 Some other statutes give specific protection against unfair terms in contracts:

Statute	Protection
Misrepresentation Act 1967	Any term excluding liability for misrepresentation is void unless it is proved the exemption was fair and reasonable in the circumstances.
Consumer Credit Act 1974	Protects the debtor during the payment period, for example, the debtor cannot be prevented from paying off what he owes at any time.
Fair Trading Act 1973	This act empowers the Department of Trade and Industry to make regulations prohibiting undesirable **consumer** trade practices.

Chapter roundup

- As a general rule, the parties to a contract may include in the agreement whatever **terms** they choose. This is the principle of **freedom of contract**. A legally binding agreement must be complete in its terms, though the parties may leave an essential term to be settled by specified means outside the contract.
- Statements made by the parties may be classified as **terms or representations**. Different **remedies** attach to breach of a term and to misrepresentation respectively.
- Statements which are classified as contract terms may be further categorised as **conditions** or **warranties**. A condition is a vital term going to the root of the contract, while a warranty is a term subsidiary to the main purpose of the contract. The remedies available for breach are different in each case. It may not be possible to determine whether a term is a condition or a warranty. Such terms are classified by the courts as **innominate terms**.
- The law may complement or replace terms by **implying** terms into a contract. Terms may be implied by the **courts**, by **statute** or by **custom**. A particularly important source of implied terms is the **Sale of Goods Act 1979**. The Supply of Goods and Services Act 1982 extends these implied terms to cover goods bought by hire purchase, barter or exchange, and contracts for services.
- An **exclusion clause** may attempt to restrict one party's liability for breach of contract or for negligence. Because of inequality of bargaining power, the **Unfair Contract Terms Act 1977** renders **void** certain exclusion clauses in sale of goods or supply of services contracts and any clause which purports to exclude liability for death or personal injury resulting from negligence.
- The courts protect customers from the harsher effects of exclusion clauses by ensuring that they are properly **incorporated** into a contract and then by **interpreting** them strictly.
- The general rules
  - A clause may not usually be disputed if it is included in a document which has been signed.
  - The clause must be put forward before the contract is made.
  - Both parties must be aware of it.
- An exclusion clause may not be sufficiently widely drawn as to cover a **fundamental breach** of contract
- The application of UCTA 1977 depends to a great extent upon whether there is a **consumer sale**. A contract between business operations is considerably less affected by the Act. Both types often have to satisfy a statutory test of **reasonableness**.
- The Unfair Terms in Consumer Contracts Regulations 1999 define what is meant by an **unfair term**.

Quick quiz

1 A term may be implied into a contract by

1 Statute

2 Trade practice unless an express term overrides it

3 The court to provide for events not contemplated by the parties

4 The court to give effect to a term which the parties had agreed upon but failed to express because it was obvious

5 The court to override an express term which is contrary to normal custom

A 2 and 3 only
B 1, 2 and 4 only
C 1, 4 and 5 only
D 1, 3, 4 and 5 only

2 In no more than 30 words, explain why it is important to distinguish between terms and representations.

3 **Fill in the blanks** in the statements below, using the words in the box.

- A (1) .... is a vital term, going to the root of the contract, breach of which entitles the injured party to treat the contract as (2) .... and claim (3) ....
- A (4) .... is a term (5) .... to the main purpose of the contract.
- The consequence of a term being classified as innominate is that the court must decide what is the actual effect of its (6) ....

• breach	• condition	• subsidiary
• warranty	• damages	• discharged

4 Give an example of a statute which identifies implied terms specifically as conditions or warranties.

5 Terms implied by custom cannot be overridden

☐ True

☐ False

6 The following definition of a consumer is contained in UCTA 77. Fill in the gaps.

(a) He neither makes the contract in course of (1) .... nor holds himself out as doing so

(b) The other (2) .... does make the contract in course of (3) ....

(c) In the case of a contract governed by the law of (4) ...., the goods are of a type ordinarily supplied for (5) ....

7 Match the section number to the SGA 1979 terms.

(a) Title	(1) 14(2)
(b) Description	(2) 12
(c) Quality	(3) 15
(d) Fitness for purpose	(4) 13
(e) Sale by sample	(5) 14(3)

8 Private sales are excluded from the implied condition that goods supplied under a contract are of satisfactory quality

☐ True

☐ False

9 What is the '*contra proferentem*' rule?

10 Match the layers of law to their jurisdictions in the law of contract

(a) Common law	(1) All contracts with specific provisions for consumer contracts
(b) UCTA 1977	(2) Applies only to consumer contracts and to non-negotiated terms
(c) UTCCR 1999	(3) All contracts

11 Delete where applicable

- A legally binding agreement must be complete in its terms/written/ signed by both parties
- The courts will seek to uphold agreements by looking at the intention of the parties/the small print of what was written down.

12 A sale of goods may be subject to statutory rules on which of the following?

- Title
- Description
- Price
- Quality
- Quantity
- Fitness for purpose
- Sale by sample

13 What is the status of exclusion clauses in the following table? (Fill in the blanks.)

		Exemption clauses in contracts for the supply of goods			
		Sale, HP, exchange and work + materials		Hire	
		Consumer transaction	*Non-consumer transaction*	*Consumer transaction*	*Non-consumer transaction*
Implied terms	Title		Void		Subject to reasonableness test
	Description		Subject to reasonableness test		Subject to reasonableness test
	Quality and suitability		Subject to reasonableness test		Subject to reasonableness test
	Sample		Subject to reasonableness test		Subject to reasonableness test

14 In no more than 30 words distinguish between conditions and warranties.

Answers to quick quiz

1 B

2 The importance of the distinction is that different remedies are available depending on whether a term is broken or a representation turns out to be untrue.

3 (1) condition (2) discharged (3) damages (4) warranty (5) subsidiary (6) breach

4 Sale of Goods Act 1979

5 False

6 (1) business, (2) party, (3) business, (4) sale of goods, (5) private use or consumption

7 (a) 2
(b) 4
(c) 1
(d) 5
(e) 3

8 True

9 In deciding what an exclusion clause means, the courts interpret any ambiguity against the person at fault who relies on the exclusion.

10 (a) (3)
(b) (1)
(c) (2)

11
- A legally binding agreement must be **complete in its terms**
- The courts will seek to uphold agreements by looking at **the intention of the parties**

12
- Title
- Description
- Quality
- Fitness for purpose
- Sale by sample

13 **Exemption clauses in contracts for the supply of goods**

		Sale, HP, exchange and work + materials		Hire	
		Consumer transaction	*Non-consumer transaction*	*Consumer transaction*	*Non-consumer transaction*
Implied terms	Title	Void	Void	Subject to reasonableness test	Subject to reasonableness test
	Description	Void	Subject to reasonableness test	Void	Subject to reasonableness test
	Quality and suitability	Void	Subject to reasonableness test	Void	Subject to reasonableness test
	Sample	Void	Subject to reasonableness test	Void	Subject to reasonableness test

14 A condition is a vital term of the contract. Breach entitles the injured party to treat the contract as discharged and claim damages. A warranty is a minor term.

The following relevant questions are included in the Exam Question Banks

You can attempt these now. However, we would advise you to attempt these as mock exams at the end of your initial stage of study

Exam Question Bank	Numbers
Paper based format	7, 8, 27
Computer based assessment	12

Chapter 5

DISCHARGE OF CONTRACT

Topic list		Syllabus reference	Ability required
1	Performance	(iii)	Comprehension
2	Agreement	(iii), (iv)	Comprehension
3	Frustration	(iii), (iv)	Comprehension
4	Breach of contract	(iii), (iv)	Comprehension
5	Damages	(iv)	Comprehension
6	Other common law remedies	(iv)	Comprehension
7	Equitable remedies	(iv)	Comprehension
8	Limitation to actions for breach	(iv)	Comprehension

Introduction

In Chapter 3 we saw how a contract comes into existence and in Chapter 4 we considered some of the factors which can affect a contract. In this chapter we examine the ways in which a contract may be **discharged** and remedies when it is discharged incorrectly.

A party who is subject to the obligations of a contract may be discharged from those obligations in one of four ways. The four ways are **performance**, **breach**, **agreement** and **frustration**.

You should remember that most business contracts are discharged by performance as the parties intended. However, if it is discharged by breach, the injured party will be able to seek remedies. There are a number of available remedies:

- **Damages** are a form of compensation for loss caused by the breach.
- An **action for the price** may be commenced where the breach is failure to pay.
- A ***quantum meruit*** is payment to the claimant for the value of what he has done.
- **Specific performance**, an equitable remedy, is a court order to the defendant to perform the contract.
- An **injunction** is a court order for the other party to observe negative restrictions.
- **Rescission** means that the contract is cancelled or rejected and the parties restored to their pre-contract positions. It is usually applied when a contract is voidable because of circumstances such as a misrepresentation.

Damages and action for the price are **common law remedies** and are most frequently sought when a remedy is needed for breach of contract, since they arise as of right. The other types of remedy are **equitable remedies** which are only appropriate in specialised circumstances.

Learning outcomes covered in this chapter

- **Explain** what the law regards as performance of the contract, and valid and invalid reasons for non-performance
- **Explain** the type of breach necessary to cause contractual breakdown
- **Describe** the remedies which are available for serious and minor breaches of contract

Syllabus content covered in this chapter

- The level of performance sufficient to discharge contractual obligations
- Valid reasons for non-performance by way of agreement, breach by the other party and frustration
- The remedies of specific performance, injunction, rescission, and requiring a contract party to pay the agreed price
- Causation and remoteness of damage
- The quantification of damages

1 PERFORMANCE — Pilot Paper, 11/01

1.1 **This is the normal method of discharge.** Each party fulfils or performs his contractual obligations and the agreement is then ended. As a general rule contractual obligations are discharged only by **complete and exact performance**.

Cutter v Powell 1795
The facts: The defendant employed C as second mate of a ship sailing from Jamaica to Liverpool at a wage for the complete voyage of 30 guineas. The voyage began on 2 August, and C died at sea on 20 September, when the ship was still 19 days from Liverpool. C's widow sued for a proportionate part of the agreed sum.

Decision: C was entitled to nothing unless he completed the voyage.

Bolton v Mahadeva 1972
The facts: The claimant agreed to install a central heating system in the defendant's home for £800. The work was defective: the system did not heat adequately and it gave off fumes. The defendant refused to pay for it.

Decision: The claimant could recover nothing.

1.2 In each of these cases the defendant might appear to have profited since he obtained part of what the claimant contracted to deliver without himself having to pay anything. The courts have developed a number of exceptions to the rule to ensure that the interests of both parties are protected. The exceptions are as follows.

- The doctrine of **substantial performance**
- Where the promisee accepts **partial performance**
- Where the promisee **prevents performance**
- Where **time** is not of the essence
- **Severable** contracts

Substantial performance

1.3 The doctrine of substantial performance may be applied, especially in contracts for building work. If the building contractor has completed a very large part of the essential work, he may claim the contract price less a deduction for the minor work outstanding.

Sumpter v Hedges 1898
The facts: The claimant undertook to erect buildings on the land of the defendant for a price of £565. He partially erected the buildings, then abandoned the work when it was only completed to the value of £333. The defendant completed the work using

materials left on his land. The claimant sued for the value of his materials used by the defendant and for the value of his work.

Decision: The defendant must pay for the materials since he had elected to use them but he had no obligation to pay the unpaid balance of the charges for work done by the claimant before abandoning it. It was not a case of substantial performance of the contract.

Hoenig v Isaacs 1952
The facts: The defendant employed the claimant to decorate and furnish his flat at a total price of £750. There were defects in the furniture which could be put right at a cost of £56. The defendant argued that the claimant was only entitled to reasonable remuneration.

Decision: The defendant must pay the balance owing of the total price of £750 less an allowance of £56, as the claimant had substantially completed the contract.

Partial performance

1.4 The promisee may accept partial performance and must then pay for it. The principle here is that although the promisor has only partially fulfilled his contractual obligations, it may sometimes be possible to infer the existence of a fresh agreement by which it is agreed that payment will be made for work already done or goods already supplied. Mere performance by the promisor is not enough; it must be open to the promisee either to accept or reject the benefit of the contract.

Question 1

Why could the doctrine of partial performance not be applied in *Cutter v Powell*?

Answer

Partial performance can only be accepted by the promisee when he has a choice of acceptance or rejection. In *Cutter v Powell,* performance consisted of Cutter's services as second mate. Once he had provided those services, they could not be returned by the shipowners after his death.

Prevention of performance

1.5 The promisee may **prevent performance**. In that case the offer of performance is sufficient discharge.

1.6 If one party is prevented by the other from performing the contract completely he may sue for damages for breach of contract, or alternatively bring a *quantum meruit* action to claim for the amount of work done.

Planché v Colburn 1831
The facts: The claimant had agreed to write a book on costumes and armour for the defendants' 'Juvenile Library' series. He was to receive £100 on completion. He did some research and wrote part of the book. The defendants then abandoned the series.

Decision: The claimant was entitled to 50 guineas as reasonable remuneration on a *quantum meruit* basis.

Time of performance

1.7 If one party fails to perform at the agreed time he may perform the contract later - the contract continues in force, unless **time is of the essence**. In that case the injured party may refuse late performance and treat the contract as discharged by breach.

1.8 If the parties expressly agree that time is of the essence and so prompt performance is to be a condition, conclusive and late performance does not discharge obligations. If they make no such express stipulation the following rules apply.

(a) In a commercial contract, time of performance is usually treated as an essential condition.

(b) In a contract for the sale of land equity may permit the claimant to have an order for specific performance even if he is late.

(c) If time was not originally of the essence, either party may make it so by serving on the other a notice to complete within a reasonable time.

Severable contracts

1.9 The contract may provide for performance by instalments with separate payment for each of them (a **divisible** or **severable** contract).

Taylor v Laird 1856
The facts: The claimant agreed to captain a ship up the River Niger at a rate of £50 per month. He abandoned the job before it was completed. He claimed his pay for the months completed.

Decision: He was entitled to £50 for each complete month. Effectively this was a contract that provided for performance and payment in monthly instalments.

Sale of Goods Act 1979

1.10 As indicated above, acceptance of goods, or part of them (unless the contract is severable), deprives the buyer of his right to treat the contract as discharged by breach of condition on the part of the seller. But he may claim damages.

1.11 The buyer must have a reasonable opportunity to examine the goods before accepting them: s 34.

1.12 Situations when the buyer loses his right to reject goods

- He waives the breached condition.
- He elects to treat the breach of condition as a breach of warranty.
- He has accepted the goods.
- He is unable to return the goods.

2 AGREEMENT

2.1 **The parties may agree to cancel the contract before it has been completely performed** on both sides.

2.2 If there are unperformed obligations of the original contract on both sides, each party provides consideration for his own release by agreeing to release the other (**bilateral discharge**). Each party surrenders something of value.

2.3 But if one party has completely performed his obligations, his agreement to release the other from his obligations (**unilateral discharge**) requires consideration, such as payment of a cancellation fee (this is called **accord and satisfaction**).

2.4 If the parties enter into a new contract to replace the unperformed contract, the new contract provides any necessary consideration. This is called **novation** of the old contract - it is replaced by a new one.

2.5 A contract may include provision for its own discharge by imposing a **condition precedent,** which prevents the contract from coming into operation unless the condition is satisfied.

2.6 Alternatively, it may impose a **condition subsequent** by which the contract is discharged on the later happening of an event; a simple example of the latter is provision for termination by notice given by one party to the other. Effectively these are contracts whereby discharge may arise through agreement.

3 FRUSTRATION **Pilot Paper, 11/01**

3.1 If it is impossible to perform the contract when it is made, there is usually no contract at all. In addition, the parties are free to negotiate escape clauses or *force majeure* clauses covering impossibility which arises after the contract has been made. If they fail to do so, they are, as a general rule, in breach of contract if they find themselves unable to do what they have agreed to do.

3.2 The rigour of this principle is modified by the doctrine that in certain circumstances a contract may be discharged by **frustration.** If it appears that the parties assumed that certain underlying conditions would continue, the contract may be frustrated if their assumption proves to be false.

KEY TERM

'The term **frustration** refers to the discharge of a contract by some outside event for which neither party is responsible which makes further performance impossible. It must be some fundamental change in circumstances such as the accidental destruction of the subject-matter upon which the contract depends. The contract is thereby brought to an end and the rights and obligations of the parties will, in many cases, be adjusted by the application of the Law Reform (Frustrated Contracts) Act 1943.'

Destruction of the subject matter

3.3 In the case which gave rise to the doctrine of frustration, the **subject matter** of the contract was destroyed before performance fell due.

> *Taylor v Caldwell 1863*
> *The facts:* A hall was let to the claimant for a series of concerts on specified dates. Before the date of the first concert the hall was accidentally destroyed by fire. The claimant sued the owner of the hall for damages for failure to let him have the use of the hall as agreed.
>
> *Decision:* Destruction of the subject matter rendered the contract impossible to perform and discharged the defendant from his obligations under the contract.

Personal incapacity to perform a contract of personal service

3.4 The principle that a physical thing must be available applies equally to a person, if that person's presence is a fundamental requirement. Not every illness will discharge a contract of personal service - personal incapacity must be established.

Condor v Barron Knights 1966
The facts: The claimant, aged 16, contracted to perform as drummer in a pop group. His duties, when the group had work, were to play on every night of the week. He fell ill and his doctor advised that he should restrict his performances to four nights per week. The group terminated his contract.

Decision: A contract of personal service is based on the assumption that the employee's health will permit him to perform his duties. If that is not so the contract is discharged by frustration.

Government intervention

3.5 Government intervention is a common cause of frustration, particularly in time of war. If maintenance of the contract would impose upon the parties a contract fundamentally different from that which they made, the contract is discharged.

Metropolitan Water Board v Dick, Kerr & Co 1918
The facts: The defendants contracted in July 1914 to build a reservoir for the claimants within six years, subject to a proviso that the time should be extended if delays were caused by difficulties, impediments or obstructions. In February 1916 the Minister of Munitions ordered the defendants to cease work and sell all their plant.

Decision: The proviso in the contract did not cover such a substantial interference with the contract. The interruption was likely to cause the contract, if resumed, to be radically different from that contemplated by the parties. The contract was discharged.

Supervening illegality

3.6 In many cases of government intervention, further performance of the contract becomes **illegal**. Supervening illegality, for example owing to outbreak of war.

Avery v Bowden 1855
The facts: The defendant entered into a contract to charter a ship from the claimant to load grain at Odessa within a period of 45 days. The ship arrived at Odessa and the charterer told the claimant that he did not propose to load a cargo. The master remained at Odessa hoping the charterer would change his. Before the 45 days (for loading cargo) had expired, the outbreak of the Crimean war discharged the contract by frustration.

Decision: The contract was discharged by frustration (the outbreak of war) without liability for either party.

Non-occurrence of an event if it is the sole purpose of the contract

3.7 Two contrasting examples of this application of the doctrine are given by the so-called coronation cases.

Krell v Henry 1903
The facts: A room belonging to the claimant and overlooking the route of the coronation procession of Edward VII was let for the day of the coronation for the purpose of viewing the procession. The coronation was postponed owing to the illness of the King. The owner of the rooms sued for the agreed fee, which was payable on the day of the coronation.

Decision: The contract was made for the sole purpose of viewing the procession. As that event did not occur the contract was frustrated.

Herne Bay Steamboat Co v Hutton 1903
The facts: A steamboat was hired for two days to carry passengers, for the purpose of viewing the naval review (at Spithead) and for a day's cruise round the fleet. The review had been arranged as part of the coronation celebrations. The naval review was cancelled owing to the King's illness but the steamboat could have taken passengers for a trip round the assembled fleet, which remained at Spithead.

Decision: The royal review of the fleet was not the sole occasion of the contract, and the contract was not discharged. The owner of the steamboat was entitled to the agreed hire charge less what he had earned from the normal use of the vessel over the two day period.

Exceptions

3.8 A contract is not discharged by frustration in the following circumstances.

(a) If an **alternative mode of performance** is still possible.

Tsakiroglou & Co v Noblee and Thorl GmbH 1962
The facts: In October 1956 the sellers contracted to sell 300 tons of Sudanese groundnuts and transport them to Hamburg. The normal and intended method of shipment from Port Sudan (on the Red Sea coast) was by a ship routed through the Suez Canal to Hamburg. Before shipment the Suez Canal was closed; the sellers refused to ship the cargo arguing that it was an implied term that shipment should be via Suez or alternatively that shipment via the Cape of Good Hope would make the contract 'commercially and fundamentally' different, so that it was discharged by frustration.

Decision: Both arguments failed. There was no evidence to support the implied term argument nor was the use of a different (although more expensive) route an alteration of the fundamental nature of the contract sufficient to discharge it by frustration.

(b) If performance becomes suddenly more **expensive**.

(c) If one party **has accepted the risk** that he will be unable to perform.

(d) If one party **has induced frustration** by his own choice between alternatives.

The Law Reform (Frustrated Contracts) Act 1943

Exam focus point

As with misrepresentation, do not overlook the importance of statute law in the area of frustration.

3.9 Where a contract is frustrated, the common law rule provides that the occurrence of the frustrating event brings the contract automatically to an end forthwith. At common law, the consequences of this can be harsh.

Chandler v Webster 1904

The facts: The defendant agreed to let the claimant have a room for £141.15s for the purpose of viewing the coronation procession of Edward VII. The contract provided that the money was payable immediately. The coronation was postponed owing to the illness of the King. The claimant sued for the return of his £100 and the defendant counterclaimed for the unpaid amount of £41.15s.

Decision: The obligation to pay rent had fallen due before the frustrating event. The claimant's action failed and the defendant's claim was upheld.

3.10 This case can be contrasted with *Krell v Henry 1903*, where the contract stipulated that payment was due on the day of the procession. Only in 1942 was the doctrine modified, so that, where there is a complete failure of consideration, the contract can be held void *ab initio*.

Fibrosa v Fairbairn 1942

The facts: The claimant placed an order for machinery to be delivered in Poland. He paid £1,000 of the contract price of £4,800 with his order. Shortly afterwards the outbreak of the Second World War frustrated the contract since the German army occupied Poland. The claimant sued to recover the £1,000 which had been paid.

Decision: The deposit was repayable since the claimant had received absolutely nothing for it - there had been a total failure of consideration.

3.11 In most cases now the rights and liabilities of parties to a contract discharged by frustration are regulated by the Law Reform (Frustrated Contracts) Act 1943 as follows.

(a) Any money paid under the contract by one party to the other is to be repaid. Any sums due for payment under the contract then or later cease to be payable.

(b) If a person has to repay money under (a), or if he must forego payment earned, he may be able to recover or set off expenses incurred up to the time the contract was frustrated.

(c) If either party has obtained a valuable benefit (other than payment of money) under the contract before it is discharged, the court may in its discretion order him to pay to the other party all or part of that value.

Question 3

Which of the following is *not* a definition of the doctrine of frustration of contract?

A Parties should be discharged from their contract if altered circumstances render the contract fundamentally different in nature from what was originally agreed

B Parties should be discharged if an event, for which neither party is responsible, occurs which was not contemplated, which renders the contract fundamentally different and which results in a situation to which the parties did not originally wish to be bound

C Parties who contract that something should be done are discharged if performance becomes more expensive

D Parties who contract that something should be done are discharged if their assumption that certain conditions would continue proves to be false

Answer

C

4 BREACH OF CONTRACT

4.1 A party is said to be in breach of contract where, without lawful excuse, he does not perform his contractual obligations precisely. A person sometimes has a **lawful excuse** not to perform contractual obligations.

- Performance is **impossible,** perhaps because of some unforeseeable event.
- He has tendered performance but this has been **rejected.**
- The **other party** has made it **impossible** for him to perform.
- The contract has been discharged through **frustration**.
- The parties have by **agreement** permitted **non-performance.**

4.2 Breach of contract gives rise to a secondary obligation to pay **damages** to the other party (see Section 5) but, the **primary obligation to perform the contract's terms remains** unless breach falls into one of two categories.

(a) Where the party in default has **repudiated** the contract, either before performance is due or before the contract has been fully performed.

(b) Where the party in default has committed a **fundamental breach.**

KEY TERM

Repudiation can be defined as 'a rejection to avoid a contract or to bring a contract to an end for breach of condition. The term may also be applied to a situation where a party renounces his/her contractual obligations in advance of the date for performance.'

Repudiatory breach

KEY TERM

A **repudiatory breach** occurs where a party indicates, either by words or by conduct, that he does not intend to honour his contractual obligations. A repudiatory breach is a serious actual breach of contract.

4.3 It does not automatically discharge the contract - indeed the injured party has a choice.

(a) He can elect to treat the contract as repudiated by the other, recover damages and treat himself as being discharged from his primary obligations under the contract.

(b) He can elect to affirm the contract.

Types of repudiatory breach

4.4 Repudiatory breach giving rise to a right either to terminate or to affirm arises in the following circumstances.

(a) **Refusal to perform (renunciation).** One party renounces his contractual obligations by showing that he has no intention to perform them: *Hochster v De la Tour 1853.* (See below.)

(b) **Failure to perform an entire obligation.** An entire obligation is said to be one where complete and precise performance of it is a precondition of the other party's performance.

(c) **Incapacitation.** Where a party prevents himself from performing his contractual obligations he is treated as if he refused to perform them. For instance, where A sells a thing to C even though he promised to sell it to B he is in repudiatory breach of his contract with B.

4.5 **Genuine mistakes**, even to one party's detriment will not necessarily repudiate a contract. This was the decision in *Vaswani Motors (Sales and Services) Ltd 1996.* A seller of a motor vehicle, acting in good faith, mistakenly demanded a higher price than that specified in the contract. However, the buyer could not evade his responsibilities under the contract, since he could have offered to pay the original price.

Anticipatory breach

4.6 Repudiation may be **explicit** or **implicit**. A party may break a condition of the contract merely by declaring in advance that he will not perform it, or by some other action which makes future performance impossible. The other party may treat this as **anticipatory breach**

- Treat the contract as discharged forthwith
- At his option may allow the contract to continue until there is an actual breach

Hochster v De La Tour 1853
The facts: The defendant engaged the claimant as a courier to accompany him on a European tour commencing on 1 June. On 11 May he wrote to the claimant to say that he no longer required his services. On 22 May the claimant commenced legal proceedings for anticipatory breach of contract. The defendant objected that there was no actionable breach until 1 June.

Decision: The claimant was entitled to sue as soon as the anticipatory breach occurred on 11 May.

4.7 Where the injured party allows the contract to continue, it may happen that the parties are discharged from their obligations without liability if the contract is later frustrated: *Avery v Bowden 1855* (detailed in Section 3).

4.8 If the innocent party elects to treat the contract as still in force the former may continue with his preparations for performance and **recover the agreed price** for his services. Any claim for damages will be assessed on the basis of what the claimant has really lost.

White & Carter (Councils) v McGregor 1961
The facts: The claimants supplied litter bins to local councils, and were paid not by the councils but by traders who hired advertising space on the bins. The defendant contracted with them for advertising of his business. He then wrote to cancel the contract but the claimants elected to advertise as agreed, even though they had at the time of cancellation taken no steps to perform the contract. They performed the contract and claimed the agreed payment.

Decision: The contract continued in force and they were entitled to recover the agreed price for their services. Repudiation does not, of itself, bring the contract to an end. It gives the innocent party the choice of affirmation or rejection.

Termination for repudiatory breach

4.9 To terminate for repudiatory breach the innocent party must notify the other of his decision. This may be by way of refusal to accept defects in performance, refusal to accept further performance or refusal to perform his own obligations.

(a) He is not bound by his future or continuing contractual obligations, and cannot be sued on them.

(b) He need not accept nor pay for further performance.

(c) He can refuse to pay for partial or defective performance already received.

(d) He can reclaim money paid to a defaulter if he can and does reject defective performance.

(e) He is not discharged from the contractual obligations which were due at the time of termination.

4.10 The innocent party can also claim damages from the defaulter. An innocent party who began to perform his contractual obligations but who was prevented from completing them by the defaulter can claim reasonable remuneration on a *quantum meruit* basis (see Section 6).

Affirmation after repudiatory breach

4.11 If a person is aware of the other party's repudiatory breach and of his own right to terminate the contract as a result but still decides to treat the contract as being in existence he is said to have **affirmed the contract**. The contract remains fully in force.

5 DAMAGES 5/01, 11/01, 5/02

KEY TERM

Damages are a common law remedy and are primarily intended to **restore the party who has suffered loss to the same position he would have been in if the contract had been performed.**

5.1 In a claim for damages the first issue is **remoteness of damage**. Here the courts consider how far down the sequence of cause and effect the consequences of breach should be traced before they should be ignored. Secondly, the court must decide how much money to award in respect of the breach and its relevant consequences. This is the **measure of damages**.

Remoteness of damage

5.2 Under the rule in *Hadley v Baxendale* damages may only be awarded in respect of loss as follows.

(a) (i) **The loss must arise naturally** from the breach.

(ii) The loss must arise **in a manner which the parties may reasonably be supposed to have contemplated**, in making the contract, as the probable result of the breach of it.

(b) A loss outside the natural course of events will only be compensated if the exceptional circumstances are within the defendant's knowledge when he made the contract.

Hadley v Baxendale 1854
The facts: The claimants owned a mill at Gloucester whose main crank shaft had broken. They made a contract with the defendant for the transport of the broken shaft to Greenwich to serve as a pattern for making a new shaft. Owing to neglect by the defendant delivery was delayed and the mill was out of action for a longer period. The defendant did not know that the mill would be idle during this interval. He was merely aware that he had to transport a broken millshaft. The claimants claimed for loss of profits of the mill during the period of delay.

Decision: Although the failure of the carrier to perform the contract promptly was the direct cause of the stoppage of the mill for an unnecessarily long time, the claim must fail since the defendant did not know that the mill would be idle until the new shaft was delivered. Moreover it was not a natural consequence of delay in transport of a broken shaft that the mill would be out of action. The miller might have a spare.

5.3 The defendant is liable only if he knew of the special circumstances from which the abnormal consequence of breach could arise.

Victoria Laundry (Windsor) v Newman Industries 1949
The facts: The defendants contracted to sell a large boiler to the claimants 'for immediate use' in their business of launderers and dyers. Owing to an accident in dismantling the boiler at its previous site delivery was delayed. The defendants were aware of the nature of the claimants' business and had been informed that the claimants were most anxious to put the boiler into use in the shortest possible space of time. The claimants claimed damages for normal loss of profits for the period of delay and for loss of abnormal profits from losing 'highly lucrative' dyeing contracts to be undertaken if the boiler had been delivered on time.

Decision: Damages for loss of normal profits were recoverable since in the circumstances failure to deliver major industrial equipment ordered for immediate use would be expected to prevent operation of the plant. The claim for loss of special profits failed because the defendants had no knowledge of the dyeing contracts.

5.4 Contrast this ruling with the case below.

The Heron II 1969
The facts: K entered into a contract with C for the shipment of a cargo of sugar belonging to C to Basra. He was aware that C were sugar merchants but he did not know that C intended to sell the cargo as soon as it reached Basra. The ship arrived nine days late and in that time the price of sugar on the market in Basra had fallen. C claimed damages for the loss due to the fall in market value.

Decision: The claim succeeded. It is common knowledge that market values of commodities fluctuate so that delay might cause loss.

5.5 If the type of loss caused is not too remote the defendant may be liable for serious consequences.

H Parsons (Livestock) v Uttley Ingham 1978
The facts: There was a contract for the supply and installation of a large storage hopper to hold pig foods. Owing to negligence of the defendant supplier the ventilation cowl was left closed. The pig food went mouldy. Young pigs contracted a rare intestinal disease, from which 254 died. The pig farmer claimed damages for the value of the dead pigs and loss of profits from selling the pigs when mature.

Decision: Some degree of illness of the pigs was to be expected as a natural consequence. Since illness was to be expected, death from illness was not too remote.

Measure of damages

5.6 As a general rule the amount awarded as damages is what is needed to put the claimant in the position he would have achieved if the contract had been performed. This is sometimes referred to as protecting the **expectation interest** of the claimant.

5.7 A claimant may alternatively seek to have his **reliance interest** protected; this refers to the position he would have been in had he not relied on the contract. This compensates for wasted expenditure.

5.8 The onus is on the defendant to show that the expenditure would not have been recovered if the contract had been performed. However, if a contract is speculative, it may be unclear what profit might result.

Anglia Television Ltd v Reed 1972
The facts: The claimants engaged an actor to appear in a film they were making for television. He pulled out at the last moment and the project was abandoned. The claimants claimed the preparatory expenditure, such as hiring other actors and researching suitable locations.

Decision: Damages were awarded as claimed. It is impossible to tell whether an unmade film will be a success or a failure and, had the claimants claimed for loss of profits, they would not have succeeded.

5.9 The general principle is to compensate for **actual financial loss**.

Thompson Ltd v Robinson (Gunmakers) Ltd 1955
The facts: The defendants contracted to buy a Vanguard car from the claimants. They refused to take delivery and the claimants sued for loss of profit on the transaction. There was at the time a considerable excess of supply of such cars over demand for them and the claimants were unable to sell the car.

Decision: The market price rule, which the defendants argued should be applied, was inappropriate in the current market. The seller had lost a sale and was entitled to the profit.

Charter v Sullivan 1957
The facts: The facts were the same as in the previous case, except that the sellers were able to sell every car obtained from the manufacturers.

Decision: Only nominal damages were payable.

Non-financial loss

5.10 In some recent cases damages have been recovered for mental distress where that is the main result of the breach. It is uncertain how far the courts will develop this concept.

Jarvis v Swan Tours 1973
The facts: The claimant entered into a contract for holiday accommodation at a winter sports centre. What was provided was much inferior to the description given in the defendant's brochure. Damages on the basis of financial loss only were assessed at £32.

Decision: The damages should be increased to £125 to compensate for disappointment and distress.

Mitigation of loss

5.11 In assessing the amount of damages it is assumed that the claimant will take any reasonable steps to reduce or **mitigate** his loss. The burden of proof is on the defendant to show that the claimant failed to take a reasonable opportunity of mitigation.

Payzu Ltd v Saunders 1919
The facts: The parties had entered into a contract for the supply of goods to be delivered and paid for by instalments. The claimants failed to pay for the first instalment when due, one month after delivery. The defendants declined to make further deliveries unless the claimants paid cash in advance with their orders. The claimants refused to accept delivery on those terms. The price of the goods rose, and they sued for breach of contract.

Decision: The seller had no right to repudiate the original contract. But the claimants should have mitigated their loss by accepting the seller's offer of delivery against cash payment. Damages were limited to the amount of their assumed loss if they had paid in advance, which was interest over the period of pre-payment.

5.12 The injured party is not required to take discreditable or risky measures to reduce his loss since these are not 'reasonable'.

Liquidated damages and penalty clauses

5.13 To avoid later complicated calculations of loss, or disputes over damages payable, the parties may include up-front in their contract a formula (**liquidated damages**) for determining the damages payable for breach.

KEY TERM

Liquidated damages can be defined as 'a fixed or ascertainable sum agreed by the parties at the time of contracting, payable in the event of a breach, for example, an amount payable per day for failure to complete a building. If they are a genuine attempt to pre-estimate the likely loss the court will enforce payment.'

5.14 A contractual term designed as a **penalty clause** to discourage breach is void and not enforceable. Relief from penalty clauses is an example of the influence of equity in the law of contract, and has most frequently been seen in consumer credit cases.

KEY TERM

A **penalty clause** can be defined as 'a clause in a contract providing for a specified sum of money to be payable in the event of a subsequent breach. If its purpose is merely to deter a potential difficulty, it will be held void and the court will proceed to assess unliquidated damages.'

Question 4

What is a liquidated damages clause?

A A penalty clause in a contract with a company
B A penalty clause in a contract payable by instalments
C A formula for pre-determining damages payable for breach
D An onerous clause which will never be enforced by the courts

Answer

C

6 OTHER COMMON LAW REMEDIES

Action for the price

6.1 If the breach of contract arises out of one party's failure to pay the contractually agreed price due under the contract, the creditor should bring a personal action against the debtor to recover that sum. This is a fairly straightforward procedure but is subject to two specific limitations.

6.2 The first is that an **action for the price** under a contract for the sale of goods may only be brought if property has passed to the buyer, unless the price has been agreed to be payable on a specific date: s 49 Sale of Goods Act 1979.

6.3 Secondly, whilst the injured party may recover an agreed sum due at the time of an anticipatory breach, sums which become due after the anticipatory breach may not be recovered unless he affirms the contract.

Quantum meruit

6.4 In particular situations, a claim may be made on a *quantum meruit* basis as an alternative to an action for damages for breach of contract.

KEY TERM

The phrase **quantum meruit** literally means '**how much it is worth**'. It is a measure of the value of contractual work which has been performed. The aim of such an award is to restore the claimant to the position he would have been in if the contract had never been made, and is therefore known as a **restitutory** award.

6.5 *Quantum meruit* is likely to be sought where one party has already performed part of his obligations and the other party then repudiates the contract.

De Bernardy v Harding 1853
The facts: The claimant agreed to advertise and sell tickets for the defendant, who was erecting stands for spectators to view the funeral of the Duke of Wellington. The defendant cancelled the arrangement without justification.

Decision: The claimant might recover the value of services rendered.

6.6 In most cases, a *quantum meruit* claim is needed because the other party has unjustifiably prevented performance: *Planché v Colburn 1831*.

6.7 Because it is restitutory, a *quantum meruit* award is usually for a smaller amount than an award of damages. However where only nominal damages would be awarded (say because the claimant would not have been able to perform the contract anyway) a *quantum meruit* claim would still be available and would yield a higher amount.

7 EQUITABLE REMEDIES — Pilot Paper, 11/01, 5/02

Specific performance

7.1 The court may at its discretion give an equitable remedy by ordering the defendant to perform his part of the contract instead of letting him 'buy himself out of it' by paying damages for breach.

KEY TERM

Specific performance can be defined as 'an order of the court directing a person to perform an obligation. It is an equitable remedy awarded at the discretion of the court when damages would not be an adequate remedy. Its principal use is in contracts for the sale of land but may also be used to compel a sale of shares or debentures. It will never be used in the case of employment or other contracts involving personal services.'

7.2 An order will be made for specific performance of a contract for the sale of land since the claimant may need the land for a particular purpose and would not be adequately compensated by damages for the loss of his bargain. However, for items with no special features, specific performance will not be given, as damages would be a sufficient remedy.

7.3 The order will not be made if it would require performance over a period of time and the court could not ensure that the defendant did comply fully with the order. Therefore specific performance is not ordered for contracts of employment or personal service nor usually for building contracts.

Injunction

KEY TERM

An **injunction** is a discretionary court order and an equitable remedy, requiring the defendant to observe a negative restriction of a contract.

7.4 An injunction may be made to enforce a contract of personal service. This would be achieved by preventing a person from taking a course of action which would breach the contract.

> *Warner Bros Pictures Inc v Nelson 1937*
> *The facts:* The defendant (the film star Bette Davis) agreed to work for a year for the claimants and not during the year to work for any other producer nor 'to engage in any other occupation' without the consent of the claimants. She came to England during the year to work for a British film producer. The claimants sued for an injunction to restrain her from this work and she resisted arguing that if the restriction were enforced she must either work for them or abandon her livelihood.
>
> *Decision:* The court would not make an injunction if it would have the result suggested by the defendant. But the claimants merely asked for an injunction to restrain her from working for a British film producer. This was one part of the restriction accepted by her under her contract and it was fair to hold her to it to that extent.

7.5 An injunction is limited to enforcement of contract terms which are in substance negative restraints. In other words, if a contract specifies acts which a party should not perform, an injunction can be granted to prevent them performing those acts.

7.6 However, an injunction will not be granted to prevent a person performing acts which seem inconsistent with the terms of a contract, if the contract does not specifically restrain them from doing so.

Question 5

The purpose of an injunction is to

A Enforce a negative restraint in a contract
B Compel compliance with the contract's terms
C Ensure timely and complete performance
D Restrain acts inconsistent with the contract's obligations

Answer

A

Rescission

7.7 Strictly speaking the equitable right to **rescind** an agreement is not a remedy for breach of contract - it is a right which exists in certain circumstances, such as where a contract is **voidable** for misrepresentation (Chapter 3).

7.8 Rescinding a contract means that it is cancelled or rejected and the parties are restored to their pre-contract condition. Four conditions must be met.

- It must be possible for each party to be returned to the pre-contract condition *(restitutio in integrum).*
- An innocent third party who has acquired rights in the subject matter of the contract will prevent the original transaction being rescinded.
- The right to rescission must be exercised within a reasonable time of it arising.
- Where a person affirms a contract expressly or by conduct it may not then be rescinded.

8 LIMITATION TO ACTIONS FOR BREACH

8.1 The right to sue for breach of contract becomes statute-barred after six years from the date on which the cause of action accrued: s 5 Limitation Act 1980. The period is twelve years if the contract is by deed.

8.2 In three situations the six year period begins not at the date of the breach but later.

(a) If the claimant is a minor or under some other contractual disability (eg of unsound mind) at the time of the breach of contract, the six year period begins to run only when his disability ceases or he dies.

(b) If the defendant or his agent conceals the right of action by fraud or if the action is for relief from the results of a mistake, the six year period begins to run only when the claimant discovered or could by reasonable diligence have discovered the fraud, concealment or mistake: s 32 Limitation Act 1980. An innocent third party who acquired property which is affected by these rules is protected against any action in respect of them: s 32(4).

(c) The normal period of six years can be extended where information relevant to the possible claims is deliberately concealed after the period of six years has started to run.

8.3 Where the claim can only be for specific performance or injunction, the Limitation Act 1980 does not apply. Instead, the claim may be limited by the equitable doctrine of delay or 'laches'.

Allcard v Skinner 1887
The facts: The claimant entered a Protestant convent in 1868 and, in compliance with a vow of poverty, transferred property worth about £7,000 to the Order by 1878. In 1879 she left the order and became a Roman Catholic. Six years later she demanded the return of the balance of her gift, claiming undue influence by the defendant, the Lady Superior of the Protestant sisterhood.

Decision: This was a case of undue influence for which a right of rescission may be available, since the rule of the Order forbade its members from seeking the advice of outsiders. But the claimant's delay in making her claim debarred her from recovering her property.

Extension of the limitation period

8.4 The limitation period may be extended if the debt, or any other certain monetary amount, is either acknowledged or paid in part before the original six (or twelve) years has expired: s 29. Hence if a debt accrues on 1.1.88, the original limitation period expires on 31.12.93. But if part-payment is received on 1.1.92, the debt is reinstated and does not then become 'statute-barred' until 31.12.97.

(a) The claim must be acknowledged as existing, not just as possible, but it need not be quantified. It must be in writing, signed by the debtor and addressed to the creditor: s 30.

(b) To be effective, the part payment must be identifiable with the particular debt, not just a payment on a running account.

Chapter roundup

- The normal method of discharge is **performance**. Obligations of the parties in the vast majority of commercial contracts are discharged by performance. Performance must be **complete and exact**. There is no right to receive payment proportionate to partially completed work unless one of the recognised exceptions applies.
- The obligations of the parties may be discharged by **agreement**.
- If the parties to the contract assumed, at the time of the agreement, that certain underlying conditions would continue, the contract is discharged by **frustration** if these assumptions prove to be false. The contract is then fundamentally different in nature from the original agreement.
- The common law consequences of frustration are modified by the **Law Reform (Frustrated Contracts) Act 1943**, which regulates the rights and obligations of the parties to a contract discharged by frustration.
- Breach of a condition in a contract may lead to the entire agreement being discharged by **fundamental breach**, unless the injured party elects to treat the contract as continuing and merely claim damages for his loss.
- If there is **anticipatory breach** (one party declares in advance that he will not perform his side of the bargain when the time for performance arrives) the other party may treat the contract as discharged forthwith, or continue with his obligations until actual breach occurs. His claim for damages will then depend upon what he has actually lost.
- **Damages** are a common law remedy intended to restore the party who has suffered loss to the position he would have been in had the contract been performed. The two tests applied to a claim for damages relate to **remoteness of damage** and **measure of damages**.
- Remoteness of damage is tested by the **two limbs** of the rule in **Hadley v Baxendale 1854**.
- The first part of the rule states that the **loss must arise either naturally**, according to the usual course of things, from the breach or in a manner which the parties may reasonably be supposed to have contemplated, in making the contract, as a probable result of its breach.
- The second part of the rule provides that a **loss outside the usual course of events** will only be compensated if the exceptional circumstances which caused it were within the defendant's **actual or constructive knowledge** when he made the contract.
- The **measure of damages** is that which will **compensate for the loss incurred**. It is not intended that the injured party should profit from a claim.
- A simple **action for the price** to recover the agreed sum should be brought if breach of contract is failure to pay the price. But property must have passed from seller to buyer, and complications arise where there is anticipatory breach.
- A **quantum meruit** is a claim which is available as an alternative to damages. The injured party in a breach of a contract may claim the value of his work. The aim of such an award is to restore the claimant to the position he would have been in had the contract never been made. It is a **restitutory** award.
- An order for **specific performance** is an equitable remedy. The party in breach is ordered to perform his side of the contract. Such an order is only made where damages are inadequate compensation, such as in a sale of land, and where actual consideration has passed.
- An **injunction** is an equitable remedy which requires that a negative condition in the agreement be fulfilled.

Quick quiz

1 **Fill in the blanks** in the statements below.

- Performance must as a rule be (1) ………… and (2) ……….
- When anticipatory breach occurs, the injured party has two options. These are

  (3) ………………..

  (4) ………………..

2 A person never has a lawful excuse not to perform contractual obligations

☐ True

☐ False

3 Which of the following is *not* a lawful excuse not to perform contractual obligations?

A The contract has been discharged through frustration
B The parties have by agreement permitted non-performance
C One party has made it impossible for the other to perform
D Performance has become more expensive than was originally anticipated

4 If the innocent party elects to treat the contract as still in force, the former may continue with his preparations for performance and recover the agreed price for his services.

☐ True

☐ False

5 **Fill in the blanks** in the statements below, using the words in the box.

- (1) ……………….. are a (2) ……………….. remedy designed to restore the injured party to the position he would have been in had the contract been (3) ………………..
- A loss outside the natural course of events will only be compensated if the (4) ……………….. circumstances are within the (5) ………………..'s knowledge at the time of making the contract.
- In assessing the amount of damage it is assumed that the (6) ……………….. will (7) ……………….. his loss.
- A contractual term designed as a (8) ……………….. is (9) ……………….. .

• mitigate	• performed	• claimant
• penalty clause	• exceptional	• damages
• common law	• void	• defendant

6 Damages are a common law remedy

☐ True

☐ False

7 The amount awarded as damages is what is needed to put the claimant in the position he would have achieved if the contract had been performed. What interest is being protected here?

expectation
reliance

8 A court will never enforce a liquidated damages clause, as any attempt to discourage breach is void.

☐ True

☐ False

9 Are each of the following remedies based on (i) equity or (ii) common law?

(a) Quantum meruit
(b) Injunction
(c) Action for the price
(d) Rescission
(e) Specific performance

10 The case of *Allcard v Skinner* illustrates the doctrine of

promissory estoppel	frustration
delay or 'laches'	mitigation of loss

11 Which of the following are lawful reasons *not* to perform contractual obligations precisely?

- Performance is impossible
- Performance has become substantially more difficult
- Performance has been tendered but rejected
- Performance has been frustrated
- Performance has not been completed by a deadline
- The parties have agreed upon non-performance.

12 Where a repudiators breach occurs, the injured party has a choice to:

- Treat the contract as repudiated by the other party, recover damages and treat himself as being discharged form his obligations under the contract.

- Affirm the contract.

True ☐

False ☐

13 Which one of the following is *not* a condition of rescinding a contract?

- The possibility of recission must have been included in the original contract.
- It must be possible for each party to be returned to the pre-contract condition.
- No innocent third party has acquired rights in the subject matter of the contract.
- Recission must take place within reasonable time.
- Contract must not have been affirmed, either expressly or through conduct.

14 Complete the definitions of each remedy.

Remedy	**Definition**
Damages	Financial compensation designed to restore the injured party to the position he would have been in, had the contract been performed.
Action for the price	
Quantum meruit	

Specific performance	
Injunction	

15 David has hired Bella, Jonathan's favourite singer, to sing at Jonathan's birthday party. Bella loses her voice and cannot sing. The contract **is/is not** discharged by frustration because...

Using no more than 20 words, delete as applicable and complete the sentence.

Answers to quick quiz

1 (1) complete (2) exact
(3) treat the contract as discharged forthwith
(4) allow the contract to continue until there is an actual breach

2 False

3 D

4 True

5 (1) damages (2) common law (3) performed
(4) exceptional (5) defendant (6) claimant
(7) mitigate (8) penalty clause (9) void

6 True

7 Expectation

8 False

9 (a) Common law
(b) Equity
(c) Common law
(d) Equity
(e) Equity

10 Delay or 'laches'

11
- Performance is impossible
- Performance has been tendered but rejected
- Performance has been frustrated
- The parties have agreed on non-performance

12 True

13 It is not necessary for recission to have been provided for in a contract for recission to take place.

14	Remedy	Definition
	Damages	Financial compensation designed to restore the injured party to the position he would have been in, had the contract been performed.
	Action for the price	Personal action taken against the debtor to recover the sum
	Quantum meruit	Measure of how much of the work has been done. Designed to restore the claimant to the position he would have been in had the contract never been made.
	Specific performance	An order of the court directing a person to perform a contractual obligation
	Injunction	A discretionary court order requiring a person to observe a negative restraint in a contract.

The following relevant questions are included in the Exam Question Banks

You can attempt these now. However, we would advise you to attempt these as mock exams at the end of your initial stage of study

Exam Question Bank	Numbers
Paper based format	9, 10
Computer based assessment	4, 13, 20, 29, 31, 37

Part C
Employment

Chapter 6

EMPLOYMENT CONTRACT

Topic list		Syllabus reference	Ability required
1	**What is an employee?**	(v)	Comprehension
2	**Why does it matter?**	(v)	Comprehension
3	**Basic contract**	(v)	Comprehension
4	**Terms implied in employment contracts**	(v)	Comprehension
5	**Employee's duties**	(v)	Comprehension
6	**Varying the terms of an employment contract**	(v)	Comprehension
7	**Vicarious liability**	(v)	Comprehension

Introduction

The law of employment was developed under common law principles as an application of the law of contract. In recent years **statutory rules** have been enacted to give the **employee protection** both against dismissal and against unsafe or unhealthy working conditions. But the basic issues in employment law remain.

(a) Is an arrangement a contract of service (**employment**) or only a contract for services (with an **independent contractor**)?

(b) What are the **terms** of a contract of employment?

Statutory references in this chapter are to the Employment Rights Act 1996 (ERA 1996) unless otherwise noted.

Learning outcomes covered in this chapter

- **Distinguish** between employees and independent contractors and **explain** the importance of the distinction
- **Explain** how the contents of a contract of employment are established

Syllabus content covered in this chapter

- The tests used to distinguish an employee from an independent contractor
- The express and implied terms of a contract of employment

1 WHAT IS AN EMPLOYEE? 11/01, 5/02

KEY TERMS

An **employee** is a person who has a relationship with an employer governed by a contract of employment (a service contract). An **independent contractor**, in contrast, sells his services to a customer under a contract for services.

1.1 It is important for a number of reasons to determine whether a **contract of employment** exists. These reasons are laid out in section 2 of this Chapter. Here we will look at the basic principles applied by the courts to distinguish between employees and independent contractors.

1.2 The court will look at the reality of the situation, rather than the form of the arrangement.

Ferguson v John Dawson & Partners 1976
The facts: A builder's labourer was paid his wages without deduction of income tax or National Insurance contributions and worked as a self-employed contractor providing services. His 'employer' could dismiss him, decide on which site he would work, direct him as to the work he should do and also provided the tools which he used. He was injured in an accident and sued his employers on the basis that they owed him legal duties as his employer.

Decision: On the facts taken as a whole, he was an employee working under a contract of employment.

Tests applied by the courts

1.3 It can be unclear whether a person is an employee or an independent contractor. The tests of **control, integration** into the employer's organisation, and **economic reality** (or the multiple test) are applied in such cases.

1.4 The fundamental prerequisite of a contract of employment is that there must be **mutual obligations** on the employer to provide, and the employee to perform, work.

Test	Criteria
Control test	Has the employee control over the way in which the employee performs his duties?
Integration test	If the employee is so skilled that he cannot be controlled in his performance of his duties, was he integrated into the employer's organisation?
Multiplc (economic reality) test	Is the employee working on his own account?

Other factors

1.5 Other significant factors are as follows.

- Does the employee use his **own tools and equipment** or does the employer provide them?
- Does the alleged employer have the power to **select or appoint** its employees, and may it dismiss them?
- **Payment of salary** is, as mentioned above, a fair indication of there being a contract of employment.
- **Working for a number of different people** is not necessarily a sign of self-employment. A number of assignments may be construed as 'a series of employments'.

1.6 In difficult cases, the court will also consider whether the employee can delegate all his obligations, whether there is restriction as to place of work, whether there is a **mutual obligation** and whether holidays and hours of work are agreed.

Question 1

In deciding whether a contract is one of service or one for services, when will the court apply the integration test?

A When it is unclear whether or not the employer has the power to select and dismiss its employees

B When it is unclear whether or not the tools and equipment used belong to the employer or the employee

C When it is clear that the employee is working on his own account

D When it is clear that the employer cannot control the employee in the conduct of his work but can direct him as to what work needs doing

Answer

D

2 WHY DOES IT MATTER?

2.1 There are several reasons why the distinction between a contract of service and a contract for services is important.

Significance of the distinction

	Employed	**Self-employed**
Implied terms	There are rights and duties implied by statute for employers and employees (see section 4)	These implied rights and duties do not apply to such an extent to a contract for services
Employment protection (see Chapter 7)	There is much legislation which confers protection and benefits upon employees under a contract of service, including • Minimum periods of notice • Remedies for unfair dismissal • Redundancy payments	
Health and safety (see Chapter 7)	There is significant common law and statutory regulation governing employers' duties to employees with regard to health and safety	The common law provisions and much of the regulation relating to employees also related to independent contractors
Social security and taxation issues	Employers must pay national insurance contributions on behalf of employees. Employees pay Class 1 NI contributions on their salary. Income tax is deducted from salary under PAYE (Schedule E). There are also differences in statutory sick pay and levies for industrial training purposes	Independent contractors pay Class 2 and 4 national insurance contributions. They must account personally to the IR for income tax under Schedule D. They may have to register for VAT as they sell services.

Significance of the distinction		
Bankruptcy	In liquidation, an employee has preferential rights as a creditor for payment of salary and redundancy payments, up to certain limits	An independent contractor is likely to rank as an ordinary creditor in liquidation. He would be low priority for payment.

3 BASIC CONTRACT

3.1 Considering how widespread and how important employment contracts are, the legal requirements as to form are remarkably fluid. Partly this is because it is difficult to incorporate every exigency which may arise during the course of work.

Question 2

As with any other contract, agreements for employment require offer and acceptance, consideration and the intention to create legal relations. How are these three essential elements manifested in a contract of employment?

Answer

Generally the offer comes from the employer and acceptance from the employee, who may write a letter or simply turn up for work at an agreed time. Consideration comprises the promises each party gives to the other - a promise to work for a promise to pay. If there is no consideration, a deed must be executed for there to be a contract of employment. The intention to create legal relations is imputed from the fact that essentially employment is a commercial transaction.

3.2 A contract of employment may be **written, oral or a mixture** of the two. At the one extreme, it may be a document drawn up by solicitors and signed by both parties; at the other extreme it may consist of a handshake and a 'See you on Monday'. Senior personnel may sign a contract specially drafted to include terms on confidentiality and restraint of trade. Other employees may sign a standard form contract, exchange letters with the new employer or supply agreed terms orally at interview.

3.3 Each of these situations, subject to the requirements outlined below as to written particulars, will form a valid contract of employment, as long as there is agreement on essential terms such as hours and wages.

Written particulars of employment **5/01, 11/01**

3.4 In general a contract of employment need not be made in writing, but within two months of the beginning of the employment the employer must give to an employee a written **statement of prescribed particulars** of his employment: s 1 ERA 1996. This requirement applies to all employees except merchant seamen, employees engaged in work wholly or mainly outside the UK and persons who already have a written contract of employment which gives all the necessary details.

3.5 The statement should identify the following.

- The names of **employer** and **employee**
- The **date** on which employment began
- Whether any service with a previous employer forms part of the employee's **continuous period** of employment

- **Pay** - scale or rate and intervals at which paid
- **Hours** of work (including any specified 'normal working hours')
- Any **holiday** and **holiday pay** entitlement
- **Sick leave** and **sick pay** entitlement
- **Pensions** and pension **schemes**
- Length of **notice** of termination to be given on either side
- The **title** of the job which the employee is employed to do

3.6 A 'principal statement', which must include the first six items above and the title of the job, must be provided, but other particulars may be given by way of separate documents.

3.7 If the employee has a **written contract of employment** covering these points and has been given a copy it is not necessary to provide him with separate written particulars.

3.8 The written particulars must also contain details of **disciplinary procedures** and **grievance procedures** or reference to where they can be found. Each employee must in this case be given a copy of the booklet. Employers with fewer than 20 employees do not need to provide particulars of disciplinary procedures: s 3 ERA 1996, but employees must still be told of grievance procedures.

3.9 Failure by an employee to initiate an established grievance procedure may, in the event of unfair dismissal, amount to contributory fault leading to a reduction in any award.

3.10 **Rules on health and safety at work need not be given, though it is common practice** for these to be included with the written statement. An employer must, however (unless he employs fewer than five employees), prepare a separate statement of his policy on health and safety at work. The Health and Safety at Work Act 1974 is the most significant piece of legislation in this area.

Changes in contract terms

3.11 Whenever any change is made in any term contained in the written particulars, the employer must within one month provide a **written statement of the change**.

Failure to give written particulars

3.12 If the employer fails to comply with these requirements the employee may apply to an employment tribunal for a declaration of what the terms should be: s 11.

Question 3

Alan countersigns his employment contract and written statement with Sheerbrow Ltd but after 2 weeks is told that the holiday entitlement of 6 weeks per annum as stated in the particulars should have read 5 weeks, as was originally agreed. What can he do?

Answer

Alan's only option is to require Sheerbrow Ltd to provide him with an amended copy of the particulars within one month. The written particulars are merely evidence of the employment contract's terms - they do not represent the contract itself, so an amendment of an error cannot be said to be a breach.

4 TERMS IMPLIED IN EMPLOYMENT CONTRACTS

4.1 Terms are implied into employment contracts from various sources:

- Statute
- Common law
- Custom (collective implied terms)

Exam focus point

It is useful to note that increasingly such terms are implied into employment contracts by statute, particularly where the UK is seeking to implement EC directives on employment issues.

4.2 There is an overriding **duty of mutual trust and confidence** between the employer and the employee.

4.3 The employer usually also has the following duties at **common law**:

- To **pay remuneration** to employees. If there is no rate fixed by the parties, this duty is to pay **reasonable** remuneration. There is statutory provision for this, see section 5.
- To **indemnify the employee** against expenses and losses incurred in the course of employment.
- To take care of the employees' **health and safety** at work. This is also provided for in statute. There are three components of the common law duty: to select proper staff, to provide adequate materials, to provide a safe system of working.
- To **select fit and competent fellow-employees**.
- To **provide work, only** where
  - Employee is an apprentice
  - Employee is paid with reference to work done
  - The opportunity to work is the essence of the contract (for example, for actors)

4.4 The importance of these common law implied duties on both parties is that:

(a) **Breach of a legal duty**, if it is important enough, may entitle the injured party to treat the contract as **discharged** and to claim damages for breach of contract at common law, and

(b) In an employee's claim for compensation for unfair dismissal, the employee may argue that it was a case of **constructive dismissal** by the employer, or the employer may seek to justify his express dismissal of the employee by reference to his conduct. We shall discuss constructive dismissal in Chapter 7.

4.5 You should note also that an employer **does not have a duty** to provide a reference for an employee. It is a common misconception that he does.

Statutory duties

4.6 Various matters are implied into contracts of employment by statute. Some of them build upon the basic matters covered by common law above. Most of the employment statutes in this area implement European Directives on employment law issues. The employer has statutory duties in the following areas:

- Pay

- Time off work
- Maternity and parental rights
- Health and safety
- Working time

Pay

4.7 There are two key pieces of legislation in relation to pay. These are the **Equal Pay Act 1970** and the **National Minimum Wage Act 1998.**

Equal Pay Act 1970

4.8 Under this Act, contractual **employment terms should be at least as favourable as those given to an employee of the opposite sex**. The Act covers other terms such as sick pay, holiday pay and working hours, and it applies to all forms of full-time and part-time work.

> *Hayward v Cammell Laird Shipbuilders 1986*
> *The facts:* The House of Lords upheld the claim of a canteen cook to equal pay with painters, joiners and thermal insulation engineers employed in the same shipyard on the ground that her work was of equal value.
>
> *Decision:* Overall the applicant was considered to be employed on work of equal value. Hayward's application was the first successful claim for equal pay for work of equal value.

4.9 A difference in pay which is connected with economic factors affecting the efficient carrying on of the employer's business or other activity may well be relevant: *Rainey v Greater Glasgow Health Board 1987*. Examples are as follows.

- Greater length of service is a material factor.
- Working at different times of day is not a material factor.
- A distinction in hourly pay between workers in London and those based in (the cheaper area of) Nottingham is based on a material factor.
- 'Market forces' do not necessarily amount to a genuine material factor.

National Minimum Wage Act 1998

4.10 A national minimum wage was introduced in the UK in 1999. The current hourly rate is £4.10. For persons between the ages of 18 and 22, the rate is £3.50.

Other matters

4.11 Employers are obliged to provide an itemised pay statement: s 8. Most employees are eligible for Statutory Sick Pay for a period of 28 weeks.

Time off work

4.12 In addition to the rights relating to maternity and parental leave discussed below, statute lists several occasions when an employee has a right to time off work.

(a) **Trade union officials** are entitled to time off on full pay at the employer's expense to enable them to carry out **trade union duties***:* ss 168-169 Trade Union and Labour Relations (Consolidation) Act 1992.

(b) An employee who has been given notice of dismissal for **redundancy** may have time off to look for work or to arrange training for other work.

(c) A member of a recognised independent **trade union** may have time off work (without statutory right to pay) for **trade union activities**, for example, attending a branch meeting: s 170 TULRCA 1992.

(d) Employees also have a duty to allow an employee to have reasonable time off to carry n out certain **public duties**, for example performing his duties as a magistrate. There is **no statutory provision** entitling an employee to time off for jury service, but prevention of a person from attending as a juror is contempt of court.

Maternity and parental leave

4.13 A woman who is pregnant is given substantial rights under statute, including:

- A right to **time off work** for ante-natal care
- The right to **ordinary maternity leave**
- The right to **additional maternity leave**
- The right to **maternity pay**
- If dismissed, a claim for unfair dismissal (this will be discussed in Chapter 7)

Maternity leave

4.14 Every woman is given the right to ordinary maternity leave which is **eighteen weeks** long, subject to her satisfying conditions giving her employer notice of her intentions. A woman who has been continuously employed for one year has a right to additional maternity leave, which allows the employee a period of **twenty-nine weeks' leave** beginning in the week childbirth occurred.

4.15 An employee on **ordinary** maternity leave has the **right to return to work** in the job she had before her absence, with her seniority, pension and similar rights which she would have had if she had not been absent and on no less favourable terms than if she had not be absent: s 71.

4.16 An employee on **additional** maternity leave has the same rights, except if it is **not practicable** for her to return to the job she had before, she has the right to another job which is **suitable and appropriate** to her.

Parental leave

4.17 Any employee with a year's continuous service who has responsibility for a child is entitled to parental leave to care for that child: s 7 Employment Relations Act 1999.

4.18 The period allowed is 13 weeks for each child born or adopted after 15 December 1999. The entitlement ceases after the child is 5 years old, or on the 5th anniversary of the child being adopted. If the child is disabled (entitled to disability allowance), the right ceases after the child's eighteenth birthday.

4.19 The leave may not be taken in periods of less than one week, unless the child is disabled.

Working time

4.20 The Working Time Regulations 1998 provide that a worker's **average working time in a seventeen week period,** (including overtime) shall **not exceed 48 hours for each 7 days period,** unless the worker has agreed in writing that this limit shall not apply.

4.21 The Regulations also give every worker the **right to paid annual leave**, which shall be a minimum of four weeks long. The employer may be able to specify when such holiday can or cannot be taken, but must give the employees notice of such occasions.

Health and safety

4.22 The key legislation under which an employer has a duty to his employees with regard to health and safety is the Health and Safety at Work Act 1974, which has been augmented by subsequent regulations, notably the Health and Safety at Work Regulations 1999. This act makes it the duty of every employer to ensure the health, safety and welfare of his employees, as far as is practicable.

4.23 This general duty includes the following issues:

- Provide and maintain plant and systems of work which are safe and without risk
- Make arrangements to ensure safe use, handling, storage and transport of articles/substances
- Provide adequate information, instruction, training and supervision
- Maintain safe places of work and ensure that there is adequate access in and out
- Provide a safe and healthy working environment

Employment rights

4.24 The contract of employment contains an implied right not to be subjected to detriment by the employer on grounds of health and safety: s 44(1). Specifically, the employee has a right not to be subjected to detriment on the ground that he intended to or did:

- Carry out activities designated to him in connection with preventing/reducing health and safety risks at work
- Perform duties as a representative of workers on issues of health and safety
- Take part in consultation with the employer under the Health and Safety (Consultation with Employees) Regulations 1996
- Leave his place of work or refused to work in circumstances which he reasonably believed to be serious or imminent and he could not reasonably be expected to avert
- Take appropriate steps to protect himself or others from circumstances of danger which he believed to be serious and imminent

Social security benefits

4.25 A person who suffers personal injury caused by accident arising out of and in the course of his employment, or who is otherwise unable to work, is entitled to **social security benefit** (ie incapacity benefit), severe disablement benefit, industrial injuries disablement benefit or death benefit as may be appropriate) under the state social security scheme.

4.26 **Incapacity benefit** can be paid to employees who are incapable of work for four or more days in a row, during a Period of Incapacity for Work (PIW). It is payable as short-term incapacity benefit, for 28 weeks at a lower rate and then a further 28 weeks at a higher rate. If the incapability continues after this time, then long-term incapacity benefit is payable.

4.27 **Industrial injuries disablement benefit** is benefit which is paid to an employee who becomes disabled as a result of an accident at work or as a result of an industrial disease.

4.28 Various supplements may be paid to augment a disablement pension. For example if the injured worker is totally disabled so that he needs to be looked after at all times, a constant attendance allowance is paid.

4.29 If a worker dies as a result of an industrial injury his widow (or dependent widower of a woman worker) receives a pension as death benefit. This may include an allowance for dependent children.

4.30 A disabled worker may also claim damages from his employer. The normal damages are reduced by one half of any industrial injury benefit which the worker receives in the five year period beginning at the date of the injury.

4.31 The Social Security Act 1989 allows the Department of Social Security to recover benefits it has paid, by claiming it out of any compensation received by the worker (ie from the employer or an insurance company).

Other employment protection

4.32 Statute also implies a number of terms into employment contracts which provide the employee with protection from the employer (perceived to be the stronger party in the contract). These are considered in more detail in Chapter 7. However, they fall into the following categories:

- Protection from discrimination
- Health and safety protection
- Protection from unfair dismissal

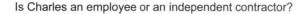

Question 4

Charles saw a sign advertising vacancies at a local building site. He contacted the foreman and was told that he would be required but that, because work depended on the weather conditions, he would not be given an employment contract - he would be accountable for his own income tax and National Insurance. The foreman added that he would be provided with tools and that at the beginning of each day he would be told which site he would work on that day. Lateness or theft of materials would lead to his dismissal.

Is Charles an employee or an independent contractor?

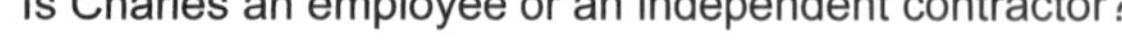

Answer

Charles is an employee. Even though he does not receive an employment contract the facts indicate a contract of service since he is controlled by the employer in that the latter provides tools, tells him where to work and reserves the right to dismiss him.

5 EMPLOYEE'S DUTIES

5.1 The employee has a **fundamental duty of faithful service** to his employer. All other duties are features of this general duty.

> *Hivac Ltd v Park Royal Scientific Instruments Ltd 1946*
> *The facts:* In their spare time certain of the claimant's employees worked for the defendant company, which directly competed with the claimant.
>
> *Decision:* Even though the employees had not passed on any confidential information, they were still in breach of their duty of fidelity to the claimants.

5.2 The **implied** duties of the employee include the following.

(a) **Reasonable competence** to do his job.

(b) **Obedience** to the employer's instructions unless they require him to do an unlawful act or to expose himself to personal danger (not inherent in his work).

(c) **Duty to account for all money and property** received during the course of his employment.

> *Boston Deep Sea Fishing and Ice Co v Ansell 1888*
> *The facts:* The defendant, who was managing director of the claimant company, accepted personal commissions from suppliers on orders which he placed with them for goods supplied to the company. He was dismissed and the company sued to recover from him the commissions.
>
> *Decision:* The company was justified in dismissing the claimant and he must account to it for the commissions.

(d) **Reasonable care and skill** in the performance of his work: *Lister v Romford Ice and Cold Storage Co 1957*. What is reasonable depends on the degree of skill and experience which the employee professes to have.

(e) **Personal service** - the contract of employment is a personal one and so the employee may not delegate his duties without the employer's express or implied consent.

(f) The same duty of **fidelity** to an employer to whom he is seconded as to a **contractual employer**.

5.3 The importance of these common law implied duties on both parties is that:

(a) **Breach of a legal duty**, if it is important enough, may entitle the injured party to treat the contract as **discharged** and to claim damages for breach of contract at common law, and

(b) In an employee's claim for compensation for unfair dismissal, the employee may argue that it was a case of **constructive dismissal** by the employer, or the employer may seek to justify his express dismissal of the employee by reference to his conduct.

Question 5

Formation of a valid contract of employment requires

1 Offer and acceptance
2 Intention to create legal relations
3 Consideration
4 Legality
5 A written document

A 1 and 2 only
B 1, 2 and 3 only
C 1, 2, 3 and 4 only
D 1, 2, 3, 4 and 5

Answer

C

---

6 VARYING THE TERMS OF AN EMPLOYMENT CONTRACT

6.1 It should be clear, from your earlier studies of general contract law, that a change in contract terms **can only be made with the consent of both parties** to the contract.

- Some terms are negotiated on a **collective** basis between employer and union(s).
- Some terms are negotiated **individually.**
- Some terms are implied by **statute.**

Varying terms without changing the contract

6.2 There may be circumstances in which an employer can vary the terms of an employment contract without actually needing to vary the contract itself. For example, there may be an **express term** in the contract which itself gives rights of variation, for example to allow a change in area of work.

6.3 Alternatively, an **implied term** may act to vary the contract.

(a) A sales representative may be required to take responsibility for such area as his employer considers necessary in order to meet changing market conditions.

(b) Terms may also be implied by custom, for example, where a steel erector is required at the request of his employer to change sites..

Changing the existing contract

6.4 Consent might be demonstrated by **oral agreement** to new terms, by the **signing** of a new statement of terms and conditions or by the employee showing acceptance by **working** under the new terms.

6.5 If an employer does not obtain willing agreement to a variation, he might give unilateral notice of the variation. The employee has a number of options.

- He may consent.
- He may stay in employment but make it clear that he does not accept the variation.
- He may resign and claim constructive dismissal.

Signing a new contract

6.6 The third broad option open to the employer is to give contractual notice to the employee and then offer a new contract on the new terms. This opens the employer to a potential claim for unfair dismissal.

7 VICARIOUS LIABILITY **Pilot Paper, 5/01**

7.1 Circumstances when vicarious liability arises

- There is the **relationship** of employer and employee
- The employee's tort is committed in the **course of his employment**

Exam focus point

You can see that negligence and employment law could overlap in a question. Indeed, the pilot paper contained a multiple choice question on the vicarious liability of employers.

Relationship of employer and employee

7.2 The existence of the employer/employee relationship is characterised by such features as a contract of service and the deduction by the employer of PAYE and national insurance from the employee's gross pay. However in certain cases it is not clear and, as described above, the courts have devised certain tests to establish whether the employer/employee relationship exists.

Torts committed in the course of employment

7.3 The employer is only liable for the employee's torts **committed in the course of employment**. Liability arises even in the following circumstances:

(a) If the employee **disobeys orders** as to how he shall do his work.

Limpus v London General Omnibus Co 1862
The facts: The driver of an omnibus intentionally drove across in front of another omnibus and caused it to overturn. The bus company resisted liability on the ground that it had forbidden its drivers to obstruct other buses.

Decision: The driver was nonetheless acting in the course of his employment, so the employers were liable.

Beard v London General Omnibus Co 1900
The facts: The same employer forbade bus conductors to drive buses. A bus conductor caused an accident while reversing a bus.

Decision: He was not doing the job for which he was employed and so the employers were not liable.

(b) If, while engaged on his duties, the employee does something for his own convenience:

Century Insurance v Northern Ireland Road Transport Board 1942
The facts: A driver of a petrol tanker lorry was discharging petrol at a garage. While waiting he lit a cigarette and threw away the lighted match. There was an explosion.

Decision: The employer was liable since the driver was, at the time of his negligent act, in the course of his employment.

Warren v Henleys 1948
The facts: A petrol pump attendant became involved in a quarrel with a customer and hit him.

Decision: The employer was not liable since the assault was not within the scope of the employment. It is not easy to distinguish this from the Century case above, but perhaps the main difference in the *Warren* case is that it was a violent personal act entirely unconnected with the employee's duty to sell petrol.

7.4 If the employer allows the employee private use of the employer's vehicle, the employer is not liable for any accident which may occur. There is the same result when a driver disobeys orders by giving a lift to a passenger who is then injured.

Twine v Bean's Express 1946
The facts: In this case there was a notice in the driver's part of the van that the firm's drivers were forbidden to give lifts. The passenger was killed in an accident.

Decision: The passenger was a trespasser and in offering a lift the driver was not acting in the course of his employment.

Rose v Plenty 1976
The facts: The driver of a milk float disobeyed orders by taking a thirteen year old boy round with him to help the driver in his deliveries. The boy was injured by the driver's negligence.

Decision: The driver was acting in the course of his employment (presumably because the boy was not a mere passenger but was assisting in delivering milk).

7.5 If the employee, acting in the course of his employment, defrauds a third party for his own advantage, the employer is still vicariously liable.

Lloyd v Grace Smith & Co 1912
The facts: L was interviewed by a managing clerk employed by a firm of solicitors and agreed on his advice to sell property with a view to reinvesting the money. She signed two documents by which the property was transferred to the clerk who misappropriated the proceeds.

Decision: The employers were liable. It was no defence that acting in the course of his employment the employee benefited himself and not them.

7.6 Where the employer is held to be vicariously liable, he may seek indemnity for the costs from his employee: *Lister v Romford Ice and Cold Storage Co 1957*.

Independent contractors

7.7 A person who has work done not by his employee but by an independent contractor, such as a freelance plumber used by a builder, is vicariously liable for torts of the contractor in the following **special circumstances**.

(a) If the operation creates a **hazard** for users of the highway.
(b) If the operation is exceptionally **risky**.

Honeywill & Stein v Larkin Bros 1934
The facts: Decorators who had redecorated the interior of a cinema brought in a photographer to take pictures of their work. The photographer's magnesium flare set fire to the cinema.

Decision: In commissioning an inherently risky operation through a contractor the decorators were liable for his negligence in causing the fire.

(c) If the duty is **personal**. For example, an employer has a common law duty to his employees to take reasonable care in providing safe plant and a safe working system. If he employs a contractor he remains liable for any negligence of the latter in his work.

(d) If there is **negligence in selecting** a contractor who is not competent to do the work entrusted to him.

(e) If the operation is one for which there is **strict liability**.

Chapter roundup

- It is important to distinguish between a **contract of service** (employment) and a **contract for services** (independent contractor). Each type of contract has different rules for taxation, health and safety provisions, protection of contract and vicarious liability in tort and contract.
- A contract of service is **distinguished** from a contract for services usually because the parties **express** the agreement to be one of service. This does not always mean that an employee will not be treated as an independent contractor by the court, however; much depends on the three tests.
  - Control test
  - Integration test
  - Economic reality test
- There are no particular legal rules relating to the commencement of employment - it is really **just like any other contract** in requiring offer and acceptance, consideration and intention to create legal relations.
- Many rights given to employees under the **Employment Rights Act 1996** are only available if an employee has a specified period of **continuous employment**.
- Most employers are required to give employees a **statement of prescribed particulars** relating to their employment within eight weeks of commencement unless the employee already has a written contract of employment covering these particulars.
- **Express terms** agreed between the parties override terms implied by common law.
- A number of terms are usually left to be **implied** by common law concerning co-operation, pay and sick pay, holidays and holiday pay, indemnity, provision of work, references, care and safety and faithful service. The recent Working Time Regulations are designed to bring UK law into line with EC directives.
- The **employer** has an implied **duty at common law** to take **reasonable care** of his employees; he must select proper staff, materials and provide a safe system of working.
- The **employee** has a duty to exercise **care and skill** in performance of his duties.
- **Statute** implies terms into employment contracts, which may not usually be overridden, regarding the effect of wage councils, maternity leave, time off and health and safety. It also implied a number of protective clauses into a contract which are the topic of Chapter 7.
- A person who suffers personal injury caused by accident arising out of and in the course of his employment is entitled to **industrial injury benefit** (ie injury benefit, disablement benefit or death benefit as may be appropriate) under the state social security scheme.

Quick quiz

1 What tests are applied by the courts to answer these questions?

- Has the employer control over the way in which the employee performs his duties? (1) ....
- Is the skilled employee part of the employer's organisation? (2) ....
- Is the employee working on his own account? (3)....................

2 Is working for a number of different people an automatic sign of self employment?

☐ Yes

☐ No

3 Give five reasons why the distinction between employed and self employed workers is important.

4 A 'principal statement' must include the following (tick all that apply)

(a) Names of parties ☐

(b) Job title ☐

(c) Date employment began ☐

(d) Notice details ☐

(e) Details of continuous employment ☐

(f) Pay details ☐

(g) Pensions and pension scheme details ☐

(h) Holiday entitlement ☐

5 An employee who only works eight hours per week is not entitled to receive an itemised pay slip

☐ True

☐ False

6 In no more than 10 words, explain an employee's fundamental duty.

7 Which of these options are open to an employer who wishes to vary the terms of an employment contract?

(i) Sign a wholly new contract
(ii) Vary the terms without changing the contract
(iii) Change the existing contract

A (iii) only
B (i) and (ii) only
C (ii) and (iii) only
D (i), (ii) and (iii)

8 Which of the following is not an implied duty of an employer?

A To pay a reasonable wage
B To provide a reasonable reference
C To ensure a safe working environment
D To reimburse expenses incurred in the course of employment

9 Which of the following factors do not constitute reasons that the distinction between contracts of and for services is important?

- The contribution rates payable under social security legislation differ for employees and the self employed.
- Employers are required to deduct income tax from the wages of independent contractors
- Employees must register for VAT.
- The employer is generally liable for the tortious acts of employees.

10 Delete where applicable

- The employer is vicariously liable for the employee's torts in the course of his employment/at any time
- Employers are liable/are not liable if the employees commit a tort while disobeying instructions during the course of their work.
- Employers are liable/not liable for torts committed in a company vehicle when the employee is undertaking private business.
- Employers are liable/not liable when an employee defrauds a client to his own advantage in the course of his employment.

Answers to quick quiz

1 (1) control test
(2) integration test
(3) multiple (economic reality) test

2 No

3 Social security
Taxation
Employment protection
Tortious acts
Health and safety

(also implied terms, VAT, rights in bankruptcy)

4 (a) (b) (c) (e) (f) (h)

5 False

6 Faithful service to his employer

7 D

8 B

9
- Employers are **not required** to deduct income tax from the wages of **independent contractors**
- **Employees** are not required to register for **VAT** (in their capacity as employees)

10
- The employer is vicariously liable for the employee's torts **in the course of his employment**
- Employers are **liable** if the employees commit a tort while disobeying instructions during the course of their work.
- Employers are **not liable** for torts committed in a company vehicle when the employee is undertaking private business.
- Employers are **liable** when an employee defrauds a client to his own advantage in the course of his employment.

The following relevant questions are included in the Exam Question Banks

You can attempt these now. However, we would advise you to attempt these as mock exams at the end of your initial stage of study

Exam Question Bank	Numbers
Paper based format	11, 12
Computer based assessment	32

Chapter 7

EMPLOYMENT PROTECTION

	Topic list	Syllabus reference	Ability required
1	Continuity of service	(v)	Comprehension
2	Discrimination at work	(v)	Comprehension
3	Health and safety	(v)	Comprehension
4	Dismissal	(v)	Comprehension
5	Wrongful dismissal	(v)	Comprehension
6	Unfair dismissal	(v)	Comprehension

Introduction

Chapter 6 provided an introduction to the contract of employment. In this chapter we consider the various protective clauses implied into a contract of employment. They fall into three areas:

- Discrimination
- Health and safety
- Dismissal

Some protection is given to employees regardless of how long they have been employed. However, for a number of the statutory provisions, the employee must have one year's continuous service. What constitutes continuous service is outlined in section 1.

Employees are given protection under the common law against being dismissed wrongly and under statute against being dismissed unfairly. What constitutes dismissal is outlined in section 4.

Statutory references in this chapter are to the Employment Rights Act 1996 unless otherwise noted.

Learning outcomes covered in this chapter

- **Explain** the distinction between unfair and wrongful dismissal
- **Demonstrate** an awareness of how employers and employees are affected by health and safety legislation, including the consequences of a failure to comply

Syllabus content covered in this chapter

- The express and implied terms of a contract of employment
- Unfair and wrongful dismissal
- An outline of the main rules relating to health and safety at work, sanctions on employers for non-compliance, and remedies for employees.

1 CONTINUITY OF SERVICE

1.1 Many of the rights given to employees under the Employment Rights Act 1996 in areas such as redundancy and unfair dismissal are only available if an employee has a specified period of **continuous employment**.

1.2 Employment is presumed to be continuous unless the contrary is proved. Continuity is preserved even where an employee's duties change within the period of service.

1.3 In calculating length of service (for all purposes including notice, redundancy pay and compensation for unfair dismissal) the following rules apply.

(a) A week is a week during which he is employed for at least eight hours or in which his employment is subject to a contract which involves employment for eight hours or more.

(b) Some periods of absence are included in reckoning continuity and length of service for example, when the employee is incapable of working owing to sickness or injury, or maternity leave.

(c) If the employee has worked in the same business before its transfer to his present employer his previous service may be counted.

Transfer of undertaking

1.4 When an 'undertaking' – a business in the UK or a part of it – is transferred, the **employees of the business are automatically transferred (on the same terms and with unbroken service) to the employment of the new owner.**

(a) **There must be a real change in the ownership of the business.** If the business is carried on by a company and ownership is changed just by selling the share capital, rather than the business assets as a whole, the regulations do not apply.

(b) **There must be continuity in the business before and after the transfer.**

1.5 An employee cannot be compelled to accept continued employment in the service of a new employer. But his **refusal would be a resignation** which disentitles him from recovering redundancy pay or compensation for unfair dismissal.

1.6 If he does go over to the service of the transferee of the business, the employee has continuity of service.

1.7 A dismissal in connection with a transfer is **automatically unfair.**

1.8 The **only exception** to dismissal being unfair is if the dismissal is for an economic, technical or organisational reason (an ETO reason). The meaning of 'economic, technical or organisational reason' which renders a dismissal a fair dismissal for which no compensation must be given is not clear-cut.

2 DISCRIMINATION AT WORK

KEY TERM

Discrimination is the practice of treating one or more members of a specified group in a manner that is unfair as compared to the treatment of other people who are not part of that group.

2.1 In recent years, legislation has been passed to prevent discrimination in the workplace. The three key areas in which legislation has been passed are:

- Sex (or marital status)
- Race
- Disability

Sex discrimination

2.2 The law implies a number of terms into an employee's contract; its working is supervised by the **Equal Opportunities Commission**.

Sex Discrimination Act 1975

2.3 This Act **prohibits discrimination on the grounds of gender** against any employee, male or female, in recruitment, promotion, training, benefits or dismissal. A Code of Practice was drawn up in April 1985 under the Act.

2.4 The two forms of discrimination can be distinguished. Direct discrimination occurs where an employer or prospective employer treats an employee or job applicant less favourably than another on grounds of sex.

2.5 The 1975 Act also prohibits **indirect** forms of discrimination such as **imposing a qualification** for promotion with which **fewer women** than men could comply.

> *Price v Civil Service Commission 1978*
> *The facts:* The Civil Service Commission imposed a maximum age limit of 28 for appointment to the civil service grade of Executive Officer. A woman argued that this was indirectly discriminating against women since women in their twenties are often prevented by care of children from taking up employment.
>
> *Decision:* The imposition of an age limit was indirect discrimination.

2.6 It is permissible however to discriminate if there is **sufficient reason**. In some jobs, it is accepted that male sex is a 'genuine occupational qualification' (GOQ).

- An advertisement for a job abroad in a country whose laws and customs might make it difficult for a woman to perform her duties would be acceptable.
- Decency may require a male attendant in a male lavatory or sports facilities.
- Some occupations such as ministers of religion and police and prison officers are exempt from the statutory rules.

2.7 The **Equal Opportunities Commission (EOC)** oversees the working of safeguards for equality of women with men. In addition to the points made above, employers should ensure that retirement ages for men and women are the same.

Race discrimination

2.8 Discrimination on the grounds of race is prohibited by the Race Relations Act 1976, which also set up the Commission for Racial Equality (CRE). The Act's provisions are similar to the Sex Discrimination Act 1975, although there are fewer grounds to justify discrimination.

- Authenticity in **entertainment, art or photography** is allowed - a black man to play Othello for instance.
- **Personal services** - recruiting a Bangladeshi housing officer in a Bangladeshi area for example.
- Maintaining **ethnic authenticity** in a **bar or restaurant**.

2.9 The CRE in 1983 published a **code of practice** which advises employers to make periodic analysis of the racial composition of their workforce and of the decisions taken on recruitment, training and promotion.

Disability discrimination

2.10 The **Disability Discrimination Act 1995** gives disabled people similar rights to those already enjoyed in relation to sex and race.

2.11 The **Disability Rights Commission Act 1999** has provided for the establishment of a **Disability Rights Commission**, which has the same powers as the Equal Opportunities Commission and the Commission for Racial Equality when determining whether unlawful discrimination has taken place.

KEY TERM

Disability is defined by the Disability Discrimination Act as 'a physical or mental impairment which has a substantial and long-term adverse effect on the ability to carry out normal day-to-day activities'.

Determining disability

2.12 For the purposes of disability discrimination, disability is a legal term, and the **tribunal** must determine whether a person has a disability. However, the tribunal must not reject medical advice: *Kapadia v London Brought of Lambeth 2000.*

Disability Discrimination Act 1995

2.13 Disability discrimination arises when an individual is treated less favourably for a reason related to disability. The employer does not have to know of the disability.

2.14 If the employer is aware of the disability, he has a statutory duty to make **reasonable adjustments.** Failure by the employer to make '**reasonable adjustments**' without justification is classed as discrimination.

Remedies for discrimination

2.15 A person who believes that they have been discriminated against should make an application to an employment tribunal within **three months** of the discrimination taking place.

2.16 If the employment tribunal decide that discrimination has taken place, they can make the following orders.

(a) Compensation.

(b) Recommendation that the employer take action to correct the situation or limit the damage done to the applicant.

(c) Appointment of an official from the Advisory, Conciliation and Arbitration Service (ACAS) to try and work out a settlement between the two parties.

2.17 The tribunal **cannot:**

- Force the employer to promote someone
- Insist the employer takes on a job applicant

3 HEALTH AND SAFETY

The Health and Safety at Work Act 1974

3.1 Aims of the 1974 Act

(a) To **integrate and extend the law on health and safety at all places of work**, that is, not only in factories

(b) To **reformulate** the previously confused, incomplete or overlapping rules of common law and statute on safety at work. This is done by making detailed regulations to be enforced by sanctions of criminal law. A person who infringes the rules, more particularly safety rules, may also have a civil liability to the injured party for breach of statutory duty

(c) To provide effective means of **shaping the policy and regulations** on health and safety at work and also effective machinery of enforcement

3.2 Under s 2 of the Act it is the **duty of every employer, as far as is practicable, to ensure the health, safety and welfare of all his employees**.

- Provide and maintain plant and systems of work which are safe and without risk
- Make arrangements to ensure safe use, handling, storage and transport of articles and substances
- Provide adequate information, instruction, training and supervision
- Maintain safe places of work and ensure there is adequate access in and out
- Provide a safe and healthy working environment

3.3 Although the 1974 Act is intended mainly to safeguard employees it also **imposes duties**, for instance on occupiers of premises, to avoid creating risks to persons who may be near their premises but outside them or who may visit them. There are also rules to control or prohibit pollution of the environment by industrial processes.

3.4 A manufacturer, designer, importer or supplier of any article or substance for use at work must take reasonable steps, say by testing, to ensure that it is safe and that adequate information for safety purposes is provided for its use.

3.5 Every **employee** is required to take reasonable care at work for the health and safety of himself and others and to co-operate with his employer in the latter's compliance with his statutory obligations.

Recent regulations

3.6 There is a range of Regulations and Codes of Practice in the UK, most of them fairly recent. They have been issued under the Health and Safety Act 1974 to implement a number of EC Directives on health and safety, and have gradually replaced existing statutes. Some of the more important regulations are as follows.

- The Health and Safety (First Aid) Regulations 1981
- The Noise at Work Regulations 1989
- The Manual Handling Operations Regulations 1992
- The Workplace (Health, Safety and Welfare) Regulations 1992
- The Provision and Use of Work Equipment Regulations 1992
- The Health and Safety (Display Screen Equipment) Regulations 1992
- The Personal Protective Equipment at Work Regulations 1992
- The Control of Substances Hazardous to Health Regulations 1994
- The Reporting of Injuries, Diseases and Dangerous Occurrences Regulations 1995
- The Management of Health and Safety at Work Regulations 1999

The Management of Health and Safety at Work Regulations 1999

3.7 These are central to the regulatory structure, and revoke the previous 1992 regulations. They cover the following issues.

- **Risk assessments** to be undertaken by employers
- **Health and safety** arrangements
- Health **surveillance**
- Health and safety **assistance**
- Procedures for **danger areas**
- Contacts with **external services**
- **Information** for employees
- **Co-operation** between employers sharing a workplace
- Working in '**host**' premises
- Taking account of **employee capabilities**
- **Employee duties**
- **Temporary workers, expectant mothers** and **young** people
- **Liability** and **exclusion** of civil liability
- Premises and activities **outside Great Britain**

Enforcement of health and safety conditions

3.8 The responsibility for making regulations rests with the government. A Health and Safety Commission, acting through the **Health and Safety Executive**, oversees the working of the system. It advises on measures to be taken, promotes research and publishes information. Its members include representatives of employers' organisations and trade unions.

KEY TERM

The **Health and Safety Commission** can be defined as follows.

'The statutory body of ten members appointed by the Secretary of State for Employment with overall responsibility for occupational health and safety. In discharging this function it may encourage research and training, disseminate information and make proposals to the Secretary of State regarding regulations and codes of practice. An annual report of its activities is published.'

3.9 The Health and Safety Executive (HSE) is the headquarters of the inspectorate. It has a director and two other members appointed by the Commission with the approval of the Department of Employment. Inspectors may, as part of routine enforcement of the safety code, issue formal notices. These may be improvement notices or prohibition notices.

Employment protection

3.10 Where there is a breach of health and safety rules, whether by employer or employee, this is usually regarded as serious by tribunals. In certain instances, employees have successfully claimed constructive dismissal.

(a) Where an employee needed safety goggles which could be worn over normal spectacles and the employer ignored repeated requests for such goggles: *British Aircraft Corporation v Austin 1978.*

(b) Where an employee was obliged to work in very cold conditions: *Graham Oxley Tool Steels Ltd v Firth 1980.*

3.11 The **Public Interest Disclosure Act 1998** protects workers from being dismissed or penalised for bringing health and safety dangers to light.

3.12 The right not to suffer a detriment means that the employee has a right not to be put under any disadvantage at work. The right not to be dismissed applies regardless of continuous employment.

Exam focus point

You should have an outline knowledge of the law in relation to health and safety at work and employers' responsibilities.

Employers' civil liability

3.13 Employees may bring claims under the tort of negligence against employers for:

- The employer's own acts
- Acts of employees which the employer is vicariously liable for

3.14 In such cases, the standard rules of negligence discussed in Chapter 3 apply.

3.15 The employee might be able to bring a case against an employer for breach of statutory duty, where the statute allows for such civil liability. For example, The Health and Safety at Work Regulations expressly exclude such civil liability.

4 DISMISSAL 11/01

Termination by notice

4.1 As regards termination by **notice,** the following rules apply.

(a) The period of notice given must **not be less than the statutory minimum,** whatever the contract may specify.

(b) It **may be given without specific reason** for so doing, unless the contract requires otherwise.

4.2 Termination of a contract by notice is modified by the statutory code, which imposes a minimum period of notice of termination to be given on either side.

Minimum period of notice

4.3 If an employer terminates the contract of employment by giving notice, the **minimum period of notice** to be given is determined by the employee's length of continuous service in the employer's service as follows: s 86.

- An employee who has been continuously employed for **one month or more** but less than two years is entitled to not less than **one week's** notice.
- An employee who has been continuously employed for **two years or more** but less than twelve years is entitled to **one week's notice for each year of continuous employment.**
- Any employee who has been employed for **twelve years** or more is entitled to not less than **twelve weeks'** notice.

Termination by dismissal

4.4 **Summary dismissal** and **constructive** dismissal are both examples of dismissal without proper notice.

KEY TERMS

In a case of **summary dismissal,** the employer dismisses the employee without notice. He may do this if the employee has committed a serious breach of contract.

In a case of **constructive dismissal,** the employer commits a breach of contract, thereby causing the employee to resign.

Summary dismissal

4.5 **Summary dismissal** occurs where the employer dismisses the employee without notice. He may do this if the employee has committed a serious breach of contract and, if so, the employer incurs no liability.

4.6 However, if he has **no sufficient justification** the employer is liable for **breach of contract** and the employee may claim a remedy for wrongful dismissal. Whether the employee's conduct justifies summary dismissal will vary according to the circumstances of the case.

Pepper v Webb 1969
The facts: A gardener was asked to put in some plants, but refused to do so, using vulgar language.

Decision: His summary dismissal was justified; he was in breach of contract for refusing to obey a lawful and reasonable order. He had a history of complaints against him for insolence.

Wilson v Racher 1974
The facts: A gardener swore at his employer using even choicer obscenities.

Decision: His action for wrongful dismissal succeeded, as the employer's own conduct had provoked the outburst. This was a solitary outburst following a history of diligence and competence.

Constructive dismissal

4.7 **Constructive dismissal** occurs where the employer, although willing to continue the employment, repudiates some essential term of the contract and the employee resigns. The employer is liable for breach of contract.

4.8 EXAMPLE

The employer unilaterally imposes a complete change in the employee's duties.

Establishing constructive dismissal

4.9 To establish constructive dismissal, an employee must show that:

- His employer has committed a serious breach of contract (a repudiatory breach).
- He left because of the breach.
- He has not 'waived' the breach, thereby affirming the contract.

4.10 Examples of breaches of contract which have led to claims of constructive dismissal include the following.

- A reduction in pay
- A complete change in the nature of the job
- A failure to follow the prescribed disciplinary procedure
- A failure to provide a suitable working environment

4.11 The breach must be a **serious** one.

5 WRONGFUL DISMISSAL 11/01

KEY TERM

Wrongful dismissal is a common law concept arising in specific circumstances and which gives the employee an action for breach of contract, for example where insufficient notice has been given.

5.1 Where the employer has **summarily dismissed** an employee without notice (as where the employer becomes insolvent), there may be a claim for **damages** at common law for **wrongful dismissal.**

Justification of dismissal

5.2 The following have been taken as justifiable circumstances.

(a) **Wilful disobedience** of a lawful order. However it **must amount to wilful and serious defiance of authority**. A single act of disobedience may not justify immediate dismissal.

Laws v London Chronicle 1957
The facts: The claimant was called to a meeting by the managing director together with her immediate superior D. The managing director criticised D sharply and D walked out calling on the claimant to leave with him. She did so although the managing director ordered her to stay. She was dismissed.

Decision: The dismissal was wrongful.

(b) **Misconduct,** in connection with the business or outside it if it is sufficiently grave. For example, acceptance of a secret commission, disclosure of confidential information, assault on a fellow employee or even financial embarrassment of an employee in a position of trust.

(c) **Dishonesty,** where the employee is in a position of particular trust.

(d) **Incompetence or neglect,** insofar as the employee lacks or fails to use skill which he professes to have.

(e) **Gross negligence**, depending on the nature of the job, for example, negligently landing a passenger aeroplane.

(f) **Immorality**, only if it is likely to affect performance of duties or the reputation of the business.

(g) **Drunkenness**, only if it occurs in aggravated circumstances such as when driving a vehicle or a train, or is repeated.

Remedies for wrongful dismissal

5.3 Generally, the **only effective remedy available to a wrongfully dismissed employee is a claim for damages based on the loss of earnings**. The measure of damages is usually the **sum that would have been earned if proper notice had been given.**

5.4 As with any other case of compensation, the wronged party is expected to **mitigate** his loss by, say, seeking other employment.

5.5 Where breach of contract leaves the employer as the injured party, he may dismiss the employee and withhold wages. The employer may recover confidential papers, or apply for an injunction to enforce a valid restrictive covenant: *Thomas Marshall (Exporters) v Guinle 1978.*

5.6 Employment tribunals have jurisdiction to deal with wrongful dismissal cases, which formerly had to be heard in the civil courts.

6 UNFAIR DISMISSAL 11/01

KEY TERM

Unfair dismissal is a statutory concept introduced by employment protection legislation. As a rule, every employee has the right not to be unfairly dismissed: s 54. Note that the distinction between wrongful and unfair dismissal depends not so much upon the nature of the dismissal, as on the **remedies available.**

6.1 **Unfair dismissal** is an extremely important element of employment protection legislation. The remedies available following a successful action for **wrongful dismissal** are **limited to damages** compensating for the sum which would have been earned **if proper notice had been given.**

6.2 Legislation seeks to **widen the scope of protection** and increase the range of remedies available to an employee who has been unfairly dismissed. Under the terms of the **Employment Relations Act 1999**, the top rate of compensation for proven unfair dismissal is £52,600.

Scope

6.3 Certain categories of employee are **excluded** from the statutory unfair dismissal code.

- Persons ordinarily employed **outside Great Britain**
- Employees dismissed while taking **unofficial strike** or other industrial action
- Other categories, including members of the police and armed forces

Subject to these exclusions, every employee who qualifies under (a) and (b) below has a statutory right not to be unfairly dismissed: s 94.

6.4 In order to obtain compensation or other remedies for unfair dismissal the employee must satisfy several criteria.

(a) Be **under the normal retiring age** applicable to his job or grade or under 65 if there is no normal age.

(b) Have been **continuously employed for one year** whether full-time or part-time.

(c) Have been **dismissed.** In the case of constructive dismissal, the tribunal may have to determine whether this is the case.

(d) Have been **unfairly** dismissed. Dismissal may be unfair even if it is not a breach of contract by the employer. This is up to the tribunal to determine.

6.5 In some cases, a person need not have been employed for the year to claim unfair dismissal. These exceptions are:

- Where the matter concerns a **safety representative** being penalised for carrying out legitimate health and safety activities

- Where an employee is being **denied a statutory** right (for example an unlawful deduction from wages)

- Where the employee is **pregnant**

6.6 The **effective date** of termination is reckoned as follows.

- Where there is termination by notice, the date on which the notice expires
- Where there is termination without notice, the date on which the termination takes effect
- Where an employee's fixed term contract is not renewed, the date on which that term expires

Making a claim

6.7 To claim **compensation** for unfair dismissal, there are three steps.

Step 1. The **employee** must apply to a tribunal **within three months** of being dismissed.

Step 2. The **employee** must show that

- He is a **qualifying employee,** and
- He has been **dismissed**

Step 3. Then the **employer** must demonstrate:

- What was the only or principal reason for dismissal
- That it was a fair reason **under the legislation (see below)**

What is dismissal?

6.8 Dismissal may be identified in three separate circumstances.

- **Actual dismissal** is usually fairly clear-cut and can be recognised from the words used by an employer.
- **Constructive dismissal**, as described earlier, involves a fundamental breach of the employment contract by the employer.
- **Expiry of a fixed-term contract** without renewal amounts to a dismissal.

6.9 The **employee must show** that **he has** in fact **been dismissed**. The courts often have to debate whether or not the use of four-letter words by employers constitutes mere abuse or indicates dismissal.

The reason for dismissal

6.10 Under Statute, there are **five potentially fair reasons** (justifications) for dismissal. The employer must state the principal reason for dismissal to the tribunal. If the reason is not one of the potentially fair reasons, the dismissal is unfair.

Potentially fair reasons for dismissal

6.11 To be able to justify dismissal as fair dismissal the employer must show that his reason related to one of the following.

(a) The **capability or qualifications** of the employee for performing work of the kind which he was employed to do

(b) The **conduct** of the employee

(c) **Redundancy**

(d) **Legal prohibition** or restriction by which the employee could not lawfully continue to work in the position which he held (for example, if a doctor or a solicitor employed as such is struck off the relevant professional register or an employee loses his driving licence which he needs to be able to do his job)

(e) **Some other substantial reason** which justifies dismissal

Capability/qualifications

6.12 The Employment Rights Act 1996 (s 98(3)) states that

> '**capability** is to be assessed by reference to skills, aptitude, health or any other physical or mental quality. '**Qualification**' means any academic or technical qualifications relevant to the position that the employee holds.'

6.13 The 1996 Act requires '**reasonableness**' on the part of the employer.

- **Consultation** with employee to determine areas of difficulty
- Allowing a **reasonable time** for improvement
- Providing **training** if necessary
- Considering **all alternatives** to dismissal

Misconduct

6.14 It is usual to apply the common law distinction between **gross misconduct** which justifies summary dismissal on the first occasion, for example, theft, and **ordinary misconduct** which is not usually sufficient grounds for dismissal unless it is persistent.

6.15 EXAMPLES

Assault on a fellow employee, conduct exposing others to danger (for example, smoking in an area prohibited for safety reasons), unpleasant behaviour towards customers and persistent absences from work have been treated as sufficient misconduct to justify dismissal.

Redundancy

6.16 If an employee is dismissed mainly or only on the ground of **redundancy**, he may claim remedies for unfair dismissal if he can show one of the following.

(a) There were one or more other employees in similar positions who might have been made redundant and that he was **selected for redundancy in breach of a customary arrangement or agreed procedure**.

(b) He was selected for a reason connected with **trade union membership**.

Other substantial reason

6.17 The category of **other substantial reason** permits the employer to rely on some factor which is unusual and likely to affect him adversely. An employer has justified dismissal on specific grounds.

- The employee was married to one of his competitors.
- The employee refused to accept a reorganisation, for example, a change of shift working, made in the interests of the business and with the agreement of a large majority of other employees.

Automatically fair reasons for dismissal

6.18 Some reasons for dismissal are automatically fair.

- **Striking** when all strikers are dismissed
- Being a **threat to national security** (to be certified by the government)

Strikes

6.19 An employee who strikes or refuses to work normally **repudiates the contract**. Where dismissal results from a lock-out or a strike, the tribunal cannot deal with it as a case of alleged unfair dismissal unless victimisation is established.

Automatically unfair reasons for dismissal

6.20 Some reasons are automatically unfair. (These are also known as '**inadmissible reasons**'.)

- Pregnancy
- A spent conviction under the Rehabilitation of Offenders Act 1974
- Trade union membership or activities
- Dismissal on transfer of an undertaking (unless there are 'economic, technical or organisational reasons' justifying the dismissal)
- Taking steps to avert danger to health and safety at work

Pregnancy

6.21 Dismissal on grounds of pregnancy or pregnancy-related illness is automatically unfair, regardless of length of service. It amounts to **gender discrimination** contrary to EC Directive 76/207: *Webb v Emo Air Cargo (UK) Ltd 1994.*

6.22 If a pregnant woman cannot do her job adequately the employer may suspend the employee while the 'hazard' continues. The employee may complain to a tribunal if not offered suitable alternative work.

Trade union membership

6.23 Automatically unfair dismissal

- **Membership** of an independent trade union
- **Taking part** at an appropriate time in the activities of such a trade union
- **Refusal** to be a member of a trade union: s 152 TULRCA 1992

Reasonableness of employer

6.24 If the principal reason for dismissal is one of the potentially fair reasons, the tribunal will still investigate. This is because the dismissal may still be unfair **if the employer acted unreasonably** in dismissing the employee.

6.25 The **employment tribunal** is required to review the circumstances and to decide whether it was reasonable to dismiss the employee for the reasons given.

6.26 Determining whether the employer has acted reasonably requires the tribunal to ask the following questions.

- Has the correct **procedure** been applied?

- Did the employer take all **circumstances** into consideration?
- What would any **reasonable employer** have done?

Remedies for unfair dismissal

6.27 An employee who alleges unfair dismissal must present his complaint to an **employment tribunal** within three months of the effective date of termination. The dispute is referred to a Conciliation Officer and only comes before the tribunal if his efforts to promote a settlement fail.

Reinstatement

6.28 If unfair dismissal is established, the tribunal first considers the possibility of making an order for reinstatement.

KEY TERM

Reinstatement is return to the same job without any break of continuity: s 114.

Re-engagement

6.29 The tribunal may alternatively order **re-engagement**. The new employment must be comparable with the old or otherwise suitable.

KEY TERM

Re-engagement means that the employee is given new employment with the employer (or his successor or associate) on terms specified in the order.

6.30 In deciding whether to exercise these powers, the tribunal must take into account whether the complainant wishes to be reinstated and, whether it is practicable and just for the employer to comply. **Such orders are in fact very infrequent**.

Compensation

6.31 If the tribunal does not order reinstatement or re-engagement the tribunal may award **compensation**, which may be made in three stages as follows.

(a) A **basic award** calculated as follows. Those aged 41 and over receive one and a half weeks' pay (up to a current maximum of £250 gross per week) for each year of service up to a maximum of 20 years. In other age groups the same provisions apply, except that the 22-40 age group receive one week's pay per year and the under 22 age group receive half a week's pay.

(b) A **compensatory award** (taking account of the basic award) for any additional loss of earnings, expenses and benefits on common law principles of damages for breach of contract: s 124. This is limited to £52, 600 by the Employment Relations Act 1999.

(c) If the employer does not comply with an order for reinstatement or re-engagement and does not show that it was impracticable to do so a **punitive additional award** is made of between 26 and 52 weeks' pay.

6.32 The tribunal may reduce the amount of the award in any of the following circumstances.

- If the employee **contributed** in some way to his own dismissal: s 123(6)
- If he has **unreasonably refused** an offer of reinstatement
- If it is **just and equitable** to reduce the basic award by reason of some matter which occurred before dismissal: s 123(1)

Question 1

The statutory definition of dismissal encompasses which of the following circumstances?

(i) Employee resigns without giving notice following employer's constructive dismissal
(ii) Employer terminates contract with notice
(iii) Employer fails to renew fixed term contract
(iv) Employer becomes insolvent and terminates contract forthwith on the appointment of a liquidator

A (i), (ii), (iii) and (iv)
B (i), (iii) and (iv) only
C (i) and (ii) only
D (iii) only

Answer

A

Question 2

What is the difference between wrongful dismissal and unfair dismissal?

Answer

- Wrongful dismissal is a common law concept arising in specific circumstances and which gives the employee an action for breach of contract, for example where insufficient notice has been given.
- Unfair dismissal is a statutory concept introduced by employment protection legislation. As a rule, every employee has the right not to be unfairly dismissed: s 54.Note that the distinction between wrongful and unfair dismissal depends not so much upon the nature of the dismissal, as on the remedies available.

Question 3

In the context of unfair dismissal, what is a compensatory award?

A An award as compensation calculated on the same scale as redundancy pay

B An award given on common law principles of damages for breach of contract so that loss may be compensated

C An award compensating the employee for loss caused by the employer's refusal to reinstate the employee following an order from the tribunal

D An award compensating the employee for loss and for distress caused by dismissal on the grounds of race and/or sex

Answer

B

Chapter roundup

- **Statute** implies terms into employment contracts, prohibit discrimination on grounds of sex, race or disability.
- Under s 2 of the **Health and Safety at Work Act 1974**, it is the duty of every employer, **as far as is practicable**, to ensure the health, safety and welfare of all his employees.

  In particular, he should

  - Provide and maintain plant and **systems of work** which are safe and without risk
  - Make arrangements to ensure health and safety in relation to the use, handling, storage and transport of **articles and substances**
  - Provide **adequate information**, instruction, training and supervision
  - Maintain **safe places** of work
  - Ensure there is **adequate access** in and out
  - Provide a **safe and healthy working environment**.
- Recent regulations, chiefly the Management of Health and Safety at Work Regulations 1999, attempt to harmonise health and safety requirements across the European Union.
- The responsibility for making health and safety regulations rests on the government (in most cases the Secretary of State for Employment). A **Health and Safety Commission** oversees the working of the system. Its members include representatives of employers' organisations and of trade unions.
- Where employment is **terminated by notice** the period given must **not be less** than the **statutory minimum**.
- If an employee is dismissed with **shorter notice** than the statutory or contractual requirements, or without notice when summary dismissal is unjustified, the employer can be sued by him for damages for **wrongful dismissal**.
- Certain employees have a right not to be **unfairly dismissed**. Breach of that right allows an employee to claim compensation from a tribunal. To claim for unfair dismissal, the employee must satisfy certain criteria.
- Dismissal must be **justified** if it related to the employee's capability or qualifications, the employee's conduct, redundancy, legal prohibition or restriction on the employee's continued employment or some other substantial reason. Some dismissals are **automatically** fair or unfair.
- Even where the reason for dismissal is justified or automatically fair, the tribunal must also decide whether the employer acted **reasonably** in the circumstances.
- Remedies for **unfair dismissal** include:
  - **Reinstatement**
  - **Re-engagement**
  - **Compensation**

Quick quiz

1 Rick has been employed for ten years by Chingtow Ltd and earns a basic salary of £24,000 pa. His company car and private health insurance are worth £3,000 pa and he has earned discretionary bonuses in the past 3 years of £3,000 pa. His contract states that he is entitled to 3 months' notice. Chingtow makes all its staff redundant on one month's notice. How much will the court award him as compensation for wrongful dismissal?

A £4,000
B £4,500
C £5,000
D £6,750

2 How much notice is an employee with 5 years' continuous service entitled to?

3 In no more than 15 words, explain whether summary dismissal is ever justified. If so, when?

4 The usual remedy for wrongful dismissal is

A Reinstatement
B Damages
C Redundancy pay
D Re-engagement

5 **Fill in the blanks** below, using the words in the box.

To claim (1) ……………….. for unfair dismissal, three issues have to be considered.

- The employee must show that he is a (2) ……………….. employee and that he has been (3) ………………..
- The (4) ……………….. must show what was the (5) ……………….. for dismissal
- Application has to be made to the (6) ……………….. within (7) ……………….. months of the dismissal

• qualifying	• dismissed	• employer
• reason	• three	• compensation
• employment tribunal		

6 Expiry of a fixed term contract without renewal amounts to a dismissal

☐ True

☐ False

7 Which of the following is *not* a question that a tribunal, when considering an employer's reasonableness in an unfair dismissal claim, will want to answer?

A What would a reasonable employer have done?
B Has the correct procedure been applied?
C Has any employee been dismissed in this way before?
D Did the employer take all circumstances into consideration?

8 Give an automatically fair reason for dismissal.

9 Which is the most frequent remedy awarded for unfair dismissal?

compensation
re-engagement
re-instalment

10 What does s 2 of the 1974 Health and Safety at Work Act provide?

11 The three steps in making a claim for compensation for unfair dismissal are given below. Fill in the blanks.

Step 1 The ……… must apply to a …………… within ………… ……………….. of being dismissed.

Step 2. The ……………………. must show that:

- He is a …………………. ……………….
- He has been ……………….

Step 3. The …………………. must demonstrate:

- What was the duty or ……………………. ………………… for ……………12
- That is was a ……………… …………… under ………………………..

12 Which of the following list of factors relating to dismissal are fair or potentially fair?

- Capabilities/qualifications of employee
- Pregnancy
- Striking
- Redundancy
- Legal prohibition
- Spent conviction
- Being a threat to national security
- Refusal of trade union membership
- Marriage to a competitor
- Dismissal on transfer of undertakings
- Refusal to accept a re-organisation

13 David is 31 and had worked for 12 years before he was unfairly dismissed. His weekly gross pay was £200. Delete as applicable.

His basic compensatory award will be: £1,200/£2,400/£3,600

His maximum compensatory award will be £50,000/£50,850/£51,200/£52,600

His maximum compensatory award includes the basic compensatory award.

True ☐

False ☐

14 The Health and Safety Commission, working though the Health and Safety Executive, oversees the working of the Health and Safety system in the UK.

True ☐

False ☐

15 Beth's employer has sent her on various computer courses to enable her to cope with the new computer system in operation. Beth, who hates computers, has not attended any of them. Beth's employer gave her a final warning last week according to company procedure, and dismissed her this morning after she did not attend another course.

Delete as applicable and complete the sentence using no more than 30 words.

Beth's dismissal is likely to be fair/unfair because…

Answers to quick quiz

1 B 2/12 × £27,000 (basic pay and benefits, excluding discretionary payments)

2 5 weeks (1 week for each year's continuous service)

3 Yes, in cases of serious breach of contract by the employee

4 B

5 (1) compensation (2) qualifying (3) dismissed (4) employer (5) reason (6) employment tribunal (7) three

6 True

7 C

8 Being a threat to national security (alternatively, striking when all strikers are dismissed)

9 Compensation

10 It is the duty of every employer, as far as is practicable, to ensure the health, safety and welfare of all his employees.

11 The three steps in making a claim for compensation for unfair dismissal are:

Step 1 The employee must apply to a tribunal within 3 months of being dismissed.

Step 2 The employee must show that:

- He is a qualifying employee
- He has been dismissed

Step 3 The employer must demonstrate:

- What was the duty or main reason for dismissal
- That it was a fair reason under legislation

12 Fair or potentially fair reasons for dismissal.

- Capabilities/qualification of employee
- Striking
- Redundancy
- Legal prohibition
- Being a threat to national security
- Marriage to a competitor
- Dismissal on transfer of undertakings
- Refusal to accept a re-organisation

13
- Basic compensatory award: £2,400
- Maximum compensatory award: £51,700
- True

14 True

15 Beth's dismissal is likely to be **fair**... Beth has been dismissed for repeated misconduct (disobeying her employer's reasonable instruction). The employer has acted reasonably, following company procedure. In the circumstances, dismissal seems fair.

The following relevant questions are included in the Exam Question Banks

You can attempt these now. However, we would advise you to attempt these as mock exams at the end of your initial stage of study

Exam Question Bank	Numbers
Paper based format	-
Computer based assessment	17, 21, 36

Part D
Company formation

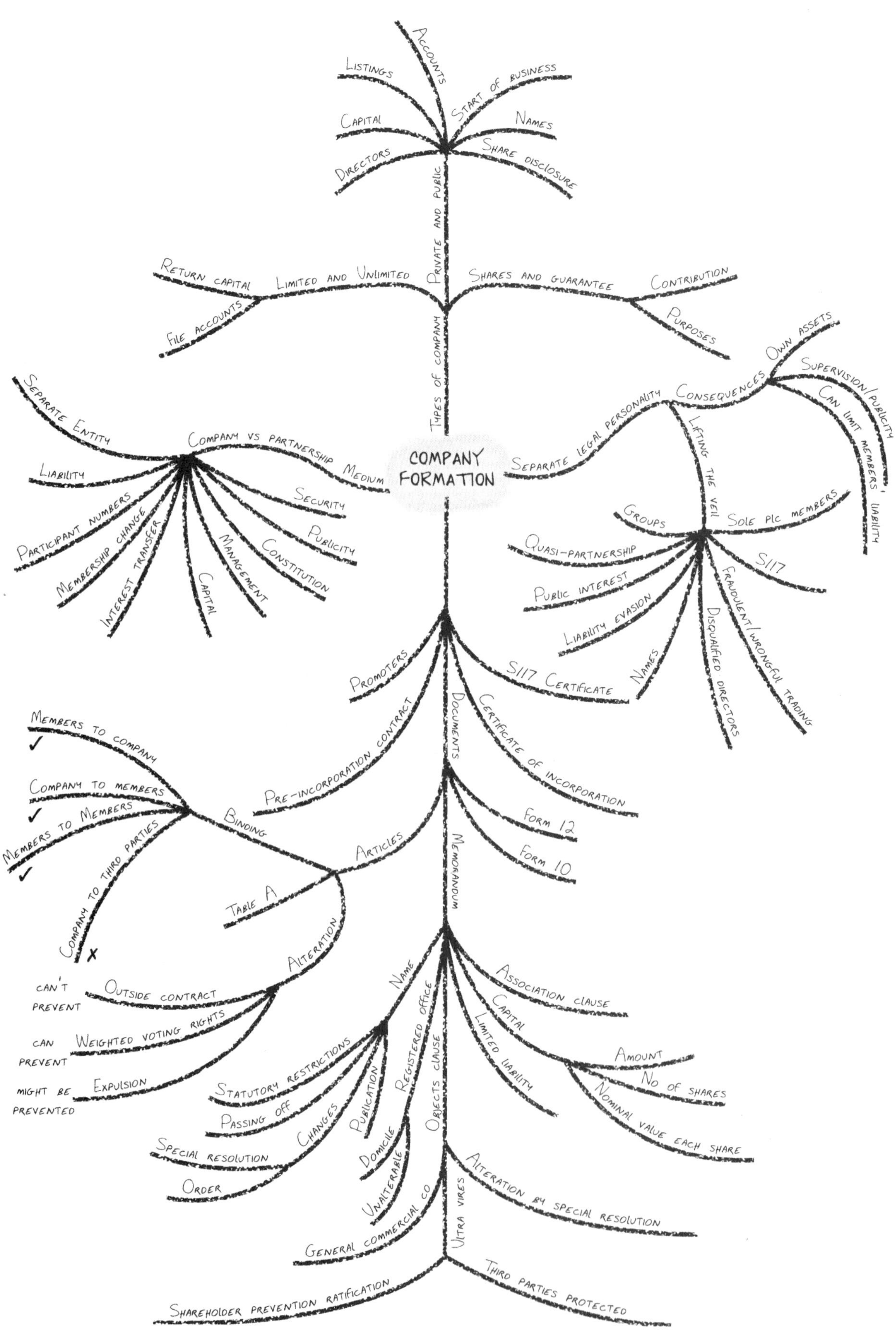

Company Formation
Types of company
Private and public
Accounts
Listings
Start of business
Capital
Names
Directors
Share disclosure
Limited and Unlimited
Return capital
File accounts
Shares and guarantee
Contribution
Purposes
Company vs partnership
Separate Entity
Liability
Participant numbers
Membership change
Interest transfer
Capital
Management
Constitution
Publicity
Security
Medium
Separate legal personality
Consequences
Own assets
Supervision/publicity
Can limit members' liability
Lifting the veil
Groups
Sole plc members
Quasi-partnership
Public interest
Liability evasion
Names
Disqualified directors
Fraudulent/wrongful trading
S117
Promoters
Pre-incorporation contract
S117 Certificate
Documents
Certificate of incorporation
Form 12
Form 10
Articles
Binding
Members to company
✓
Company to members
✓
Members to Members
✓
Company to third parties
✗
Table A
Alteration
Outside contract
can't prevent
Weighted voting rights
can prevent
Expulsion
might be prevented
Memorandum
Name
Statutory restrictions
Passing off
Changes
Special resolution
Order
Publication
Registered office
Domicile
Unalterable
Objects clause
General commercial co
Ultra vires
Alteration by special resolution
Shareholder prevention ratification
Third parties protected
Association clause
Capital
Amount
No of shares
Nominal value each share
Limited liability

Chapter 8

ORGANISATIONS AND CORPORATE PERSONALITY

Topic list		Syllabus reference	Ability required
1	Sole traders	(vi)	Comprehension
2	Partnerships	(vi)	Comprehension
3	Limited liability partnerships	(vi)	Comprehension
4	Legal personality	(vi)	Comprehension
5	Comparison of companies and partnerships	(vi)	Comprehension
6	Limited and unlimited companies	(vi)	Comprehension
7	Public and private companies	(vi)	Comprehension
8	Additional classifications	(vi)	Comprehension
9	The veil of incorporation	(vi)	Comprehension

Introduction

The concept of legal personality and in particular a company as a separate legal personality is fundamental to your understanding of company law.

Questions about the legal personalities of different types of organisation are particularly popular in law exams. You may be asked about the differences between **public** and **private** companies, **companies limited** by **shares** and **guarantee**, and **companies** and **partnerships**. Questions may also be asked about the **advantages** and **disadvantages** of **incorporation**.

The other main area this chapter covers is the concept and consequences of a company's **separate legal personality**, also when '**the veil of incorporation**' will be lifted and a company identified with its members or directors.

Learning outcomes covered in this chapter

- **Explain** the essential characteristics of the different forms of business organisations
- **Explain** the concept and practical effect of corporate personality
- **Explain** the differences between public and private companies
- **Explain** the main advantages of carrying on business through the medium of a company limited by shares

Syllabus content covered in this chapter

- The essential characteristics of sole traderships/practitionerships, partnerships and companies limited by shares
- Corporate personality and its legal consequences
- Lifting the corporate veil both at common law and by statute
- The distinction between public and private companies

1 SOLE TRADERS 5/02

KEY TERM

A **sole trader** is a person carrying on business with total legal responsibility for his/her actions, neither in partnership nor as a company. (CIMA, *Official Terminology*)

1.1 A sole trader owns and runs a business, contributes the capital to start the enterprise, runs it with or without employees, and earns the profits or stands the loss of the venture.

1.2 Sole traders are found mainly in the retail trades (local newsagencies), small scale service industries (plumbers), and small manufacturing and craft industries. An accountant may operate as a sole trader.

1.3 Whilst the business is a separate accounting entity the business is **not legally distinct** from the person who owns it. In law, the person and the business are viewed as the same entity.

1.4 The **advantages** of being a sole trader are as follows.

- **No formal procedures** are required to set up in business, except that for certain classes of business a licence must be obtained (eg retailing wines and spirits).
- **Independence** and **self-accountability**. A sole trader need consult nobody about business decisions and is not required to reveal the state of the business to anyone (other than the tax authorities each year).
- **Personal supervision** of the business by the sole trader should ensure its effective operation. Personal contact with customers may enhance commercial flexibility.
- **All** the **profits** of the business **accrue** to the sole trader. This can be a powerful motivator, and satisfying to the individual whose ability/energy results in reward.

1.5 The **disadvantages** of being a sole trader include the following.

- If the business gets into debt, a sole trader's personal wealth (for example, private house) might be lost if the debts are called in, as they are the same legal entity.
- Expansion of the business is usually only possible by **ploughing back** the **profits** of the business as further capital, although loans or overdraft finance may be available.
- The business has a **high dependence** on the **individual** which can mean long working hours and difficulties during sickness or holidays.
- The **death** of the proprietor may make it **necessary** to **sell** the **business** in order to pay the resulting tax liabilities, or, family members may not wish to continue the business anyway.
- The **individual** may **only have one skill**. A sole trader may be, say, a good technical engineer or craftsman but may lack the skills to market effectively or to maintain accounting records to control the business effectively.
- **Disadvantages** associated with small size, lack of diversification, absence of economies of scale, problems of raising finance etc.

2 PARTNERSHIPS Pilot Paper, 5/01, 11/01, 5/02

2.1 Partnership is the normal organisation in the professions as most professions prohibit their members from carrying on practice through limited companies.

2.2 A partner is **personally liable** for all the debts of the firm (incurred while he is a partner and sometimes even after he has ceased to be a partner).

Definition of partnership

KEY TERM

'**Partnership** is the relation which subsists between persons carrying on a business in common with a view of profit.'

2.3 A partnership exists whenever the facts satisfy the statutory definition above (s 1 Partnership Act 1890), which is as follows.

The relation which subsists between persons

2.4 'Person' includes a corporation such as a registered company as well as an individual living person.

2.5 There must be at least **two** partners. If, therefore, two men are in partnership, one dies and the survivor carries on the business, he is a sole trader. There is no longer a partnership.

2.6 The standard maximum number of partners permitted by law is 20: s 716 Companies Act 1985. The intention of this rule is that if more than 20 persons wish to carry on a commercial business, they should form a registered company for that purpose.

2.7 However, as professional practice cannot usually be carried on by a registered company, accountants, solicitors, chartered surveyors and many other **professions** are permitted to form partnerships with any number of partners.

Carrying on a business

2.8 Business is defined to include 'every trade, occupation or profession': s 45.

In common

2.9 Broadly this phrase means that the partners must be associated in the business as **joint proprietors**. The evidence that this is so is found in their taking a share of the profits.

A view of profit

2.10 If persons enter into a partnership with a view to making profits but they actually suffer losses, it is still a partnership. The test to be applied is one of **intention**.

Consequences of definition

2.11 In most cases there is no doubt about the existence of a partnership. The partners declare their intention by such steps as signing a written partnership agreement and adopting a firm name. These outward and visible signs of the existence of a partnership are not essential - a partnership can exist without them.

Liability of the partners

2.12 Every partner is liable **without limit** for the debts of the partnership. It is possible to register a limited partnership in which sole partners have limited liability, but the limited partners may not take part in the management of the business: Limited Partnerships Act 1907.

2.13 Under the Limited Liability Partnership Act 2000 it is possible to register a partnership with limited liability (an LLP). LLPs are discussed in Section 3.

Changes of membership

Death of a partner

2.14 The death of a partner may itself dissolve the partnership. This is usually avoided by expressly agreeing that so long as there are two or more surviving partners the partnership shall continue.

Retirement of a partner

2.15 The partner who retires is still **liable** for any **outstanding debts** incurred while he was a partner, unless the creditor has agreed to release him from liability. He is **also liable** for debts of the firm **incurred after his retirement** if the creditor knew him to be a partner (before retirement) and has not had notice of his retirement.

New partner

2.16 A new partner admitted to an existing firm is liable for **debts incurred** only **after** he becomes a partner. He is not liable for debts incurred before he was a partner unless he agrees to become liable.

Partnership property

2.17 The initial property of the partnership is that which the partners expressly or impliedly agreed shall be partnership property. Property used in the business need not be partnership property but may be the sole property of one of the partners.

A partner's authority as agent of the firm

2.18 The Partnership Act 1890 defines the apparent authority of a partner to make contracts as follows.

> 'Every partner is an agent of the firm and his other partners for the purpose of the business of the partnership; and the acts of every partner who does any act for carrying on in the **usual way business** of **the kind carried on** by the firm of which he is a member bind the firm and his partners, unless the partner so acting has in fact no authority to act for the firm in the particular matter, and the person with whom he is dealing either knows that he has no authority, or does not know or believe him to be a partner': s 5.

The Act also states that the partnership is only bound by acts done by a partner in the firm's name and not apparently for the partners personally: ss 6 and 7.

The partnership agreement

2.19 A written partnership agreement is *not* legally required. In practice there are advantages in setting down in writing the terms of their association.

(a) It **fills** in the **details** which the law would not imply - the nature of the firm's business, its name, and the bank at which the firm's will maintain its account.

(b) A written agreement serves to **override terms** otherwise implied by the Partnership Act 1890 which are inappropriate to the partnership. The Act for example implies (unless otherwise agreed) that partners share profits equally.

Terms implied by the Partnership Act 1890

2.20 Some of the more important areas covered by this Act are as follows.

Areas of the Partnership Act	Description
Freedom of variation	The partnership agreement may be varied with the consent of all the partners. This may be formal or informal: s.19.
Good faith	There is a duty of utmost good faith once the partnership is established.
Profits and losses	These are shared equally in the absence of contrary agreement. However, if the partnership agreement states that profits are to be shared in certain proportions then, losses are to be shared in the same proportions: s 24.
Interest on capital	None is paid on capital except by agreement. However, a partner is entitled to 5% interest on **advances** beyond his original capital: s 24.
Indemnity	The firm must indemnify any partner against liabilities incurred in the ordinary and proper conduct of the partnership business or in doing anything necessarily done for the preservation of the partnership property or business: s 24.
Management	Every partner is entitled to take part in managing the firm's business; ordinary management decisions can be made by a majority of partners: s 24.
Change in business	Any decision on changing the nature of the partnership's business must be unanimous: s 24.
Remuneration	No partner is entitled to remuneration such as salary for acting in the partnership business: s 24.
Records and accounts	These must be kept at the main place of business, and must be open to inspection by all partners: s 24.
New partners	New partners must only be introduced with the consent of all existing partners: s 24.
Expulsion	A partner may only be expelled by a majority of votes when the partnership agreement allows; even then, the power must only be used in good faith and for good reason: s 25.
Dissolution	The authority of the partners after dissolution continues so far as is necessary to wind up the partnership affairs and complete transactions already begun. On dissolution, any partner can insist on realisation of the firm's assets, payment of the firm's debts and distribution of the surplus.
Capital deficiency	The remaining partners share the capital deficiency (what a partner owes but cannot pay back) not as a loss but in ratio to the amounts of capital which they originally contributed to the firm. This is the rule in *Garner v Murray 1904*.

Dissolution

2.21 Dissolution of a partnership occurs in the following situations.

- **Passing of time,** if the partnership was entered into for a fixed term
- **Termination of the venture,** if entered into for a single venture
- The **death or bankruptcy** of a partner (partnership agreement may vary)
- **Subsequent illegality**
- **Notice** given by a partner if it is a partnership of indefinite duration
- **Order of the court** granted to a partner

Supervision

2.22 There is no formal statutory supervision of partnerships. Their accounts need not be in prescribed form nor is an audit necessary. The public has no means or legal right of inspection of the firm's accounts or other information such as companies must provide.

2.23 If, however, thc partners carry on business under a firm name which is not the surnames of them all, say, 'Smith, Jones & Co', they are required to disclose the **names** of the **partners** on their letterheads and at their places of business. They are required to make a **return** of their **profits** for income tax and **usually** to **register** for VAT.

Exam focus point

The key features of partnerships are often the subject of MCQs in law exams.

3 LIMITED LIABILITY PARTNERSHIPS

Definition of limited partnership

3.1 A recent development in partnership law has been the introduction of a new form of business vehicle, the limited liability partnership. These are permitted under the Limited Liability Act 2000 and have been in use since 6 April 2001.

KEY TERM

A **limited liability partnership (LLP)** formed under the 2000 Act is a corporate body which has separate legal personality from its members and therefore some of the advantages and disadvantages of a company.

Formation

3.2 A limited liability partnership may be formed by persons associating to carry on lawful business with a view to profit, but it **must be incorporated** to be recognised.

3.3 To be incorporated, the subscribers must send the correct document to the Registrar of Companies and must sign that document. The form must state the following:

- The **name** of the LLP
- The **location** of its **registered office** (England and Wales/Wales/Scotland)
- The **address** of the registered office
- The name and address of all the **members** of the LLP
- Which of the members are to be **designated members** (see below)

3.4 There is also a registration fee of £95.

Internal regulation

3.5 The members of the LLP are those who subscribe to the original incorporation document, and those admitted afterwards in accordance with the terms of the partnership agreement.

3.6 The rights and duties of the partners will usually be set out in a **partnership agreement.** In the absence of a partnership agreement, the rights and duties are set out in regulations under the Act.

3.7 LLPs must have designated members, who must take responsibility for the publicity requirements of the LLP, see below.

External relationships

3.8 Every member is an **agent** of the LLP. As such, where the member has authority, the LLP will be bound by the acts of the member.

3.9 The **LLP will not be bound by the acts of the member where:**

- He has **no authority** and the **third party is aware** of that fact
- He has **ceased to be a member**, and the **third party is aware** of that fact

Dissolution

3.10 An LLP **does not dissolve on a member leaving** it, in the same way that a traditional partnership does. Where a member has died or (for a corporate member) been wound up, that member ceases to be a member, but the LLP continues in existence.

3.11 An **LLP must therefore be wound up** when the time has come for it to be dissolved. This is achieved under provisions **similar to company winding up** provisions.

Supervision

3.12 As can be seen in the incorporation procedures, LLPs come under the supervision of the **Registrar of Companies.**

3.13 LLPs are required to have **designated members** who are responsible for signing relevant documents and returning them to the Registrar. Each LLP must have two designated members.

3.14 Designated members are required to:

- Sign notices sent to the Registrar
- Appoint auditors (if they are required)
- Sign the accounts
- Deliver the accounts to the Registrar

3.15 The Registrar will maintain a file containing the publicised documents of the LLP at Companies House.

4 LEGAL PERSONALITY

4.1 A legal person possesses legal rights and is subject to legal obligations. In law, the term person is used to denote two categories of legal person.

- An individual human being is a **natural person.**
- The law also recognises **artificial persons** in the form of corporations.

4.2 A corporation, such as a limited company, is distinguished from an unincorporated association. An **unincorporated association** (for example a partnership) is not a separate legal entity; it does not have a legal identity separate from that of its members.

Artificial persons

KEY TERM

Corporate personality is a common law principle which grants a company a legal entity, separate from the members who comprise it. It follows that property of a company belongs to that company, debts of the company must be satisfied from the assets of that company, and a company has perpetual succession until wound up.

4.3 A corporation is a **legal entity** separate from the natural persons connected with it, for example as members. Corporations are classified in one of the following categories.

Categories	Description
Corporations sole	A corporation sole is an **official position** which is filled by one person who is replaced from time to time. The Public Trustee and the Treasury Solicitor are corporations sole.
Chartered corporations	These are usually **charities** or bodies such as the Association of Chartered Certified Accountants.
Statutory corporations	Statutory corporations are formed by special Acts of Parliament. This method is little used now, as it is slow and expensive. It was used in the nineteenth century to form railway and canal companies.
Registered companies	Registration under the Companies Act 1985 is the normal method of incorporating a commercial concern. Any body of this type is properly called a company.

Incorporation **Pilot Paper, 5/01**

4.4 The most important consequence of registration is that a company becomes a **legal person distinct from its owners**. The owners of a company are its members, or shareholders.

4.5 The first case which clearly demonstrated the separate legal personality of the company is of great significance to any study of company law, and is therefore set out in some detail below.

Salomon v Salomon & Co Ltd 1897

The facts: The claimant had carried on business as a leather merchant and boot manufacturer for 30 years. He decided to form a limited company to purchase the business, he and six members of his family each subscribing for one share. The company then purchased the business for £38,782, the purchase price being payable to the claimant by way of the issue of 20,000 £1 shares, the issue of debentures for £10,000 (effectively making Salomon a secured creditor) and the payment of £8,782 in cash. The company did not prosper and was wound up a year later, at which point its liabilities exceeded its assets. The liquidator, representing unsecured trade creditors of the company, claimed that the company's business was in effect still the claimant's (he owned 20,001 of 20,007 shares) and that he should bear liability for its debts and that payment of the debenture debt to him should be postponed until the company's trade creditors were paid.

Decision: At first instance, and in the Court of Appeal, that the other shareholders were 'mere puppets' and that the company had been irregularly incorporated. Salomon should indemnify the company against its liabilities. The House of Lords however held that the business was owned by, and its debts were liabilities of, the company. The claimant was under no liability to the company or its creditors, his debentures were validly issued and the security created by them over the company's assets was effective.

4.6 The principle of separate legal personality has been confirmed by more recent cases.

Lee v Lee's Air Farming Ltd 1960
The facts: Mr Lee, who owned the majority of the shares of an aerial crop-spraying business, and was the sole working director of the company, was killed while piloting the aircraft.

Decision: Although he was the majority shareholder and sole working director of the company, he and the company were separate legal persons and therefore he could also be an employee with rights against it when killed in an accident in the course of his employment.

Liability

4.7 A key consequence of the fact that the company is distinct from its members is that its members therefore have **limited liability.**

Limited liability for members

> **KEY TERM**
>
> **Limited liability** is a protection offered to members of certain types of company. In the event of business failure, the members will only be asked to contribute identifiable amounts to the assets of the business.

Protection offered to members

4.8 The **company** itself is **liable without limit for its own debts.** If the company buys plastic from another company, for example, it owes the other company money.

4.9 Limited liability is a benefit to members for its members (shareholders). They own the business, so might be the people who the creditors logically asked to pay the debts of the company if the company is unable to pay them itself.

4.10 Limited liability prevents this by stipulating the creditors of the company cannot demand the company's debts from members of the company.

Business failure

4.11 As the company is liable for all its own debts, limited liability only becomes an issue in the event of a business failure when the company is unable to pay its own debts.

4.12 This will result in the winding up of the company which will enable the creditors to be paid from the proceeds of any assets remaining in the company. It is at winding up that limited liability becomes relevant.

Members asked to contribute identifiable amounts

4.13 Although the creditors of the company cannot ask the members of the company to pay the debts of the company, there are some amounts that members are required to pay, in the event of a winding up.

Type of company	Amount owed by member at winding up
Company limited by shares	Any outstanding amount from when they originally purchased their shares. If the member's shares are fully paid, they do not have to contribute anything in the event of a winding up.
Company limited by guarantee	The amount they guaranteed to pay in the event of a winding up

Liability for the company 11/01

4.14 As mentioned above, the company is liable without limit for its own debts.

4.15 A company, as a separate legal entity, may also have liabilities in tort and crime. Criminal liability of companies is a topical area following recent disasters such as the Paddington train disaster.

4.16 It is currently extremely difficult to prosecute a company on criminal charges, as it is necessary to show a '*mens rea*', or controlling mind. Unless a company is very small it is difficult to show that the mind controlling the company was connected with the criminal act.

4.17 However, the Law Commission have issued proposals which include a charge of killing by gross carelessness, which it would be easier to charge companies with. There is, at present, no such criminal offence in the United Kingdom.

Question 1

Which of the following statements about limited liability are correct?

A A main reason for converting a private company into a public company is to enable shareholders to gain the benefits of limited liability.

B By law, at least one director of a registered company must have unlimited personal liability for debts incurred by the company.

C If a limited company is unable to meet its liabilities there may be circumstances in which the directors can be declared personally bankrupt.

D In the event of incurring business debts, an unincorporated sole trader cannot benefit from limited liability.

Answer

C and D are correct. A private company can have the benefit of limited liability so A is incorrect. B is not true of companies; however in certain circumstances (fraudulent and wrongful trading) directors may be liable for a company's debts and hence face bankruptcy (C). An unincorporated sole trader cannot claim limited liability as he or she is not a separate legal entity, therefore D is correct.

5 COMPARISON OF COMPANIES AND PARTNERSHIPS

5.1 It is important to know what the key differences between companies and partnerships are.

5.2 The most important difference between a company and a partnership is that a company has a **separate legal personality** from its members, while a traditional partnership does not.

5.3 This basic quality of a company gives rise to a number of characteristics which mark it out from a partnership. These are outlined below. The other key differences relate to the **formality** of a company as opposed to a partnership and the **regulations** it has to adhere to.

Factor	Company	Partnership
Entity	Is a legal entity separate from its members.	Has no existence outside of its members.
Liability	Members' liability can be limited	Partner's liability is usually unlimited
Size	May have any number of members (at least 2 for a public company)	Some partnerships are limited to twenty members (professional partnerships excluded)
Succession	Perpetual succession – change in ownership does not affect existence	Partnership is dissolved when any of the partners leaves it
Owners' interests	Members own transferable shares	Partners cannot assign their interests in a partnership
Assets	Company owns the assets	Partners own assets jointly
Management	Company must have at least one director	All partners can participate in management
Constitution	Company must have a written constitution (memorandum)	A partnership may have a written partnership agreement
Accounts	A company must usually deliver accounts to the registrar	Partners do not have to send their accounts to a registrar
Security	A company may offer a floating charge over its assets	A partnership may not usually give a floating charge on assets
Withdrawal of capital	Strict rules concerning repayment of subscribed capital	More straightforward for a partner to withdraw capital

5.4 **Revise** this table above when you have studied the rest of the book and know more of the details concerning the distinctive factors of companies above.

6 LIMITED AND UNLIMITED COMPANIES 5/02

6.1 The meaning of limited liability has already been explained. It is the **member**, not the company, whose liability for the company's debts may be limited.

Liability limited by shares

> **KEY TERM**
>
> A **company limited by shares, joint stock company, limited liability company** is a company in which the liability of members for the company's debts is limited to the amount, if any, unpaid on the shares taken up by them. (CIMA, *Official Terminology*)

6.2 Liability is usually limited by shares.

Limitation by guarantee

> **KEY TERM**
>
> A **company limited by guarantee** is a company in which each member undertakes to contribute (to the limit of his guarantee), on a winding-up, towards the payment of the liabilities of the company. (CIMA, *Official Terminology*)

6.3 A creditor has no direct claim against a member under his guarantee, nor in this case can the company require a member to pay up under his guarantee until the company goes into liquidation.

6.4 Companies limited by guarantee are appropriate to **non-commercial activities,** such as a charity or a trade association which aim to keep income and expenditure in balance but also have the members' guarantee as a form of reserve capital if it becomes insolvent.

Unlimited liability companies

6.5 A company may also be formed with unlimited liability: its memorandum makes **no reference** to **members' liability**. If the company goes into insolvent liquidation the liquidator can then require members to contribute as much as may be required to enable the company to pay its debts in full. An unlimited company can only be a private company since a public company is by definition always limited: s 1.

6.6 An unlimited company has two main advantages.

(a) It need not **file** a copy of its **annual accounts** and reports. There are some exceptions, the most notable of which being if the unlimited company is a subsidiary of a limited company.

(b) An unlimited company **may without formality purchase its shares** from its own members.

6.7 The unlimited company certainly has its uses. It provides a corporate body (a separate legal entity) which can conveniently hold assets to which liabilities do not attach.

Re-registering a limited company as unlimited

6.8 A private company originally formed with limited liability may re-register as unlimited under the procedure of ss 49 – 50, which requires **application** in the prescribed form signed

by a director or by the secretary made to the **registrar**. The application sets out the necessary changes to the memorandum. It must be accompanied by the **written consent** of **every member** of the company.

6.9 A company can only change from limited liability to unlimited once; it cannot change back again.

Re-registering an unlimited company as limited

6.10 An unlimited company may re-register as limited under a similar procedure except that the decision is taken by passing a **special resolution** (75% majority). The members may still be liable in the event of liquidation within three years of re-registering.

6.11 In this case also only one change, from unlimited to limited liability, is permitted. The company may not reverse the change.

6.12 A company limited by shares **cannot** re-register as a company limited by guarantee or **vice versa**.

7 PUBLIC AND PRIVATE COMPANIES — Pilot Paper, 5/01, 11/01, 5/02

KEY TERMS

A **public company** is a company limited by share or by guarantee, with a share capital, whose memorandum states that it is public and that it has complied with the registration procedures for such a company.

A **private company** is a company which has not been registered as a public company under the Companies Act. The major practical distinction between a private and public company is that the former may not offer its securities to the public. (CIMA, *Official Terminology*)

7.1 Since 1980 a **public** company is a company registered as such under the Companies Acts with the Registrar of Companies. Any company not registered as public is a private company: s 1(3). A public company may never be unlimited.

Conditions for being a public company

7.2 The conditions are:

(a) The **name** of the company identifies it as a public company by ending with the words 'public limited company' or 'plc' or their Welsh equivalents

(b) The **memorandum of association** of the company states that 'the company is to be a public company' or words to that effect: s 1(3)(a).

(c) The **authorised capital** of the company is not less than the authorised minimum (s 11) which is currently £50,000: s 118. (Of this, ¼ of the nominal value must be paid up, ie £12,500, plus all of any premium on the nominal value.)

(d) It is a **limited company**.

(e) It must have a minimum of **two members**: s 1.

Private companies

7.3 A private company is the residual category and so need not satisfy any special conditions.

7.4 Private companies are generally small enterprises in which some if not all shareholders are also directors and **vice versa**. Ownership and management are often combined in the same individuals. In that situation, it is unnecessary to impose on the directors complicated restrictions to safeguard the interests of members and thus a number of rules that apply to public companies are reduced for private companies.

Differences between private and public companies

7.5 The more important differences between public and private companies imposed by law relate to the following factors.

Directors

7.6 (a) A **public** company must have at least **two directors:** a **private** company need only have **one director**: s 282.

(b) The rules on **loans to directors** are much **more stringent** in their application to **public companies** and their subsidiaries than to private companies: s 330.

(c) A **public company**, except by ordinary resolution with special notice, may **not appoint a director aged over 70**: s 293.

Capital

7.7 (a) There is a minimum amount of **£50,000 authorised share capital** for a **public** company, **no minimum** for a **private** company.

(b) A public company may **raise capital** by **offering** its **shares** or debentures to the public; a **private** company is **prohibited** from doing so.

Dealings in shares

7.8 Only a **public company** can obtain a **Stock Exchange** or other investment exchange **listing** for its shares.

Commencement of business

7.9 A **private** company can commence business **as soon** as it is **incorporated**. A **public** company if incorporated as such must first **obtain a s117 certificate from the registrar**.

Question 2

Alex, Barry and Carol have operated as a partnership for five years trading in domestic carpets. The business has been successful and they are now considering expanding the business operations by opening three new shops and an additional wholesale unit. The partners are aware that the expansion will require new business capital. They are considering the formation of a company rather than continuing as a partnership.

What types of company may be formed under the Companies Act 1985? Which type of company is suitable for this business?

Answer

The main categories of companies which may be formed under the Companies Act 1985 are a public company, limited by shares, and a private company, which may be limited by shares or by guarantee or be an unlimited company.

A private company limited by shares is the most suitable type for a small business venture of this kind. It offers the advantages of being a corporate entity separate from its members, giving them the protection of limited liability.

The main restriction on a private company is that it may not offer its shares or debentures to the public. But it is subject to fewer restrictions than a public company in respect of dividends and loans to directors. It may use capital to finance the purchase of its own shares and it may give financial assistance for the purchase of its shares. If the company ranks as a small or a medium-sized company for purposes of its annual accounts, the accounts delivered to the registrar need not contain all the material required in the accounts of a public company. The 'elective regime' of the Companies Act 1989 allows further elements of new flexibility to a private company in respect of the AGM, share allotment, auditors, accounts and required majorities for authorisation of meetings at short notice.

	Re-registering as a public company	**Re-registering as a private company**
Resolution	The **shareholders must agree** to the company going public • Convene a general meeting • Pass a **special resolution** (75% majority – Alters the memorandum and if necessary, the articles	The **shareholders must agree** to the company going private • Convene a general meeting • Pass a **special resolution** (75% majority - Alters the memorandum and if necessary, the articles
Application	The **company must** then **apply** to the registrar to go public	The **company must** then **apply** to the registrar to go private
Approval	The registrar must be convinced the **application is in order.** If he is, he issues a certificate of re-registration.	The registrar issues a certificate of re-registration.
Minority protection	**No application can be made** to the registrar to cancel the resolution to become public.	**Members who did not vote in favour** of the resolution **may apply** to the registrar to cancel the resolution. • Application must be made by either - Holders of 5% of issued share capital, or - Holders of 5% of any type of share capital, or - 50 members • Within 28 days of the resolution being passed • Company is notified of objection which is considered
Compulsory re-registration	If the **share capital** of a public company **falls below £50,000,** it must re-register as a private company.	There is **no such compulsion** for a private company.

Single member private companies

7.10 It is possible to form **private** companies which have only one member. The following regulations apply to them.

Single member private companies	
Minimum share capital	£1
Officers	Company must have at least 1 director and 1 secretary who must be different people.
Meetings	Quorum: 1 person
	Member should provide company with a written record of resolutions made.

Exam focus point

Specific rules that affect public and private companies are often examined in MCQs, whilst a longer question may require a general comparison of the two types, and also a discussion of their advantages and disadvantages.

Question 3

Which one of the following statements is incorrect?

A A public company limited by shares must have at least two directors.
B A public company limited by shares must have at least two shareholders.
C A private company limited by shares must have at least one director.
D A private company limited by shares must have at least two shareholders.

Answer

D. It is possible to form a private company with only one shareholder.

8 ADDITIONAL CLASSIFICATIONS

Holding and subsidiary companies

8.1 The Companies Act draws a distinction between an 'accounting' and a 'legal' definition of group companies. Under the Act, s 736 applies only to the latter 'legal' category. A company will be the **subsidiary company** of another company, its **holding company**, if:

(a) The latter **holds** the **majority of the voting rights** in the former.

(b) The **latter** is a **member** of the former and in addition has the right **by voting control** to remove or appoint a majority of its board of directors.

(c) The **latter** is a **member** of the former and **controls a majority** of the **voting rights**, pursuant to an agreement with other members or shareholders.

(d) It is a subsidiary of a company which is itself a subsidiary of that other company: s 736 (1).

In parts (a) and (b) of the definition the references to voting rights in a company are to the rights conferred on members, to vote at general meetings of the company on all, or substantially all, matters: s 736A(2).

8.2 A company (A Ltd) is a **wholly owned subsidiary** of another company (B Ltd) if it has no other members except B Ltd and its wholly owned subsidiaries, or persons acting on B Ltd's or its subsidiaries' behalf: s 736 (2).

8.3 The importance of the holding and subsidiary company relationship is recognised in company law in a number of rules.

(a) A holding company must generally prepare **group accounts** in which the financial situation of holding and subsidiary companies is consolidated as if they were one person: s 227.

(b) A subsidiary may **not ordinarily be a member** of its holding company or give financial assistance for the purchase of the shares of its holding company: s 23 and s 151(1).

(c) Since directors of a holding company can **control** its **subsidiary** some rules designed to regulate the dealings of a public company with its directors also apply to its subsidiaries even if they are private companies, particularly loans to directors: s 330.

Quoted companies

8.4 Public companies may seek a listing on a public exchange. This option is not open to private companies, who are not allowed to offer their shares for sale to the public. Listed companies are sometimes referred to as quoted companies (because their shares are quoted publicly).

8.5 To obtain the advantages of listing the company must agree to elaborate conditions contained in a **listing agreement** with The International Stock Exchange. Not all public companies however are listed; the shares of a public company must have a market value of at least £1,000,000 before a listing can be obtained.

Small companies

8.6 Small companies benefit from reduced legal requirements in terms of filing accounts with the registrar and obtaining an audit. The definitions of a small company for the purposes of accounting and auditing are different.

8.7 In accounting terms, a company is small if it meets two of the following criteria:

(a) Balance sheet total of £2.8 million
(b) Turnover of £1.4 million
(c) Less than 250 employees

8.8 For the purposes of audit, a company is small if it has a turnover of less than £1 million. In the future it is anticipated that this turnover limit will rise to £4.8 million.

9 THE VEIL OF INCORPORATION — Pilot Paper

9.1 To recap, the reason that members have limited liability and do not have to pay the debts of the company is that through incorporation, the company establishes a separate legal personality from the people who own it (the members/shareholders).

9.2 This means that people can look at a company and not know who or what owns it.

9.3 The fact that members are 'hidden' in this way is referred to as the '**veil of incorporation**'. Literally, the members are 'veiled' from view.

Lifting the veil

9.4 It is sometimes necessary by law to look at who the owners of a company are. This is referred to as lifting the veil. It can be done to:

- **Identify** the **company** with its **members** and directors.
- Treat a **group of companies** as a **single commercial entity** (if a company is owned by another company).

9.5 The more important of these two reasons is the first one, although the second reason can sometimes be more complex. The main instances for lifting the veil are given below.

Lifting the veil by statute to enforce the law

Liability of a sole member for a company's debts

9.6 Every public company must have a minimum membership of at least two members: s 1. If therefore a public company has two members and one dies or transfers his shares to the other, the one surviving member is made liable (with the company) for its debts if:

(a) The company **carries on business** after **six months** from the time when the membership is reduced to one, and

(b) The **surviving member knows** that it is carrying on business with himself as sole member.

9.7 The member's liability is not retrospective and extends only to debts of the company incurred **after** the **six months** have expired: s 24.

Liability for trading without trading certificate

9.8 A public company must, under s 117, obtain a certificate from the Registrar before it may commence to trade. Failure to do so leads to **personal liability** for the directors for any loss or damage suffered by a third party to a transaction entered into by the company in contravention of s 117.

Fraudulent and wrongful trading

9.9 If, when a company is wound up, it appears that its business has been carried on with **intent** to **defraud creditors** or others, the court may decide that the persons (usually the directors) who were knowingly parties to the fraud shall be **personally responsible** for debts and other liabilities of the company: s 213 Insolvency Act 1986. Fraudulent and wrongful trading are discussed later in this text.

Disqualified directors

9.10 Directors who participate in the management of a company in contravention of an order under the Company Directors Disqualification Act 1986 will be **jointly** or **severally liable** along with the company for the company's debts.

Abuse of company names

9.11 There have been a large number of instances where directors of a company which went into insolvent liquidation formed another company with an identical or similar name, which bought the original company's business and assets from its liquidator.

9.12 S 216 Insolvency Act 1986 now prevents a director or shadow director of a company that goes into insolvent liquidation being involved for the next five years with the directing, managing or promoting of a business which has an **identical name** to the original company, or a **name similar** enough to suggest a connection.

9.13 Breach of these rules is an offence of strict liability and proof of intent is not required: *R v Cole & Others 1997*. The directors concerned will be **jointly** or **severally liable** along with the company for its debts if they contravene this section.

Liability for use of company name in incorrect form

9.14 A company is identified by its name which distinguishes it from other companies. Every company is required to exhibit its name in its correct form outside every place of business, on its seal (if it has one) and on its business letters and other documents such as bills of exchange.

9.15 If the rule is broken an **officer** of the company responsible for the default may be fined. As regards business documents, he is **personally liable** to the creditor if the company fails to pay the debt: s 349.

> *Penrose v Martyr 1858*
> *The facts:* A company secretary accepted a bill of exchange drawn on the company on which its name was incorrectly written by omitting the word 'limited' from the name. The company defaulted.
>
> *Decision:* The secretary was personally liable on the bill.

9.16 Until recently, when a company's name was given wrongly on a cheque or other financial instrument, this was a mistake and it was unfortunate for the officer responsible that the creditor could proceed against him personally. This applied even to trifling errors in the company's name: *Hendon v Adelman 1973*.

9.17 However, more recently the High Court gave an interpretation of s 349 which is more generous to company directors and other officers.

> *Jenice Ltd and Others v Dan 1993*
> *The facts:* Mr Dan was a director of a company called Primekeen Ltd. The bank incorrectly printed the company's cheques in the name of 'Primkeen Ltd'. Mr Dan signed several of these. They were dishonoured and returned by the various claimants including Jenice. Primekeen Ltd then went into creditors' voluntary winding up and the various claimants sued Mr Dan as personally liable on the cheques because of s 349(4).
>
> *Decision:* Mr Dan was not liable. The purpose of s 349(4) was to ensure that outsiders knew they were dealing with a company and that the liability of its members was limited. There was no doubt that in this case outsiders would have known that they were dealing with a limited company, so no mischief had been done.

Exam focus point

It is very important to know the statutory ways of lifting the veil as their omission can be a serious weakness in many answers.

Evasion of obligations

9.18 A company may be identified with those who control it, for instance to determine its residence for tax purposes. The courts may also ignore the distinction between a company and its members and managers if the latter use that distinction to **evade** their **legal obligations**.

Gilford Motor Co Ltd v Horne 1933
The facts: The defendant had been employed by the claimant company under a contract which forbade him to solicit its customers after leaving its service. After the termination of his employment he formed a company of which his wife and an employee were the sole directors and shareholders. However he managed the company and through it evaded the covenant by which he himself was prevented from soliciting customers of his former employer.

Decision: An injunction requiring observance of the covenant would be made both against the defendant and the company which he had formed as 'a mere cloak or sham'.

Public interest

9.19 In time of war it is not permitted to trade with 'enemy aliens'. The courts may draw aside the veil if, despite a company being registered in the UK, it is suspected that it is controlled by aliens: *Daimler Co Ltd v Continental Tyre and Rubber Co Ltd 1916*. The question of nationality may also arise in peacetime.

Evasion of liabilities

9.20 The veil of incorporation may also be lifted where directors themselves ignore the separate legal personality of two companies and transfer assets from one to the other in disregard of their duties in order to avoid a contingent liability: *Creasey v Breachwood Motors Ltd 1992.*

Re H and Others 1996
The facts: The court was asked to rule that various companies within a group, together with the minority shareholders, should be treated as one entity in order to restrain assets prior to trial.

Decision: The order was granted. The court thought there was evidence that the companies had been used for the fraudulent evasion of excise duty.

Evasion of taxation

9.21 The court may lift the veil of incorporation where it is being used to conceal the nationality of the company.

Unit Construction Co Ltd v Bullock 1960
The facts: Three companies, wholly owned by a UK company, were registered in Kenya. Although the companies' constitutions required board meetings to be held in Kenya, all three were in fact managed entirely by the holding company.

Decision: The companies were resident in the UK and liable to UK tax. The Kenyan connection was a sham, the question being not where they ought to have been managed, but where they were managed.

Quasi-partnership

9.22 An application to wind up a company on the 'just and equitable' ground under s 122(1)(g) Insolvency Act 1986 may involve the court piercing the veil to reveal the company as a **quasi-partnership.** This may happen where the company only has a few members, all of whom are actively involved in its affairs. The individuals who have operated contentedly as a company for years fall out, and one or more of them seeks to remove the others.

9.23 The courts are willing in such cases to treat the central relationship between the directors as being that of partners, and rule that it would be unfair therefore to allow the company to continue with only some of its original members. This was illustrated by the case of *Ebrahimi v Westbourne Galleries Ltd 1973* which is discussed further in Chapter 13

Group situations

9.24 The principle of the veil of incorporation extends to the holding company/subsidiary relationship. Although holding companies and subsidiaries are part of a group under company law, they retain their **separate legal personalities**.

9.25 In, *Adams v Cape Industries 1990,* three reasons were put forward for identifying the companies as one, and lifting the veil of incorporation. They are:

- The subsidiary is acting as **agent** for the holding company.
- The group is to be treated as a **single economic entity.**
- The **corporate structure** is being used as a **facade** (or sham) to conceal the truth.

Adams v Cape Industries plc 1990
The facts: Cape, an English company, headed a group which included many wholly-owned subsidiaries. Some of these mined asbestos in South Africa, and others marketed the asbestos in various countries including the USA. Several hundred claimants had been awarded damages by a Texas court for personal injuries suffered as a result of exposure to asbestos dust. The defendants in Texas included one of Cape's subsidiaries NAAC. The courts also considered the position of AMC, another subsidiary, and CPC, a company linked to Cape Industries.

Decision: The judgement would not be enforced against the English holding company, Cape, either on the basis that Cape had been 'present' in the US through its local subsidiaries (an argument which would have involved lifting the veil) or because it had carried on business in the US through the agency of NAAC. Slade LJ commented in giving the judgement that English law 'for better or worse recognises the creation of subsidiary companies ... which would fall to be treated as separate legal entities, with all the rights and liabilities which would normally be attached to separate legal entities'. Whether desirable or not, English law allowed a group structure to be used so that legal liability fell on an individual member of a group rather than the group as a whole.

Lifting the veil and limited liability

9.26 The above examples of lifting the veil include examples of where, if they have broken the law, **directors** can be made **personally liable** for a company's debts.

9.27 If those directors are also members, limited liability **does not apply** in these instances. This is the only time that limited liability is overridden and that the **member** becomes **personally liable** for the company's debts **due to his actions as a director.**

Chapter roundup

- In this chapter we have looked at a number of different types of organisation, but in particular limited companies.
- The word 'person' is used to denote both individual human beings (natural persons) and other bodies. The law attaches rights to a person and imposes legal obligations on him. Legal persons include **natural persons** and **artificial legal persons** (for example corporate bodies and local authorities).
- Because it is a separate legal entity a company has the following features.
    - **Limited liability** of its **members,** not of the company itself (except for unlimited companies)
    - **Transferable shares** in its ownership
    - **Perpetual succession**
    - **Ownership** of a company's assets, rights and liabilities is vested in the company, not its members
    - **Capital** is provided by members whose liability for the company's debts is then limited to that amount
    - **Detailed supervision**
    - **Management** by directors
    - A written **constitution**
- Companies may be distinguished as to whether they are **public** or **private** companies or as to whether they have **limited** or **unlimited** liability of members.
- **Partnership** is defined as 'the relation which subsists between persons carrying on a business in common with a view of profit'. A partnership is *not* a separate legal person distinct from its members, it is merely a 'relation' between persons. Each partner (there must be at least two) is **personally liable** for all the debts of the firm.
- Each partner is an **agent** of the firm when he acts in carrying on in the usual way business of the kind carried on by the firm, although his authority may be restricted by the other partners.
- A '**veil of incorporation**' is drawn between the company and the members, but it may be '**lifted**' in certain situations so as either to identify the company with its members or directors, or to treat a group of companies as a single commercial entity. The veil may be lifted:
    - Where the membership has fallen below the minimum number
    - Where directors have traded with intent to defraud creditors
    - For tax purposes if the company is a 'close company'
    - Where the rules governing the company seal or documents are broken
    - To determine the company's residence for tax purposes
    - To determine the company's nationality
    - If, within a group of companies, one is acting as agent or trustee of another, or they are both carrying on a 'single business'

Quick quiz

1 Which of the following types of company can be incorporated under the Companies Act 1985?

A A private limited company
B A public limited company
C A company limited by guarantee with a share capital
D A company limited by guarantee with no share capital
E A private unlimited company
F A public unlimited company

2 Which one of the following statements is incorrect?

A In England a partnership has no existence distinct from the partners.
B A partnership must have a written partnership agreement.
C A partnership is subject to the Partnership Act.
D Each partner is an agent of the firm.

3 A private company needs to obtain a s 117 certificate if it re-registers as a public company.

☐ True

☐ False

4 Which of the following statements is true? A private company

A Is defined as any company that is not a public company

B Sells its shares on the junior stock market known as the Alternative Investment Market and on the Stock Exchange

C Must have at least one director with unlimited liability

D Is a significant form of business organisation in areas of the economy that do not require large amounts of capital

5 What are the main effects of lifting the veil of incorporation?

6 The minimum allotted and paid up share capital of a public limited company is

£12,500	£50,000
£100,000	£500,000

7 What is meant by perpetual succession?

8 Which of the following are correct? A public company or plc

A Is defined as any company which is not a private company
B Has a legal personality that is separate from its members or owners
C Must have at least one director with unlimited liability
D Can own property and make contracts in its own name

9 Give two advantages of forming an unlimited company.

(a) ....
(b) ....

10 What was the name of the case that demonstrated the principle of separate legal personality?

11 Complete the blank squares in the table below

Factor	Company	Partnership
	Is a legal entity separate from its members.	Has no existence outside of its members.
Liability		Partner's liability is usually unlimited
Size		Some partnerships are limited to twenty members (professional partnerships excluded)
Succession	Perpetual succession – change in ownership does not affect existence	

BPP PUBLISHING

Factor	Company	Partnership
Owners' interests		Partners cannot assign their interests in a partnership
	Company owns the assets	Partners own assets jointly
Management		All partners can participate in management
Constitution	Company must have a written constitution (memorandum)	
Accounts	A company must usually deliver accounts to the registrar	Partners do not have to send their accounts to a registrar
Security	A company may offer a floating charge over its assets	
Withdrawal of capital		More straightforward for a partner to withdraw capital

12 Complete the table

Type of company	Amount owed by member at winding up
Company limited by shares	
	The amount they guaranteed to pay in the event of a winding up

13 Put the examples given below in the correct category box.

WHEN THE VEIL OF INCORPORATION IS LIFTED		
To enforce law	To enforce obligations	To expose groups

- Liability of sole member for a company's debts
- Liability for use of company name in the wrong form
- Legal obligations
- Quasi partnership
- Disqualified directors
- Fraudulent and wrongful trading
- Need to treat as single economic entity
- Corporate structure a sham
- Public interest

Answers to quick quiz

1 A,B,D and E are correct. It is not possible to incorporate a company limited by guarantee with a share capital, so C is incorrect. A public limited company is by definition limited, so F is wrong.

2 B. A written agreement is not needed.

3 False. Only public companies that are registered as public companies need obtain this certificate.

4 A and D are correct. A private company cannot sell its shares to the public on any stock market, so B is incorrect. No directors need have unlimited liability, so C is incorrect.

5 The main effects are to identify the company with its members or directors and to treat a group of companies as a single commercial entity.

6 £12,500. The authority is s 101.

7 Perpetual succession means that a change of membership is not a change in the company itself.

8 B and D are correct. A public company has to be defined as such in its memorandum so A is incorrect. No directors *need* have unlimited liability, so C is incorrect.

9 An unlimited company

(a) Need not file annual accounts, and
(b) Can purchase its own shares without formality.

10 *Salomon v Salomon Ltd 1897.*

11

Factor	Company	Partnership
Entity	Is a legal entity separate from its members.	Has no existence outside of its members.
Liability	Members' liability can be limited	Partner's liability is usually unlimited
Size	May have any number of members (at least 2 for a public company)	Some partnerships are limited to twenty members (professional partnerships excluded)
Succession	Perpetual succession – change in ownership does not affect existence	Partnership is dissolved when any of the partners leaves it
Owners' interests	Members own transferable shares	Partners cannot assign their interests in a partnership
Assets	Company owns the assets	Partners own assets jointly
Management	Company must have at least one director	All partners can participate in management
Constitution	Company must have a written constitution (memorandum)	A partnership may have a written partnership agreement
Accounts	A company must usually deliver accounts to the registrar	Partners do not have to send their accounts to a registrar
Security	A company may offer a floating charge over its assets	A partnership may not usually give a floating charge on assets
Withdrawal of capital	Strict rules concerning repayment of subscribed capital	More straightforward for a partner to withdraw capital

12

Type of company	Amount owed by member at winding up
Company limited by shares	Any outstanding amount from when they originally purchased their shares. If the member's shares are fully paid, they do not have to contribute anything in the event of a winding up.
Company limited by guarantee	The amount they guaranteed to pay in the event of a winding up

13

WHEN THE VEIL OF INCORPORATION IS LIFTED		
To enforce law	**To enforce obligations**	**To expose groups**
Liability of a sole member for debts	Legal obligation	Single economic entity
Wrong use of company name	Quasi partnership	Corporate structure a sham
Disqualified directors	Public interest	
Fraudulent / Wrongful } trading		

The following relevant questions are included in the Exam Question Banks

You can attempt these now. However, we would advise you to attempt these as mock exams at the end of your initial stage of study

Exam Question Bank	Numbers
Paper based format	13, 14, 26
Computer based assessment	25, 28

Chapter 9

FORMATION AND CONSTITUTION

	Topic list	Syllabus reference	Ability required
1	Promoters and pre-incorporation contracts	(vi)	Comprehension
2	Registration and commencement of business	(vi)	Comprehension
3	Memorandum of association	(vi)	Comprehension
4	Company name	(vi)	Comprehension
5	Company objects and capacity	(vi)	Comprehension
6	Articles of association	(vi)	Comprehension
7	Memorandum and articles as contracts	(vi)	Comprehension
8	Shareholder agreements	(vi)	Comprehension
9	Publicity	(vi)	Comprehension

Introduction

In Chapter 8 of this Study Text you were introduced to the idea of the separate legal personality of a company.

Sections 1 and 2 of this chapter concentrate on the **procedural aspects** of **company formation**. Important topics in these sections include the formalities that a company must observe in order to be formed, and the liability of promoters for pre-incorporation contracts.

Sections 3 to 7 of this chapter consider the constitution of a company, that is, the memorandum and articles of association. The memorandum governs the external relationships of a company, and the articles govern internal relationships. Of particular importance in the memorandum is the **objects clause**, which determines the legal capacity of the company.

Section 8 of this chapter looks at the contracts which members of a company may make to supplement the articles of association. Such shareholder agreements can determine the way that the business will operate.

Lastly in this chapter, the publicity requirements of a company are considered. These will be referred to later in the text also, in relation to specific issues as they are covered.

Learning outcomes covered in this chapter

- **Explain** the distinction between establishing a company by registration and purchasing 'off the shelf'
- **Explain** the purpose and legal status of the memorandum of association
- **Explain** the ability of a company to contract
- **Explain** the purpose and legal status of the articles of association

Syllabus content covered in this chapter

- The procedure for registering a company, the advantages of purchasing a company 'off the shelf'
- The purpose and contents of the memorandum of association
- Corporate capacity to contract
- The purpose and contents of the articles of association

1 PROMOTERS AND PRE-INCORPORATION CONTRACTS

1.1 A company cannot form itself. The person who does so is called a 'promoter'.

KEY TERM

A **promoter** is 'one who undertakes to form a company with reference to a given project and to set it going and who takes the necessary steps to accomplish that purpose': *Twycross v Grant 1877.*

1.2 In addition to the person who takes the procedural steps to get a company incorporated, the term 'promoter' includes anyone who makes **business preparations** for the company. However a person who acts merely in a professional capacity in company formation, such as a solicitor or an accountant, is not on that account a promoter.

Duties of promoters

1.3 Promoters have the general duty to exercise **reasonable skill and care.**

1.4 If some or all the shares of the company when formed are to be allotted to persons other than the promoter, the promoter as an agent has a number of fiduciary duties.

(a) A promoter must account for any **benefits obtained** through acting as a promoter.

(b) A promoter must not put himself in a position where his own **interests conflict** with those of the company.

(c) A promoter must provide **full information** on his transactions and account for all monies etc arising from them.

1.5 A promoter has a duty not to make a wrongful profit. A wrongful profit one made when a promoter enters into a makes a profit personally in a contract as a promoter. If he makes a legitimate profit (say by selling the company a building which he owned prior to being a promoter) he may retain it, as long as it is sufficiently disclosed to the shareholders.

Pre-incorporation expenses

1.6 A promoter usually incurs expenses in preparations, such as drafting legal documents, made before the company is formed. He has no automatic right to recover his expenses from the company. However he can generally arrange that the first directors, of whom he may be one, agree that the company shall pay the bills or refund to him his expenditure.

Pre-incorporation contracts

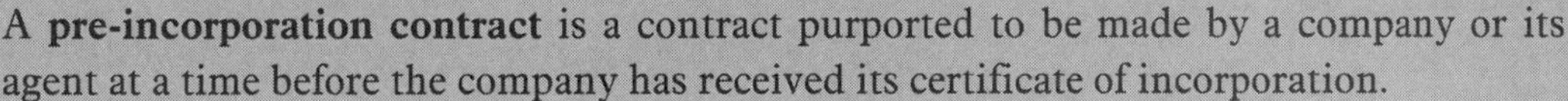

KEY TERM

A **pre-incorporation contract** is a contract purported to be made by a company or its agent at a time before the company has received its certificate of incorporation.

1.7 A company cannot enter into a contract before it exists as it does not have contractual capacity. Neither can a company **ratify** a contract made on its behalf **before it was incorporated**. It did not exist when the pre-incorporation contract was made; it cannot be made a party to it

Liability of promoters for pre-incorporation contracts

1.8 As the company is not bound by a pre-incorporation contract the person who made the contract on its behalf was warranting to the other party that his principal (the company) existed when in fact it did not. He is therefore liable for damages for breach of warranty of authority: *Kelner v Baxter 1866.*

1.9 Liability is now determined by s 36C(1).

> 'A contract which purports to be made by or on behalf of a company at a time when the company has not been formed has effect, subject to any agreement to the contrary, as one made with the person purporting to act for the company or as agent for it, and he is personally liable on the contract accordingly.'

Ways of avoiding promoter liability

1.10 There are various ways for promoters to avoid liability for a pre-incorporation contract.

(a) Novation.

(b) 'Off the shelf' companies.

(c) The contract remains as a **draft** until the company is formed. The promoters are the directors, and the company has the power to enter the contract. Once the company is formed, the directors take office and the company enters into the contract.

(d) If the contract has to be finalised before incorporation it should contain a clause that the personal liability of promoters is to cease if the company, when formed, enters a **new contract** on identical terms.

(e) The promoters in the contract declare themselves to be **trustees** for the company. (You can have an unborn beneficiary of a trust.)

Novation

1.11 A company may enter into a **new contract** (novation) on **similar terms** after it has been incorporated.

'Off the shelf companies'

1.12 A common way to avoid the problem concerning pre-incorporation contracts is to buy a company '**off the shelf**' (see Section 2 of this chapter). Even if a person contracts on behalf

of the new company before it is bought the company should be able to ratify the contract since it existed 'on the shelf' at the time the contract was made.

Exam focus point

A favourite MCQ in law exams is recognition of a pre-incorporation contract.

1.13 **Section summary**

- A promoter has the following duties.
  - A duty to exercise reasonable skill and care
  - A fiduciary duty to disclose to independent directors/members interest in transactions entered by the company
  - A fiduciary duty not to make personal profits from his role as a promoter
- A company cannot ratify a **pre-incorporation contract.** A **new contract** (novation) is required.
- Promoters may be **personally liable** on pre-incorporation contracts. They can avoid personal liability by:
  - Use of draft contracts
  - Acting as a trustee for the new company
  - Buying an off the shelf company
  - Stating the company will enter a new contract on identical terms when formed

Question 1

Fiona is the promoter of Enterprise Ltd. Before the company is incorporated, she enters into a contract on its behalf. After the certificate of incorporation is issued, the contract is breached. Who is liable?

A The directors and Enterprise Ltd
B Enterprise Ltd and Fiona
C Enterprise Ltd only
D Fiona only

Answer

D. A company cannot retrospectively ratify a pre-incorporation contract: s 36(4), confirmed in *Phonogram Ltd v Lane 1981*.

2 REGISTRATION AND COMMENCEMENT OF BUSINESS Pilot Paper, 5/02

2.1 Most companies are formed by registration under the Companies Act 1985.

2.2 A company is formed by the issue of a **certificate of incorporation** by the Registrar of Companies. The certificate identifies the company by its **name** and **serial number** at the registry and states (if it be so) that it is **limited** and (if necessary) that it is a public company.

Documents to be delivered to the registrar

2.3 The documents to be delivered to the registrar to obtain registration are as follows.

Documents	Description
Memorandum of association	The memorandum is signed by at least two **subscribers** or one in the case of single member private companies, dated and witnessed. Each subscriber agrees to subscribe for at least one share: s 1(1).
Articles of association	Articles are signed by the same subscriber(s), dated and witnessed. **Alternatively** the memorandum of a company limited by shares may be endorsed 'registered without articles of association'. The statutory **Table A articles** then become the company's articles in their entirety.
Statement in the prescribed form (known as Form 10)	The statement gives the particulars of the first **director(s)** and **secretary** and of the **first address** of the registered office. The persons named as directors and secretary must sign the form to record their consent to act in this capacity. When the company is incorporated they are deemed to be appointed.
Statutory declaration (Form 12)	The declaration is made by a solicitor engaged in the formation of the company or by one of the persons named as director or secretary that the **requirements** of the **Companies Act** in respect of registration have been **complied** with: s 12(3).
Registration fee	A registration fee of £20 is also payable on registration.

Certificate of incorporation

2.4 The registrar considers whether the documents are formally in order and whether the objects specified in the memorandum appear to be **lawful.** If he is satisfied he issues a **certificate of incorporation**.

KEY TERM

The **certificate of incorporation** is a certificate issued by the Registrar of Companies which denotes that a company has been formed and has legal incorporated status.

2.5 The certificate of incorporation is conclusive evidence that:

- All the **requirements** of the **Companies Act** have been **followed.**
- The company is a **company authorised** to be **registered** and has been **duly registered.**
- If the certificate states that the company is a **public company** it is conclusive.

Companies 'off the shelf' **Pilot Paper, 5/02**

2.6 Because the registration of a new company can be a lengthy business, it is often easiest for people wishing to operate as a company to purchase an **'off the shelf' company**. This is possible by contacting enterprises specialising in registering a stock of companies, ready for sale when a person comes along who needs the advantages of incorporation.

2.7 Normally the persons associated with the company formation enterprise are registered as the company's subscribers, and its first secretary and director. When the company is

purchased, the **shares** are **transferred** to the **buyer**, and the registrar is notified of the director's and the secretary's resignation.

2.8 The principal advantages of purchasing an off the shelf company are as follows.

(a) The **following documents** will **already have been filed** with the Registrar of Companies:

- Memorandum and articles
- Statement in the prescribed form
- Statutory declaration
- Fee

It will therefore be a quicker, and very possibly cheaper, way of incorporating a business.

(b) There will be **no risk** of **potential liability** arising from pre-incorporation contracts.

2.9 The disadvantages relate to the changes that will be required to the off-the-shelf company to make it compatible with the members' needs. For example, the constitution (memorandum and articles) may need to be changed. The subscriber shares will need to be transferred.

Question 2

What are the documents which must be delivered to the registrar on formation of a company?

Answer

Look back to Paragraph 2.3.

Commencement of business

Private company

2.10 A **private company** may do business and exercise its borrowing powers from the date of its incorporation.

Public company

2.11 A **public company** incorporated as such may not do business or exercise any borrowing powers unless it has obtained a **trading certificate** from the registrar: s 117. A private company which is re-registered as a public company is not subject to this rule.

2.12 To obtain the registrar's certificate under s 117 a public company makes application on **Form 117** signed by a director or by the secretary with a statutory declaration made by the director or secretary which states:

(a) That the **nominal value** of the **allotted share capital** is not less than **£50,000**

(b) The **amount paid up** on the allotted share capital, which must be **at least one quarter** of the nominal value and the entire premium if any; effectively this imposes a minimum of paid up capital of **£12,500**: s 101

(c) Particulars of **preliminary expenses** and **payments** or **benefits to promoters**

2.13 If a public company does business or borrows before obtaining a certificate the other party is protected since the transaction is valid. However the company and any officer in default is **punishable** by a **fine**. Moreover the other party may call on the directors to obtain a s 117 certificate. If they fail to do so within 21 days they must **indemnify him** against any loss: s 117(7) and (8).

2.14 If a public company fails to obtain a s 117 certificate within a year of incorporation a petition may be presented for its compulsory winding up: s 122(1)(b) Insolvency Act 1986.

Exam focus point

Remember these rules only apply to public companies.

3 MEMORANDUM OF ASSOCIATION 5/02

KEY TERM

The **memorandum of association** is the document which, with the articles of association, provides the legal constitution of a company. (CIMA, *Official Terminology*)

3.1 The purpose of the memorandum and articles of association (for short 'the memorandum' and 'the articles' in the remainder of this text) is to define what the company is and how its business and affairs are to be conducted.

3.2 Together the memorandum and articles bind the company and its members in a contractual relationship: s 14. For historical reasons these are two separate documents.

3.3 If there is any inconsistency between them the **memorandum** prevails.

3.4 The original memorandum must be presented to the registrar to obtain registration of the new company. Whenever the memorandum is altered a copy of the complete altered text must be delivered to the registrar for filing: s 18.

Contents of the memorandum

3.5 The memorandum of a **private** company limited by shares is required by s 2 to state the following.

- The **name** of the company
- Whether the **registered office** is to be situated in England and Wales, or Scotland
- The **objects** of the company
- The **limited liability** of members
- The **authorised share capital**

Exam focus point

You should memorise this list. Remember a private company limited by shares has no discretion: all these clauses **must** be in its memorandum.

3.6 S 1(3) and s 2 prescribe the form of the memorandum for other types of company as below:

MEMORANDUM OF ASSOCIATION

	Private company limited by shares	*Private company limited by guarantee*	*Public company*	*Unlimited company*
Name	✓	✓	✓	✓
Statement company is a public company			✓	
Location of registered office	✓	✓	✓	✓
Objects clause	✓	✓	✓	✓
Limited liability	✓	✓	✓	
Authorised share capital	✓		✓	
Statement of amount each member will contribute in winding up		✓		
Declaration of association	✓	✓	✓	✓

3.7 In addition to the above clauses, which are obligatory, the memorandum may include optional clauses if so desired.

The registered office clause

KEY TERM

The **registered office** is a business address to which all communications with a company may be sent.

3.8 The memorandum does **not** state the address of the registered office but only that it will be situate in England and Wales (or Wales alone if it is to be a Welsh company - s 2(2)). This fixes the **domicile** of the company which, unlike other matters comprised in the memorandum, is **unalterable**.

Limited liability

3.9 The memorandum states, if it is so, that the liability of the members is limited. If the company is a guarantee company, the memorandum also states the amount which the members are liable to contribute in a winding up.

3.10 The memorandum of association of a limited liability company may provide that the liability of its managing director, directors and managers for the company's debts shall be unlimited: s 306 (1).

The capital clause

KEY TERM

The **capital clause** is a clause that appears in the memorandum of association of a company which specifies the amount of share capital and its division into shares of a fixed amount.

3.11 A limited company which has a share capital must in its memorandum state:

- The **amount** of share capital with which it proposes to be registered
- The **division** of that capital into shares of a fixed amount: s 2(5)(a)
- The **nominal value** of each share

3.12 As a simple example: 'the capital of the company is £100 divided into 100 shares of £1 each'. represents the company's **authorised share capital.**

Name and objects clauses

3.13 These clauses are discussed in more detail in the next two sections of this Chapter.

Additional clauses

3.14 The contents of the memorandum are normally restricted to the compulsory clauses as described above. All additional material goes into the articles. However there is no rule which requires that this should be so. It sometimes happens that particular clauses are included in the memorandum rather than the articles because it is then **more difficult** to **alter them**.

Declaration of association

3.15 Every memorandum must also end with a **declaration of association** by which the subscribers state their wish to form the company. For a private company limited by shares the declaration is as follows.

'We, the subscribers to this memorandum of association, wish to be formed into a company, pursuant to this memorandum, and we agree to take the number of shares shown opposite our respective names.'

Names and addresses of subscribers	*Number of shares taken by each subscriber*
Henrietta Carrot (Address)	One
Henry Jones (Address)	One
Total number of shares taken	Two

Dated the first day of February 19XX
Witness to the above signatures

George Brown
(Address)

Alteration of the memorandum

3.16 The compulsory clauses of the memorandum may be altered as follows.

BPP PUBLISHING

Clause	Means of alteration
Name clause	Special resolution (75% majority) and registrar's certificate
Country of registered office	Unalterable
Objects clause	Special resolution (75% majority) with right of minority objection (see next chapter)
Limited liability - unlimited to limited	Special resolution (75% majority) and registrar's certificate.
Limited liability - limited to unlimited	Consent of all members and registrar's certificate
Removal of clause stating public company is such	Special resolution and re-registration as a private company
Authorised capital	Whatever resolution articles prescribe (generally ordinary resolution)

Alteration of optional additional clauses

3.17 As regards optional additional clauses included in the memorandum instead of the articles, there is a general power of **alteration by special resolution**. Members who hold at least 15% in nominal value of the company's shares or any class can apply to the court to prevent the alteration. Moreover this general power of alteration is subject to the following exceptions and restrictions of s 17.

(a) The clause can be '**entrenched**' by expressly providing that it shall not be altered. The general power of alteration is then excluded: s 17(2)(b).

(b) If the memorandum specifies a **special alteration procedure** it must be followed.

(c) If the clause defines the **rights** attached to a class of shares, those rights may only be varied by **variation of rights procedure**.

(d) If the **court has ordered** that an alteration shall be made to a clause of the memorandum or that an existing clause shall not be altered then it cannot be altered except with the **consent of the court**.

(e) **No alteration** of the memorandum or articles can compel a member to **subscribe** for additional shares or to pay more than he previously agreed in respect of shares already held unless the member agrees in writing: s 16.

3.18 When the memorandum is altered in any way the company must deliver to the registrar within 15 days of making the alteration:

- A **signed copy** of the resolution by which the alteration is made: s 380
- A **copy** of the **altered memorandum** itself

4 COMPANY NAME

Statutory rules on the choice of company name

4.1 The choice of name (whether the first name or a name adopted by change of name later) of a limited company must conform to ss 25 to 31, as follows.

(a) The name must **end** with the word(s):

 (i) **Public limited company** (abbreviated **plc**) if it is a public company

 (ii) **Limited** (or Ltd) if it is a private limited company, unless permitted to omit 'limited' from its name

 (iii) The Welsh equivalents of either (i) or (ii) may be used by a Welsh company (s25)

(b) No company may have a name which is the **same** as that of any existing company appearing in the statutory index at the registry. For this purpose two names are treated as 'the same' in spite of minor or non-essential differences; for instance the word 'the' as the first word in the name is ignored. 'John Smith Limited' is treated the same as 'John Smith' (an unlimited company) or 'John Smith & Company Ltd': s 26(3).

(c) No company may have a name the use of which would in the registrar's opinion be a **criminal** offence or which he considers **offensive:** s 26(1).

(d) Official approval is required for a name which in the registrar's opinion suggests a **connection** with the **government** or a **local authority** or which is subject to **control**: s 26(2).

Words such as 'International' or 'British' are only sanctioned if the size of the company matches its pretensions.

A name which suggests some professional expertise such as 'optician' will only be permitted if the appropriate representative association has been consulted and raises no objection.

The general purpose of the rule is to **prevent** a company **misleading** the public as to its real circumstances or activities. Certain names may be approved by the Secretary of State on written application.

Omission of the word 'limited'

4.2 A private company limited by guarantee and a company licensed to do so before 25 February 1982 may omit the word 'limited' from its name if the following conditions of s 30 are satisfied.

(a) The objects of the company must be the **promotion** of either commerce, art, science, education, religion, charity or any profession (or anything incidental or conducive to such objects).

(b) The memorandum or articles must require that the **profits** or other income of the company are to be **applied to promoting** its objects and no dividends may be paid to its members. Also on liquidation the **assets** (otherwise distributable to members) are to be **transferred** either to **another body** with similar objects or to a **charity**.

(c) A **statutory declaration** in the prescribed form must be delivered to the registrar stating that the company satisfies conditions (a) and (b) above.

Change of name

4.3 A company may change its name by:

(a) Passing a **special resolution**

(b) Obtaining the **registrar's certificate of incorporation** that he has registered the company under a new name: s 28

4.4 The change is effective from when the certificate is issued, although the company is still treated as the same legal entity as before. The same limitations as above apply to adoption of a name by change of name as by incorporation of a new company.

4.5 The **Registrar** may impel a company to change its name:

- If the name is the same as, or too similar to, another name on the register (within 12 months of the name being registered)
- If the name gives so misleading a view of its activities so as to harm the public (within 5 years of the name being registered)

Passing off action

4.6 A person who considers that his rights have been infringed can apply for an injunction to restrain a company from using a name (**even if** the name has been duly registered) which suggests that the latter company is carrying on the business of the complainant or is otherwise connected with it.

4.7 A company can be **prevented** by an **injunction** issued by the court in a **passing-off action** from **using** its **registered name** if in doing so it causes its goods to be confused with those of the claimant, who need not be another company.

> *Ewing v Buttercup Margarine Co Ltd 1917*
> *The facts:* The claimant, a sole trader, had since 1904 run a chain of 150 shops in Scotland and the north of England through which he sold margarine and tea. He traded as 'The Buttercup Dairy Co'. The defendant was a registered company formed in 1916 with the name above. It sold margarine as a wholesaler in the London area. The defendant contended that there was unlikely to be confusion between the goods sold by the two concerns.
>
> *Decision:* An injunction would be granted to restrain the defendants from the use of its name since the claimant had the established connection under the Buttercup name; he planned to open shops in the south of England and if the defendants sold margarine retail, for which their objects clause provided, there could be confusion between the two businesses.

4.8 If, however, the two companies' businesses are different, confusion is unlikely to occur, and hence the courts will refuse to grant an injunction: *Dunlop Pneumatic Tyre Co Ltd v Dunlop Motor Co Ltd 1907.*

4.9 The complaint will not succeed if the complainant lays claim to the exclusive use of a word which has a general use: *Aerators Ltd v Tollit 1902.*

Question 3

National Shaving Products Ltd was incorporated on 1 June 20X0. On 1 November 20X0 the directors received a letter from Nottinghamshire Shaving Products Ltd stating that it was incorporated in 19X4, that its business was being adversely affected by the use of the new company's name, and demanding that National Shaving Products Ltd change its name.

Advise National Shaving Products Ltd.

Answer

Nottinghamshire Shaving Products Ltd may seek to bring a 'passing-off action', a common law action which applies when one company believes that another's conduct (which may be the use of a company name) is causing confusion in the minds of the public over the goods which each company sells. Nottinghamshire Shaving Products Ltd would apply to the court for an injunction to prevent National Shaving Products Ltd from using its name.

However, in order to be successful, Nottinghamshire Shaving Products Ltd will need to satisfy the court, first, that confusion has arisen because of National Shaving Products Ltd's use of its registered name and, secondly, that it lays claim to something exclusive and distinctive and not something in general use: *Aerators Ltd v Tollit 1902.*

Appeal to Registrar

Alternatively Nottinghamshire Shaving Products Ltd might object to the Registrar of Companies that the name National Shaving Products Ltd is too like its own name and is causing confusion, thus appealing to the Registrar of Companies to exercise its power under s 28 CA 1985 to compel a change of name. In these circumstances, the Registrar would invite written submissions from each company, on which he would base his decision (against which there is no appeal).

Publication of the company's name

4.10 The company's name must appear legibly and conspicuously:

- **Outside** the **registered office** and **all places of business**: s 348
- On the **common seal** (if the company has one): s 350
- On all **business letters, notices** and **official publications**
- On all **cheques, orders, receipts** and **invoices** issued on the company's behalf: s 349

Business names other than the corporate name

KEY TERM

A **business name** is a name used by a company which is different from the company's corporate name or by a firm which is different from the name(s) of the proprietor or the partners.

4.11 Most companies trade under their own registered names. However a company may prefer to use some other name. If it does so it becomes subject to the Business Names Act. The rules require any person (company, partnership or sole trader) who carries on business under a different name from his own:

(a) To **state** its **name** (the registered name of the company if it is a company) and **address** on all **business letters**, invoices, receipts, written orders for goods or services and written demands for payment of debts: s 4(1)(a) BNA

(b) To **display** its **name** and **address** in a **prominent position** in any **business premises** to which its customers and suppliers have access: s 4(1)(b) BNA

(c) On **request** from any **person** with whom it does business to give **notice** of its name and address: s 4(2)

4.12 Section summary

- A company is subject to **statutory** rules on its choice of name.
  - The name must end in Ltd/plc (apart from some exceptions).
  - The name cannot be the same as another name on the registry.
  - The name cannot be a criminal offence or offensive.
  - Certain names require permission before they can be used.
- A company may also be subject to a **passing-off action** if its name is similar to another business's.
- The company's **name** must be **displayed** on **documents** and at its **place of business**.
- Further rules govern a company which has a different **business name** to its company name.

5 COMPANY OBJECTS AND CAPACITY — Pilot Paper, 5/02

KEY TERM

The **objects clause** is a clause in the memorandum of association of a company which states the activities which a company intends to follow. If a company pursues an activity outside the scope of that clause, any such actions are *ultra vires*.

5.1 The objects clause sets out the 'aims' and 'purposes' of the company. There are two main reasons for including it in the memorandum.

(a) Firstly, the investor wants to know for what **purpose** his capital is going to be used.

(b) The objects clause also allows a third party to know whether his proposed contract is within the company's capacity, and therefore whether it will be **enforceable**. A transaction outside the terms of the objects clause is *ultra vires* ('beyond the power') and, in principle at least, unenforceable.

Content of the objects clause

5.2 The contents of many objects clauses are lengthy and fairly complex, since they were originally designed to cover as many purposes as possible so that the company's activities would not be caught by the *ultra vires* rule.

Object as a 'general commercial company'

5.3 The Companies Act 1989 reformed the rules relating to the objects clause so that there would be no necessity for the objects clause to be long and complex to cover every eventuality. A company's objects clause can merely state that the company's object is to '**carry on business as a general commercial company**': s 3A. The legislation specifically states this to mean that:

(a) The object of the company is to carry on any **trade** or **business** whatsoever.

(b) The company has power to do all such things as are **incidental** or **conducive** to the carrying on of any trade or business by it.

Alteration of the objects

5.4 A company may under s 4(1) alter its objects by **special resolution** for any reason.

5.5 S 5 provides a procedure for a dissenting minority to apply to the court to modify an otherwise valid alteration of the objects clause. The conditions are as follows.

(a) Application to the court must be made **within 21 days** from the passing of the special resolution to alter the objects.

(b) The applicants must hold in aggregate at least **15 per cent** of the issued share capital or 15 per cent of any class of shares. They must not originally have voted in favour of the alteration nor consented to it. They may appoint one or more of their membership to apply to the court on their behalf: s 5(3).

5.6 Once such an objection is made the alternative which was approved can only come into effect insofar as the court allows: s 4(2).

Contractual capacity and *ultra vires*

> **KEY TERM**
>
> **Ultra vires** is where a company exceeds the objects specified in the memorandum of association it acts outside its capacity.

5.7 Since a company's capacity to contract is defined in its objects clause it has always followed that, however widely this is drawn, some acts went beyond its capacity or 'power'. The Latin term for this is **ultra vires**; in principle, the law would not allow such an act to be legally enforceable because of lack of capacity.

Ashbury Railway Carriage & Iron Co Ltd v Riche 1875
The facts: The company had an objects clause which stated that its objects were to make and sell, or lend on hire, railway carriages and wagons and all kinds of railway plant, fittings, machinery and rolling stock; and to carry on business as mechanical engineers. The company bought a concession to build a railway in Belgium, subcontracting the work to the defendant. Later the company repudiated the contract.

Decision: Constructing a railway was not within the company's objects so the company did not have capacity to enter into either the concession contract or the sub-contract. The contract was void for *ultra vires* and so the defendant had no right to damages for breach. The members could not ratify it and the company could neither enforce the contract nor be forced into performing its obligations.

5.8 The approach taken by the Companies Act 1989 is to give security to commercial transactions for third parties, whilst preserving the rights of shareholders to restrain an action on the grounds that it is *ultra vires*.

5.9 S 35(1) provides as follows:

> 'the validity of an act done by a company shall not be called into question on the ground of lack of capacity by reason of anything in the company's memorandum.'

5.10 S 35A(1) provides as follows:

> 'in favour of a person dealing with a company in good faith, the power of the board of directors to bind the company, or authorise others to do so, shall be deemed to be free of any limitation under the company's constitution.'

5.11 There are a number of points to note about s 35A(1).

(a) The section applies in favour of the **person dealing with the company** (the company is protected under s 35(3)).

(b) In contrast with s 35(1), **good faith** is required. The company has, however, to prove lack of good faith in the third party and this may turn out to be quite difficult: s 35A(2).

(c) The section covers not only acts beyond the capacity of the company, but acts beyond **'any limitation under the company's constitution'.**

5.12 The effect of the *ultra vires* rule continues to operate **internally** between the company and its members. S 35(2) provides that a member can gain an injunction to restrain the doing of an *ultra vires* act **before** it is done. However, **after** the event, there will be no right to challenge the action (by virtue of its validation under s 35(1)). The members are, in practice, unlikely to learn of the action until after it has been done.

5.13 The directors have a duty (to the company) to ensure that the assets of the company are not used for *ultra vires* purposes. If they have breached this duty, the action can only be **ratified** by **special resolution**: s 35(3). **Relief** from **liability** from the directors or any other person will require a **separate special resolution.**

Protection of the company in contracts with directors

5.14 The wide scope of ss 35 and 35A could be used to validate questionable transactions between the directors and the company. S 322A deals with this situation, allowing any **ultra vires** transactions with a director or connection of a director to be **voidable** at the instance of the company. The transaction will not however be voidable if ratified, where third party rights intervene, or where restitution can no longer be made.

5.15 The section also provides that, whether or not the transaction is avoided, the persons covered by the section (and any director who authorised the transaction) is liable to account to the company for profit made or loss and damage caused.

Powers of the company

5.16 The objects clause may contain a list of permissible transactions, **express powers.** These include the ability to borrow funds, to give security by creating charges over property, to give guarantees, and possibly to make gifts. Other powers may be implied by what the company does.

5.17 Certain powers are held to be **subordinate** to **the main objects**, and cannot be converted into independent objects. The most important example is **borrowing.** In *Re Introductions Ltd 1970,* the court held that the power to borrow 'cannot mean something in the air.' Borrowing is not an end in itself and must be used for the purposes of the company.

5.18 If transactions are entered into to **further** the **objects** of the company or to exercise its powers, it does not matter that in the absence of fraud, the transaction does not benefit the company.

5.19 If the company's powers have been misused, normally the members may **ratify** the **contract.** However this cannot be done when the company property is **misappropriated,** since to ratify a misappropriation would be a fraud on the minority.

5.20 If powers are used **illegally,** the transaction will always be void.

5.21 Section summary

- The objects clause sets out the **purpose** and **capacity** of the company.
- If the company acts **beyond its capacity,** it acts *ultra vires.*
- **Third parties** can enforce *ultra vires* transactions, and in addition can enforce transactions that the company's directors have no authority to enter.
- Nowadays a company can avoid the threat of *ultra vires* by adopting the '**general commercial company**' objects clause.
- Certain **powers** of the company, particularly the power to borrow, are **not independent**, and must be used for the purposes of the company.
- A company's objects clause may be **altered** by **special resolution.**

Question 4

Which of the following statements is correct?

(i) A company's capacity to contract is regulated by the objects clause of its memorandum of association.

(ii) A company now has the same ability to contract as a human being.

A (i) only
B (ii) only
C Both (i) and (ii)
D Neither (i) nor (ii)

Answer

A.

Exam focus point

Make sure you understand how s 35 protects third parties.

6 ARTICLES OF ASSOCIATION 11/01

KEY TERM

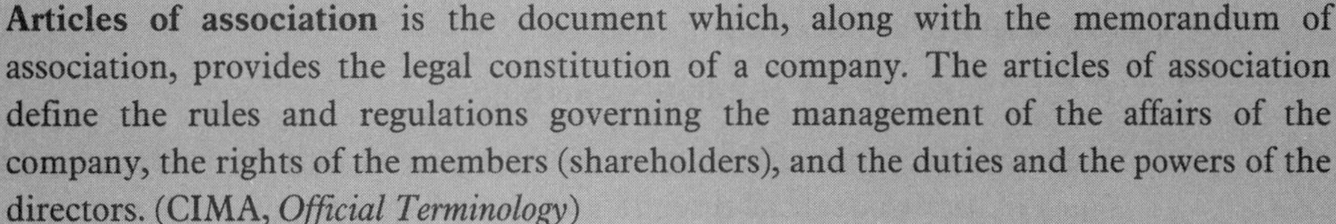

Articles of association is the document which, along with the memorandum of association, provides the legal constitution of a company. The articles of association define the rules and regulations governing the management of the affairs of the company, the rights of the members (shareholders), and the duties and the powers of the directors. (CIMA, *Official Terminology*)

Difference between memorandum and articles

6.1 The articles of association deal mainly with matters affecting the **internal conduct** of the company's affairs. The memorandum differs from the articles in that it deals with the constitution of the company mainly as it affects **outsiders**.

CONTENTS OF ARTICLES	
Appointment of directors	Accounts
Powers of directors	Class rights
Board meetings	Issue of shares
Calling general meetings	Transfer of shares
Conduct of general meetings	Alterations of capital structure
Dividends	Company secretary

Table A articles

6.2 A company limited by shares may adopt all or any part of the statutory standard Table A model articles made under s 8.

6.3 A company limited by shares may have its own full-length special articles. Listed companies must, since Stock Exchange rules require that the articles shall include a number of special provisions differing from the standard model.

6.4 The articles of a company limited by shares usually make clear how far Table A applies by starting with:

(a) Either a **statement** that **Table A shall not apply** (because full length special articles follow), or

(b) That **Table A shall apply** with **only the modifications** and exclusions which follow

If no such statement is made the special articles override Table A where they cover the same subjects, but Table A applies to any matter on which there is nothing in the special articles.

6.5 A company **limited by guarantee**, an **unlimited company** and a '**partnership company**' must adopt **special articles.** However there are statutory models to which these special articles must conform so far as the circumstances permit: s 8.

Interaction of statute and articles

6.6 There are two aspects to consider.

(a) The Companies Act may permit companies to do something **if** their **articles** also authorise it. For example a company may reduce its capital if its articles give power to do this: s 135. If, however, they do not, then the company must alter the articles to include the necessary power before it may exercise the statutory power.

(b) The Companies Act will **override** the articles:

(i) If the Companies Act **prohibits something**

(ii) If something is permitted by the Companies Act **only** by a **special procedure** (such as passing a special resolution in general meeting)

Form of articles

6.7 The articles must be printed and divided into numbered paragraphs: s 7(3). The first articles presented to obtain registration of a new company are signed by the subscribers to the memorandum, dated and witnessed.

Alteration of the articles

6.8 A company has a statutory power to alter its articles by **special resolution:** s 9(1). The alteration will be valid and binding on **all** members of the company.

6.9 An article **cannot** be made unalterable by:

(a) **Declaring** it to be **unalterable** in the articles

(b) **Making** a **separate contract** by which the company undertakes not to alter it

(c) Providing that a **larger majority** shall be required than three quarters of the votes cast on a special resolution to make an alteration: *Malleson v National Insurance & Guarantee Corporation 1894*

6.10 If all the members of the company agree to an alteration of the articles but do not hold a general meeting and pass a special resolution, this is still an effective alteration under the '**assent principle**': *Cane v Jones 1980*.

Making the company's constitution unalterable

6.11 There are devices by which some provisions of the company's constitution can be made unalterable (without the consent of the member who wishes to prevent any alteration).

(a) The clause can be **inserted in the memorandum** instead of the articles and be described as unalterable (an 'entrenched' article). The right to alter an item in the memorandum which would have been in the articles does not apply in this case: s 17.

(b) The articles may give to a member **additional votes** so that he can block a resolution to alter articles on particular points (including the removal of his weighted voting rights from the articles): *Bushell v Faith 1970*. However, to be effective, the articles must also limit the powers of members to alter the articles that give extra votes.

(c) The articles may provide that when a meeting is held to vote on a proposed alteration of the articles the **quorum present must include** the **member concerned.** He can then deny the meeting a quorum by absenting himself.

(d) Where a clause that could have been in the articles is in the memorandum it may be altered by a special resolution; however, **application may be made to the court** to have the alteration cancelled: s 17(1).

Restrictions on alteration

6.12 Even when it is possible to hold a meeting and pass a special resolution, alteration of the articles is restricted by the following principles.

(a) The alteration is **void** (under s 9 itself) if it **conflicts with the Companies Act** or with the **memorandum:** *Welton v Saffery 1897*.

(b) In various circumstances, such as to protect a minority (s 459) or in approving an alteration of the objects clause (s 5(5)), the **court may order** that an alteration be made or, alternatively, that an existing article shall not be altered.

(c) A **member may not be compelled** by alteration of the articles to **subscribe for additional shares** or to accept increased liability for the shares which he holds unless he has given his consent: s 16.

(d) An alteration of the articles which varies the rights attached to a class of shares may only be made if the **correct rights variation procedure** has been followed to obtain the consent of the class: s 125. A 15 per cent minority may apply to the court to cancel the variation under s 127.

(e) An alteration may be **void** if the **majority** who approve it are **not acting *bona fide* in what they deem to be the interests of the company as a whole** (see below).

6.13 The case law on this subject is an effort to hold the balance between two principles:

(a) The **majority** is **entitled** to **alter articles** even though a minority considers that the alteration is prejudicial to its interests.

(b) A minority is entitled to protection against an alteration which is intended to **benefit** the **majority** rather than the company and which is **unjustified discrimination** against the minority.

6.14 Principle (b) tends to be restricted to **some cases** where the majority seeks to **expel** the minority from the company.

6.15 The most elaborate analysis of this subject was made by the Court of Appeal in the case of *Greenhalgh v Arderne Cinemas Ltd 1950*. Two main propositions were laid down by Evershed MR.

(a) '**Bona fide for the benefit of the company as a whole**' is a **single test** and also a **subjective test** (what did the majority believe?). The court will not substitute its own view.

(b) 'The company as a whole' means, in this context, **the general body of shareholders.** The test is whether every 'individual hypothetical member' would in the honest opinion of the majority benefit from the alteration.

Shuttleworth v Cox Bros & Co (Maidenhead) Ltd 1927
The facts: Expulsion of director appointed by the articles who had failed to account for funds was held to be valid.

Brown v British Abrasive Wheel Co 1919
The facts: The company needed further capital. The majority who held 98 per cent of the existing shares were willing to provide more capital but only if they could buy up the 2 per cent minority. As the minority refused to sell the majority proposed to alter the articles to provide for compulsory acquisition on a fair value basis. The minority objected to the alteration.

Decision: The alteration was invalid since it was merely for the benefit of the majority. It was not an alteration 'directly concerned with the provision of further capital' and therefore not for the benefit of the company.

Filing of alteration

6.16 Whenever any alteration is made to the articles a **copy** of the **altered articles** must be delivered to the registrar **within 15 days**, together with a signed copy of the special resolution by which the alteration is made: ss 18 and 380. The registrar gives notice in the *Gazette*: s 711.

6.17 Section summary

- Articles deal with the **internal conduct** of a company's business.
- Most companies limited by shares have their articles in **Table A form.**
- The Companies Act allows companies to do certain things if their **articles permit.**
- However, articles cannot override **statutory prohibitions** or **procedures.**
- Articles can be **altered** by **special resolution.**
- Alteration of articles must be **bona fide** for the **benefit of the company** as a whole, that is the general body of shareholders.
- There are **other restrictions** on altering articles in certain circumstances (subscription for additional shares, variation of class rights).
- There are **various methods** for **making articles unalterable.**

7 MEMORANDUM AND ARTICLES AS CONTRACTS

7.1 A company's memorandum and articles bind, under s 14:

- **Members** to **company**
- **Company** to **members** (but see below)
- **Members** to **members**

The company's articles do **not** bind the company to third parties.

7.2 This principle applies only to rights and obligations which affect members **in their capacity as members**.

7.3 The principle that only rights and obligations of members are covered by s 14 applies when an outsider who is also a member seeks to rely on the articles in support of a claim made **as an outsider**.

> *Eley v Positive Government Security Life Assurance Co 1876*
> *The facts:* E, a solicitor, drafted the original articles and included a provision that the company must always employ him as its solicitor. E became a member of the company some months after its incorporation. He later sued the company for breach of contract in not employing him as a solicitor.
>
> *Decision:* E could not rely on the article since it was a contract between the company and its members and he was not asserting any claim **as a member**.

Articles as contract between members

7.4 S 14 gives to the memorandum and articles the effect of a contract made between (a) the company and (b) its members individually. It can also impose a contract on the members **in their dealings with each other**.

> *Rayfield v Hands 1958*
> *The facts:* The articles required that (a) every director should be a shareholder and (b) the directors must purchase the shares of any member who gave them notice of his wish to dispose of them. The directors, however, denied that a member could enforce the obligation on them to acquire his shares.
>
> *Decision:* There was 'a contract ... between a member and member-directors in relation to their holdings of the company's shares in its article' and the directors were bound by it.

7.5 Articles are usually drafted so that each stage is a **dealing between** the **company** and the **members**, to which s 14 clearly applies, so that:

(a) A member who intends to transfer his shares must, if the articles so require, give notice of his intention to the company.

(b) The company must then give notice to other members that they have an option to take up his shares.

Articles as supplement to contracts

7.6 If an outsider makes a separate contract with the company and that contract contains no specific term on a particular point but the articles do, then the contract is deemed to incorporate the articles to that extent. One example is when services, say as a director, are provided under contract without agreement as to remuneration: *Re New British Iron Co, ex parte Beckwith 1898.*

7.7 If a contract incorporates terms of the articles it is subject to the company's **right** to **alter** its articles: *Shuttleworth v Cox Bros & Co (Maidenhead) Ltd 1927.* However a company's articles cannot be altered to deprive another person of a right already earned, say for services rendered **prior** to the alteration.

7.8 Section summary

- Articles bind the **members** to the **company**, the **company** to **members** and **members** to other **members**.
- They do **not** bind the **company** to **third parties.**
- The articles only **apply** to **rights of membership**; they **do not apply** to **rights other than membership rights** that members possess.
- Articles can be used to **supplement contracts,** to supply missing contract terms.

Exam focus point

Remember the articles only create contractual rights/obligations in relation to rights **as a member**.

Question 5

S 14(1) Companies Act 1985 provides as follows.

> 'Subject to the provisions of the Act, the memorandum and the articles when registered, bind the company and its members to the same extent as if they respectively had been signed and sealed by each member, and contained covenants on the part of each member to observe all the provisions of the memorandum and of the articles.'

In your own words explain what this provision means.

Answer

The effect of s 14 Companies Act 1985 is that, without obtaining from a new member any express agreement to that effect, the memorandum and articles of the company are a **binding agreement** between the member and the company.

A member must comply with the obligations imposed on him in relation to his shares. The company on its side must permit him to exercise his member's rights to vote or to receive a dividend.

The articles, if so expressed, may also constitute a contract between members: *Rayfield v Hands 1960.*

8 SHAREHOLDERS' AGREEMENTS

8.1 Shareholders' agreements sometimes supplement a company's memorandum and articles of association. They are concerned with the running of the company; in particular they often contain terms by which the shareholders agree how they will vote on various issues.

8.2 Shareholders' agreements often offer more protection to the interests of shareholders than do the articles of association. Individuals have a **power of veto** over any proposal which is contrary to the terms of the agreement. This enables a minority shareholder to protect his interests against unfavourable decisions of the majority.

9 PUBLICITY

9.1 Under company law the privilege of trading through a separate corporate body is matched by the duty to provide information which is available to the public about the company. This duty is fulfilled in several ways:

- Sending certain documents to the Registrar of Companies:
  - Accounts Assistant
  - Resolutions
  - Constitutional documents on formation and when changed subsequently
  - An annual return containing details of shareholdings and officers
- Maintaining statutory registers

Statutory registers

9.2 A company must keep **registers** of certain aspects of its constitution. To make inspection of the registers reasonably easy for persons who are entitled to have access to them, the company must keep them at specified places. Members are entitled to inspect the registers for free, others must may a reasonable fee.

STATUTORY REGISTERS		
Register	*Must be kept at registered office?*	*Relevant CA85 section*
Register of **members**	NO	s 352
Register of **directors and secretaries**	YES	s 288
Register of **directors' interests** in shares and debentures of the company	NO	s 325
Register of **charges**	YES	s 411
Minutes of general meetings of the company	YES	s 382
Minutes of directors' and **managers' meetings**	YES	s 382
Register of **written resolutions**	YES	s 382A
Register of **substantial interests** in shares (Public company ONLY) (a substantial interest is 3% or more of the nominal value of any class of share)	NO	s 211

Register of members

9.3 Every company must, under s 352, keep a register of members and enter in it:

(a) The **name** and **address** of **each member**

(b) **The class** (if more than one) to which he belongs unless this is indicated in the particulars of his shareholding

(c) If the company has a share capital, the **number of shares** held by each member. In addition:

(i) If the shares have **distinguishing numbers**, the member's shares must be identified in the register by those numbers

(ii) If the company has more than one class of shares the member's shares must be **distinguished** by their **class**, such as preference, ordinary, non-voting etc shares

(d) The date on which each member **became** and eventually the date on which he **ceased** to be a member

Location of register of members

9.4 The register of members may be kept:

- At the registered office
- At another office of the company
- At the office of a professional registrar

where in the latter two cases it is made up provided that:

- The other place is in England and Wales.
- Its address is notified to the registrar: s 353.

Register of charges

9.5 The register must contain:

- **Details of charges** affecting the company property or undertaking
- **Brief descriptions** of property charged
- The **amount** of the charge
- The **name** of the person entitled to the charge

Register of directors and secretaries

9.6 The register of directors and secretaries must contain the following details in respect of a director who is an individual: s 288.

- Present and former forenames and surnames*
- Residential address*
- Nationality
- Business occupation
- Particulars of other current and former directorships held in the last five years
- Date of birth

Only the * items are required for company secretaries.

9.7 The register must include shadow directors (discussed in a later chapter) as well as normal directors.

Register of directors' interest in shares and debentures

9.8 The register of **directors' interests in shares** and debentures must be maintained by the company (s 324), showing details of holdings and rights under s 325 and Schedule 13 para 14. Interests include those of a **director's spouse** and **minor children** (under 18).

9.9 The register of directors' interests and any register of substantial interests in the voting shares of a public company must be kept in the same place, **either** at the company's **registered office** or where the **register of members is kept**.'

Register of debentureholders

9.10 Companies with debentures issued nearly always keep a **register of debentureholders,** but there is no statutory compulsion to do so. If a register of debentureholders is maintained, it should not be held outside England and Wales, and should generally be kept at the **registered office**.

Directors' service agreements

9.11 Copies of directors' service agreements should be kept with the register of members, at the company's principal place of business, or at the registered office.

Annual accounts and returns

9.12 The directors must, in respect of each accounting reference period of the company:

- **Prepare** a **balance sheet** and **profit and loss account** which give a **true and fair view:** s 226
- **Lay** before the company in general meeting **accounts** for the period: s 241 (with exceptions as described below)
- Deliver to the registrar a copy of those accounts: s 242

Chapter roundup

- A **promoter** is a person who **undertakes** to **form** a company.
- A promoter is in a **fiduciary position** to the company and must disclose any personal advantage he obtains from acting as promoter. If a contract purports to be made by a company before the company has been formed, the person making the contract is held **personally** liable.
- A company is formed by the issue of a **certificate of incorporation**.
- To obtain a certificate of incorporation, various documents must be sent to the registrar.
    - **Memorandum** of association
    - **Articles** of association
    - Forms 10 and 12 giving **particulars** of **first director(s)** and **secretary** and **address** of registered office and a statutory declaration by the directors
    - **Registration fee**
- A private company may carry on business as soon as it is incorporated. A public company requires a **s 117 certificate.**
- In this chapter we have seen that the memorandum is extremely important to a company because it governs the relation of a company to the outside world. Its contents (and the individual rules relating to its content) should be thoroughly learnt.
- The contents are summarised as follows.
    - The **name** of the company
    - Whether the **registered office** is to be situated in England and Wales, or Scotland
    - The **objects** of the company
    - The **limited liability** of members
    - The **authorised share capital**
    - **Declaration of association**
- Except in certain circumstances the name must end with the words limited (Ltd), public limited company (plc) or the Welsh equivalents.
- No company may use a name which is:
    - The **same** as that of an existing company
    - A **criminal offence** or offensive
    - Suggest a **connection** with the **government or local authority** (unless approved)
- If a company enters into a contract which is outside its objects, that contract is said to be **ultra vires.** However the rights of third parties to the contract are protected.

- Members have the right to restrain a company from an ultra vires act, but that right is only effective if exercised prior to the act being done.
- Under the provisions of the Companies Act 1989, a company may opt out of the ultra vires rule by stating that the object of the company is to carry on business as a **general commercial company**.
- A company's **objects** can be **altered** by passing a **special resolution**.
- **Table A** contains the specimen format for the articles. It applies unless excluded expressly or by implication.
- The articles constitute a contract between:
  - Company and members
  - Members and the company
  - Members and members
- The articles **do not constitute** a contract between the **company** and **third parties**, or members in a **capacity** other than as **members** (the *Eley* case).
- The articles can be used to establish the terms of a contract existing elsewhere.
- The articles may be altered by a **special resolution**. The basic test is whether the alteration is for the **benefit of the company as a whole.**
- A company can, by various measures (for example **weighted voting rights**), ensure that articles are unalterable.

Quick quiz

1 A company must keep at its registered office a register of directors and secretary. What details must be revealed concerning the secretary?

A Full name
B Address
C Nationality
D Date of birth
E Directorships in other companies currently held
F Directorships in other companies held in the last five years

2 A company can confirm a pre-incorporation contract by performing it or obtaining benefits from it.

☐ True

☐ False

3 Which one of the following statements about the formation of a company in the United Kingdom is correct?

A A company comes into existence following the registration of a certificate of incorporation at Companies House.

B Following the formation of a company, articles of association must be submitted to the Registrar of Companies.

C After receiving a certificate of incorporation, a private company must issue a prospectus to people who may wish to buy shares in the company.

D A memorandum of association must be included with the application to form a company.

4 Which of the following details is the register of members required to include?

A Names, addresses and date of birth of members
B The amount paid to the company for the shares
C Date of presentation of the share certificate
D Date on which a person ceases to be a member
E Nominal value of the shares

5 Percy Limited has recently entered a contract with a third party which is not authorised by the objects clause of the company's Memorandum of Association.

Which of the following statements is correct?

A The validity of the act cannot be questioned on the grounds of lack of capacity by reason of anything in the company's memorandum.

B The act may be restrained by the members of Percy Ltd.

C The act may be enforced by the company and the third party.

D The directors have a duty to observe any limitation on their powers flowing from the company's memorandum.

6 If a company wishes to alter its objects clause, what kind of resolution is required?

A Special resolution
B Extraordinary resolution
C Ordinary resolution with special notice
D Ordinary resolution

7 A company has been formed within the last six months. Another long-established company considers that because of similarity there may be confusion between it and the new company. The long-established company must bring a passing-off action if it is to prevent the new company using its name.

☐ True

☐ False

8 The memorandum can contain additional optional clauses in addition to the compulsory clauses, and these can be 'entrenched' by providing that they cannot be altered.

☐ True

☐ False

9 Which of the following persons are bound to one another by the memorandum and articles?

A Members to company
B Company to members
C Members to members
D Company to third parties

10 Which one of the following statements concerning a company's memorandum and articles is correct?

A The articles but not the memorandum are involved in the legal process of company formation.

B In the case of public companies, both documents must be sent to the shareholders each year with the company report.

C The articles, but not the memorandum, set out the benefits of limited liability which the shareholders gain.

D The memorandum describes the constitution of the company, whereas the articles represent the rules of the company by which the members must abide.

11 Complete the table using the factors given below.

PURCHASING AN OFF THE SHELF COMPANY	
Advantages	*Disadvantages*

- May need to increase authorised share capital
- No requirement to file memorandum/articles/statutory declaration with the Registrar
- Quicker than incorporating a business
- Objects in the company's memorandum might not be appropriate
- Likely to be cheaper than incorporating a business
- Need to transfer subscriber shares
- May need to change the name of the company

12 Fill in the blanks.

STATUTORY REGISTERS		
Register	*Must be kept at registered office?*	*Relevant CA85 section*
Register of **members**		s 352
Register of **directors and secretaries**		s 288
Register of **directors' interests** in shares and debentures of the company		s 325
Register of **charges**		s 411
Minutes of general meetings of the company		s 382
Minutes of directors' and **managers' meetings**		s 382
Register of **written resolutions**		s 382A
Register of **substantial interests** in shares (Public company ONLY) (a substantial interest is 3% or more of the nominal value of any class of share)		s 211

13 Delete where applicable

- Promoters have a duty to exercise absolute/reasonable skill and care
- If a promoter does not make proper disclosure of legitimate profits the company may/must rescind the contract.
- A company can/can never ratify a contract made by a promoter on its behalf before it was incorporated.

14 Tick the clauses which are obligatory in each types of company's memorandum.

	Private company limited by shares	*Private company limited by guarantee*	*Public company*	*Unlimited company*
Name				
Statement company is a **public company**				
Location of **registered office**				
Objects clause				
Limited liability				
Authorised share capital				
Statement of amount each member will **contribute in winding up**				
Declaration of association				

15 (a) A company may change its name by passing a special/extraordinary/ordinary resolution

(b) For which of the following reasons can the Registrar intervene and compel a company to change its name?

- Name is the same as another company
- Misleading information was given to secure registration
- Name gives misleading indication of company's activities

16 Delete where applicable

- The articles do/do not bind the company to third parties
- An article may/may not be made unalterable by declaring it to be unalterable in the articles
- Articles can be altered by special/ordinary/extraordinary resolution

17 In which of the following situations will an alteration of the articles of association be ineffective?

(i) Where alteration of the articles would result in a breach of the contract by the company
(ii) Where the alteration conflicts with any provision of the Companies Acts
(iii) Where the alteration compels 5% or fewer of the members to subscribe for additional shares

A (i) and (ii) only
B (ii) only
C (ii) and (iii) only
D (i), (ii) and (iii)

Answers to quick quiz

1 A and B. C to F are required of directors, but not of the secretary.

2 False. The company must make a *new* contract on similar terms

3 D is correct. A is incorrect because Companies House issues, not registers, the certificate of incorporation. B is untrue because articles must be submitted with the application for registration. C is incorrect because a private company cannot issue shares to the public.

4 B, D and E are correct. The date of presentation is not required, so C is incorrect. The register should include the members' names and addresses, but not their dates of birth, so A is incorrect.

5 A, C and D are true under s 35 (1). Members can only act before the contract is signed, so B is incorrect.

6 A

7 False. The long-established company can also complain to the Registrar within 12 months of the date that the new company was registered.

8 True: s 17 (2) (b) provides.

9 A, B and C are correct: s 14. D is incorrect, illustrated by *Eley v Positive Government Security Life Assurance Co Ltd 1876.*

10 D is correct. A is incorrect as both documents need to be sent to the registrar when the company is incorporated. There is no need to send either document to shareholders annually, so B is wrong. C is incorrect because the memorandum contains the limited liability clause.

11

PURCHASING AN OFF THE SHELF COMPANY	
Advantages	**Disadvantages**
• No requirement to file memorandum/ articles/statutory declaration with the Registrar • Quicker than incorporating a business • Likely to be cheaper than incorporating a business	• May need to increase authorised share capital • Objects in the company's memorandum might not be appropriate • Need to transfer subscriber shares • May need to change the name of the company

12

STATUTORY REGISTERS		
Register	*Must be kept at registered office?*	*Relevant CA85 section*
Register of **members**	NO	s 352
Register of **directors and secretaries**	YES	s 288
Register of **directors' interests** in shares and debentures of the company	NO	s 325
Register of **charges**	YES	s 411
Minutes of general meetings of the company	YES	s 382
Minutes of directors' and **managers' meetings**	YES	s 382
Register of **written resolutions**	YES	s 382A
Register of **substantial interests** in shares (Public company ONLY) (a substantial interest is 3% or more of the nominal value of any class of share)	NO	s 211

- If a promoter does not make proper disclosure of legitimate profits the company **may** rescind the contract
- A company **can never** ratify a contract made by a promoter on its behalf before it was incorporated

14 **MEMORANDUM OF ASSOCIATION**

	Private company limited by shares	*Private company limited by guarantee*	*Public company*	*Unlimited company*
Name	✓	✓	✓	✓
Statement company is a **public company**			✓	
Location of **registered office**	✓	✓	✓	✓
Objects clause	✓	✓	✓	✓
Limited liability	✓	✓	✓	
Authorised share capital	✓		✓	
Statement of amount each member will **contribute in winding up**		✓		
Declaration of association	✓	✓	✓	✓

15 (a) A company may change its name by passing a special resolution

(b) All the given reasons.

16
- The articles **do not** bind the company to third parties
- An article **may not** be made unalterable by declaring it to be unalterable in the articles
- Articles can be altered by **special** resolution

17 C (See Southern Foundries v Shirlaw 1940). The articles cannot be altered in such a way as to compel any member to subscribe for additional shares or to accept increased liability for his existing shares (s16).

The following relevant questions are included in the Exam Question Banks

You can attempt these now. However, we would advise you to attempt these as mock exams at the end of your initial stage of study

Exam Question Bank	Numbers
Paper based format	15, 16, 17, 21, 22, 23, 26
Computer based assessment	1, 7, 35, 38

Part E
Corporate administration and management

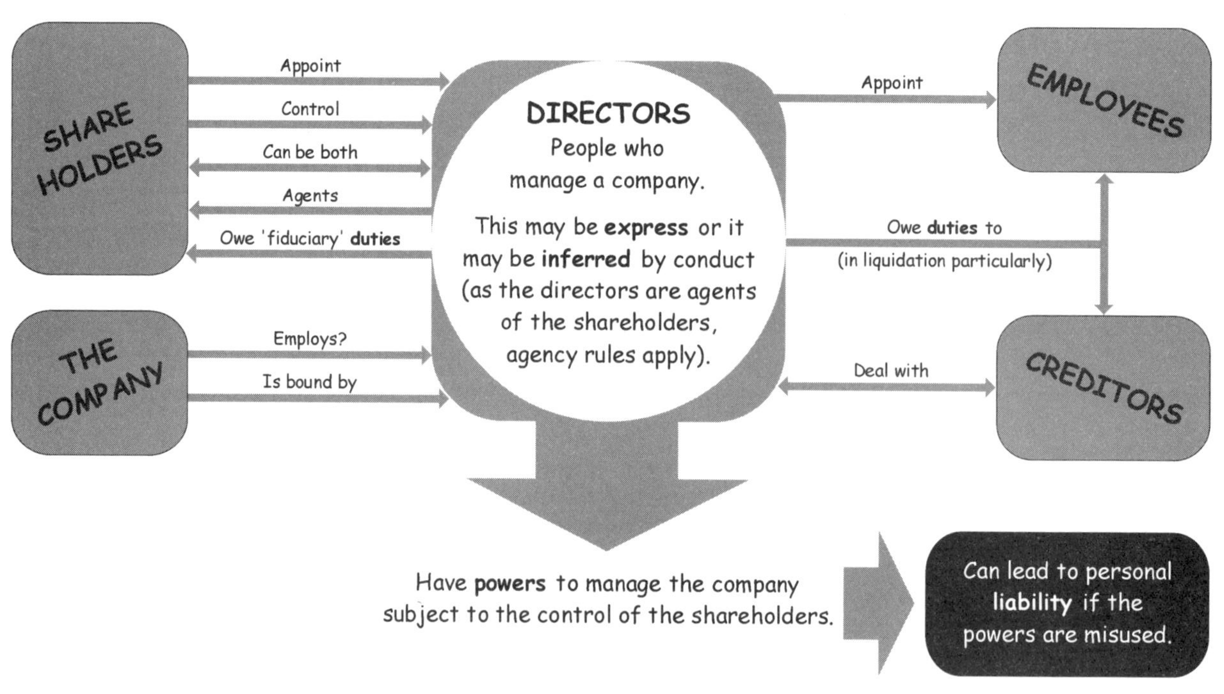

SHARE HOLDERS
Appoint
Control
Can be both
Agents
Owe 'fiduciary' duties
THE COMPANY
Employs?
Is bound by
DIRECTORS
People who manage a company.
This may be express or it may be inferred by conduct (as the directors are agents of the shareholders, agency rules apply).
Appoint
EMPLOYEES
Owe duties to
(in liquidation particularly)
Deal with
CREDITORS
Have powers to manage the company subject to the control of the shareholders.
Can lead to personal liability if the powers are misused.

The shareholders' powers are exercised in:

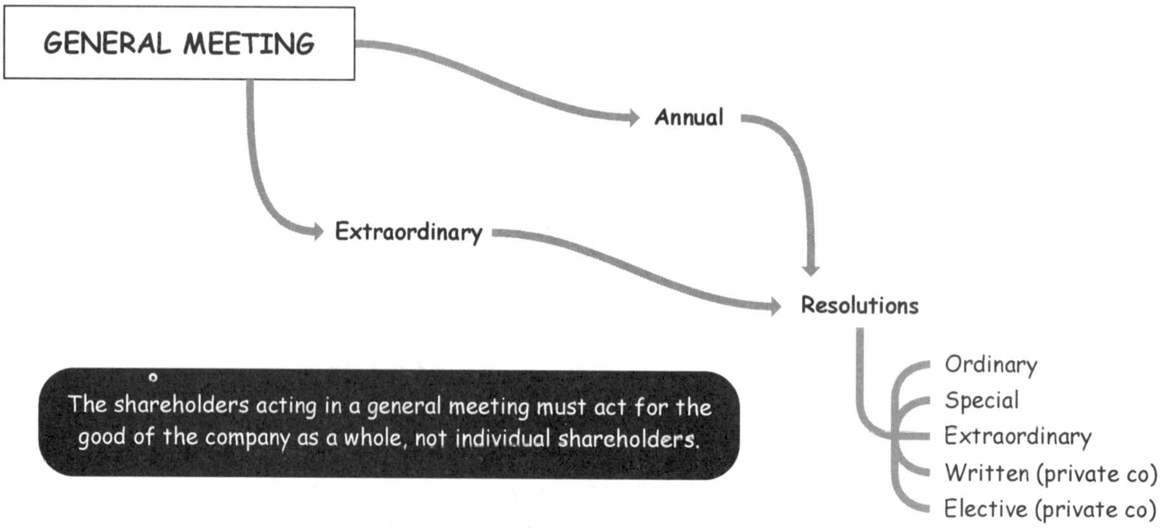

GENERAL MEETING
Annual
Extraordinary
Resolutions
Ordinary
Special
Extraordinary
Written (private co)
Elective (private co)
The shareholders acting in a general meeting must act for the good of the company as a whole, not individual shareholders.

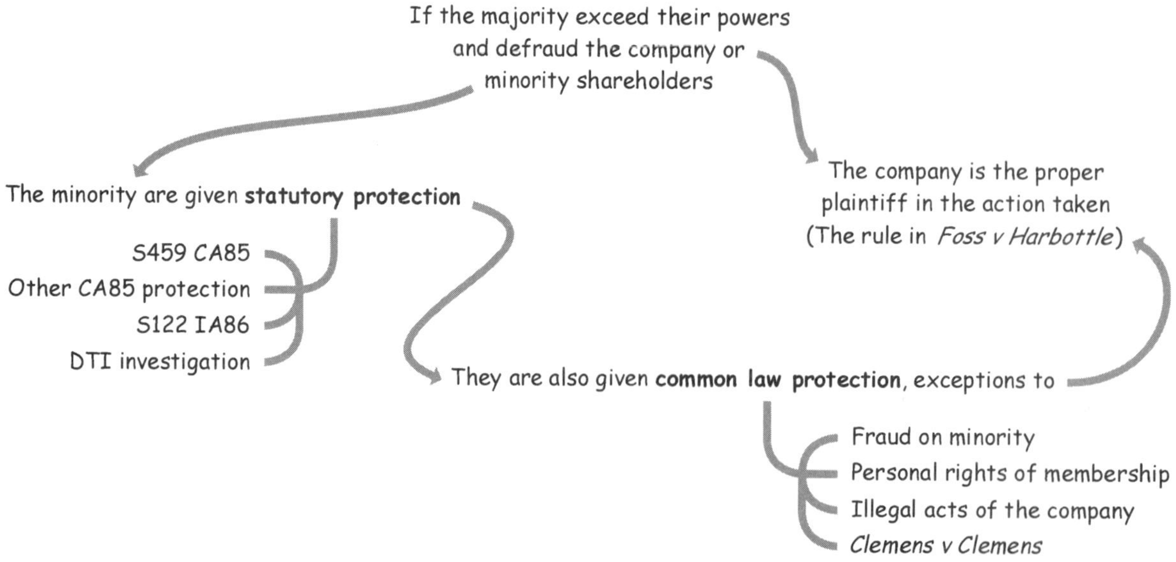

If the majority exceed their powers and defraud the company or minority shareholders
The minority are given statutory protection
S459 CA85
Other CA85 protection
S122 IA86
DTI investigation
The company is the proper plaintiff in the action taken (The rule in Foss v Harbottle)
They are also given common law protection, exceptions to
Fraud on minority
Personal rights of membership
Illegal acts of the company
Clemens v Clemens

Chapter 10

MEETINGS

Topic list		Syllabus reference	Ability required
1	The importance of meetings	(vii)	Comprehension
2	Board meetings	(vii)	Comprehension
3	General meetings	(vii)	Comprehension
4	Types of resolution	(vii)	Comprehension
5	Convening a meeting	(vii)	Comprehension
6	Proceedings at meetings	(vii)	Comprehension
7	Class meetings	(vii)	Comprehension

Introduction

In this chapter we consider the **procedures** by which companies are managed and controlled, namely board and general meetings. **Board meetings** are where directors meet to discuss management issues. **General meetings** afford members a measure of protection of their investment in the company. There are many transactions which, under the Act, cannot be entered into without a **resolution** of the company in general meeting.

Moreover, a general meeting at which the annual accounts and the auditors' and directors' reports will be laid must normally be held annually, thus affording the members an opportunity of questioning the directors on their **stewardship**.

For the exam you must be quite clear about the different types of resolution, when each type is used, and the percentage vote needed for each type to be passed.

Learning outcomes covered in this chapter

- Explain the use and procedure of board meetings and general meetings of shareholders
- Explain the voting rights of directors and shareholders
- Identify the various types of shareholder resolutions

Syllabus content covered in this chapter

- Board meetings; when used and the procedure at the meeting
- Annual and Extraordinary General Meetings; when used and the procedure at the meeting
- Company resolutions and the uses of each type of resolution

1 THE IMPORTANCE OF MEETINGS

Decisions reserved for members

1.1 Although the management of a company, including important decisions on, for instance, making business contracts, is in the hands of the directors, the **decisions which affect the existence of the company**, its structure and scope, (that is, constitutional issues) are **reserved to the members** in general meeting.

Control over directors

1.2 The members in general meeting can exercise control over the directors, though only to a limited extent.

(a) Under normal procedure (Table A Article 73) one third of the directors retire at each annual general meeting though they may offer themselves for re-election. The company may remove directors from office by **ordinary resolution**: s 303.

(b) Member approval in general meeting is required if the directors wish to:

- **Exceed their delegated power** or to use it for other than its given purpose
- **Allot shares**
- **Make a substantial contract** of sale or purchase with a director
- Grant a director a **long-service agreement**: ss 80, 320 and 319

(c) The **appointment and removal of auditors** is normally done in general meeting: s 385.

Resolution of differences

1.3 Finally, general meetings are the means by which **members resolve differences** between themselves by voting on resolutions.

2 BOARD MEETINGS

KEY TERM

The **board of directors** is the elected representative of the shareholders acting collectively in the management of a company's affairs.

2.1 One of the basic principles of company law is that the powers which are delegated to the directors under the articles (Table A Article 70) are given to them as a **collective body.** The **board meeting** is the proper place for the exercise of those powers.

2.2 The directors can unanimously assent on issues without meeting by a 'signed resolution procedure' . Any resolution signed by all the directors entitled to attend a board meeting will be valid, as if it had been decided at a board meeting.

Content of the notice

2.3 Notice of the business, in the form of an agenda, is usually given. Some items of business are discussion of lengthy papers, such as management reports or proposals for new projects. Directors cannot usually discuss such matters adequately without having read the papers before the meeting.

2.4 The period of notice given to convene a board meeting need be **no longer** than is **reasonable** to enable directors to attend. Even five minutes' notice has been held reasonable, where the director in question was free to attend and close at hand.

Quorum for a board meeting

2.5 In order to constitute a board meeting, as any other a properly appointed chairman must preside, and a quorum must be present.

2.6 Most companies have articles (Table A Article 89) which provide that:

> 'The quorum for the transaction of the business of the directors may be fixed by the directors and unless so fixed at any other number shall be two.'

2.7 Table A Article 90 provides for a fall in number of directors to less than quorum level.

> 'The continuing directors or a sole continuing director may act notwithstanding any vacancies in their number but, if the number of directors is less than the number fixed as the quorum, the continuing directors or director may act only for the purpose of *filling vacancies* or of *calling a general meeting*.'

2.8 Note also that on each item of business, any director who is disqualified from voting by having a personal interest may have to be excluded in reckoning the quorum for that item.

The chairman

2.9 The directors of a company may appoint one of their number to be **chairman** of the board of directors.

2.10 The directors may at any time remove the chairman of the board from his office.

2.11 The chairman presides at meetings of the board, and is responsible for:

- **Ensuring** that the **functions** of the **board** are **carried out**
- Ensuring that the **meeting proceeds** in an **efficient manner**, without unnecessary or irrelevant discussion, and with a reasonable cross-section of views being heard
- **Providing** an **agenda** for the board meetings (and any necessary documentation, although the secretary would handle the paperwork)

Agenda for a board meeting

2.12 The agenda will vary according to the type and formality of the meeting and the particular business to be discussed. A typical agenda might include the following.

- Membership
- Apologies for absence
- Minutes of the last meeting
- Matters arising from the minutes
- Business of the present meeting, presentation of reports, resolutions etc.
- Any other business
- Date of the next meeting

Conduct of board meetings

Pilot Paper

2.13 There are some aspects of procedure which should be strictly observed.

(a) The discussion should **follow** the **sequence** of the **agenda**, and be confined at each stage to the item currently under discussion.

(b) Although it is not usually necessary to take a vote, the chairman should sum up '**the sense of the meeting**', so that a suitably worded decision or conclusion may be formulated for inclusion in the minutes.

(c) If a vote does appear to be necessary, it will be along the lines of a show of hands or voice vote. The usual procedure is to '**go round the table**' inviting each member of the board to declare his vote for or against. If any member abstains, perhaps because a personal interest does not allow him to vote, this should be noted and recorded.

(d) Each member of the board, including the chairman, has **one vote**. The **articles** may provide otherwise, say by weighted voting or a veto given to a particular. The chairman **may** also be given a casting vote, with which to resolve a tied issue.

Sole director and board meetings

2.14 In *Re Neptune Vehicle Washing Equipment Ltd 1995* it was held that a sole director could hold a meeting with a company secretary or by himself. Even if holding a meeting alone a director had to make and minute a declaration of interests in contracts, pausing for thought over potential conflicts of interest.

3 GENERAL MEETINGS

3.1 There are two kinds of general meeting of members of a company:

- **Annual general meeting** (AGM)
- **Extraordinary general meeting** (EGM)

Exam focus point

You should appreciate the difference between AGMs and EGMs.

Annual general meetings

3.2 The AGM plays a major role in the life of a company although often the business carried out seems fairly routine. It is a statutorily protected way for members to have a regular assessment and discussion of their company and its management.

Rules for directors calling an AGM	
Timing s 366	• Every company **must** hold an AGM in **each** (calendar) **year** • Not more than **fifteen months** may elapse between meetings • First AGM must be held within **eighteen months** of incorporation (i.e. the first AGM doesn't necessarily have to be in the first or following calendar year.
Notice s 369	• Must be in **writing** and **in accordance with the articles** • At least **21 days** notice should be given • **Shorter** notice is only valid if **all** members agree to attend • The notice **must specify** the meeting of an AGM

Rules for directors calling an AGM	
Dispensation s 366A	• **Private** companies may **dispense** with holding an AGM • They must pass an **elective resolution** (see later)
Default s 357	• If the directors **fail to call an AGM**, the members may apply to the DTI • If they do, the **DTI may call the AGM** • They may give any direction necessary: modify the articles or file a quorum of one.

3.3 The business of an annual general meeting usually includes:

- Considering the accounts
- Receiving the directors' report and the auditors' report
- Dividends
- Electing directors

Extraordinary general meetings

Directors

3.4 The **directors** have power under the articles to convene an EGM whenever they see fit: Table A Article 37.

Members

3.5 The directors may be required to convene an EGM by **requisition of the members.**

Rules for members requisitioning an EGM (s 368)	
Shareholding	• The requisitioning members **must hold** at least **1/10** of the **paid up** share capital **holding voting rights** • If there is no share capital, they **must** represent **1/10** of the **voting rights**
Requisition	• They must deposit a **signed requisition** at the **registered office** • This must state the 'objects of the meeting': the **resolutions proposed**
Date	• The meeting must be called within **28 days** of the notice • If the directors have not called the meeting within 21 days of the members issuing the notice, **the members** may convene the meeting for a date within 3 months of the deposit of the requisition
Quorum	• Under Table A (Article 41) if no quorum is present, the meeting is adjourned.

Court order

3.6 The court, on the application of a director or a member, may order that an EGM shall be held and may give instructions for that purpose including fixing a quorum of one.

3.7 This is a method of last resort to resolve a deadlock such as the refusal of one member out of two to attend (and provide a quorum) at an EGM: s 371.

Auditor requisition

3.8 An auditor who gives a statement of circumstances for his resignation or other loss of office (s 394) in his written notice may also requisition a meeting to receive and consider his explanation: s 392A.

Loss of capital by public company

3.9 The directors of a public company must convene an extraordinary general meeting if the net assets fall to half or less of the amount of its called-up share capital: s 142.

4 TYPES OF RESOLUTION 5/01, 11/01, 5/02

4.1 A meeting reaches a decision by passing a resolution. There are three major kinds of resolution, and an additional two introduced by the Companies Act 1989.

TYPE OF RESOLUTION	
Ordinary	Requires simple (50%+) majority 14 days notice
Extraordinary	Requires 75% majority 14 days notice
Special	Requires 75% majority 21 days notice
Elective	Five situations (see below) All members must vote in favour 21 days notice
Written	Can be used for all GM resolutions except those needing special notice All members must vote in favour

Differences between ordinary, special and extraordinary resolutions

4.2 Apart from the required size of the majority and period of notice, the main differences between the types of resolution are as follows.

(a) The **text** of **special** and **extraordinary** resolutions must be **set out** in **full** in the notice convening the meeting (and they must be described as special or extraordinary resolutions): s 378. This is not necessary for an ordinary resolution if it is routine business.

(b) A **signed copy** of every **special** and **extraordinary resolution** (and equivalent decisions by unanimous consent of members) must be **delivered** to the **registrar** for filing. **Some ordinary resolutions**, particularly those relating to share capital, have to be **delivered** for filing but many do not.

Special resolutions

4.3 A special resolution is required for major changes in the company such as the following.

- A change of name
- Alteration of the objects or of the articles
- Reduction of share capital
- Winding up the company
- Presenting a petition by the company for an order for a compulsory winding up

Question 1

The period of notice for an EGM at which a special resolution is proposed is:

A 14 days
B 21 days
C 28 days
D 42 days

Answer

B.

Extraordinary resolutions

4.4 An extraordinary resolution suffices to put the company into creditors' voluntary liquidation (where the shorter period of notice may be an advantage).

Elective resolutions

4.5 The elective resolution required is part of a wider scheme of de-regulation for private companies introduced by the 1989 Companies Act. An elective resolution may be passed by a **private** company in any one of five situations.

- To confer **authority to issue shares indefinitely** or for a **fixed period** which may **exceed five years**: s 80A
- To **dispense with the laying of accounts** before a general meeting, unless a member or the auditors require it: s 252
- To **dispense with holding an AGM** unless a member requires it: s 366A
- To **reduce the 95% majority** needed to consent to short notice under ss 369(4) or 378(3), to a figure of not less than **90%**
- To **dispense with the annual appointment of auditors** (so that the incumbent auditors are automatically re-appointed): s 386

4.6 To pass such a resolution, **all** the members entitled to attend and vote must agree: s 379A. **21 days notice** is required. This can be waived provided all members entitled to attend and vote at the meeting agree. The resolution must be registered within 15 days.

4.7 An elective resolution may be revoked by ordinary resolution (s 379A(3)) but this must also be registered: s 380(4).

Written resolutions

4.8 Anything that a private company could do by a resolution of a general meeting or a class meeting may be done by a written resolution.

4.9 All **members entitled** to **attend** and **vote** must **sign** the **resolution**: s 381A(1). This may be achieved by sending each member a separate document, as long as they all set out the resolution.

4.10 The procedure can be used to bypass **any** of the other four types of resolution: s 381(A)(b). A written resolution suffices, because such a resolution is provided to be **equivalent** to a resolution passed in general meeting.

4.11 Three further points should be noted concerning written resolutions.

(a) Written resolutions can be used **notwithstanding any provisions** in the company's **articles**.

(b) A written resolution **cannot** be **used to remove a director or auditor** from office, since such persons have a right to **speak** at a **meeting**.

(c) **Copies of written resolutions** should be **sent to auditors** at or before the time they are sent to shareholders. Under s 381B auditors do not have the right to object to written resolutions. If the auditors are not sent a copy, the resolution remains valid; however the directors and secretary will be liable to a fine. The purpose of this provision is to ensure auditors are kept informed about what is happening in the company.

Question 2

Briefly explain the main features of the following types of resolution which may be passed at a general meeting of a company:

(a) An ordinary resolution
(b) An extraordinary resolution
(c) A special resolution

Answer

(a) Ordinary resolutions require a simple majority of votes cast (ie over 50%). Usually 14 days notice is sufficient. Ordinary resolutions of a routine nature need not be set out in full in the notice of an annual general meeting, and most ordinary resolutions need not be filed with the Registrar of Companies.

In certain circumstances, however, special notice of 28 days is required, namely for removal of an auditor or appointment of an auditor who was not appointed at the previous year's meeting (s 391A), for reappointment of a director aged over 70 where the age limit applies (s 293) and for removal of a director or appointment of a substitute director following such removal (s 303).

In these cases, 28 days special notice must be given to the company and to all company members at the same time and in the same form as notice of the meeting. If it is impracticable, however, to include notice of the resolution in the notice of the meeting, the company may give notice to members by newspaper advertisement or other means permitted by the articles, not less than 21 days before the meeting.

(b) Extraordinary resolutions require a majority of 75% of the votes cast at the meeting (in person or by proxy) and 14 days' notice of the intention to propose such a resolution. The text of the resolution should be set out in the notice of the meeting and the resolution should be filed with the Registrar within 15 days of being passed: s 380.

Matters for which an extraordinary resolution will be required may be specified in the company's articles. An extraordinary resolution is required under the Companies Act to vary class rights in certain circumstances. The Insolvency Act 1986 also provides that an extraordinary resolution is required to begin a voluntary winding up where the company is unable to meet its debts and to give certain powers to the liquidator in a member's voluntary winding-up.

(c) Special resolutions also require a 75% majority of votes cast (in person or by proxy) but require 21 days notice of the intention to propose such a resolution (members holding shares constituting 95% or more of share capital can waive the notice requirement: s 378(3)). Various provisions in the Companies Acts specify that a special resolution will be required, including a change of name, alteration of the articles (s 9) or objects clause (s 4) of the company, reduction of the share capital (s 135), re-registration as a public (s 43) or private (s 53) company, authorisation of the redemption or purchase of the shares of a private company out of capital (s 173) and presentation of a petition for a compulsory winding-up order.

As with extraordinary resolutions, the text of the notice should be set out in the notice of the meeting, and the resolution should be filed with the Registrar within 15 days of being passed: s 380.

5 CONVENING A MEETING

5.1 A meeting cannot make valid and binding decisions until it has been properly convened.

(a) The meeting must generally be **called by** the **board of directors** or other competent person or authority.

(b) The notice must be issued to members in advance of the meeting so as to give them **14 to 21 days** 'clear notice' of the meeting. The members may agree to waive this requirement.

(c) The **notice** must be sent to every member (or other person) entitled to receive the notice.

(d) The notice need **not** be sent to:

- A member whose only shares do not give him a right to attend and vote (as is often the position of **preference shareholders**)
- A **joint holder** of voting shares who is **not the first named holder** on the register

(e) If, however, the business to be done must by law be '**disclosed**' to all members, then notice of it must be sent **even** to members who are not entitled to vote on it.

(f) The notice must include any information **reasonably necessary** to enable shareholders to know in advance what is to be done.

Timing of notices **Pilot Paper**

5.2 For an AGM, or an EGM at which a special resolution is proposed, the required period of notice is **21 days**. In any other case the standard period is **14 days:** s 369.

5.3 Members may - and in small private companies often do - waive the required 21 or 14 days notice. For a waiver:

(a) All **members** must consent in respect of an **AGM**.

(b) In **any other case** a **majority of members** who hold at least **95 per cent** of the **issued shares** carrying voting rights (or if the company has no share capital, who represent 95 per cent of the voting rights) is required. This may be reduced (under s 369(4)) for a private company which passes an elective resolution to this effect, but not to less than **90 per cent.**

5.4 The following specific rules by way of exception should be remembered.

(a) When **special notice** of a resolution is given to the company in three circumstances mentioned below, it must be given **28 days or 6 weeks** in advance as prescribed.

(b) In a **creditors' voluntary winding up** there must be at least **7 days notice** of the **creditors' meeting** (to protect the interests of creditors). The members may shorten the period of notice down to 7 days but that is all: s 98 IA.

5.5 **Notices** may be given to members **personally** or sent to them by **post** or other delivery to their registered address. If the notice is properly addressed and stamped the addressee is deemed to receive it **48 hours** after posting.

Special notice of a resolution

KEY TERM

Special notice is notice of 28 days which must be given to a company of the intention to put certain types of resolution at a company meeting.

5.6 **Special notice** must be given **to the company** of the intention to propose a resolution for any of the following purposes.

- To **remove** an **auditor** or to **appoint** an **auditor other** than the **auditor** who was **appointed** at the **previous year's meeting**: s 391A
- To **reappoint** a **director aged more than 70** where the age limit applies: s 293
- To **remove a director from office** or to appoint a substitute in his place after removal: s 303

5.7 When special notice is given under s 379 the sequence is as follows.

Step 1. **Member** gives **notice** to the **company** of intention to propose relevant resolution **28 days** prior to the meeting.

Step 2. **Company** determines whether it is **required to include** the **resolution in the AGM notices** it issues to members.

Step 3. **Company** gives **notice** of the resolution to members **21 days** prior to the meeting (via Step 2 or in newspaper or other permitted methods).

Step 4. For resolutions to remove **directors** or **auditors,** the company must send a copy to the relevant director or auditor.

Requisitioning a resolution

5.8 The directors normally have the right to decide what resolutions shall be included in the notice of a meeting. However (apart from the requisition of an EGM) members can take the initiative if they represent at least **one-twentieth of the voting rights** or are at least 100 members holding shares on which there has been paid up an average per member of at least £100: s 376. These members may, under s 377:

(a) By **requisition** delivered at least **6 weeks in advance** of an **AGM or EGM** require the company to **give notice** to members of a **resolution** which they wish to move (these may include any type of resolution)

(b) By **requisition** delivered at least **one week in advance** of an **AGM or EGM** require the company to circulate to members a **statement** not exceeding 1,000 words in length

5.9 In either instance, the **requisitionists** must bear the incidental costs unless the company otherwise resolves.

Content of notices

5.10 The notice of a general meeting must contain adequate information on the following points.

- The **date, time** and **place** of the meeting must be given.
- An **AGM** or a **special** or **extraordinary resolution** must be described as such.

- Information must be given of the business of the meeting **sufficient** to enable members (in deciding whether to attend or to appoint proxies) to **understand what will be done** at the meeting.

Special business

5.11 The nature of non-routine business makes it necessary to set out in the notice convening the meeting the full **verbatim** text of the relevant resolution.

5.12 Section summary

- Meetings must be called by a **competent person** or authority.
- **Clear notice** (21 days AGM/EGM with special resolutions, 14 days otherwise) must be given to members.
- **Notice** must be **sent to all members** entitled to receive it.
- **Special notice of 28 days** of intention to propose certain resolutions (removal of directors/auditors) must be given.
- The notice convening the meeting must give certain details.
  - Date, time and place of the meeting
  - Identification of AGM, special and extraordinary resolutions
  - Sufficient information about business to be discussed at the meeting to enable shareholders to know what is to be done

Question 3

(a) How can members remove a director from office? What is the significance of special notice in this context?

(b) When is a company compelled to call an extraordinary general meeting?

Answer

(a) There is a procedure under ss 303-304 Companies Act 1985 by which a company may by ordinary resolution remove any director from office, notwithstanding any provision to the contrary in the articles or in a contract such as a director's service agreement.

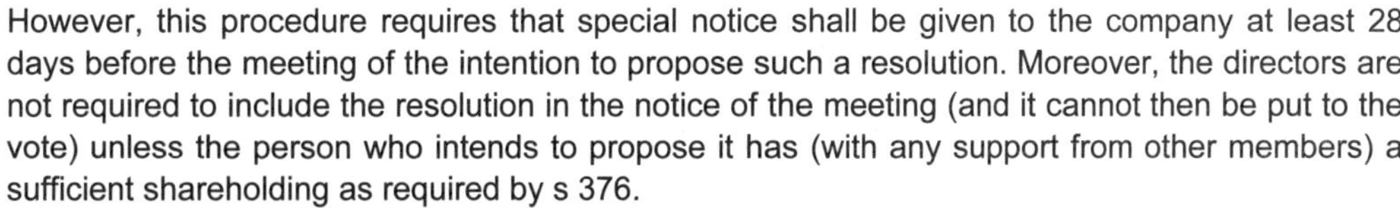

However, this procedure requires that special notice shall be given to the company at least 28 days before the meeting of the intention to propose such a resolution. Moreover, the directors are not required to include the resolution in the notice of the meeting (and it cannot then be put to the vote) unless the person who intends to propose it has (with any support from other members) a sufficient shareholding as required by s 376.

If a company receives special notice it must forthwith send a copy to the director concerned who has the right to have written representations of reasonable length circulated to members and to speak before the resolution is put to the vote at the meeting.

(b) Members of a company who hold not less than one tenth of the company's paid up share capital carrying voting rights, may requisition the holding of a extraordinary general meeting. As this is a public company it must have a share capital and the alternative qualification does not arise. The directors are then required within 21 days of the deposit of the requisition to issue a notice convening the meeting to transact the business specified in the requisition, for a date not more than 28 days hence: s 368.

An auditor who resigns giving reasons for his resignation may requisition an extraordinary general meeting so that he may explain to members the circumstances of his resignation: s 392A.

If the net assets of a public company are reduced to less than half in value of its called-up share capital, it is the duty of the directors to convene (within 28 days of becoming aware of this situation) an extraordinary general meeting to consider what, if any, steps should be taken: s 142.

The Department of Trade (s 367) and the court (s 371) have statutory power in certain circumstances to direct that a meeting shall be held.

6 PROCEEDINGS AT MEETINGS

6.1 A meeting can only reach binding decisions if:

- It has been properly **convened** by notice. (See Section 6.)
- A **quorum is present.**
- A **chairman presides**.
- The **business** is **properly transacted** and **resolutions** are **put to the vote.**

6.2 There is no obligation to allow a member to be present if his shares do not carry the right to attend and vote. Full general meetings and class meetings can be held when shareholders not entitled to vote are present.

Quorum

KEY TERM

A **quorum** is the minimum number of persons required to be present at a particular type of (company) meeting. For a meeting of a board of directors, the number is two under Table A unless the directors have provided to the contrary. In the case of shareholders' meetings, again the Table A figure is two, in person or by proxy, but the articles may make other provisions.

6.3 There is a legal principle that a 'meeting means a coming together of more than one person'.

6.4 The rule that at least two persons must be present to constitute a 'meeting' does not require that both persons must be members, because every member has a **statutory right** to **appoint a proxy** (who does not have to be a member – see below) to attend as his representative. Hence one member and another member's proxy may together provide the quorum (if it is fixed, as is usual, at 'two members present in person or by proxy').

6.5 However one member who is also the proxy appointed by another member cannot by himself be a meeting, since a minimum of two individuals present is required.

6.6 There may, however, be a meeting attended by one person only, if:

(a) It is a **class meeting** and all the **shares** of that class are **held** by **one member.**

(b) The **DTI** or the **court**, in exercising a power to order a general meeting to be held, **fixes** the **quorum** at one: ss 367 and 371; this means that in a two-member company, a meeting can be held with one person if the other deliberately absents himself to frustrate business.

(c) The company is a **single member private company**: s 370A.

6.7 The articles usually fix a quorum for general meetings which may be as low as two (the minimum for a meeting) but may be more - though this is unusual. The Table A quorum is two persons **entitled to vote** who may be members, proxies or authorised representatives of corporate members: Article 40.

The chairman

6.8 The articles usually provide that the chairman of the board of directors is to preside at general meetings; in his absence another director chosen by the directors shall. In the last resort a member chosen by the members present can preside.

6.9 The chairman derives his authority from the articles and he has no casting vote unless the articles give him one. His duties are to **maintain order** and to **deal** with the **agenda** in a methodical way so that the business of the meeting may be properly transacted.

Adjournment

6.10 The chairman may **dissolve** or **adjourn** the **meeting** if it has become disorderly or if the members present agree. He must adjourn if the meeting instructs him to do so.

6.11 The articles may provide that the chairman of a meeting can adjourn a general meeting **only with its consent**. The chairman, however has a residual common-law power to hold a meeting over if this is essential for the business to be conducted in a proper way and where the machinery of the articles has effectively broken down.

Amendments to resolutions

6.12 Members may propose amendments to the resolution. The chairman should reject any amendment which is outside the limits set by the notice convening the meeting.

6.13 If the relevant business is an ordinary resolution it may be possible to amend it so as to **reduce its effect** to something less (provided that the change does not entirely alter its character). An ordinary resolution authorising the directors to borrow £100,000 might be amended to substitute a limit of £50,000 (but not to increase it to £150,000 as £100,000 would have been stated in the notice). It is not possible to pass a special or extraordinary resolution which differs in substance from the text set out in the notice.

Proxies

KEY TERM

A **proxy** is a person appointed by a shareholder to vote on behalf of that shareholder at company meetings.

6.14 Any member of a company which has a share capital, if he is entitled to attend and vote at a general or class meeting of the company, has a **statutory right** (s 372) to **appoint** an agent, called a '**proxy**', to attend and vote for him. The rules are as follows.

Rules for appointing proxies		
Basic rule	• Any member may appoint a proxy • The proxy does not have to be a member	
Private company	• Member may appoint **one** proxy • Proxy may **speak** at meeting	ARTICLES MAY VARY THIS RIGHT
Public company	• Member may appoint **more than one** proxy • Proxy may **not speak** at meeting	
Voting	• Proxy **may vote** on **poll** but **not** on **show of hands**	ARTICLES MAY VARY THIS RIGHT
Notice	• Every notice of a meeting must **state** the member's right to a proxy	
Cards	• Directors may issue proxy appointment cards to all members • Articles may require that cards are **only valid** if received up to 48 hours before meeting	ARTICLES MAY **NOT** LENGTHEN THIS PERIOD

6.15 Although a proxy may not vote on a show of hands he has the same right to demand or join with other members in demanding a poll as the member whom he represents: s 373.

Voting and polls

6.16 The **rights of members** to **vote** and the **number of votes** to which they are entitled in respect of their shares are fixed by the **articles**. One vote per share is normal but some shares, for instance preference shares, may carry no voting rights in normal circumstances. To shorten the proceedings at meetings the procedure is as follows.

Voting on a show of hands

KEY TERM

A **show of hands** is a method of voting for or against a resolution by raising hands. Under this method each member has one vote irrespective of the number of shares held, in contrast to a poll vote.

6.17 On putting a resolution to the vote the chairman calls for a show of hands. One vote may be given by each member present in person; proxies do not vote.

6.18 Unless a poll is then demanded, the chairman's declaration of the result is conclusive. However it is still possible to challenge the chairman's declaration on the grounds that it was fraudulent or manifestly wrong.

Polls

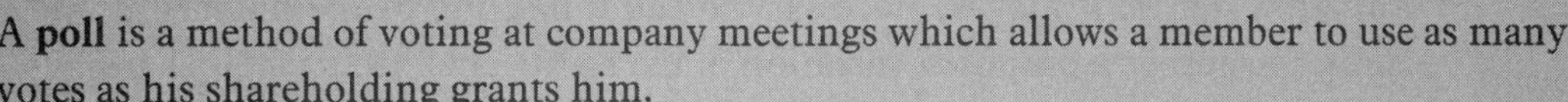

KEY TERM

A **poll** is a method of voting at company meetings which allows a member to use as many votes as his shareholding grants him.

6.19 If a real test of voting strength is required a poll may be demanded. The result of the previous show of hands is then disregarded. On a poll every member and also proxies representing absent members may cast the full number of votes to which they are entitled. A poll need not be held forthwith but may be postponed so that arrangements to hold it can be made.

6.20 A poll may be demanded by:

- Not **less than five members** (unless the articles permit a lesser figure)
- Member(s) representing **not less than one tenth of the total voting rights**
- Member(s) holding shares which represent **not less than one tenth of the paid-up capital**

Result of a vote

6.21 In voting either by show of hands or on a poll, the number of votes cast determines the result. Votes which are not cast, whether the member who does not use them is present or absent, are simply disregarded. Hence the majority vote may be much less than half (or three quarters) of the total votes which could be cast.

Minutes

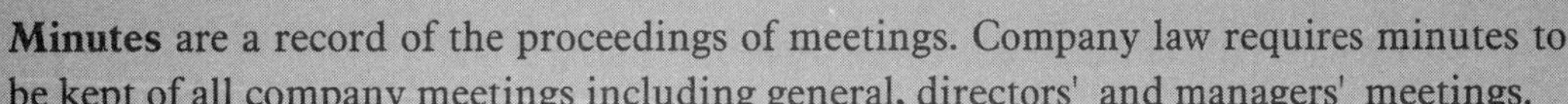

KEY TERM

Minutes are a record of the proceedings of meetings. Company law requires minutes to be kept of all company meetings including general, directors' and managers' meetings.

6.22 Every company is required to keep minutes which are a formal written record of the proceedings of its general meetings and of the meetings of its directors (and managers if any): s 382.

6.23 Members of the company have the right to inspect minutes of general meetings but not of board meetings: s 383. The minutes of general meetings must be held at the registered office available for inspection by members who are also entitled to demand copies.

The assent principle

6.24 A unanimous decision of the members is often treated as a substitute for a formal decision in general meeting properly convened and held, and is equally binding.

7 CLASS MEETINGS

7.1 Class meetings are of two kinds.

(a) If the company has more than one class of share, for example if it has 'preference' and 'ordinary' shares, it may be necessary to call a meeting of the holders of one class of shares, to approve a proposed **variation** of the **rights** attached to their shares.

(b) Under the procedure for a '**scheme of arrangement**' (s 425), the holders of shares of the same class may nonetheless be divided into **separate** classes (for whom separate meetings are required) if the scheme proposed will affect each group differently.

7.2 When separate meetings of a class of members are held, the same procedural rules as for general meetings apply (but there is a different rule on quorum).

Quorum for a class meeting

7.3 Under s 125 the standard general meeting rules, on issuing notices and on voting, apply to a class meeting.

7.4 However the **quorum** for a class meeting is fixed at two persons who hold, or represent by proxy, at least one third in nominal value of the issued shares of the class (unless the class only consists of a single member).

7.5 If no quorum is present, the meeting is **adjourned** (under the standard adjournment procedure for general meetings). When the meeting resumes, the quorum is **one** person (who must still hold at least one third of the shares).

Question 4

Which one of the following is *not* a situation in which a meeting may be validly held that is attended by only one person?

A A class meeting where all the shares are held by one member

B Where the articles provide a quorum of one for a general meeting, and the company is not a single member company

C Where the DTI has fixed a quorum for a general meeting at one

D A board meeting

Answer

B. The articles cannot override the general principle that a meeting consists of more than one person, although the DTI can (C). A is however a situation where only one person is eligible to attend, and a private company may only have one director (D).

Chapter roundup

- In this chapter we have discussed the various types of meeting that a company holds.
- In particular we have concentrated on the formalities and proceedings of general meetings.
- The directors can exercise their powers by holding **board meetings.**
- There are two types of general meeting of a company.
  - **Annual general meeting**
  - **Extraordinary general meeting**
- Notice of general meetings must be given **14 or 21 days** in advance of the meeting.
- The notice should contain **adequate information** about the meeting.
- The **quorum** for meetings may be two or more (except for single member private companies).
- **Proxies** can attend and vote on behalf of members. Only private company proxies have the right to speak.
- A meeting can pass three types of resolution.
  - An **ordinary resolution**, carried by a simple majority of votes cast and requiring 14 days notice
  - An **extraordinary resolution**, carried by a 75 per cent majority of votes cast and requiring 14 days notice
  - A **special resolution**, requiring a 75 per cent majority of votes cast and 21 days notice
- An **elective resolution** may be passed by a private company in certain situations, for example to dispense with the annual appointment of auditors.
- Anything that a private company can do by a resolution of a general meeting or a class meeting may also be done by a **written resolution**.
- Voting at general meetings may be on a **show of hands** or a **poll**.
- A unanimous decision of the members is often treated as a substitute for a formal decision for general meetings and is equally binding (the **assent principle)**.

Quick quiz

1 Which of the following decisions can only be taken by the members in general meeting?

A Alteration of objects
B Alteration of articles
C Change of name
D Reduction of capital
E Appointment of a managing director

2 **Fill in the blanks** in the statements below

A poll may be demanded:

A By not less than .... members
B By members representing not less than .... of the total voting rights
C By members holding shares representing not less than .... of the paid-up capital

3 Before a private company can hold an extraordinary general meeting on short notice, members holding a certain percentage of the company's shares must agree. Which one of the following percentages is correct?

51%	60%
75%	90%

4 A company holds an AGM on 1 November 20X0 and holds its next AGM on 2 January 20X2. Explain, in no more than 40 words, whether this is legal.

5 Which one of the following statements is correct?

A A board of directors reaches decisions by a simple majority vote.

B A board of directors reaches decisions by following the procedure set down in the company's memorandum of association.

C A board of directors reaches decisions by following the procedure set down in the company's articles of association.

D A board of directors reaches decisions in the manner set down by the chairman of the board.

6 Give three examples of routine items of business of the AGM for which it is unnecessary to include in the notice the text of the relevant resolutions.

7 Under s 372, a member of a public company may only appoint one proxy, but the proxy has a statutory right to speak at the meeting.

☐ True

☐ False

8 An auditor may be removed from office before the expiry of his appointment by the passing of:

A A special resolution
B An extraordinary resolution
C An ordinary resolution
D An ordinary resolution with special notice

9 Match the following with the relevant notice period.

A Special resolution	(i)	14 days
B Extraordinary resolution	(ii)	21 days
C Special notice given to a company of an ordinary resolution	(iii)	28 days

10 List the purposes for which a private company may use an elective resolution.

11 Fill in the blanks.

Rules for directors calling an AGM	
Timing s 366	• Every company **......** hold an AGM in **each** .... • Not more than **...........** **months** may elapse between meetings • First AGM must be held within **.......................** of incorporation • That is first AGM doesn't have to be in the first or following calendar year.
Notice s 369	• Must be .... and **in accordance with the articles** • At least **.....** **days** notice should be given • **Shorter** notice is only valid if **.....** members agree to attend • The notice **must specify** the meeting of an AGM
Dispensation s 366A	• **.........** companies may **dispense** with holding an AGM • They must pass an **...........** **resolution**
Default s 357	• If the directors **fail to call an AGM**, the members may apply to .... • If they do, ... **may call the AGM** • They may give any direction necessary: modify the articles or file a quorum of one.

12 Re-order the steps associated with special notice for a resolution.

Step ... For resolutions to remove **directors** or **auditors,** the company must send a copy to the relevant director or auditor.

Step ... **Member** gives **notice** to the **company** of intention to propose relevant resolutions **28 days** prior to her meeting.

Step ... **Company** gives **notice** of the resolution to member **21 days** prior to the meeting (via Step 2 or in newspaper or other permitted methods).

Step ... **Company** determines whether it is **required to include** the **resolution in the AGM notice** it issues to members.

13 Link the resolution with its correct majority and notice period.

(a) Ordinary	(i) 14 days	(1) 100%
(b) Extraordinary	(ii) 21 days	(2) 75%
(c) Special	(iii) 14 days	(3) 75%
(d) Elective	(iv) 21 days	(4) 50(+)%

Answers to quick quiz

1 A, B, C and D. The board can appoint someone to be managing director, so E is incorrect.

2 A poll may be demanded:

A By not less than five members
B By members representing not less than one tenth of the total voting rights
C By members holding shares representing not less than one tenth of the paid-up capital

3 90%

4 No. Although the company has held the second AGM within 15 months of the first AGM, it should also have held the second AGM in the following calendar year, 20X1.

5 C

6 Declaration of dividends
Election of directors
Appointment of auditors and fixing of their remuneration

7 False. A *private* company member has the right only to appoint one proxy who can speak. Public company members can appoint more than one proxy, but they have no statutory right to speak.

8 D

9 Special resolution *21 days*
Extraordinary resolution *14 days*
Special notice given to a company of an ordinary resolution *28 days*

10 To confer authority to issue shares indefinitely or for a fixed period which may exceed five years

To dispense with the laying cf accounts before a general meeting, unless a member or the auditors require it

To dispense with holding an AGM unless a member requires it

To reduce the 95% majority needed to consent to short notice to a figure of not less than 90%

To dispense with the annual appointment of auditors

11

Rules for directors calling an AGM	
Timing s 366	• Every company **must** hold an AGM in **each** (calendar) **year** • Not more than **fifteen months** may elapse between meetings • First AGM must be held within **eighteen months** of incorporation • that is first AGM doesn't have to be in the first or following calendar year.
Notice s 369	• Must be in **writing** and **in accordance with the articles** • At least **21 days** notice should be given • **Shorter** notice is only valid if **all** members agree to attend • The notice **must specify** the meeting of an AGM
Dispensation s 366A	• **Private** companies may **dispense** with holding an AGM • They must pass an **elective resolution** (see later)
Default s 357	• If the directors **fail to call an AGM**, the members may apply to the DTI • If they do, the **DTI may call the AGM** • They may give any direction necessary: modify the articles or file a quorum of one.

12 ***Step 1.*** Member gives notice to the company of intention to propose relevant resolution 28 days prior the meeting.

Step 2. **Company** determine whether it is **required to include** the **resolution in the AGM notice** it issues to members.

Step 3. **Company** gives **notice** of the resolution to members **21 days** prior to the meeting (via Step 2 or in newspaper or other permitted methods).

Step 4. For resolutions to remove directors or auditors, the company must send a copy to the relevant director or auditor.

13 (a), (i), (4)
(b), (iii), (2)
(c), (ii), (3)
(d), (iv), (1)

The following relevant questions are included in the Exam Question Banks

You can attempt these now. However, we would advise you to attempt these as mock exams at the end of your initial stage of study

Exam Question Bank	Numbers
Paper based format	27
Computer based assessment	8, 30

Chapter 11

SECRETARY

Topic list		Syllabus reference	Ability required
1	Defining the company secretary	(ix)	Comprehension
2	Appointment the company secretary	(ix)	Comprehension
3	Powers of the company secretary	(ix)	Comprehension
4	Duties of the company secretary	(ix)	Comprehension

Introduction

The secretary is an important officer of the company. As you will see as you work through this and the next chapter, the secretary has less power and consequently fewer apparent duties to shareholders than a director, but they are nonetheless important in the running of the company.

Historically, the powers of a company secretary were extremely limited. Today, the law recognises the administrative role which the secretary has consequent powers to act in.

Public company secretaries are required to have certain qualifications, as discussed in section 2.

Learning outcomes covered in this chapter

- Explain the qualifications of the company secretary
- Explain the powers and duties of the company secretary

Syllabus content covered in this chapter

- The qualifications of the company secretary
- The powers and duties of the company secretary

1 DEFINING THE COMPANY SECRETARY

KEY TERM

A **company secretary** is an officer of a company appointed to carry out general administrative duties.

1.1 Every company must have a company secretary.

1.2 If there is only one director, the company secretary must be a different person to the **sole director**.

1.3 A **corporation** may be a secretary to a company, but Company A cannot have Company B as its secretary if Company B has a sole director who is also the sole director of Company A.

2 APPOINTMENT OF A COMPANY SECRETARY **Pilot Paper**

2.1 Any person or corporation can be the company secretary to a private limited company. There is no qualification requirement.

2.2 The directors of a **public company** must take all reasonable steps to ensure that the secretary is suitably qualified for the post by **knowledge and experience**. Under s 286, a public company secretary may be anyone who fulfils one of the following criteria:

- Was the **secretary** or **secretary's assistant** on **22 December 1980**
- Has been a **public company secretary** for at least **three** out of the **five years** previous to appointment
- Is a **member** of ACCA, ICAEW, ICAS, ICAI, ICSA, CIMA or CIPFA
- Is a **barrister, advocate** or **solicitor** in the UK
- Is a **person** who, by virtue of holding or **having** held **any other position** or being a member of any other body, **appears** to the directors to be **capable**

2.3 Two or more persons may be appointed **joint secretaries**. A company may appoint a deputy secretary who assists or acts in place of the secretary: s 283.

2.4 The term 'officer' (used in legislation) includes the secretary.

Exam focus point

Do not forget the distinction between the rules affecting the appointment of a secretary of a private company with that of a public company.

3 POWERS OF THE COMPANY SECRETARY

3.1 Many of the functions of the company secretary have **developed in recent years** as the size of companies has increased and their administration has come to require a specialist competent to deal with a variety of complicated matters.

3.2 At one time the functions of the secretary were very limited and he dealt with them strictly in accordance with instructions given to him. The law therefore treated him as a mere subordinate lacking authority to enter into contracts or to speak for the company.

3.3 In 1971 however the Court of Appeal **applied the principle of apparent authority** and recognised that it is a normal function of a company secretary to enter into contracts connected with the **administration** of the company, and hence the secretary has **apparent authority** to enter such contracts as far as a third party is concerned.

Panorama Developments (Guildford) Ltd v Fidelis Furnishing Fabrics Ltd 1971
The facts: B, the secretary of a company, ordered cars from a car hire firm, representing that they were required to meet the company's customers at London Airport. Instead he used the cars for his own purposes. The bill was not paid, so the car hire firm claimed payment from B's company.

Decision: B's company was liable, for he had apparent authority to make contracts such as the present one, which were concerned with the administrative side of its business. The decision recognises the general nature of a company secretary's duties.

3.4 The court also said that, if the issue had arisen, it **might not have treated the secretary as having apparent authority to make commercial contracts** such as buying or selling trade goods, since that is **not a normal duty** of the company secretary.

3.5 The company might by its actions give the secretary apparent authority to make commercial contracts but **positive actions** would be required; merely appointing someone company secretary would not be enough.

Exam focus point

The *Panorama* case was an important development in the law on the authority of the secretary.

4 DUTIES OF THE COMPANY SECRETARY

4.1 The Companies Act does not define the general duties of a company secretary since these will vary according to the size of the company and of its headquarters. The **standard minimum duties** of the secretary are as follows.

To make the arrangements incidental to meetings of the board of directors.

4.2 The secretary usually convenes the meetings (Table A Article 88), issues the agenda, collects or prepares the papers for submission to each meeting, attends the meeting, drafts the minutes and communicates decisions taken to employees or to outsiders.

To maintain the register of members

4.3 The secretary has this responsibility unless the work is contracted out to professional registrars. The secretary also keeps the other statutory registers and prepares the notices, returns and other documents which must be delivered to the registrar.

Acting as general administrator and head office manager

4.4 Duties include:

(a) Dealing with staff matters, office equipment and pensions, and conducting the company's correspondence with its legal advisers, members, government departments, trade associations and so on

(b) Being responsible for the accounts and taxation aspects of the company's business, unless the company has an accountant or finance department

Question 1

Faith is the company secretary of Recycle Ltd. In March 20X5 she hired a car from Kingfisher Ltd. She told Kingfisher Ltd that the car was for company business, but she asked for it to be delivered to her home address. Faith then used the car for private purposes and has now disappeared without paying the hire charge.

Advise the directors of Recycle Ltd whether they are bound by the agreements with Conifer Bank Ltd and Kingfisher Ltd.

Answer

The general duties and authority of a company secretary are not defined in the Companies Act. It is now accepted that a company secretary's general function is to enter into contracts connected with the administration of the company. In *Panorama Developments (Guildford) Ltd v Fidelis Furnishing Fabrics*

Ltd 1971 it was accepted that a company secretary was usually held out as having authority to enter into contracts of an administrative nature (as opposed to commercial contracts such as buying or selling trade goods) and so such activity would be regarded as being within his or her ostensible authority.

The contract entered into by Faith in the name of the company is one of an administrative nature within her apparent authority as company secretary. As a result Recycle Ltd is bound by the contract with Kingfisher Ltd.

Chapter roundup

- Every company must have a secretary
- A public company must appoint a secretary who meets one of the following criteria:
  - Was the secretary or secretary's assistant on 22 December 1980
  - Has been a public company secretary for 3 out of the last 5 years
  - Is a member of ACCA, ICEAW, ICAS, ICAI, ICSA, CIMA, CIPFA
  - Is a barrister, advocate of solicitor in the UK
  - Is any person who, by virtue of holding or having held any other position or being a member of any other body, appears to the directors to be capable.
- A secretary has apparent authority to bind the company in a contract relating to administrative matters.
- The standard minimum duties of a secretary are to make incidental arrangements for board meetings, to maintain the register of members and to act as a general administrator.

Quick quiz

1 In relation to the company secretary, which one of the following statements is incorrect?

A Both a public company and a private company must have a company secretary
B In a private company, a sole director cannot also act as the company secretary
C In a public company, the company secretary must be qualified
D A company secretary can bind a company in contract if acting outside his or her actual or apparent authority

2 What details must the register of directors give about the company secretary?

3 What are the conditions, one of which must be fulfilled by a public company secretary?

4 The judgement in the *Panorama Developments* case made it clear that a company secretary has full authority to make commercial contracts on a company's behalf.

☐ True

☐ False

Answers to quick quiz

1 D

2 Present and former forenames and surnames, and residential address.

3 A public company secretary may be anyone who:

- Was the secretary or secretary's assistant on 22 December 1980, or
- Has been a public company secretary for at least three out of the five years previous to appointment, or
- Is a member of ACCA, ICAEW, ICAS, ICAI, ICSA, CIMA or CIPFA, or
- Is a barrister, advocate or solicitor in the UK, or
- Is a person who, by virtue of holding or having held any other position or being a member of any other body, appears to the directors to be capable

4 False. Under the judgement the secretary has authority to make contracts of an *administrative* nature.

The following relevant questions are included in the Exam Question Banks

You can attempt these now. However, we would advise you to attempt these as mock exams at the end of your initial stage of study

Exam Question Bank	Numbers
Paper based format	-
Computer based assessment	10

Chapter 12

DIRECTORS

	Topic list	Syllabus reference	Ability required
1	Defining directors	(ix)	Comprehension
2	Appointment of directors	(ix)	Comprehension
3	Vacation of office	(ix)	Comprehension
4	Control of directors	(ix)	Comprehension
5	Directors' powers	(ix)	Comprehension
6	Directors' duties	(ix)	Comprehension
7	Breach of duties	(ix)	Comprehension

Introduction

A company, being an abstract person, cannot manage itself. Company law therefore requires that every company shall have one or more directors and a secretary. Since directors are in control of the assets (which are often very valuable), they are subject to an elaborate code of rules which broadly cover three main topics:

(a) **Who is a director** (and therefore subject to the rules), how a director is appointed to his office and when he ceases to be a director, also who should be appointed as a secretary

(b) **What standard of honest and disinterested service is required of directors** and also what standard of competence; this principle is developed by a number of statutory rules on particular transactions

(c) **What are the powers of directors** and how they exercise those powers, whether the members of the company control them in their management function and whether the company whom they represent is liable if the directors exceed their delegated powers

The duties of directors can conveniently be discussed under two headings.

- **Fiduciary duties** of loyalty and good faith
- **Duties of care and skill**

We then consider the specific statutory offences of **insider dealing**, and **fraudulent and wrongful trading**. Fraudulent and wrongful trading relate to insolvency situations, where directors have been guilty of fraud or failed to take appropriate steps to minimise the losses of creditors.

Both fraudulent and wrongful trading are grounds for disqualifying directors; we look here at why directors might be disqualified.

The important principle to grasp in relation to the powers of directors is that the **extent of directors' powers is defined by the articles**. Table A Article 70 provides that 'the business of the company shall be managed by the directors who may ... exercise all the powers of the company'. Also 'No alteration of the memorandum or articles and no such direction shall invalidate any prior act of the directors'.

Thus, if shareholders do not approve of the directors' acts they must either remove them under s 303 or alter the articles to regulate their future conduct. They cannot simply take over the functions of the directors. The directors also have powers as **agents**. This ties in with the agency part of your business law studies discussed in connection with partnerships.

Learning outcomes covered in this chapter

- Explain the procedure for the appointment, retirement and removal of directors

- **Explain** the procedure for the disqualification of directors
- **Identify** the duties owed by directors to the company, shareholders, creditors and employees
- **Explain** the rules dealing with the possible imposition of personal liability upon the directors of insolvent companies
- **Identify** the power of directors
- **Identify** and **contrast** the rights of shareholders with the board of a company

Syllabus content covered in this chapter

- The appointment, retirement and removal of directors
- Directors' duties
- Fraudulent and wrongful trading
- Directors' powers
- The division of powers between the board and the shareholders

1 DEFINING DIRECTORS

KEY TERM

A **director** is a person who is responsible for the overall direction of the company's affairs.

1.1 Every company must have at least **one** director and for a **public** company the minimum is **two**: s 282. There is no statutory maximum but the articles usually impose a limit.

1.2 Any person who occupies the position of director is treated as such: s 741

1.3 A person who is given the title of director, such as 'sales director', is not a director in company law unless by virtue of his appointment he is a **member** of the **board** of **directors**, or he carries out functions that would be properly discharged only by a director.

1.4 Anyone who is held out by a company as a director, and who acts as a director although not validly appointed as one, is known as a **de facto** director. A key example of a de facto director is a **shadow director**. Company law relating to directors extends to individuals who are de facto directors.

KEY TERM

A **shadow director** is a person in accordance with whose instructions other directors are accustomed to act.

1.5 A person might seek to avoid the legal responsibilities of being a director by not accepting formal appointment as a director but using his power, say as a major shareholder, to manipulate the acknowledged board of directors. This would make him a shadow director.

KEY TERM

An **alternate director** is a person who acts as a director in place of another.

1.6 A director may appoint an **alternate director** to attend and vote for him at board meetings which he himself is unable to attend, if the articles permit him to do so.

KEY TERMS

An **executive director** is a director who performs a specific role in a company under a service contract which requires a regular, possibly daily involvement in management.

A **non-executive director** does not generally have a function to perform in a company's management. His usual involvement is to attend board meetings only.

1.7 In listed companies, boards of directors are felt more likely to be fully effective if they comprise both able executive directors and strong, independent non-executive directors.

1.8 The main tasks of the NEDs are as follows:

- **Contribute** an **independent view** to the board's deliberations
- **Help the board provide** the company with **effective leadership**
- **Ensure** the **continuing effectiveness** of the **executive directors** and management
- **Ensure high standards** of **financial probity** on the part of the company

1.9 Non-executive and shadow directors are subject to the same duties as executive directors. Duties are discussed below in section 6.

Managing directors

KEY TERM

A **managing director** is one of the directors of the company appointed to carry out overall day-to-day management functions.

1.10 If the articles provide for it the board may appoint one or more directors to be **managing directors**. A Managing Director ('MD') does have a special position and has wider apparent powers than any director who is not appointed an MD.

Director-members

1.11 A director **may** be a member, but he doesn't have to be one unless the articles require it.

2 APPOINTMENT OF DIRECTORS

Appointment of first directors

2.1 The documents delivered to the registrar to form a company include **Form 10** giving particulars of the first directors and signed by them to signify their consent: s 13(5). On the formation of the company those persons become the first directors.

Appointment of subsequent directors

2.2 Most companies follow Table A in providing for **co-option** of new members by existing directors and **election of** directors in general meeting.

2.3 When the appointment of directors is proposed at a general meeting of a **public** company a **separate** resolution should be proposed for the election of each director. However the rule may be waived if a resolution to that effect is first carried without any vote being given against it.

2.4 A company may by its **articles** or by a **separate agreement** permit a director to assign, or transfer his office to another person. However any such transfer is valid only if approved by **special resolution** passed in general meeting: s 308.

3 VACATION OF OFFICE

3.1 A director may leave office in the following ways.

- **Resignation**
- Not **offering himself for re-election** when his term of office ends
- **Death**
- **Dissolution of the company**
- Being **removed** from office (this is discussed below in section 4)
- Being **disqualified** (this is discussed below in section 7)

However the director leaves office, Form 288b should be filed with the Registrar.

Rotation and re-election of directors

3.2 Table A Articles 73-80 on retirement and re-election of directors ('rotation') contains the following provisions.

(a) Every year **one-third** (or the number nearest to one-third) shall **retire**; at the first AGM of the company they all retire (Article 73).

(b) **Retiring directors** are **eligible** for **re-election** (Article 80).

(c) Those retiring shall be those **in office longest** since their last election (Article 74).

(d) If directors fail to agree who should retire and be offered for re-election, the question should be decided by lot (Article 74).

(e) A director shall be **deemed** to be **re-elected unless** the **meeting decides otherwise** (Article 75).

(f) The **directors** themselves **may fill** a **casual vacancy** by **co-option**. Such an appointee must stand for re-election at the next AGM after his appointment and does not count in determining the one-third to retire by rotation (Article 79).

(g) The company in general meeting may also elect new directors (Article 79).

(h) A managing director or any other director holding **executive** office is **not subject** to **retirement by rotation** and is excluded in reckoning the one-third in (a) above (Article 84).

Question 1

The board of Teddy plc has the following directors at the start of its AGM on 31 December 20X7.

	Age	*When last re-elected*
Mr Timothy	42	31 December 20X4
Mr Paul	64	31 December 20X5
Mr Henry	70	31 December 20X6
Mr Maurice	38	31 December 20X6
Mr Edgar	34	31 December 20X6
Mr Gordon	43	2 May 20X7
Mr Edward	41	2 May 20X7

At the board meeting on 2 May 20X7 Mr Gordon and Mr Edward were appointed to fill casual vacancies and Mr Timothy was appointed managing director. The company's articles follow Table A as regards rotation of directors; the articles do not contain any provision about re-appointing directors who are over the statutory age limit. Which directors would be due for re-election at the AGM on 31 December 20X7?

Answer

Mr Gordon and Mr Edward must stand for re-election since they have been appointed during the year. Mr Henry must stand for re-election as he has reached the age of 70 and Teddy plc is a public company with no provision in its articles for automatic appointment of directors who are 70.

Calculation of who is to retire by rotation excludes Mr Gordon, Mr Edward, Mr Henry and Mr Timothy (as Managing Director), thus leaving three directors. One of those must therefore retire, and as Mr Paul has been in office the longest, it must be him.

Directors' retirement

3.3 A director of a public company is deemed to retire at the end of the AGM following his 70th birthday: s 293(3). This rule is disapplied if the **articles** permit him to continue or if his continued **appointment** is **approved** by the **general meeting**.

3.4 A director may, if the articles permit, **assign** his office to another person, because for example he is to be abroad. Assignment must be approved by a **special resolution**: s 308.

4 CONTROL OF DIRECTORS 5/02

4.1 Directors manage the company on behalf of the members. They are **stewards** and **agents** of the members. Therefore, while the **directors** have **powers to manage** the company (discussed in section 5), the **members** have some **controls** over the **actions of the directors,** which we will consider now.

Removal of directors 5/02

4.2 The members always have the power to remove a director in general meeting **by ordinary resolution** under s 303. **Special notice** of the resolution must be given by the person proposing it.

4.3 The limits on the power to propose such a resolution are as follows:

(a) The member can only insist on the resolution being included in the meeting if he represents members who:

- Either, have **1/20th** of the **voting rights,**
- Or, are at least **100 members** on whose shares an average of £100 has been paid up

(b) A director may have 'weighted' voting rights given to him in the articles, so he may be able to prevent the resolution being passed.

Bushell v Faith 1970
The facts: The company had three members who were also the directors and each held 100 shares. The shares carried one vote per share in normal circumstances but the articles provided that on a resolution for his removal the director to be removed should have 3 votes for each share. On a resolution for his removal the director concerned cast 300 votes against and the other members cast 200 votes for the resolution.

Decision: It was permissible to have weighted voting rights. The director could only be removed if the resolution were carried; it had been defeated.

(c) It is possible that a director's removal could be prevented by class rights.

Power restricted to members in general meeting

4.4 Certain transactions or acts require the approval of the members in general meeting. Key examples are:

- Changing the company's name
- Changing the company's objects in the memorandum
- Changing the nominal share capital of the company
- Changing the articles of the company (see below)

Alteration of the articles

4.5 The members have power to change the articles, by special resolution. This means that they can change the balance of power between the members and the directors set out in the articles.

4.6 The articles can contain constraints on the power of the directors. For example, a common constraint inserted in the articles is an upper limit on the amount of money which the directors can borrow in the name of the company. If the directors want to borrow more than that sum, they would have to ask the company in general meeting.

4.7 However, the directors' powers do not come from individual members, but are derived from the company as a whole. They are to be exercised as the directors think is best for the company as a whole.

Shareholders' approval

4.8 Certain acts require the approval of the shareholders in general meeting. These tend to be transactions where the directors stand to make an advantage, or are being benefited in some way. Statute requires that they are disclosed to the company in general meeting.

4.9 The key examples of transactions for which shareholder approval is required are as follows:

(a) **Substantial property transactions** (s 320). Shareholders must approve any company contract with a director relating to property which falls within the following criteria:

- It exceeds £100,000 in value, or
- It exceeds 10% of the net assets of the company (subject to a minimum value, £2,000)

If a director does not gain shareholder's approval for such a transaction, it is **voidable** by the company.

(b) **Non contractual compensation** (ss 312-315). Shareholders must approve any non-contractual compensation given to directors for loss of office.

(c) **Funding directors to perform their duties** (under the exception to s330). Loans to directors are generally prohibited, but the general meeting may approve funding being given to a director to allow him to perform his duties.

(d) **Directors' service contracts which exceed 5 years.**

5 DIRECTORS' POWERS 11/01, 5/02

5.1 Subject to the controls discussed in the previous section, the directors must have certain powers to be able to manage the company on behalf of the shareholders.

5.2 The extent of the directors' powers is defined by the articles. So, for example, Table A, Article 70 provides:

> "The business of the company shall be managed by the directors who may...exercise all the powers of the company."

5.3 The directors may therefore take any decision in the running of the company, unless:

- It is outside the scope of the objects clause in the memorandum
- Statute requires the decision to be made by the shareholders in general meeting

5.4 When the directors have the necessary power to make decisions, their decision may be challenged if they have **exercised their power in the wrong way**. The powers are restricted to the **purposes** for **which they were given**. If the directors infringe this rule by exercising their powers for a collateral purpose the transaction will be invalid **unless** the **company** in **general meeting gives approval**, which may be retrospectively.

5.5 If the irregular use of directors' powers is the allotment of shares the votes attached to the new shares may not be used in reaching a decision in general meeting to sanction it.

Howard Smith Ltd v Ampol Petroleum Ltd 1974
The facts: Shareholders who held 55% of the issued shares intended to reject a take-over bid for the company. The directors honestly believed that it was in the company's interest that the bid should succeed. The directors therefore allotted new shares to the prospective bidder so that the shareholders opposed to the bid would then have less than 50% of the enlarged capital and the bid would succeed.

Decision: The allotment was void. 'It must be unconstitutional for directors to use their fiduciary powers over the shares in the company purely for the purpose of destroying an existing majority or creating a new majority which did not previously exist'.

5.6 Any **shareholder** may thus **apply to the court** to declare the transaction void. However the practice of the courts is generally to **remit the issue** to the **members in general meeting**. If the majority approve what has been done (or have authorised it in advance) that decision is treated as a proper case of majority control to which the minority must normally submit.

Hogg v Cramphorn 1966
The facts: The directors of a company issued shares to trustees of a pension fund for employees to prevent a take-over bid which they honestly thought would be bad for the company. The shares were paid for with money belonging to the company provided

from an employees' benevolent and pension fund account. The shares carried 10 votes each and as a result the trustees and directors together had control of the company. The directors had power to issue shares but not to attach more than one vote to each. A minority shareholder brought the action on behalf of all the other shareholders.

Decision: If the directors have acted honestly in the best interest of the company, the company in general meeting can ratify the use of their powers for an improper purpose, so the allotment of the shares would be valid. But only one vote could be attached to each of the shares because that is what the articles provided.

5.7 The rules on minority protection are considered in more detail in Chapter 13.

5.8 If the company permits people to act as if they were directors and to **hold themselves out** as directors, then those people have **apparent authority** to bind the company in any contacts they negotiate with third parties.

5.9 The powers delegated to the directors are given to them as a **collective body**, the board of directors. The board meeting is the proper place for the powers to be exercised.

5.10 If the directors are unable to exercise their powers because of deadlock, then the shareholders may have a **residual power** in general meeting which they may exercise to solve the problem.

5.11 The directors may permit the director to behave as if he were a managing director. If so, he has **apparent authority** as a managing director. The company will be bound by any contracts he negotiates in that capacity.

Question 2

The articles of a company provide that certain transactions must be approved by unanimous vote of the directors. One director dissents from a resolution that the rest of the board wishes to pass. By ordinary resolution in general meeting, the company ratified the board's resolution. Is this ratification valid?

A Yes. The general meeting can exercise the power of management if the board is deadlocked.

B No. This is an attempt to alter the terms of the contract (the articles) between the parties by an ordinary and not a special resolution.

C Yes. The meeting can confirm a majority decision of the board.

D No. The meeting cannot exercise this sort of control in any circumstances.

Answer

B. C is incorrect. The articles can be changed by special resolution, hence D is incorrect. A is a correct statement, but is not relevant here, as the board is not deadlocked.

---

6 DIRECTORS' DUTIES

6.1 Directors owe duties to various sets of people. The key people that directors owe duties to are:

- **Shareholders**
- **Creditors** of the company
- **Employees** of the company

6.2 In section 7 we will look at the effects of the duties being breached. The duties to creditors and employees are often highlighted in an insolvency situation and provision has been made for them in statute.

Duties owed to shareholders

6.3 Directors owe the following duties to shareholders:

- **Fiduciary** duties of loyalty and good faith arising from their agency relationship
- Duties of **care** and skill (in tort)
- **Statutory** duties, primarily duties to keep the shareholders informed about their actions

Fiduciary duties

KEY TERM

Fiduciary duty is a duty imposed upon certain persons because of the position of trust and confidence in which they stand in relation to another. The duty is more onerous than generally arises under a contractual or tort relationship. It requires full disclosure of information held by the fiduciary, a strict duty to account for any profits received as a result of the relationship, and a duty to avoid conflict of interest.

6.4 Broadly speaking directors must be **honest** and **not seek personal advantage**. The directors are said to hold a **fiduciary position** since they make contracts as **agents** of the company and have control of its property.

6.5 The directors owe a fiduciary duty to the company to exercise their powers *bona fide* in what they honestly consider to be the interests of the company and to exercise them for a proper purpose. This duty is owed **to the company** and not generally to individual shareholders.

6.6 Many of the cases arising in this area concern the **duty of directors** to exercise their power to allot shares. This is only one of the many powers given to directors which are subject to this **fiduciary duty**, including the powers to **borrow** and **give security**, to **refuse** to **register** a **transfer** of shares, to **call general meetings** and to **circulate information** to shareholders.

6.7 As agents, directors have a **duty to avoid a conflict of interest**. In particular:

(a) The directors must retain their **freedom of action** and not fetter their discretion by agreeing to vote as some other person may direct.

(b) The directors owe a fiduciary duty to **avoid a conflict of duty** and **personal interest.**

(c) The directors must **not obtain any personal advantage** from their position as directors **without the consent of the company** for whatever gain or profit they have obtained.

6.8 Directors may not obtain **personal advantages** gained through their being **directors unless the company allows**.

Regal (Hastings) Ltd v Gulliver 1942
The facts: The company owned a cinema. It had the opportunity of acquiring two more cinemas through a subsidiary to be formed with an issued capital of £5,000. However the company could not proceed with this scheme since it only had £2,000 available for investment in the subsidiary. The directors and their friends therefore subscribed £3,000 for shares of the new company to make up the required £5,000. The chairman

acquired his shares not for himself but as nominee of other persons. The company's solicitor also subscribed for shares. The share capital of the two companies (which then owned three cinemas) was sold at a price which yielded a profit of £2.80 per share of the new company in which the directors had invested. The new controlling shareholder of the company caused it to sue the directors to recover the profit which they had made.

Decision:

(a) The directors were **accountable** to the company for their profit since they had obtained it from an opportunity which came to them as directors.

(b) It was **immaterial** that the **company** had **lost nothing** since it had been unable to make the investment itself.

(c) The directors might have kept their profit if the company had **agreed** by resolution passed in general meeting that they should do so; the directors might have used their votes to approve their action since it was not fraudulent (there was no misappropriation of the company's property.)

(d) The chairman was not accountable for the profit on his shares since he did not obtain it for himself. The solicitor was not accountable for his profit since he was **not a director** and so was not subject to the rule of accountability as a director for personal profits obtained in that capacity.

Exam focus point

Questions with facts similar to the *Regal Hastings* case often occur in law exams.

Duty of care

6.9 Directors have a common law duty of care to show reasonable competence. In the case of *Re City Equitable Fire and Insurance Co Ltd 1925*, this duty was analysed into three propositions.

(a) A director is expected to show the **degree of skill** which may **reasonably be expected** from a person of his knowledge and experience. The standard set is personal to the person in each case. An accountant who is a director of a mining company is not required to have the expertise of a mining engineer, but he should show that of an accountant.

(b) A director is required to attend board meetings when he is able but he has no duty to concern himself with the affairs of the company at other times (unless he has undertaken to do so). His duties are of an **intermittent** nature. If he is also a working executive of the company his extra duties are performed as an employee and not as a director.

(c) In the absence of ground for suspicion and subject to normal business practice, he is **entitled to leave** the **routine conduct** of the business **in the hands of its management** and may trust them, accepting the information and explanation which they provide, if they appear to be honest and competent.

6.10 The duty to be competent extends to non-executive directors, who may be liable if they fail in their duty. Again the test is personal.

Dorchester Finance Co Ltd v Stebbing 1977
The facts: Of all the company's three directors, S, P and H, only S worked full-time. P and H signed blank cheques at S's request; he used them to make loans which became irrecoverable. The company sued all three; P and H, who were experienced accountants, claimed that as non-executive directors they had no liability.

Decision: All three were liable, P's and H's acts in signing blank cheques being negligent and not showing the necessary skill and care.

Statutory duties **11/01**

6.11 Under statute, the directors are required to disclose various matters. Often this is done through the financial statements, which are then audited to ensure that they show a true and fair view.

6.12 Under 2 317 CA 1985, a director must '**declare in nature of his interest**', direct or indirect, in a contract or a proposed contract with the company. This disclosure must take place at:

- The first meeting of the directors at which the contract is considered, or
- (If later), the first meeting after the director becomes interested in the contract.

6.13 If a director fails to give such notice he commits an offence and may be fined, the contract is **voidable** at the instance of the company, he may be **accountable** to the company for **any profit made** on the contract.

6.14 A company must disclose in the annual accounts any **company contract in which a director has an material interest**. Material is determined by the directors. The following contracts would be **exempt**:

- Contracts of a value **not exceeding £1,000,** or
- Contracts not exceeding **one per cent of the company's assets** (maximum of £5,000)

6.15 The annual accounts must include information of **directors' emoluments** distinguishing directors' fees and management salaries (if any) and certain directors' pensions: s 231 and Sch 5.

6.16 A company must make available for inspection by members a copy or particulars (if there is no written service agreement) of **contracts of employment** between the company or a subsidiary with a director of the company: s 318.

6.17 There are two exceptions to the s 318 disclosure requirements (s 319):

(a) If the contract requires the director to work **wholly** or **mainly outside the UK,** only brief particulars (the director's name and the duration of the contract) need be given.

(b) If the contract will **expire** or if the company can **terminate it without compensation within a year,** no copy or particulars need be kept available for members' inspection.

6.18 The copy or particulars must be available either at the **registered office,** or at the **principal place of business** in England: s 318(4).

6.19 If any loan to directors, whether **prohibited or permitted,** existed during the year prescribed particulars must be **included** in the **annual accounts** for the year: s 232. Loans are generally prohibited, however, there are some exceptions:

- Allowed to lend less than £5,000
- Holding companies may make loans to directors of subsidiary companies (if they are not directors of the holding company)
- A company may make a loan to a director who is also its holding company
- A money-lending company may make a loan on normal commercial terms to a director (maximum £100,000 for a plc)

- A company may fund a director to carry out his duties if the loan is approved in general meeting (maximum £20,000 for a plc)

Insider dealing

6.20 Statute has also forbidden (as a criminal offence) 'insider dealing'. Insider dealing is when directors (among others) might take unfair advantage of individual shareholders by purchasing shares at an advantage to themselves due to their inside knowledge of company affairs. The Criminal Justice Act 1993 defines the offence as 'dealing in securities while in possession of insider information as an insider, the securities being price-affected by the information'.

6.21 The maximum penalites for insider dealing are **seven years' imprisonment** and/or an **unlimited fine**.

Duties owed to employees and creditors — 11/01, 5/02

6.22 The statutory obligation placed on directors to have regard to the interests of employees in general is a duty to the **company**, to be enforced by **the company** (that is a majority of shareholders), **not** by the **employees**: s 309. For that reason it is mainly significant as a justification for directors if they consider the employees' interests and shareholders complain of it.

6.23 If the company is insolvent directors have a **duty to the company** to consider creditors' interests.

6.24 A director may be held personally liable to the creditors when the company has become insolvent. The main instances of this are fraudulent trading and wrongful trading (discussed below).

KEY TERMS

Fraudulent trading is where the court finds that the business of a company in liquidation has been carried on with the intent to defraud creditors, or for any fraudulent purpose.

Wrongful trading is where the court finds that directors of an insolvent company knew, or ought to have known, that there was no reasonable prospect that the company could have avoided going into insolvent liquidation, and the directors did not take sufficient steps to minimise the potential loss to creditors.

Both are offences under the Insolvency Act 1986.

7 BREACH OF DUTIES

7.1 There are various effects and remedies arising from breach of directors' duties. The **key statutory effect** is that a **director can be disqualified** under the Company Directors Disqualification Act 1986.

7.2 This could be the result of a breach of many of the duties discussed above and so is the most important aspect of this section. However, we shall look at some specific remedies in relation to the duties discussed above also.

Breach of fiduciary duties **11/01**

7.3 The **company** itself (that is a majority of shareholders in general meeting) **would take action** in the event of a breach of the directors' fiduciary duties. If an individual member wanted to take action, he would have to do so under the rules of minority protection (outlined in Chapter 13).

7.4 The type of remedy varies with the breach of duty.

(a) The director may have to **account for a personal gain:** *Regal (Hastings) Ltd v Gulliver*

(b) He may have to **indemnify the company** against loss caused by his negligence by an unlawful transaction which he has approved.

(c) If he contracts with the company in a conflict of interest the **contract may be rescinded by the company**.

(d) The **court** may declare that a transaction is *ultra vires* or unlawful.

7.5 A company may, either by its **articles** or by **passing a resolution** in general meeting, **authorise or ratify** the conduct of directors in breach of duty. There must be **full disclosure** to members of the relevant facts. At the meeting a director who is a shareholder **may** use his votes as he wishes to approve his own conduct.

7.6 There are some limits on the power of members in general meeting to sanction a breach of duty by directors or to release them from their strict obligations.

(a) If the directors **defraud** the company and vote in general meeting to approve their own fraud, their votes are invalid (*Cook v Deeks*).

(b) If the directors **allot shares** to alter the balance of votes in a general meeting the votes attached to those shares may not be cast to support a resolution approving the issue.

7.7 A **director is not liable for acts of fellow directors**. However if he becomes aware of serious breaches of duty by other directors, he himself may have a duty to inform members of them or to take control of assets of the company without having proper delegated authority to do so.

7.8 In such cases the director is liable for his own negligence in what he allows to happen and not directly for the misconduct of the other director.

Negligence

7.9 The company may recover damages from its directors for loss caused by their negligence. However something more than imprudence or want of care must be shown. It must be shown to be a case of **gross negligence**, defined in *Overend Gurney & Co v Gibb 1872* as conduct which 'no men with any degree of prudence acting on their own behalf, would have entered into such a transaction as they entered into'.

7.10 In the absence of fraud therefore it was difficult to control careless directors effectively. The new statutory provisions on disqualification of directors of insolvent companies and on liability for wrongful trading (CDDA and IA 1986) both set out how to judge a director's competence, and provide more effective enforcement (discussed below).

7.11 The company by decision of its members in general meeting decides whether to sue the directors for their negligence. As we have seen, even if it is a case in which they could be liable **the court has discretion under s 727 to relieve directors of liability** if it appears to the court that:

- The directors acted **honestly** and **reasonably**
- They **ought**, having regard to the circumstances of the case, **fairly to be excused**.

Re D' Jan of London Ltd 1993
The facts: D, a director of the company, signed an insurance proposal form without reading it. The form was filled in by D's broker. An answer given to one of the questions on the form was incorrect and the insurance company rightly repudiated liability for a fire at the company's premises in which stock worth some £174,000 was lost. The company became insolvent and the liquidator brought this action under s 212 of the Insolvency Act 1986 alleging D was negligent.

Decision: In failing to read the form D was negligent. However, he had acted honestly and reasonably and ought therefore to be partly relieved from liability by the Court under s 727 of the Companies Act 1985.

7.12 In the absence of **fraud, bad faith** or **ultra vires** the members may vote unanimously to forgive the director's negligence, even if it is those negligent directors who control the voting and exercise such forgiveness: *Multinational Gas & Petrochemical Co v Multinational Gas and Petrochemical Services Ltd 1983*. Where there is no fraud on the minority, a majority decision is sufficient: *Pavlides v Jensen 1956*.

Directors' personal liability

7.13 As a general rule a director has no personal liability for the debts of the company. But there are certain exceptions.

- Personal liability **may arise** by **lifting the veil** of incorporation.
- A **limited company** may by its memorandum or by **special resolution** provide that its directors shall have unlimited liability for its debts: ss 306 - 307.
- A director may be **liable** to the **company's creditors** in certain circumstances (see below).

Fraudulent and wrongful trading

7.14 If the liquidator considers that there has been **fraudulent or wrongful trading** he should apply to the court for an order that those responsible (usually the directors) are liable to make good to the company all or some specified part of the **company's debts**.

7.15 The liquidator should also report the facts to the Director of Public Prosecutions so that the DPP may **institute criminal proceedings.**

Disqualification of directors

7.16 As mentioned above, the **statutory disqualification** of directors is governed by the Company Directors Disqualification Act 1986.

7.17 The court **may** make an order on any of the following grounds.

(a) Where a **person is convicted** of an **indictable offence in connection with the promotion, formation, management or liquidation of a company** or with the receivership or management of a company's property (s 2).

(b) Where it appears that a person has been **persistently in default in relation to provisions of company legislation.**

(c) Where it appears in the course of the winding up of a company that a person has been guilty of **fraudulent trading**, carrying on business with intent to defraud creditors or for any fraudulent purpose.

(d) Where the **Secretary of State** acting on a report made by the inspectors or from information or documents obtained under the Companies Act, **applies to the court** for an order believing it to be expedient **in the public interest.**

(e) Where a director has participated in **wrongful trading** (s 10).

7.18 The court **must** make an order where it is satisfied that the following apply:

(a) A person has been a director of a company which has at any time become **insolvent** (whether while he was a director or subsequently).

(b) His conduct as a director of that company makes him **unfit** to be **concerned** in the **management** of a company (s 6). The courts may also take into account his conduct as a director of other companies, whether or not these other companies are insolvent:. Directors can be disqualified under this section even if they take no active part in the running of the business.

Examples of conduct leading to disqualification

7.19 Offences for which directors have been disqualified include the following.

- **Insider dealing**
- **Failure** to **keep proper accounting records**
- **Failure to read the company's accounts**
- **Loans** to another company for the purposes of purchasing its own shares with **no grounds for believing the money would be repaid**
- **Loans** to associated companies on **uncommercial terms** to the detriment of creditors

Procedures for disqualification

7.20 Administrators, receivers and liquidators all have a statutory duty to report to the DTI on directors of companies in whose affairs they have become involved, where they believe the conditions in s 6 for a disqualification order have been satisfied: s 7.

7.21 The Secretary of State then decides whether to apply to the court for an order, but if he does decide to apply he must do so within two years of the date on which the company became insolvent.

Disqualification under the articles

7.22 The disqualification discussed above is all statutory. The articles of a company often embody the statutory grounds and add some optional extra grounds. Table A, article 81 provides that a director must vacate office if:

- He is **disqualified** by the **Act** or any rule of law (for example if he ceases to be the registered holder of qualification shares).
- He becomes **bankrupt** or enters into an arrangement with his creditors.
- He becomes of **unsound mind.**
- He **resigns** by notice in writing.

- He is **absent** for a period of **six consecutive months** from board meetings held during that period, without obtaining leave of absence **and** the other directors resolve that he shall on that account vacate office.

Question 3

In what circumstances can a court make a disqualification order against a director of a company?

Answer

The provisions for disqualification of directors are now contained in the Company Directors Disqualification Act 1986. A court may, by order, disqualify a person from being a director, liquidator, administrator, receiver or manager of a company, and from being concerned in the promotion or management of any company: CDDA s 1.

The order may be made in any one of the following circumstances.

(a) The director concerned is convicted of an indictable offence in connection with a company: s 2.

(b) The director concerned has been persistently in default in relation to company law requirements requiring the delivery to the Companies Registry of annual accounts, the annual return and other documents. A previous decision of a court on three previous occasions in five years that the person concerned has been in default in compliance with these requirements is conclusive evidence of 'persistent' default: s 3.

(c) The director concerned has been guilty of fraud in connection with a company then in liquidation: s 4.

(d) The court is satisfied that a director's conduct is such as to make him unfit to be concerned in the management of a company. There is a procedure and subsidiary rules for this ground of disqualification including the criteria that the company must have become insolvent either during the period the person was a director or subsequently. In this case the court must make an order if it finds that the grounds exist and a minimum of 2 years disqualification is prescribed: ss 6 and 7.

(e) Where the Secretary of State applies for disqualification in the public interest. This would arise from an investigation by DTI inspectors or documents obtained under the Companies Act: s 8.

(f) The director has participated in wrongful trading in insolvency: s 10.

In general disqualification may be ordered for up to 15 years. But the maximum is 5 years in case (b) above or when the order is made by a magistrates' court: s 2. A person subject to disqualification may apply to the court for remission of the order.

Bankruptcy

An undischarged bankrupt may not, without leave of the court, act as a director of a company or be concerned in the management or promotion of a company: s 11. Here the disqualification is the automatic result of the bankruptcy order made against him by the court.

Question 4

Briefly describe the fiduciary duties owed to a company by a director.

Answer

The fiduciary duties of directors can be summarised under two headings.

(a) To exercise their powers properly
(b) To avoid a conflict of interest

Proper exercise of powers

(a) Is the transaction reasonably incidental to the company's business?

(b) Is the transaction bona fide?

(c) Is the transaction done for the benefit of and to promote the prosperity of the company (for a proper purpose)?

Use of powers for a proper purpose means directors must use powers for the purposes for which they were given. Directors should not use powers for a collateral purpose, for example, allotting shares to prevent a takeover bid: *Howard Smith Ltd v Ampol Petroleum Ltd 1974*.

If, however, the directors use their powers for a proper purpose but act honestly in the best interests of the company, the breach of duties may be ratified retrospectively by the company.

Conflict of interest

Case law provides a number of examples of conflicts of interest directors must avoid.

(a) Directors must retain their freedom of action. In certain circumstances a director may be appointed to represent the interests of a shareholder or debentureholder. If then his duty to the company conflicts with the interests of whoever appointed him, he should resign.

(b) Directors should not, except with the company's consent make any arrangement where their personal interests conflict with the company's interests.

(c) A director should not make personal profits from his position except with the company's consent. If no consent is given the director will be liable to account to the company for the profit. This rule extends to profits obtained from transactions with a director in that capacity with third parties. Although he does not profit at the company's expense he is nonetheless accountable to it.

In *Regal (Hastings) Ltd v Gulliver 1942* which concerned investments in shares, it was held that it was immaterial that the company would not have been able to obtain the profit from share dealings the directors obtained, since it did not have sufficient capital to make the required investment. The directors were accountable since the opportunity to make a profit had come from their being directors.

The same principle applies even if the director has ceased to be a director, if the opportunity came because the person had been a director.

Chapter roundup

- In this chapter we have concentrated on the formalities of appointing and removing company directors and their powers and duties.
- Any person who occupies the position of director is treated as such, the test being one of **function.**
- Every company must have at least **one** director, and for a public company the minimum is **two.**
- The method of appointing directors, along with their rotation and co-option is **controlled** by the **articles.** The articles may provide regulations for the removal of a director from office, but any such provisions are overridden by statute which allows removal by **ordinary resolution** with **special notice.**
- Directors may also be required to vacate office because they have been disqualified on grounds dictated by the articles. Directors **may** be disqualified from a very wide range of company involvements under the Company Directors Disqualification Act 1986 (CDDA).
- The **powers** of the directors are **defined** by the **articles**.
- The directors have a duty to exercise their powers in what they honestly believe to be the **best interests** of the company and for the **purposes** for which the powers are given.
- If the articles provide for it, one or more directors may be appointed by the board as **managing director**. The managing director has **apparent** authority to make business contracts on behalf of the company. The managing director's **actual** authority is whatever the board gives him. The directors may appoint one of their number to be **chairman** of the board.
- The members **cannot retrospectively restrict** the directors or **take over** the company **management**.
- If the principal (the company acting through the board) **holds out** a person as its authorised agent, then it is estopped from denying that he is its authorised agent.
- Directors are said to be in a **fiduciary position** in relation to the company. Because of their special position, directors owe a number of strictly applied fiduciary duties to the company.
- They must exercise their powers **bona fide in** what they consider to be the best interest of the company. Breach of this rule leads to the act being ultra vires, and the directors become liable to indemnify the company against any loss.
- The **powers of directors** must only be used for a **proper purpose**. Unlike the requirement for bona fides, breach of this rule does not lead to the act being ultra vires, but the transaction will still be invalid unless the company in general meeting ratifies it.
- The directors must **retain their freedom of action** and not fetter their discretion by agreeing to vote as some other person may direct. The directors must **avoid conflicts** of duty and **personal interest**. This rule is very strictly applied.
- Directors have a duty of care to show **reasonable competence**.

Quick quiz

1 Table A Articles 73-80 provide a number of rules on retirement and re-election of directors. These include which of the following?

A Every year one-third (or the nearest number thereto) shall retire.

B The managing director and any other director holding executive office are not subject to retirement by rotation and are excluded from the reckoning of the one third figure.

C A director shall be deemed to be re-elected unless the meeting decides otherwise.

D If the directors fail to agree on who should retire, the question is decided by lot.

E A co-opted director must stand for re-election at each AGM after his appointment.

2 **Fill in the blanks** in the statements below.

……………….. directors are directors who give directions in accordance with which the board usually act.

……………….. directors are directors who perform a specific role in the company and are generally given a service contract.

3 **Fill in the blanks** in the statements below.

Under Table A Article 70 directors are authorised to ……………….. the ……………….. of the company, and ……………….. the ………………..of the company.

4 Using no more than 10 words, explain the extent of a managing director's actual authority.

5 What are the two principal ways by which members can control the activities of directors? (Max 15 words)

6 George is a director of Kitten Ltd. The board of directors delegate to him the job of negotiating the purchase of a lorry. George's actual authority in relation to this transaction is

A Implied actual authority
B Express actual authority
C Ostensible authority
D Apparent authority

7 The directors of a company are in breach of the rule requiring them to act *bona fide* in what they honestly believe to be the best interests of the company. A general meeting can

A Do nothing that will authorise the transaction
B Authorise the transaction by ordinary resolution
C Authorise the transaction by special resolution only
D Relieve the directors of any liability under the transaction by special resolution only

8 What were the three principles laid down in the case of *Re City Equitable Fire Insurance Co Ltd 1925* in relation to a director's duty of skill and competence?

9 Directors have a duty under s 309 to consider the interests of the company's employees. The duty is owed to:

A The recognised trade unions
B Each employee individually
C The employees as a body
D The company itself

10 Under which of the following grounds *may* a director be disqualified if he is guilty, and under which *must* a director be disqualified?

A Conviction of an indictable offence in connection with a company

B Persistent default with the provisions of company legislation

C Fraudulent trading

D Public interest, as a result of an inspectors' report

E Wrongful trading

F Director of an insolvent company whose conduct makes him unfit to be concerned in the management of the company

11 Fill in the gaps in the following definitions, using the words in the box below

(a) A …………………. is a person responsible for the overall direction of the company.

(b) An …………………… is a person who acts as a director in place of another.

(c) An …………………… is a director who performs a specific role in a company under a service contracts, which requires a regular, possibly daily involvement in management.

(d) A …………………… is a person in accordance with those instructions other directors are accustomed to act.

(e) A ……………… is one of the directors of the company appointed to carry out overall day-to-day management functions.

Managing director		Alternate director
	Director	
Executive director		Shadow director

12 Which of the following items listed must be kept on a register of

(a) Directors
(b) Secretaries

- Present and former forenames and surnames
- Residential address
- Nationality
- Business occupation
- Current/former directorships of previous 5 years
- Date of birth

13 Which of the following reasons disqualify a director under Table A?

- Disqualified by Companies Act 1985
- Becomes bankrupt
- Becomes of unsound mind
- Resigns orally
- Resigns in writing
- Makes an arrangement with his creditors
- Other directors decide he should be disqualified after six months absence without leave

14 Directors have a duty to avoid conflicts of interest. In particular:

- The directors must retain their ………….. …. ………… and not fetter their …………….. by agreeing to vote as another person may direct.
- The directors owe a fiduciary duty to avoid a conflict of duty and ……………. …………
- The directors must not obtain any ……………. ……………. from their position as directors without the …………………… of the company.

15 In his dealings with outsiders the managing director has apparent authority as agent of the company to make business contracts.

☐ True

☐ False

Answers to quick quiz

1 A, B, C and D are correct. Article 79 provides that a co-opted director should stand for re-election at the *next* AGM after his appointment.

2 *Shadow* directors are directors who give directions in accordance with which the board usually act.

Executive directors are directors who perform a specific role in the company and are generally given a service contract.

3 Under Table A Article 70 directors are authorised to *manage* the *business* of the company, and *exercise* all the *powers* of the company.

4 The actual authority is whatever the board gives him.

5 Appointing and removing directors in general meeting
Reallocating powers by altering the articles

6 B is correct

7 B

8 A director is expected to show the degree of skill which may reasonably be expected from a person of his knowledge or experience.

A director is required to attend board meetings when he is able, but has no duty to concern himself with the affairs of the company at other times.

In the absence of grounds for suspicion and subject to normal business practice, a director is entitled to leave the routine conduct of the business in the hands of its management.

9 D

10 A to E are grounds under which a director may be disqualified; F is grounds under which a director must be disqualified.

11 (a) Director
(b) Alternate director
(c) Executive director
(d) Shadow director
(e) Managing director

12

• Present and former forenames and surnames	D	S
• Residential address	D	S
• Nationality	D	
• Business occupation	D	
• Current/former directorships of previous 5 years	D	
• Date of birth	D	

13 The following reasons disqualify a director under Table A

- Disqualified by companies Act 1985
- Become bankrupt
- Becomes of unsound mind
- Resigns in writing
- Makes an arrangement with his creditors
- Other directors decide he should be disqualified after six months absence without leave

14 Directors have a duty to avoid conflicts of interest. In particular:

- The directors must retain their **freedom of action** and not fetter their **discretion** by agreeing to vote as another person may direct.
- The directors owe a fiduciary duty to avoid a conflict of duty and **personal interest**
- The directors must not obtain any **personal advantage** from their position as directors without the approval of the company.

15 True

The following relevant questions are included in the Exam Question Banks

You can attempt these now. However, we would advise you to attempt these as mock exams at the end of your initial stage of study

Exam Question Bank	Numbers
Paper based format	24, 25
Computer based assessment	9, 14, 15, 18, 27

Chapter 13

MAJORITY CONTROL AND MINORITY PROTECTION

	Topic list	Syllabus reference	Ability required
1	The rule of the majority	(ix)	Comprehension
2	Statutory protection for the minority	(ix)	Comprehension
3	Other protection for the minority	(ix)	Comprehension

Introduction

Every member of a company is bound by the articles to the company and to his fellow members as we saw in an earlier chapter. By implication, a member agrees to be bound by the decisions of the **majority** as expressed at a general meeting. This principle of majority rule was established in *Foss v Harbottle*.

However, while *directors* must exercise their power *bona fide* for the benefit of the company, shareholders are under no such obligation. Clearly shareholders may exercise their votes in their own interests and not those of the company. There must, therefore, be some restraint on the power of those able to command a majority vote. Minorities are therefore protected by **common law** and **statute**, and the various rules are all covered in this chapter.

You should concentrate more on the statutory rules for minority protection under s 459 than on the common law rules.

This topic may be examined along with the duties of directors and other actions a shareholder may take, including a shareholder's right to remove directors under s 303.

Learning outcomes covered in this chapter

- **Identify** the rights of shareholders

Syllabus content covered in this chapter

- The rights of majority and minority shareholders

1 THE RULE OF THE MAJORITY

1.1 Directors owe their duties to company (the members as a body in general meeting), not to individual members. Therefore, if they breach their duties, it is the company who should bring proceedings.

Foss v Harbottle 1843
The facts: A shareholder (Foss) sued the directors of the company alleging that the directors had defrauded the company by selling land to it at an inflated price. The company was by this time in a state of disorganisation and efforts to call the directors to account at a general meeting had failed.

Decision: The action must be dismissed.

(a) The **company** as a person separate from its members is the **only proper plaintiff** in an action to protect its rights or property.

(b) The **company** in **general meeting** must decide whether to bring such legal proceedings.

1.2 In laying down the general principles of procedure the court did nonetheless recognise that 'the claims of justice' must prevail over 'technical rules'. A shareholder minority may have an effective voice in general meeting, and if **directors or majority shareholders** make use of this fact to **take a course of action** which is **detrimental to the minority,** then the minority must have some **protection** against them.

1.3 The protection of a minority in various situations is provided by (most importantly) **statute,** and (rarely in modern times) in common law by making **exceptions** to the rule laid down in *Foss v Harbottle*.

2 STATUTORY PROTECTION FOR THE MINORITY

S 459: Unfairly prejudical conduct

2.1 Any member may apply to the court for relief under s 459 on the grounds that the company's affairs are being or have been conducted in a manner which is **unfairly prejudicial** to the interests of the members **generally or of some part** of the members. Application may also be made in respect of a single prejudicial act or omission.

2.2 There is **no** statutory definition of what constitutes unfairly prejudicial conduct. Applications against unfairly prejudicial conduct often arise from:

(a) **Exclusion of a director** from participation in the management of a quasi-partnership company (A 'quasi-partnership' company is a small, generally private and often family-owned company where essentially the relationship between the directors and members is equivalent to partners in a partnership.)

(b) **Discrimination against a minority**

Examples of conduct that has been held to be unfairly prejudicial

2.3 Examples of conduct that has been held to be unfairly prejudicial include the following.

- **Exclusion** and **removal** from the **board**
- **Improper allotment** of shares
- **Failure** to **call a meeting**
- **Making** an **inaccurate statement** to **shareholders**
- A managing director using **assets** for his own **personal benefit** and the personal benefit of his family and friends
- **Diversion of company's business** to a director-controlled company
- Making a **rights issue** which minority shareholders could not take up
- Payment of **excessive directors' bonuses** and **pension contributions**

2.4 The courts will not generally intervene in cases of **management** (even bad management). However, on occasions the courts have intervened where continued mismanagement caused serious financial damage to the company and the minority's interests.

2.5 There are other instances where the courts have held that conduct was **not unfairly prejudicial.**

- **Late presentation** of **accounts**
- **Failure** by a parent company **to pay** the debts of a **subsidiary**
- **Non-compliance** with the **Stock Exchange rules**, the City Code and the Cadbury Code

2.6 The limits on the application of s 459 remain under debate. It has been argued for example that a s 459 action could be used as a check on excessive board remuneration packages.

Court orders

2.7 When a petition is successful the court may make whatever order it deems fit. Courts may give, under s 461:

(a) An order regulating the **future conduct** of the company's affairs, for example that a controlling shareholder shall conform to the decisions taken at board meetings: *Re H R Harmer Ltd 1958*

(b) An authorisation to any person to bring **legal proceedings** on behalf of the company; the company is then responsible for the legal costs

(c) An order requiring the company to **refrain** from doing or continuing an act complained of

(d) Provision for the **purchase of shares** of the **minority**

(e) **Inclusion in the memorandum or articles** of provisions which may only be altered or removed thereafter by leave of the court

2.8 Perhaps the most common type of relief is an order that either the controlling shareholder or the company shall purchase the petitioner's shares at a fair price; this ends a relationship which has probably broken down beyond repair.

- The shares should be valued on the basis of their **worth before** the controlling shareholders' conduct had diminished it
- The **court** may determine what is **fair**; in particular no allowance need be made because the shares to be bought are only a minority holding and do not give control

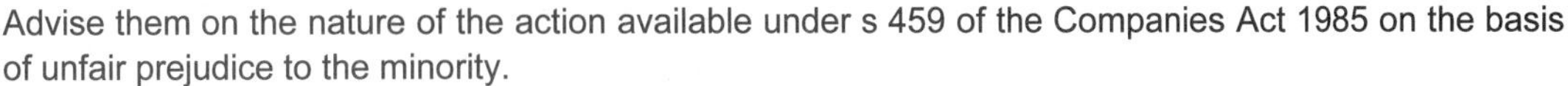

Question 1

James is the majority shareholder in Elan Ltd, holding 52% of the issued shares. The other shareholders are Chris, Martin, Jennifer and Henry, each of whom holds 12% of the shares. The minority shareholders feel that James has been abusing his position as majority shareholder and have lost confidence in him. They approach you for general advice.

Advise them on the nature of the action available under s 459 of the Companies Act 1985 on the basis of unfair prejudice to the minority.

Answer

Under s 459, any member may now apply to the court for relief on the grounds that the company's affairs are being or have been conducted in a manner which is unfairly prejudicial to the interests of the members generally or some part of the members or in respect of a particular act or omission which has been or will be prejudicial. Applications are commonly made in cases of discrimination against a minority or exclusion of a partner in a quasi-partnership company.

The prejudice complained of must affect the plaintiff-member in his capacity as member and not as an employee or unpaid creditor. The member need not prove bad faith or even an intention to discriminate.

The court will take into account the surrounding circumstances including the parties' conduct and may make such orders as it deems fit. It might regulate the company's future affairs in some way, order the purchase of the minority's shares by the majority or by the company itself, authorise some person to bring proceedings on the company's behalf, order the company to refrain from doing the act complained of or include in the company's constitution provisions which could then only be altered by the court.

The types of conduct that have been held to be unfairly prejudicial are as follows.

(a) Exclusion and removal from the board

(b) Where a managing director uses assets for his own personal benefit and the personal benefit of his family and friends

(c) Where a majority shareholder transfers sources of profit into another company owned by the majority shareholder

(d) The diversion of a company's business to a director-controlled company or the making of a rights issue which minority shareholders were not permitted to take up or the payment of excessive directors' bonuses and pension contributions

(e) The improper allotment of shares

(f) The failure to call a meeting as requisitioned by the petitioner-minority

(g) Failure to pay dividends

Exam focus point

A shareholder who is unhappy about the conduct of the company's affairs will often try to obtain a remedy under s 459.

S 122 Insolvency Act 1986

2.9 A member who is dissatisfied with the directors or controlling shareholders over the management of the company may petition the court for a winding up on the **just and equitable ground**.

2.10 For such a petition to be successful, the member must show that no other remedy is available. It is not enough for a member to be dissatisfied to make it just and equitable that the company should be wound up, since winding up what may be an otherwise healthy company is a drastic step. This makes it very **rare**, given the protection given to the minority under S459 Companies Act 1985, discussed above.

2.11 Orders have been made for winding up in the following situations.

(a) The substratum of the company has gone - **the only main object(s) of the company** (its underlying basis or substratum) **cannot be** or can no longer be **achieved**.

(b) The company was **formed for an illegal or fraudulent purpose or** there is a **complete deadlock** in the management of its affairs.

(c) The **understandings between members or directors** which were **the basis of the association** have been **unfairly breached** by lawful action.

(d) The **directors deliberately withheld information** so that the shareholders have no confidence in the company's management

Other Companies Act protection

2.12 A minority of members is given a number of specific statutory rights, including the following.

MINORITY RIGHTS		
Subject	**Required**	**Reference**
Ultra vires transactions	Any shareholder may obtain an injunction from the court to prevent an ultra vires act prior to the act being committed (s35(2))	Page 195
Decisions wrongly taken outside a general meeting	The general meeting can ratify the acts of the board of directors, but if the directors have taken a decision which required a special or extraordinary resolution, the general meeting cannot ratify this by a simple majority.	
Alteration of the articles	The minority have a right to resist an alteration to the articles where the alteration was not *bona fide* for the company as a whole.	Page 199
Variation of class rights	Holders of 15%+ of class of shares can apply to court for cancellation	
Alteration of objectives	Holders of 15%+ of issued shares can apply to court for cancellation	Page 194
Company meeting	Can be requisitioned by holders of 10%+ of company's voting capital	Page 219
Notice of members' resolutions	Must be given by company on requisition of members holding 5%+ of voting rights/100 or more members holding shares in the company on which an average sum of £100+ per member has been paid up	Page 224
Full notice of special resolution	Must be given if members with 5%+ of voting capital insist	Page 223
Conversion of public company to private	50+ members or members holding 5%+ of issued share capital can apply to court for cancellation	Page 169
Purchase of own shares out of capital by private company	Holders of 10%+ of shares/any class of shares can apply to court to prohibit the transaction	Page 293
Financial assistance by private company	Any member can apply to court to prohibit the transaction	Page 294
Poll	Can be demanded by at least 5 members/members holding 10%+ of voting rights or have 10%+ of total of all paid up shares	Page 229
Off-market purchase of own shares	Poll can be demanded by individual members	
Full notice of AGM	Can be demanded by individual members	Page 218
Registration of limited company as unlimited	Can be prevented by individual members	Page 167
DTI investigation into affairs/ownership of company	Can be requested by 200+ members/members holding 10%+ of issued shares	Page 266
Public company investigation into membership of company	Can be demanded by holders of 10%+ of company's voting capital	

BPP PUBLISHING

DTI Investigations

2.13 The DTI has statutory power to appoint an inspector (or joint inspector) to investigate:

- The **affairs** of a company
- The **ownership** of a company
- Suspected **infringement** by directors of **statutory** rules relating to their interests or dealings in options over shares or debentures of their company
- **Suspected insider dealing**

2.14 The DTI **must** appoint inspectors to investigate the affairs of a company if the **court** makes an **order** to that effect.

2.15 The DTI **may** in its discretion appoint inspectors to investigate the affairs of a company in any of the following situations.

(a) If the **company** itself **applies**

(b) If application is made by members:

- Who are **not less than 200** in number
- Who **hold at least one tenth** of the **issued shares**
- If the company has no share capital, by at **least one fifth** of the **members**

(c) If the DTI considers that the affairs of the company have been conducted in a **fraudulent or unlawful manner** (or that it was formed for a fraudulent or unlawful purpose) or in a manner **unfairly prejudicial** to some part of its members or that members have not been given all the information with respect to its affairs which they might reasonably expect.

Reports of inspectors

2.16 The inspectors submit a report to the DTI. Their report is usually published and may well contain severe criticism of the shortcomings of the persons involved.

2.17 The outcome of the investigation may be civil or criminal proceedings or a petition (by the DTI) for compulsory winding up of the company or for a court order for the protection of a minority.

3 OTHER PROTECTION FOR THE MINORITY

3.1 In addition case law recognises a number of limitations to the principle of majority control (the rule in *Foss v Harbottle*). In those cases a minority can bring legal proceedings.

(a) No majority vote can be effective to sanction an act of the company which is **illegal**.

(b) If those who control the company use their control to **defraud** it (or possibly to **act oppressively** to a minority) the minority may bring legal proceedings against the fraudulent (or oppressive) majority.

(c) If the company under majority control deprives a member of his **individual rights of membership**, he may sue the company to enforce his rights.

Illegal decisions

3.2 Illegal decisions taken in general meeting are not binding because a majority of members cannot decide that the company shall break the law. If they attempt to do so any member may apply to the court for a declaration that the decision is void and (if necessary) for an **injunction** to restrain the company from acting on the decision.

Fraud on the company

3.3 The exception to the rule (in *Foss v Harbottle*) over fraud by a controlling majority is to protect the company (by a member's action) since the company cannot protect itself. It must be shown that:

- What was taken **belonged to the company**
- It **passed to those against** whom the claim is made
- Those who **appropriated the company's property are in control** of the company

Diversion of contracts

3.4 To divert away from the company profitable contracts which it was about to make is to deprive it of its 'property' (for the purposes of this rule).

Cook v Deeks 1916
The facts: The directors who were also controlling shareholders negotiated a contract in the name of the company. They took the contract for themselves and passed a resolution in general meeting declaring that the company had no interest in the contract. A minority shareholder sued them as trustees for the company of the benefit of the contract.

Decision: The contract 'belonged in equity to the company' and the directors could not, by passing a resolution in general meeting, bind the company to approving this action of defrauding it.

Passing of property to controlling shareholders

3.5 Likewise passing property to controlling shareholders (though **not** to **other third parties**: *Pavlides v Jensen 1956*) may well be equivalent to fraud even though no dishonesty is shown.

Daniels v Daniels 1978
The facts: The company was controlled by its two directors, husband and wife. It bought land for £4,250 (probate value) from the estate of a deceased person and later resold it at the same price to the lady director. She re-sold it for £120,000. A minority shareholder sued the directors but did not allege fraud. Objection was raised that a member could not sue the directors on the company's behalf for negligence (*Pavlides*' case above) but only for fraud.

Decision: The circumstances required investigation and a member might sue the directors and controlling shareholders for negligence if one of them secured benefit from the company by reason of it.

Discrimination against minority

3.6 The courts have taken fraud to mean not just misappropriation of company property but also discrimination against the minority.

Clemens v Clemens Bros Ltd 1976
The facts: A and B (who were aunt and niece) held 55% and 45% respectively of the shares with voting rights. A proposed to vote in favour of ordinary resolutions to increase the authorised share capital and to approve the allotment of new shares to or for the benefit of employees of the company. No more shares would be allotted to A or B but the effect of the scheme would be to reduce B's shareholding from 45% to 24.5% with the object of depriving B of her power to block a special resolution to alter the articles as A desired. B sought a declaration that A could not use her votes in this way.

Decision: A should be restrained from using her votes to deprive B of her 'negative control' (her ability to block an alteration of the articles to which B objected).

Enforcement of individual rights of membership

3.7 A member may sue the company to enforce his personal rights against it. This is a different kind of minority action. In the other cases the minority is usually seeking to protect **the company** (and their interests in it) against others. In protecting his personal rights the member is **protecting himself against** the company.

Pender v Lushington 1877
The facts: The articles gave members one vote for each 10 shares held by them but subject to a maximum of 100 votes for each member. A company which was a large shareholder transferred shares to the plaintiff to increase its voting power. At the meeting the chairman rejected the plaintiff's votes. The plaintiff sued and the company relied on the argument that only the company itself could object to an irregularity of voting procedure.

Decision: The plaintiff's votes were a 'right of property' which he was entitled to protect by proceedings against the company.

3.8 The principle of *Pender's* case is restricted to protection of **personal rights** of **membership** such as the right to vote or receive a due dividend.

Usefulness of common law remedies

3.9 Owing to changes in the statutory code the dissatisfied minority is now more likely to apply to the court for relief under ss 459 - 461 than to attempt to sue the majority under common law rules.

3.10 There are also procedural points in bringing a minority shareholders' action.

(a) The plaintiff may bring a **derivative** action on behalf of the company to enforce its rights or recover its property. Any benefit obtained will accrue to the company since the claim is derived from and made on behalf of the company.

(b) The plaintiff usually combines a derivative action with a **representative** action - he asserts that he sues on behalf of all other shareholders (except the defendants). He may however combine a representative action with a personal claim for damages.

Question 2

In which of the following circumstances can an action for fraud on the minority not be brought?

A Where profitable contracts have been diverted away from the company to the directors but the general meeting has ratified this action

B Where the directors have caused the company to sell the property at a price lower than valuation to a third party

C Where the property has passed to the directors, but there is no evidence of dishonesty

D Where the minority attempting to bring the action hold only non-voting shares, and could therefore not have influenced the decision

Answer

B. This is illustrated by *Pavlides v Jensen 1956.*

Question 3

Austen Ltd has three directors. Darcy, Bingley and Benett. Together they own 85% of the shares in the company. They agree to sell a plot of land to Wickham for £50,000 which is what they honestly believe it to be worth. They do not, however, have the land professionally valued until later when it is shown to be worth nearer £100,000. Elizabeth and Jane are two minority shareholders who are considering bringing an action against the directors and the company.

Advise Elizabeth and Jane whether they are likely to be successful.

Answer

The type of action open to Elizabeth and Jane would be a derivative action, that is one brought by Elizabeth or Jane on behalf of the company, with the directors as defendants. However, they would be unlikely to succeed. The facts of this case resemble those of *Pavlides v Jensen 1956.* In this case it was held that mere negligence did not justify a minority action to protect the company's rights. Thus, in the absence of fraud, the sale could legitimately be approved by a majority of the shareholders.

Question 4

Where the court orders the purchase of shares of a dissentient minority, which of the following is *not* the case?

A The court decides the fair price.

B The basis of the valuation is the worth of the shares before the minority's actions diminished it.

C An allowance must be made for the fact that the shares are a minority (and therefore a non-controlling holding).

D Such a purchase may be ordered to be made by the company or its shareholders.

Answer

C

Chapter roundup

- In this chapter we have shown that ultimate control of a company rests with its members voting in general meeting.
  - If the directors hold a majority of the voting shares or represent a majority shareholding, the minority has no remedy unless the rules of **minority protection apply.**
  - *Foss v Harbottle 1843* made it clear that the **company**, as a separate person from its members, is the **only proper plaintiff** in an action to protect the rights or property, and that the decision to bring an action must be taken by the company in general meeting.
- The principal **statutory** remedy for minorities is a s 459 action alleging the company's affairs have been conducted in an **unfairly prejudicial manner.**
- The court may make **whatever order** it sees fit to settle a s 459 action (generally purchase of the petitioner's shares).
- A number of common law exceptions for the protection of the minority have been accepted since *Foss v Harbottle*. A minority has been allowed to bring proceedings in the following situations.
  - To restrain an **illegal** or **ultra vires decision**
  - To remedy certain **errors in procedure**
  - To enforce **individual rights** of membership
  - To prevent a **fraud** on the minority
- Dissatisfied shareholders also have these statutory remedies.
  - To petition for winding-up of the company on the **just and equitable ground**
  - To demand a **DTI investigation**
  - To object to certain specific actions (for example changing the company's articles)

Quick quiz

1 *Foss v Harbottle* established the rights of minority shareholders to obtain relief from oppressive acts by the majority.

☐ True

☐ False

2 Give four examples of remedies a court may provide under s 461.

3 **Fill in the blanks** in the statements below.

S 459 gives relief on the grounds that the company's affairs are being or have been conducted in a manner that is .... to the interests of .... or ....

4 What is the position of a minority shareholder who wishes to bring an action in the company's name against the directors, who are the majority shareholders and have purchased company assets at a considerable under-valuation.

A No action may be brought by the minority.
B An action may only be brought if there is deliberate fraud on the part of the directors.
C An action will only be allowed if the articles of association permit.
D An action will be permitted since the directors have used their position to make personal gain at the expense of the company.

5 What are the four main common law exceptions to *Foss v Harbottle*?

6 Which of the following are statutory rights of individual members?

A To demand full notice of an AGM
B To prevent re-registration of a limited company as unlimited
C To apply for a cancellation of a variation of class rights
D To demand a poll on a resolution for an off-market purchase of own shares
E To require the DTI to investigate a company's membership
F To insist on full notice for a special resolution

7 **Fill in the blanks** in the statements below.

Petitions under s 459 often arise from exclusion of a director from participation in the management of a ……………….. company, or ……………….. against a minority.

8 Give four grounds under which the DTI can use its statutory power to appoint inspectors.

9 What point of law was confirmed by the case of *Pender v Lushington 1877*?

10 Give four examples of instances where the court has ordered a company to be wound up on the just and equitable grounds.

11 Which of the following are examples of conduct held to be unfairly prejudicial to a minority?

- Removal from the board
- Improper allotment of shares
- Failure to call a meeting
- Making inaccurate statement to shareholders
- Diverting company business to a director controlled company

12 What three things must be shown when bringing an action that there has been a fraud on the minority?

(1) ……………………………

(2) ……………………………

(3) ……………………………

13 Complete the table, giving the reasons illustrated by the cases.

Reasons for just and equitable winding up	
	Re German Date Coffee Co 1882
	Re Yenidje Tobacco Co Ltd 1916
	Ebrahimi v Westbourne Galleries 1973

Answers to quick quiz

1 False. *Foss v Harbottle* emphasised the principle of *majority* rule. (It was thus evident that the minority needed protection.)

2 An order regulating the future conduct of the company's affairs
Authorising the company to bring legal proceedings
Ordering the company to refrain from actions
Providing for the purchase of shares of the minority

3 S 459 gives relief on the grounds that the company's affairs are being or have been conducted in a manner that is *unfairly prejudicial* to the interests of *members generally* or *some part of the members.*

4 D

5 The majority cannot sanction an illegal act.
Special procedures under law or the company's articles should be observed.
Individual rights of membership should be preserved.
The majority may be brought to account for defrauding the company.

6 A, B and D represent individual rights. Under s 127, C requires application by holders of at least 15% of the shares of the class. E requires 200 members or the holders of at least 10% of issued shares: s 431. F requires members holding at least 5% of voting shares: s 378.

7 Petitions under s 459 often arise from exclusion of a director from participation in the management of a *quasi-partnership* company, or *discrimination* against a minority.

8 To investigate the affairs of a company

To investigate the ownership of a company

To investigate suspected infringement by directors of statutory rules relating to interests or dealings in share or debentures

To investigate suspected insider dealing

9 That a member's votes are a right of property which can be protected by proceedings against a company

10 The substratum of the company has gone.

The company was formed for an illegal or fraudulent purpose, or there is complete deadlock in its affairs.

The understandings between members or directors which were the basis of association have been unfairly breached.

The directors deliberately withhold information so that the shareholders have no confidence in the company's management.

11 All of them.

12 (1) What was taken belonged to the company
(2) It passed to those against whom the claim is made
(3) Those who appropriated the company's property are in control of the company

13

Reasons for just and equitable winding up	
Object of the company has finished	*Re German Date Coffee Co 1882*
Management deadlock	*Re Yenidje Tobacco Co Ltd 1916*
Quasi-partnership breaks down	*Ebrahimi v Westbourne Galleries 1973*

The following relevant questions are included in the Exam Question Bank

You can attempt these now. However, we would advise you to attempt these as mock exams at the end of your initial stage of study

Exam Question Bank	Numbers
Paper based format	-
Computer based assessment	2, 39

Part F

Corporate finance

Chapter 14

SHARE CAPITAL

Introduction

In this chapter the nature of share capital is explained. You should note (and **not** confuse) the different types of capital that are important for company law purposes.

The rest of the chapter discusses procedural matters relating to the **issue** and **transfer** of shares. You will see that there are built-in safeguards to protect members'rights, **pre-emption rights** and the necessity for directors to be voted **authority** before they can **allot** shares. There are also safeguards that ensure that a company receives **sufficient consideration** for its shares. This is an aspect of **capital maintenance**. Capital maintenance is a fundamental principle of company law, the price that members of a limited company pay for limited liability. There are a number of rules governing how capital must be maintained, which we explore in the second half of this chapter.

Learning outcomes covered in this chapter

- **Explain** the nature of a share and the essential characteristics of different types of shares
- **Explain** the procedure for the issue of shares, and the acceptable forms of payment
- **Explain** the legal repercussions of issuing shares for an improper purpose
- **Explain** the procedure to increase share capital
- **Explain** the maintenance of capital principle and the exceptions to the principle
- **Explain** the procedure to reduce share capital

Syllabus content covered in this chapter

- The rights attaching to the different types of shares issued by companies
- The procedure for issuing shares
- The purposes for which shares may be issued
- The rules for the increase of share capital

- The maintenance of capital principle and the ability of a company to redeem, purchase and provide financial assistance for the purchase of its own shares, and the situations in which such powers are useful
- The rules for the reduction of share capital

1 THE NATURE OF SHARES

KEY TERM

A **share** is 'the interest of a shareholder in the company measured by a sum of money, for the purpose of a liability in the first place, and of interest in the second, but also consisting of a series of mutual covenants entered into by all the shareholders *inter se*': *Borland's Trustee v Steel Bros & Co Ltd 1901.*

1.1 The key points in this definition are:

- The share must be **paid for** ('liability').
- It gives a **proportionate entitlement** to dividends, votes and any return of capital ('interest').
- It is a form of **bargain** ('mutual covenants') between shareholders which underlies such principles as majority control and minority protection.

1.2 A share is a form of property, carrying rights and obligations. It is by its nature **transferable**. A member who holds one or more shares is a **shareholder**. However some companies (such as most companies limited by guarantee) do not have a share capital. So they have members who are not also shareholders.

Becoming a member

KEY TERM

A **member** of a company is a person who has agreed to be a member and whose name has been entered in the register of members: s 22(2).

1.3 Entry in the register is **essential**. Mere delivery to the company of a transfer of shares does not make the transferor a member - until the transfer is entered in the register.

Subscriber shares

1.4 Subscribers to the memorandum are deemed to have agreed to become members of the company. As soon as the company is formed their names should be entered in the register of members.

1.5 Other persons may acquire shares and become members:

- By **applying** for shares (which signifies their agreement to become members) and the company allotting shares to them

- By presenting to the company for registration a **transfer** of shares to them (again this signifies their agreement)

The number of members

1.6 The minimum number of members is **two** for public companies of any type. There is no legal maximum: some large public companies have more than 100,000 members.

1.7 A private limited company may be formed or operate with only **one member**.

2 TYPES OF CAPITAL 11/01, 5/02

2.1 The term 'capital' is used in several senses in company legislation.

Authorised share capital

KEY TERM

Authorised share capital (nominal share capital, registered share capital) is the type, class, number and amount of the shares which a company may issue, as empowered by its memorandum of association. (CIMA, *Official Terminology*)

2.2 This total must be divided into shares of fixed amount (called the '**nominal**' or '**par**' value of the shares).

2.3 A company which has a share capital may, if authorised by its articles and by resolution passed in general meeting, **increase** the amount of its **authorised share capital**: s 121. The standard form of articles (Table A Article 32) requires only that an **ordinary** resolution shall be passed.

2.4 The effect of such an increase of authorised share capital is merely to add to the unissued shares which the company has available for issue. There is no increase in issued share capital unless new shares are then allotted.

Issued share capital

KEY TERM

Issued share capital (or subscribed share capital) is the type, class, number and amount of the shares held by shareholders. (CIMA, *Official Terminology*)

2.5 A company need not issue all its share capital at once. If it retains part this is unissued share capital.

Called up share capital

KEY TERMS

Called up share capital is the amount which the company has required shareholders to pay on the shares issued.

Paid up share capital is the amount which shareholders are deemed to have paid on the shares issued and called up. (CIMA, *Official Terminology*)

2.6 If for example a company has issued 70 £1 (nominal) shares, has received 25p per share on application and has called on members for a second 25p, its **called up** share capital is £35 (50p per share). When the members pay the call the '**paid up**' share capital is then £35 also. Capital not yet called is '**uncalled capital**'.

Loan capital

KEY TERM

Loan capital is debentures and other long-term loans to a business. (CIMA, *Official Terminology)*

2.7 Loan capital, in contrast with the above, is the term used to describe **borrowed money** obtained usually by the issue of debentures. This is discussed in Chapter 15.

3 TYPES OF SHARE — Pilot Paper

KEY TERM

Equity is the issued ordinary share capital plus reserves, statutory and otherwise, which represents the investment in a company by the ordinary shareholders. **Equity share capital** is a company's issued share capital less capital which carries preferential rights. Equity share capital normally comprises ordinary shares. (CIMA, *Official Terminology*)

3.1 If no differences between shares are expressed then all shares are equity shares with the **same rights**, known as ordinary shares.

KEY TERM

Ordinary shares are shares which entitle the holders to the remaining divisible profits (and, in a liquidation, the assets) after prior interests, eg creditors and prior charge capital , have been satisfied. (CIMA, *Official Terminology*)

Class rights

KEY TERM

Class rights are those rights which by the company's constitution are attached to particular types of shares.

3.2 A company may at its option attach special rights to different shares.

- Dividends
- Return of capital
- Voting
- The right to appoint a director

Any share which has different rights from others is grouped with the other shares carrying **identical** rights to form a class.

3.3 Information about any special rights attached to shares is obtainable from one of the following documents which are on the file at the registry:

- The **articles**, which are the normal context in which share rights are defined, or the memorandum
- A **resolution** or agreement incidental to the creation of a new class of shares; a copy must within 15 days be delivered to the registry: s 380(4)(c)
- **Particulars** of the rights of shares must be given to the registry within one month of **allotment** if the class rights are not disclosed by (a) or (b) above: s 128

3.4 The most common types of share capital with different rights are **preference shares** and **ordinary shares;** there may also be ordinary shares with voting rights and ordinary shares without voting rights.

Preference shares

KEY TERM

Preference shares are shares carrying a fixed rate of dividend, the holders of which have a prior claim to any company profits available for distribution. (CIMA, *Official Terminology*)

3.5 A preference share will carry a **prior right** to receive an annual dividend of fixed amount, say a six per cent dividend. There are no other **implied** differences between preference and ordinary shares though there are often **differences** between them **expressed** in the **articles** or **resolution creating them.**

3.6 As regards the priority dividend entitlement, four points should be noted.

(a) **The right is merely to receive a dividend at the specified rate before any other dividend may be paid or declared.** It is **not** a right to compel the company to pay the dividend.

(b) **The right to receive a preference dividend is deemed to be cumulative unless the contrary is stated.** If, therefore, a 6% dividend is not paid in year 1, the priority

entitlement is normally carried forward to Year 2, increasing the priority right for that year to 12% - and so on.

(c) **If a company which has arrears of unpaid cumulative preference dividends goes into liquidation, the preference shareholders cease to be entitled to the arrears unless:**

- A **dividend** has been **declared** though **not yet paid** when liquidation commences.
- The **articles** (or other terms of issue) **expressly provide** that in a liquidation arrears are to be paid in priority to return of capital to members.

(d) Holders of preference shares have **no entitlement to participate in any additional dividend** over and above their specified rate.

3.7 The criteria above are the common features of a preference share. However, class rights can be tailored in the articles.

Advantages and disadvantages of preference shares

3.8 The advantages of preference shares are **greater security of income** and (if they carry priority in repayment of capital) **greater security** of capital. However in a period of persistent inflation, the entitlement to fixed income and to capital fixed in money terms is an illusion.

Variation of class rights

KEY TERM

A **variation of class rights** is an alteration in the position of shareholders with regard to those benefits or duties which they have by virtue of their shares.

3.9 The holders of issued shares have vested rights which can only be varied by the company with the consent of all the holders or with such consent of a majority as is specified (usually) in the articles.

3.10 The standard procedure for variation of class rights requires that an **extraordinary resolution** shall be passed by a **three quarters majority** cast either at a **separate meeting** of the class, or by **written consent:** s 125(2).

3.11 If any other requirements are imposed by the company's articles then these must also be followed.

Redeemable shares

3.12 Redeemable shares, shares that are issued on terms that they may be bought back by a company either at a future specific date or at the shareholder's or company's option, are discussed further in section 8.

Question 1

Give brief definitions of the following types of share.

(a) Equity share
(b) Ordinary share
(c) Preference share

Answer

(a) An equity share is a share which gives the holder the right to participate in the company's surplus profit and capital. There is no limit to the size of the dividend which may be paid except the size of the profit itself. In a winding up the holder is entitled to a repayment of the nominal value plus a share of surplus assets. The term equity share embraces ordinary shares, but it can also include a preference share when the terms of issue include either the right to an additional dividend or the right to surplus assets in a winding up.

(b) An ordinary share is the more common type of equity share, as discussed in (i) above. The dividend is payable only when preference dividends, including arrears have been paid.

(c) The essential characteristic of a preference share is that it carries a prior right to receive an annual dividend of a fixed amount. There are no other implied differences between preference and ordinary shares, although there may be express differences between them, for example the preference shares may carry a priority right to return of capital. Generally preference shares do not carry voting rights in the company other than those relating to their own class. Unless otherwise stated, preference shares are assumed to be cumulative. This means that, if the company does not make sufficient profits to pay a dividend in one year, the arrears are carried forward to future years.

3.13 Section summary

- The only specific right all preference shareholders have is a **prior right** to receive a fixed dividend.
- This right is not a right to **compel payment** of a dividend.
- The right to receive a dividend is **cumulative** unless otherwise stated.
- Unless otherwise stated, preference shareholders:
  - **Cannot participate** in a dividend over and above their fixed dividend
  - **Cease to be entitled to arrears of undeclared dividends** when the company goes into liquidation
- Preference shares have **equal rights** to ordinary shares in all other respects, **unless** the **contrary** is **stated**.

4 ALLOTMENT OF SHARES

Pilot Paper, 5/01, 5/02

> **KEY TERM**
>
> **Allotment of shares** is the allocation to a person of a certain number of shares under a contract of allotment. Once the shares are allotted and the holder is entered in the register of members, the holder becomes a member of the company. The member is sent a share certificate.

4.1 The allotment of shares is a form of contract. The intending shareholder applies to the company for shares, and the company accepts the offer.

Public company allotment of shares

4.2 There are various methods of selling shares to the public.

KEY TERMS

Public offer: where the public subscribe directly to the company for shares.

Offer for sale: an invitation to apply for shares in a company based on information contained in a prospectus *(CIMA Official Terminology)*.

Placing: a method of raising share capital in which there is no public issue of shares, the shares being issued, rather, in a small number of large 'blocks', to persons or institutions who have previously agreed to purchase the shares at a predetermined price. *(CIMA Official Terminology)*.

4.3 In order to encourage the public to buy shares in a public company, it may issue a prospectus, or in the case of a company listed on the Stock Exchange, listing particulars. Listing particulars are subject to Stock Exchange rules.

Prospectus

4.4 The Companies Act definition of a prospectus covers all public advertisements for shares. It is an invitation to treat, such as we read about in Chapter 5. A prospectus has to comply with certain legal requirements under the Financial Services and Markets Act 2000.

Listing particulars

4.5 This document is similar to a prospectus, but, as mentioned above, it is governed by the rules of the Stock Exchange.

Private company

4.6 The allotment of shares in a private company is more straightforward. The key rule to remember is that private companies cannot sell shares to the public. An application will be made to the directors in a private company.

Directors' powers to allot shares

4.7 Directors may neither allot shares (except to subscribers to the memorandum and to employees' share schemes) nor grant options or convertible securities, without **authority from the members.**

4.8 Authority may be given either by the **articles** or by **ordinary resolution** passed in general meeting in conformity with s 80 or under the provisions of s 80A.

Director's power to allot shares	
Timescale	**Public companies** • Authority to allot must be given until a **specified date** • Authority to allot must be given for a **specified period** • Authority can be received by ordinary resolution in general meeting • Extension cannot be for more than five years **Private companies** • Authority to allot can be given **indefinitely** • Authority to allot can be given for fixed periods greater than five years
Maximum	**All companies** must specify a maximum number of shares which may be allotted.
Additional conditions	**All companies** may give additional conditions.
Resolution	An **ordinary** resolution is required. Signed copy must be sent to the Registrar with in 15 days.
General authority	Directors may have been given general authority to allot without further reference to general meeting. A **general meeting** must be called if • **No authority** has been given in advance • Authority is subject to certain **conditions** • Authority has **lapsed** or been used up
Breach of law	If directors have allotted wilfully without authority • The allotment is valid • Directors are punishable by fine

Exam focus point

Remember the basic distinction that (a) directors can only allot shares if they have the power to do so (given by the Articles, generally as part of their power of management) *and* (b) if they have the authority to *exercise* the power (given by the Articles or ordinary resolution under s 80).

Pre-emption rights: s 89 5/02

KEY TERM

Pre-emption rights are the rights of existing company shareholders to be offered new equity shares issued by the company *pro rata* to their existing holding of that class of shares.

4.9 If a company proposes to allot shares described as 'equity securities' (basically ordinary shares issued for cash) wholly for cash it generally has a **statutory obligation** to offer those shares first to holders of similar shares in **proportion to their holdings**: s 89 (a rights issue).

4.10 The offer must be made **in writing** in the same manner as a notice of a general meeting is sent to members. It must specify a period of **not less than 21 days** during which the offer may be accepted. If not accepted within that period the offer is deemed to be declined: s 90.

4.11 Equity securities which have been offered to members in this way but are not accepted may then be allotted on the same (or less favourable) terms to non-members.

4.12 If the **memorandum** or **articles** confer special rights of pre-emption on certain members of the company only, the offer must first be made to them; shares which they do not accept must then be offered to shareholders under s 89.

4.13 If equity securities are allotted in breach of these rules the members to whom the offer should have been made may within the ensuing two years recover **compensation** for their loss from those in default: s 92. The allotment will generally be valid.

Exclusion of pre-emption rights: s 91

4.14 A **private** company may by its memorandum or articles permanently exclude these rules so that there is no statutory right of first refusal: s 91.

Disapplication of pre-emption rights: s 95

4.15 **Any** company may, by special resolution resolve that the statutory right of first refusal shall not apply: s 95. Such a resolution to 'disapply' the right may either:

(a) Be **combined** with the **grant to directors** of **authority to allot shares** under s 80, or

(b) May simply **permit an offer** of shares to be made for cash to a non-member (without first offering the shares to members) on a particular occasion

4.16 In case (b) the directors, in inviting members to 'disapply' the right of first refusal, must issue a circular setting out their reasons, the price at which the shares are to be offered direct to a non-member and their justification of that price.

Issues for an improper purpose

4.17 We discussed in Chapter 13 the rules that directors may issue shares for a proper purpose, and that issues to manipulate the company's shareholdings were void, unless approved by the members in general meeting. Remember that holders of shares that have been issued irregularly **cannot vote** in a general meeting to sanction the directors' actions.

Rights issues

KEY TERM

A **rights issue** is a right given to a shareholder to subscribe for further shares in the company, usually *pro rata* to his/her existing holding in the company's shares.

4.18 As indicated above a rights issue is an allotment (or the offer of it by renounceable allotment letter) of additional shares made to existing members. If the members do not wish to subscribe for additional shares under a rights issue they may be able to sell their rights to other persons and so obtain the value of the option.

Bonus issues

> **KEY TERM**
>
> A **bonus issue** is the capitalisation of the reserves of a company by the issue of additional shares to existing shareholders, in proportion to their holdings. Such shares are normally fully paid-up with no cash called for from the shareholders. (CIMA, *Official Terminology*)

4.19 A bonus issue is more correctly but less often called a 'capitalisation issue' (also called a 'scrip' issue). The articles of a company usually give it power to apply its reserves (including its undistributed profits and reserves which could never be distributed as dividends) to paying up unissued shares wholly or in part and then to allot these shares as a bonus issue to members.

4.20 Table A Article 110 is the standard form of articles on **bonus issues**, requiring an **ordinary** resolution. Obviously **sufficient authorised capital** must be available to make the issue; if not it must be **increased** under s 121.

4.21 Section summary

- In order to allot shares **directors**:
  - Must have the **power** given by the articles
  - Must be given **authority** to allot
- The maximum number of shares to be allotted must be specified.
- The time period during which allotment can take place must not exceed five years (private companies can disapply this rule).
- Current members have pre-emption rights unless permanently excluded (private companies) or disapplied for a specific offer or set time (all companies).

5 CONSIDERATION FOR SHARES — Pilot Paper

5.1 Every share has a **nominal value** and **may not be allotted at a discount** to that.

ISSUES	
Partly paid shares	The no-discount rule only requires that, in allotting its shares, a company shall not fix a price which is less than the nominal value of the shares. It may leave part of that price to be paid at some later time. Thus £1 shares may be issued partly paid - 75p on allotment and 25p when called for or by instalment. The unpaid capital passes with the shares, if they are transferred, as a debt payable by the holder at the time when payment is demanded.
Underwriting fees	A company may pay underwriting or other commission in respect of an issue of shares if so permitted by its Articles (s 97 and Table A Article 4). This means that, if shares are issued at par the net amount received will be below par value. This is not a contravention of s 100 (prohibiting allotment of shares at a discount).
Bonus issue	The allotment of shares as a 'bonus issue' is for full consideration since reserves, which are shareholders' funds, are converted into fixed capital and used to pay for the shares: s 99(4).

Money's worth	The price for the shares may be paid in **money** or '**money's worth**', including goodwill and know-how: s 99. It need not be paid in cash and the company may agree to accept a '**non-cash' consideration** of sufficient value. For instance, a company may issue shares in payment of the price agreed in the purchase of a property. The rules on non-cash consideration are different for public and private companies (see below).

Private companies

5.2 A private company may allot shares for inadequate consideration by acceptance of goods or services at an over value. This loophole has been allowed to exist because in some cases it is very much a matter of opinion whether an asset is or is not of a stated value.

5.3 The courts therefore have refused to overrule directors in their valuation of an asset acquired for shares if it appears reasonable and honest: *Re Wragg 1897*. However a blatant and unjustified overvaluation will be declared invalid.

Public companies

5.4 The more **stringent rules** which apply to public companies regarding consideration and payment are as follows.

(a) **Future services are not to be accepted as consideration:** s 99(2). A public company may, however, allot shares to discharge a debt in respect of services already rendered.

(b) The company must, at the time of allotment, receive **at least one quarter of the nominal value** of the shares and the **whole** of any premium.

(c) **Non-cash consideration** may **not** be accepted as payment for shares if an undertaking contained in such consideration is to be, or may be, **performed more than five years after the allotment: s** 102. This relates to, say, a property or business in return for shares.

(d) Any **non-cash consideration** accepted must be **independently valued:** s 103. The valuation report must be madc to the company within the six months before the allotment. On receiving the report the company must send a copy to the proposed allottee and later to the registrar.

(e) Within **two years of receiving its certificate** under s 117, a public company **may not receive a transfer of non-cash assets from a subscriber** to the memorandum, unless its value as consideration is less than 10% of the issued nominal share capital and it has been independently valued and agreed by an ordinary resolution: s 104.

Allotment of shares at a premium

KEY TERM

Premium is an amount paid to a company for a share in excess of the nominal value of the share.

5.5 An established company may be able to obtain consideration for new shares in excess of their nominal value. The excess, called 'share premium', must be credited to a **share premium account** (s 130).

5.6 EXAMPLE

If a company allots its £1 (nominal) shares for £1.50 in cash, £1 per share is credited to the share capital account, and 50p to the share premium account.

5.7 The general rule is that reduction of the share premium account is subject to the **same** restrictions as reduction of share capital; a company cannot distribute any part of its share premium account as dividend: s 130.

Bonus issues

5.8 Share premium may be used to pay up fully paid shares under a bonus issue since this operation merely converts one form of fixed capital into another.

Other uses of the share premium account

5.9 The other permitted uses of share premium are to pay:

- **Capital expenses,** such as the preliminary expenses of forming the company
- A **discount on the issue of debentures** (NB shares cannot be issued at a discount)
- **A premium (if any) paid on the redemption of debentures:** s 130(2)
- Purchase of own shares out of capital by private companies

Exam focus point

The prohibition on offer of shares at a discount on *nominal* value is often confused with a company issuing shares at a price below *market* value (which is not prohibited).

6 CAPITAL MAINTENANCE

KEY TERM

Maintenance of capital is a fundamental principle of company law that limited companies should not be allowed to deplete their assets by making payments out of capital to the detriment of company creditors. Thus the Companies Act contains many examples of control upon capital payments. These include provisions restricting dividend payments, financial assistance to aid share purchases, the uses to which share premiums may be put, the freedom of a company to purchase its own shares, and capital reduction schemes.

6.1 The capital which a limited company obtains from its members as consideration for their shares is sometimes called 'the creditors' buffer'.

6.2 No one can prevent an unsuccessful company from losing its capital by trading at a loss. However, what capital the company does have must be held for the payment of the company's debts and may not be returned to members (except under procedures which safeguard the interest of creditors). It is these procedures which the remainder of this chapter are primarily concerned with.

6.3 However, there are some other aspects of capital maintenance for you to be aware of before you consider these detailed rules. The first is dividends and the second is the issue of loss of capital in a plc.

Dividends

6.4 As discussed earlier, ownership of a share gives the member a right to receive any dividends declared by the directors. There are certain rules governing the payment of dividends.

6.5 Dividends may only be paid by a company out of profits available for the purpose. In other words, they may not be paid out of capital. In the event of liquidation, a **liquidator** may take action against directors who have paid dividends out of capital. A **company** may recover unlawful dividends from members, if the member knew the distribution was unlawful.

KEY TERM

Profits available for distribution are accumulated realised profits (which have not been distributed or capitalised) less accumulated realised losses (which have not been previously written off in a reduction or reorganisation of capital).

6.6 A public company may only make a distribution if its **net assets** are equal to or greater than the aggregate of its called up share capital and undistributable reserves. Undistributable reserves are:

- Share premium account
- Capital redemption reserve
- Revaluation reserve
- Any reserve restricted by the articles

Loss of capital in a plc

6.7 If the net assets of a public company are half or less of the amount of its called up share capital there must be an extraordinary general meeting: s 142.

6.8 Where the directors' duty arises they must issue a notice to **convene a meeting** within **28 days** of becoming aware of the need to do so. The meeting must be convened for a date within 56 days of their coming to know the relevant facts.

6.9 The purpose of this procedure is to enable shareholders to consider 'whether any, and if so what, measures should be taken to deal with the situation'. If the capital falls below £50,000, the company must re-register as private.

7 REDUCTION OF SHARE CAPITAL **Pilot Paper**

7.1 A limited company is permitted without restriction to cancel **unissued** shares and in that way to **reduce** its **authorised** share capital. That change does not alter its financial position.

7.2 If a limited company with a share capital wishes to **reduce** its **issued** share capital (and so its authorised capital of which the issued capital is part) it may do so provided that:

- It has **power** to do so in its articles (if not it can alter the articles by special resolution).
- It passes a **special resolution.**
- It obtains **confirmation** of the reduction **from the court: s 135.**

7.3 A company may wish to reduce its capital for one or more of the following reasons.

- The company has suffered a **loss** in the **value** of its **assets** and it reduces its capital to reflect that fact.
- The company wishes to **extinguish** the **interests** of some members entirely.
- The capital reduction is part of a **complicated arrangement** of capital which may involve, for instance, replacing share capital with debt capital.

7.4 There are three basic methods of reducing share capital specified in s 135(2).

Method	What happens	Effects
Extinguish or reduce liability on partly paid shares	Eg Company has nominal value £1 shares 75p paid up. Either (a) reduce nominal value to 75p; or (b) reduce nominal value to figure between 75p and £1.	Company gives up claim for amount not paid up (nothing is **returned** to shareholders).
Pay off part of paid up share capital out of surplus assets	Eg Company reduces nominal value of fully paid shares from £1 to 70p and repays this amount to shareholders	Assets of company are reduced by 30p in £.
Cancel paid up share capital which has been lost/ which is no longer represented by available assets.	Eg Company has £1 nominal fully paid shares but net assets only worth 50p per share. Difference debit balance on reserves. Company reduces nominal value to 50p, and applies amount to write off debit balance	Company can resume payments out of future profits without having to make good past losses.

7.5 A company could also reduce capital by cancelling statutory capital reserves such as the share premium amount, or allotting debenture stock to shareholders.

Role of court in reduction of capital

Protection of creditors

7.6 When the court receives an application for reduction of capital its first concern is the effect of the reduction on the company's ability to pay its debts: s 136. If the reduction is by extinguishing liability or paying off part of paid up share capital, the court **must** generally require that **creditors** shall be **invited** by advertisement to state their objections (if any) to the reduction. Where paid up share capital is cancelled, the court **may** require an invitation to creditors.

7.7 Normally the company persuades the court to dispense with advertising for creditors' objections (which can be commercially damaging to the company). Two possible approaches are:

- To **pay off** all **creditors** before application is made to the court; or, if that is not practicable

- To produce to the court a **guarantee**, say from the company's bank, that its existing debts will be paid in full

Effect on different classes of shareholder

7.8 The court also considers whether, if there is more than one class of share, the reduction is fair in its effect on different classes of shareholder. If the reduction is, **in the circumstances**, a **variation of class rights** (for example removal of the right to an interest in the surplus on a winding-up) the **consent** of the class must be obtained under the variation of class rights procedure.

7.9 Within each class of shares it is usual to make a uniform reduction of every share by the same amount per share, though this is **not** obligatory.

Other issues

7.10 The court may be concerned that the reduction should not confuse or mislead people who may deal with the company in future; for instance, it may insist that the company add 'and reduced' to its name or publish explanations of the reduction.

Approval by the court

7.11 If the court is satisfied that the reduction is in order, it approves the reduction by making an order to that effect.

7.12 A **copy of the court order** and of a **minute**, approved by the court, to show the altered share capital is delivered to the registrar who issues a certificate of registration.

Question 2

Which one of the following statements is incorrect in relation to the maintenance of capital rule?

A Share capital must be put aside as a fund to pay creditors in the event of the company becoming insolvent.

B A company cannot simply give share capital back to its members.

C Share capital may be returned to members following an approved reduction of capital scheme.

D Share capital should be used to further the company's lawful objects.

Answer

A. The money raised can always be used in the company's business, and thus the company may lose it through its trading activities.

8 REDEMPTION AND PURCHASE BY A COMPANY OF ITS OWN SHARES

8.1 S 143 states that **a company cannot acquire its own shares** by purchase, subscription or other method.

8.2 A company can however accept shares as a gift. It would then usually cancel those shares.

8.3 The prohibition is subject to exceptions. A company may:

- Purchase its own shares in compliance with a **court order**
- Issue and redeem **redeemable** shares

- **Purchase** its **own shares** under certain specified procedures
- Forfeit or **accept** the **surrender** of its shares

Redeemable shares

Pilot Paper

KEY TERM

Redeemable shares are shares which are issued on terms which may require them to be bought back by the issuer at some future date, either at the discretion of the issuer or of the holder. Redemption must comply with the conditions of the Companies Act, 1985. (CIMA, *Official Terminology*)

8.4 Both ordinary and preference shares may be issued on terms which allow the company to redeem them. The expression redeemable shares means only shares which are redeemable from the time of issue, so shares not issued as redeemable cannot later be made so.

8.5 The conditions for the issue and redemption of redeemable shares are set out in ss 159 and 160.

The articles must give **authority** for the issue of redeemable shares (Table A does). If the articles do not, they must be altered before the shares are issued: s 159(1).
Redeemable shares may only be issued if, at the time of issue, the company also has **issued shares** which are **not redeemable**. A company's capital may not consist entirely of redeemable shares: s 159(2).
Redeemable shares may only be redeemed if they are **fully paid**: s 159(3).
The terms of redemption must provide for **payment on redemption**: s 159(3).
The shares may be redeemed out of: • **Distributable profits** • The **proceeds of a new issue** of shares • **Capital** (if it is a **private** company) In accordance with the relevant rules: s 160(1).
Any **premium payable on redemption** must generally be provided out of **distributable profits**.
The company may redeem shares on such **terms** and in such manner as may be provided by the company's **articles**, subject only to the specific provisions set out in Chapter VII of the Act.

8.6 When shares are redeemed they are cancelled and may not be reissued.

(a) The amount of the company's **issued** share capital is **reduced** by the **nominal amount** of the shares but its authorised capital is unaltered: s 160(4).

(b) Any new shares issued to raise money to redeem shares are treated as a **replacement** for them to the extent that the nominal value of the new shares does not exceed the nominal value of the shares redeemed: s 160(5).

(c) If shares are redeemed wholly out of profits an amount equal to the nominal value of shares redeemed must be transferred to a **capital redemption reserve** which is to be treated as if it were share capital, except that it may be applied in paying up unissued shares as a bonus issue.

Purchase of own shares

8.7 A limited company may purchase its own shares by market or off-market purchase:

- **Out of profits or the proceeds of an issue of new shares** under the same rules that apply to redemption of shares
- If it is a **private company,** out of **capital;** this must by definition be an off-market purchase since no market purchase may be made of a private company's shares

8.8 A company cannot, however, purchase ordinary shares if, as a result, only redeemable shares are left.

8.9 An **unlimited** company can reduce its share capital or purchase its own shares without complying with any statutory rules.

8.10 There are two methods of carrying out the purchase, off-market or market purchase. Either can be used for any type of share, but only public companies can use the market method, as private companies will not have shares available on a public market.

- **Market purchase** is purchase under the normal market arrangements of a recognised investment exchange.
- **Off-market purchase** is any other purchase, usually by private treaty. This will apply to shares of private companies.

Market purchase of own shares (s166)	
Authority	The purchase must be authorised by ordinary resolution specifying • **Maximum** number of **shares** to be acquired • Maximum and minimum prices to be paid ◦ By global sum, or ◦ By price formula • Specify a date (< 18 months after resolution) on which authority expires
Filing	A copy of the resolution must be sent to the **Registrar** within 15 days
Changes	The authority may be **varied, revoked** or **renewed**

Off market purchase of own shares (s 164)	
Authority	A contract for the purchase of shares must be approved in advance by **special resolution**
Inspection	A copy of the proposed contract must be available for inspection by members • At the registered office • For 15 days before the meeting for approval • At the meeting It must disclose the names of the seller
Voting	The **member** who intends to **sell** the shares should **not vote** If he does vote and the resolution would not have been carried without his vote, it is invalid He may cast votes attached to other shares which he is not selling
Public company	A public company may only be given **authority** for a **limited period** (maximum 6 months)

Filing	The company must make a **return** to the Registrar giving prescribed particulars within **28 days** of making the purchase
Changes	The authority may be **varied, revoked** or **renewed**

Payment for shares out of capital - private companies only

8.11 A private limited company which has a share capital may redeem or purchase its shares 'out of capital' by a '**permissible capital payment**' to which elaborate rules apply: s 171. These rules are designed to ensure that the company does not make itself insolvent.

8.12 The conditions are as follows.

(a) There must be general **authority** in the **articles** for redemption or purchase of shares out of capital (such as Table A Article 35).

(b) Capital may only be used to '**top up**' distributable profits and the proceeds of any issue of new shares in cases where those resources, fully used, do not suffice to make up the required amount,

$$\text{Cost of redemption or purchase} = \text{Available distributable profits} + \text{Proceeds of fresh issue} + \text{Permissible capital payment}$$

(c) A **capital redemption reserve** must be created where the amount of the permissible capital payment is less than the nominal amount of the shares redeemed or purchased: s 171(4).

If the payment is greater than the nominal amount then the capital redemption reserve, share premium account, share capital or revaluation reserve of the company may be reduced by the excess: s 171(5).

(d) A **statutory declaration of the directors** must be made and supported by a report of the auditors to the effect that after the payment is made the company will be able to pay its debts and to carry on its business for at least a year to come: s 173. These must also be delivered to the registrar: s 195.

(e) Shareholders must approve the payment by passing a **special resolution**. In this decision any vendor of shares may **not** use the votes attached to the shares which he is to sell to the company: s 173.

(f) A member who did not vote for the resolution and a creditor (for any amount) may within five weeks **apply to the court to cancel the resolution**, which may not be implemented until the five weeks have elapsed: s 176.

(g) A **notice** must be placed in the *Gazette* and in an appropriate national newspaper, **or** every creditor must be informed: s 175.

8.13 If the company goes into insolvent liquidation within a year of making a payment out of capital the persons who received the payment and the directors who authorised it may have to make it good to the company.

Subsidiary not to be a member of its holding company

8.14 The restrictions on acquisition by a company of its own shares are extended by a general prohibition against a subsidiary being a member of its holding company: s 23.

8.15 Section summary

- All companies can issue and redeem **redeemable shares** provided their **articles allow it**.
- A company issuing redeemable shares must have **non-redeemable shares** in issue.
- Various conditions apply to redemption, including shares being fully paid and payment being made on redemption.
- All companies can purchase their own shares out of **profits** or the **proceeds** of a **fresh issue**.
- Purchase can be by **market** or **off-market** purchase.
- A private company can purchase its shares out of capital subject to **strict conditions.**

9 FINANCIAL ASSISTANCE FOR PURCHASE OF SHARES 5/01

KEY TERM

Financial assistance is the provision of benefit by a company to a person to put that person in funds so that s/he may purchase shares in the company.

The rule against financial assistance

9.1 The general rules apply to all public companies, and all private companies who do not follow the procedures outlined below.

(a) A company is **prohibited** from **giving** any **financial assistance** for the **purpose** of the **acquisition** of **shares** either of the company or of its holding company or to **discharge liabilities** incurred in making the acquisition (subject to certain exceptions).

(b) 'Financial assistance' is elaborately defined to mean:

- A loan
- A guarantee indemnity or security
- Purchase of such rights from a third party
- 'Any other financial assistance given by a company which reduces to a material extent, its net assets': s 152

9.2 A company may give a person financial assistance as part of a wider purpose of the company and in good faith, so two main tests have to be applied to any suspect transaction.

What was its **purpose**? It is not objectionable if its **principal purpose** was **not** to give financial assistance for the purchase of the shares nor if it was an incidental part of some **larger purpose** of the company: s 153(1)(a).
What was the state of mind of the directors in approving the transaction? Did they act in **good faith** in what they deemed to be the interests of the company and not of a third party: s 153 (1)(b).

Giving financial assistance: private companies

9.3 A private company may give financial assistance for the acquisition of its own shares or the shares of its holding company, subject to the following conditions of ss 155 - 158.

The financial assistance given **must not reduce the net assets** of the company or, if it does, the financial assistance is to be provided out of distributable profits.
There must be a **statutory declaration of solvency** by the directors of the company (with a report by the auditors) of the same type as is prescribed when a private company purchases its own shares by a payment out of capital.
A **special resolution** must be passed to approve the transaction. Normally this is a resolution of the company which gives the assistance.
A right to **apply to the court** is given to members holding at least 10% of the issued shares (or of a class of shares). To permit them to exercise this right there is a four week standstill on the implementation of the resolution.
The procedure described above is not available to any group of companies which includes a public company.

Other exceptions from the financial assistance rules

9.4 Three specific exceptions are also made. A company is not prohibited from entering into any of the following transactions: s 153(4).

(a) Making a loan if **lending is part of its ordinary business,** and the loan is made in the ordinary course of its business; this exception is restricted to money-lending companies

(b) Providing money in good faith and in the best interests of the company for the purpose of an **employees' share scheme** or for other share transactions by *bona fide* employees or connected persons

(c) **Making loans** to persons (other than directors) employed in good faith by the company with a view to those **persons acquiring fully paid shares** in the company or its holding company to be held by them as beneficial owners

9.5 Section summary

- S 151 prohibits a company giving **financial assistance** for the purchase of its own shares.
- Financial assistance is defined to include many arrangements, although certain transactions do not count as financial assistance.
- **Private companies** are allowed to give financial assistance under certain stringent conditions.

Exam focus point

Do not confuse a company purchasing its own shares with a company providing financial assistance for **someone else** to purchase its shares.

Chapter roundup

- A **share** is a transferable form of property, carrying rights and obligations, by which the interest of a member of a company limited by shares is measured.
- A **public** company must have a minimum of **two** members. A **private** company may be formed and operate with only **one** member.
- If the constitution of a company states no differences between shares, it is assumed that they are all **ordinary** shares with parallel rights and obligations. There may, however, be other types, notably **preference shares** and **redeemable shares**.
- The holders of **issued** shares have **vested rights** which can only be altered by using a strict procedure. The standard procedure is by **extraordinary resolution** passed by at least **three quarters** of the votes cast at a **separate class meeting** or by written consent.
- Directors may receive the **delegated power** to allot shares, either from the articles or a resolution in general meeting.
- If the directors propose to allot 'equity securities' wholly for cash, there is a general requirement to offer these shares to **holders** of **similar shares** in proportion to their holdings.
- In issuing shares, a company must fix a **price** which is **equal** to or **more than** the **nominal value of the shares**. If shares are issued at a premium, the **excess** must be credited to a **share premium** account.
- A limited company may reduce its issued share capital provided:
  - It has **power** to do so in its articles.
  - A **special resolution** is passed.
  - The court **confirms** the reduction under s 135.
- Elaborate rules govern the ability of private and public companies to **redeem** or **purchase** their own shares.
- A **private** company may **purchase its own shares out of capital** subject to restrictions.
- A **public** company may not give **financial assistance** to a third party to purchase shares in the company. A private company can do so, however, under certain conditions.

Quick quiz

1. What is the difference between authorised and called up share capital?
2. If a company fails to pay preference shareholders their dividend, they can bring a court action to compel the company to pay the dividend.

   ☐ True

   ☐ False
3. Which of the following are implied rights of preference shareholders

   A The right to receive a dividend is cumulative.

   B If the company goes into liquidation, preference shareholders are entitled to claim all arrears of dividend from the liquidator.

   C As well as rights to their preference dividends, preference shareholders can share equally in dividends payable to ordinary shareholders.

   D Preference shareholders have a priority right over ordinary shares for the return of their capital.

   E Preference shareholders have equal voting rights to ordinary shareholders.

4 If class rights are defined otherwise than by the memorandum, and there is no variation procedures in the articles, consent of a three quarters majority of the class is required to alter the class rights.

☐ True

☐ False

5 If a company issues new ordinary shares for cash, the general rule is that:

A The shares must first be offered to existing members in the case of a public but not a private company.

B The shares must first be offered to existing members whether the company is public or private.

C The shares must first be offered to existing members in the case of a private but not a public company.

D The shares need not be issued to existing members.

6 **Fill in the blanks** in the statements below.

A ……………….. issue is an allotment of additional shares to existing members in exchange for consideration payable by the members.

A ……………….. issue is an allotment of additional shares to existing members where the consideration is effectively paid by using the company's reserves.

7 **Fill in the blanks** in the statements below.

If there has been a variation of class rights, a minority of holders of shares of the class (who have not consented or voted in favour of the variation) may apply to the court to have the variation cancelled. The objectors must hold not less than ……………….. of the issued shares of that class, and apply to the court within ……………….. days of the giving of consent by that class.

8 Where application is made to the court for approval of a reduction in capital, the court may require that creditors should be invited by advertisement to state their objections. In which of the following ways can the need to advertise be avoided?

A Paying off all creditors before application to the court
B Producing a document signed by the directors stating the company's ability to pay its debt
C Producing a guarantee from the company's bank that its existing debts will be paid in full
D Renouncement by existing shareholders of their limited liability in relation to existing debts
E Production of a comfort letter from a holding company

9 Which of the following statements are true of redeemable shares?

A The articles must give authority for the issue of redeemable shares.
B A company's capital cannot consist entirely of redeemable shares.
C Redeemable shares may only be redeemed if they are fully paid.
D Redeemable shares may only be redeemed from distributable profits, not capital.
E The terms of redemption must provide for payment on redemption.

10 No company may give financial assistance for the purchase of its own shares unless that assistance is for certain specified purposes.

☐ True

☐ False

11 Put the steps to complete an unlisted company transfer procedure in the correct order.

Step … The **company issues** to him a **new share certificate** within two months (s 185) and cancels the old one.

Step … The **buyer becomes** the **holder** and legal owner of the shares only when his **name is entered in the register of members:** s 22.

Step … The **registered holder** (the 'seller') **completes** and **signs** the **stock transfer form** and **delivers** it with his share certificate to the **transferee** (the 'buyer').

Step … The buyer **completes** the **transfer** and **pays stamp duty** before **delivering** it to the **company** (with the seller's share certificate) for registration.

12 Match the definitions to the correct type of capital

(a) Authorised share capital
(b) Issued share capital
(c) Called up share capital
(d) Paid up share capital

(i) The amount which the company has required shareholders to pay on shares issued.
(ii) The type, class, number and amount of the shares held by the shareholders.
(iii) The type, class, number and amount of the shares which a company may issue.
(iv) The amount which shareholders are deemed to have paid on the shares issued and called up.

13 Which of the following transactions are not prohibited by CA 85?

- Payment of a dividend out of profits
- Distribution of assets in a winding up
- Allotment of bonus shares
- Giving financial assistance to a public company director to buy shares in the company
- Court approved reduction of capital

Answers to quick quiz

1 Authorised share capital is the total amount of capital that a company can issue under the terms of the capital clause in its memorandum. Called up share capital is the amount payable by shareholders on the capital that has been issued

2 False. The company may decide not to pay any dividend, or may be unable to because it does not have any distributable profits. What the preference shareholders have is a right to receive their dividends before other dividends are paid or declared.

3 A and E are implied rights; the others have to be stated explicitly.

4 True

5 B

6 A *rights* issue is an allotment of additional shares to existing members in exchange for consideration payable by the members.

A *bonus* issue is an allotment of additional shares to existing members where the consideration is effectively paid by using the company's reserves.

7 If there has been a variation of class rights, a minority of holders of shares of the class (who have not consented or voted in favour of the variation) may apply to the court to have the variation cancelled. The objectors must hold not less than *15%* of the issued shares of that class, and apply to the court within *21* days of the giving of consent by that class.

8 A and C. The only guarantee that the courts will accept is from the company's bank.

9 A, B, C and E are correct. D is wrong, as shares can be redeemed out of the proceeds of a fresh issue, and a private company can redeem shares out of capital.

10 False. A private company may give financial assistance for any reason providing it follows the procedures in ss 155-158.

11 ***Step 1.*** **The** registered holder **(the 'seller')** completes **and** signs **the** stock transfer form **and** delivers **it with his share certificate to the** transferee **(the 'buyer').**

Step 2. The buyer **completes** the **transfer** and **pays stamp duty** before **delivering** it to the **company** (with the seller's share certificate) for registration.

Step 3. The **buyer becomes** the **holder** and legal owner of the shares only when his **name is entered in the register of members**: s 22.

Step 4. The **company issues** to him a **new share certificate** within two months (s 185) and cancels the old one.

12 (a) (iii)
(b) (ii)
(c) (i)
(d) (iv)

13
- Payment of a dividend out of profits
- Distribution of assets in a winding up
- Allotment of bonus shares
- Court approved reduction in capital

The following relevant questions are included in the Exam Question Banks

You can attempt these now. However, we would advise you to attempt these as mock exams at the end of your initial stage of study

Exam Question Bank	Numbers
Paper based format	18, 19, 20, 26, 27
Computer based assessment	23, 34

Chapter 15

BORROWING AND LOAN CAPITAL

	Topic list	Syllabus reference	Ability required
1	Borrowing	(vii)	Comprehension
2	Debentures	(vii)	Comprehension
3	Charges	(vii)	Comprehension
4	Registration of charges	(vii)	Comprehension
5	Debentureholders' remedies	(vii)	Comprehension
6	Transactions at an undervalue and preferences	(vii)	Comprehension

Introduction

The last chapter was concerned with share capital. In this chapter on borrowing and loan capital, you should note that the interests and position of a lender are very different from that of a shareholder.

This chapter covers how loan capital holders protect themselves, specifically through taking out **fixed or floating charges**.

You need to understand the differences between fixed and floating charges, and also how they can protect loan creditors, for example by giving chargeholders the ability to appoint a receiver.

Learning outcomes covered in this chapter

- **Explain** the ability of a company to take secured and unsecured loans, the different types of security and the registration procedure

Syllabus content covered in this chapter

- The ability of a company to borrow money and the procedure to be followed
- Unsecured loans, and the nature and effect of fixed and floating charges

1 BORROWING

1.1 A company whose objects are to carry on a trade or business has an implied power to borrow for purposes incidental to the trade or business. A non-trading company must have an express power to borrow since it is not implied.

1.2 In delegating the company's power to borrow to the directors it is usual, and essential in the case of a company whose shares are listed on the Stock Exchange, to impose a **maximum** limit on the **borrowing** arranged by directors.

1.3 When they need to raise capital, the directors will often be faced by a straight choice between issuing shares and borrowing. They will consider factors such as: comparative costs of issue, the timescale of the money requirement, and the associated ongoing costs in terms of dividends and interest.

2 DEBENTURES

> **KEY TERM**
> A **debenture** is the written acknowledgement of a debt by a company, usually given under its seal, and normally containing provisions as to payment of interest and the terms of repayment of principal. A debenture may be secured on some or all of the assets of the company or its subsidiaries. (CIMA, *Official Terminology*)

2.1 A debenture may create a **charge** over the company's assets as security for the loan. Charges are discussed in section 3. However a document relating to an unsecured loan is also a debenture in company law.

2.2 A debenture is usually a formal legal document, often in printed form. Broadly, there are three main types.

(a) **A single debenture**

If, for example, a company obtains a secured loan or overdraft facility from its bank, the latter is likely to insist that the company seals the bank's standard form of debenture creating the charge and giving the bank various safeguards and powers.

(b) **Debentures issued as a series and usually registered**

Different lenders may provide different amounts on different dates. Although each transaction is a separate loan, the intention is that the lenders should rank equally *(pari passu)* in their right to repayment and in any security given to them. Each lender therefore receives a debenture in identical form in respect of his loan.

The debentures are transferable securities. The normal conditions require the company to maintain a register of debentureholders (unless they are bearer debentures).

(c) **The issue of debenture stock subscribed to by a large number of lenders**

Only a public company may use this method to offer its debentures to the public and any such offer is a prospectus; if it seeks a listing on The Stock Exchange then the rules on listing particulars must be followed.

Each lender has a right to be **repaid** his **capital** at the **due time** and to receive **interest** on it until **repayment**. This form of borrowing is treated as a single global loan 'stock' in which each debenture stockholder has a specified fraction (in money terms) which he or some previous holder contributed when the stock was issued. Debenture stock is transferable in multiples of, say, £1 or £10.

A company will maintain a register of debenture stockholders.

The terms of the debenture stock are expressed in a trust deed, and a trustee for the debenture stockholders is appointed to represent their interests and to enforce their rights. Each debenture stockholder receives a debenture stock certificate.

2.3 One advantage of debenture stock over debentures issued as single and indivisible loan transactions is that the holder of debenture stock can sell part of his holding, say £1,000 (nominal) out of a larger amount.

Debenture trust deed

2.4 A **debenture trust deed** usually contains the following major elements.

(a) **The appointment usually of a trustee for prospective debenture stockholders**. The trustee is usually a bank, insurance company or other institution but may be an individual.

(b) **The nominal amount of the debenture** stock is defined, which is the maximum amount which may be raised then or later. The date or period of repayment is specified, as is the rate of interest and half-yearly interest payment dates.

(c) If the debenture stock is secured **the deed creates a charge or charges** over the assets of the company.

(d) The trustee is authorised to **enforce the security** in case of default and, in particular, to appoint a receiver with suitable powers of management.

(e) The company enters into **various covenants**, for instance to keep its assets fully insured or to limit its total borrowings; breach is a default by the company.

(f) There may be elaborate provisions for a **register** of debenture stockholders, **transfer of stock** and **meetings** of debenture stockholders.

2.5 The main **advantages** of the use of a debenture trust deed are as follows.

(a) The **trustee** with appropriate powers can **intervene promptly** in case of default.

(b) **Security** for the debenture stock in the form of charges over property can be **given to a single trustee**.

(c) The **company** can **contact a representative of the debentureholders** with whom it can negotiate.

(d) By calling a **meeting of debentureholders**, the trustee can consult them and obtain a decision binding on them all.

(e) The **debentureholders** will be able to **enjoy the benefit of a legal mortgage** over the company's land. This would not be possible without trustees since under the Law of Property Act 1925, a legal estate in land cannot be vested in more than four persons.

Register of debentureholders

2.6 Company law does not require a register of debentureholders be maintained. The company may choose to do so.

Rights of debentureholders

2.7 The position of debentureholders is best described by comparison with that of shareholders. At first sight the two appear to have a great deal in common.

(a) Both **own transferable company securities** which are usually long-term investments in the company.

(b) The **issue procedure** is much the same. An offer of either shares or debentures to the public is a prospectus as defined by s 744.

(c) The **procedure** for **transfer** of registered shares and debentures is the same.

2.8 There are however important and more fundamental differences.

FACTOR	SHAREHOLDER	DEBENTURE HOLDER
Role	Is a proprietor or **owner** of the company	Is a **creditor** of the company
Voting rights	May vote at general meetings	May not vote
Cost of investment	Shares **may not** be issued at a discount	Debentures **may** be offered at a discount
Return	Dividends are only paid • Out of distributable profits • When directors declared them	Interest **must** be paid when it is due
Redemption	Statutory restrictions on redeeming shares	No restriction on redeeming debentures
Liquidation	Shareholders arc the last people to be paid in a winding up	Debentures must be paid back before shareholders are paid

2.9 From the investor's standpoint debenture stock is often preferable to preference shares since the former offers greater security and either yields a fixed income.

Advantages and disadvantages of debentures (for the company)

Advantages	Disadvantages
Easily traded	May have to pay high interest to make them attractive
Terms clear and specific	Interest payments mandatory
Asset floating charged may be traded	Interest payments may upset shareholders if dividends fall
Popular due to guaranteed income	Debentureholder's remedies of liquidators or receivers may be disastrous for the company
Interest tax-deductible	
No restrictions on issue or purchase by a company	Crystallisation of a floating charge can cause trading difficulties for a company

Question 1

Explain how the rights of the shareholders of a company differ from the rights of its debentureholders.

Answer

Rights of shareholders and debentureholders

Shareholders are members of the company. Debentureholders are creditors but not members of the company. Their relationships with the company differ in the following principal respects.

What governs the relationship

A company's relationship with its shareholders is governed by

(a) Its memorandum and articles which operate as a contract between them and between the shareholders and each other (s 14), and

(b) The Companies Act

The relationship between a company and its debentureholders is regulated by:

(a) The terms of the trust deed or other formal document, and
(b) (Different) provisions of the Companies Act

The major practical differences are set out below.

Voting

As members of the company, shareholders have the right to attend and vote at meetings. Debentureholders have no such automatic rights; they may however have votes if the articles and deed allow.

Income

A shareholder, even if he holds preference shares on which fixed dividends are due on specific days, can only receive dividends out of distributable profits. In addition he cannot force the company to pay dividends: *Bond v Barrow Haematite Steel Co 1902.*

By contrast interest at the agreed rate must be paid on debentures even if that interest has to be paid out of capital.

Rights on securities

The Companies Act confers pre-emption rights on shareholders, entitling them to first call on any new shares which are to be issued: s 89.

Debentureholders have no right of objection to further loans and debentures being taken out, unless the trust deed sets out restrictions. However there is no statutory restriction on debentureholders having debentures redeemed or purchased by the company. By contrast there are detailed rules regulating redemption or purchase of a company's own shares.

Rights if aggrieved

Shareholders have the right to complain to the court if directors are allowing ultra vires transactions (s 35 (2)) or acting in a manner unfairly prejudicial to their interests (s 459). Shareholders can by simple majority remove directors from the board: s 303.

Debentureholders may have rights under the trust deed if the company breaches the agreement. These include:

(a) The right to appoint a receiver, or

(b) The right if given to enforce charges and sell the property under the charge to realise their debts

Their consent may also be required before the company deals with certain of its assets, when the debentureholders have secured their loan by means of a fixed charge over those assets.

Rights on liquidation

In liquidation debentureholders must be repaid in full before anything is distributed to shareholders.

3 CHARGES 5/01, 11/01, 5/02

KEY TERM

A **charge** is an encumbrance upon real or personal property granting the holder certain rights over that property, usually as security for a debt owed to the charge holder. The most common form of charge is by way of legal mortgage, used to secure the indebtedness of borrowers in house purchase transactions. In the case of companies, charges over assets are most frequently granted to persons who provide loan capital to the business.

3.1 A charge **secured** over a company's assets gives to the creditor (called the 'chargee') a prior claim (over other creditors) to payment of his debt out of those assets. Charges are of two kinds, fixed and floating.

KEY TERM

A **fixed charge** is a form of protection given to secured creditors relating to specific assets of a company. The charge grants the holder the right of enforcement against the identified asset (in the event of default in repayment) so that the creditor may realise the asset to meet the debt owed. Fixed charges rank first in order of priority in receivership or liquidation. (CIMA, *Official Terminology*)

3.2 **Fixed or specific charges** attach to the relevant asset as soon as the charge is created. By its nature a fixed charge is best suited to fixed assets which the company is likely to retain for a long period. If the company does dispose of the asset it will either repay the secured debt out of the proceeds of sale so that the charge is discharged at the time of sale, or pass the asset over to the purchaser still subject to the charge.

KEY TERM

A **floating charge** has been defined (*Re Yorkshire Woolcombers Association Ltd 1903*) as:

- A charge on a class of assets of a company, present and future . . .
- Which class is, in the ordinary course of the company's business, changing from time to time and . . .
- Until the holders enforce the charge the company may carry on business and deal with the assets charged.

3.3 **Floating charges** do not attach to the relevant assets until the charge crystallises. A floating charge is not restricted however to current assets such as book debts or stock in trade. A floating charge over 'the undertaking and assets' of a company (the most common type) applies to fixed as well as to current assets.

Crystallisation of a floating charge

KEY TERM

Crystallisation of a floating charge occurs when it is converted into a fixed equitable charge: that is, a fixed charge on the assets owned by the company at the time of crystallisation: *Re Griffin Hotel Co Ltd 1941.*

3.4 Events causing crystallisation are as follows:

(a) The **liquidation** of the company

(b) **Cessation** of the company's **business**

(c) **Active intervention** by the chargee, generally by way of appointing a receiver

(d) If the **charge contract so provides**, when notice is given by the chargee that the charge is converted into a fixed charge (on whatever assets of the relevant class are owned by the company at the time of the giving of notice)

(e) The **crystallisation** of **another floating charge** if it causes the company to cease business.

3.5 Floating charge contracts sometimes make provision for 'automatic crystallisation': that is, the charge is to crystallise when a **specified event** - such as a breach of some term by the company - occurs, whether or not:

- The chargee learns of the event.
- The chargee wants to enforce the charge as a result of the event.

Comparison of fixed and floating charges

3.6 A fixed charge is normally the more satisfactory form of security since it confers immediate rights over identified assets. A floating charge has some advantage in being applicable to current assets which may be easier to realise than fixed assets subject to a fixed charge. If for example a company becomes insolvent it may be easier to sell its stock than its empty factory.

3.7 The principal **disadvantages** of **floating charges** are as follows.

(a) The **holder** of a floating charge **cannot be certain** until the charge crystallises (often through the company failing) which assets will form his security.

(b) Even when a floating charge has crystallised over an identified pool of assets the **chargeholder** may find himself **postponed** to the claim of **other creditors** as follows.

(i) A **judgement creditor or landlord** who has seized goods and sold them may retain the proceeds if received before the appointment of the debentureholder's receiver: s 183 IA.

(ii) **Preferential debts** such as taxation may be paid out of assets subject to a floating charge unless there are other uncharged assets available for this purpose: ss 40 and 175 IA.

(iii) The **holder** of a **fixed charge** over the same assets will usually have priority over a floating charge on those assets even if that charge was created before the fixed charge (see below).

(iv) A creditor may have sold goods and delivered them to the company on condition that he is to retain legal ownership until he has been paid (a **Romalpa** clause).

(c) A **floating charge** may become **invalid automatically** if the company creates the charge to secure an existing debt and goes into liquidation within a year thereafter (s 245 IA); the period is only six months with a fixed charge.

Priority of charges

3.8 If different charges over the same property are given to different creditors their priority must be determined.

3.9 EXAMPLE

If charges are created over the same property to secure a debt of £5,000 to X and £7,000 to Y and the property is sold yielding only £10,000 either X or Y is paid in full and the other receives only the balance remaining out of £10,000 realised from the security.

3.10 Leaving aside the question of registration (discussed below), the main points to remember in connection with the priority of any charges are as follows.

(a) **Legal charges** rank according to the **order of creation**. If two successive legal charges over the same factory are created on 1 January and 1 February the earlier takes priority over the later one.

(b) An equitable charge created before a legal charge will only take priority over the latter if, when the latter was created, the **legal chargee** had **notice** of the equitable charge.

(c) A **legal charge created before** an **equitable one** has **priority**.

(d) **Two equitable charges** take priority according to the **time of creation**.

3.11 If a floating charge is created and a fixed charge over the same property is created later, the **fixed** charge will rank **first** since it attached to the property at the time of **creation** but the **floating** charge attaches at the time of **crystallisation**. Once a floating charge has crystallised it becomes a fixed charge and a fixed charge created subsequently ranks after it.

3.12 A creditor to whom a floating charge is given may seek to protect himself against losing his priority by including in the terms of his floating charge a prohibition against the company creating a fixed charge over the same property which would otherwise take priority (sometimes called a '**negative pledge clause**'). If the company breaks that prohibition the creditor to whom the fixed charge is given nonetheless obtains priority, unless at the time when his charge is created he has actual knowledge of the prohibition.

3.13 If a company sells a charged asset to a third party the following rules apply.

(a) A chargee with a legal charge still has recourse to the property in the hands of the third party - the **charge** is **automatically** transferred with the property.

(b) Property only remains charged by an equitable charge if the **third party** had **notice** of it when he acquired the property.

Question 2

A floating charge is created on 1 January 20X1. A fixed charge over the same property is created on 1 April 20X1. Assuming both are registered within the prescribed time limits, which ranks first?

A The floating charge

B The fixed charge

C The floating charge becomes a fixed charge on crystallisation, and at that point ranks before the original fixed charge

D On crystallisation of the floating charge to a fixed charge, both rank pari passu (as fixed charges)

Answer

B. The fixed charge attaches to the asset on creation; the floating charge only attaches on crystallisation, and the effect of crystallisation is not retrospective.

Avoidance of floating charges

3.14 Liquidation automatically renders void, under s 245, any floating charge created within the period of 12 months (or in the case where the charge was created in favour of a 'connected person', two years) subject to the following exceptions.

(a) The charge is **valid** if the company was **solvent** at the time when the charge was created, unless as a result of the transaction under which the charge was created the company became unable to pay its debts. This exception does not apply where the charge was created in favour of a '**connected person**'. Note that a company is not solvent unless it can pay its **debts in full** as they fall **due**.

(b) If the company was not solvent at the time the charge was created, the floating charge is still valid to the extent of **money paid** or **goods and services** received by the company at the same time or after the charge is created, or discharge or reduction of the company's liability.

3.15 Only the charge (as security), not the debt, becomes void: s 247.

3.16 Section summary

- **Fixed charges** attach to assets (generally fixed assets) from **creation**.
- Floating charges have three characteristics.
  - A charge on a **class** of assets
  - The **class** is **changing from time to time**
  - The **company can deal** with the **assets** until the charge is enforced
- Floating charges **crystallise** (conversion into a fixed equitable charge) on the happening of certain relevant events.
- Floating charges rank behind a number of other creditors on liquidation, in particular preferential creditors such as tax authorities.

Exam focus point

This is an important section for your exam. You should be aware of what fixed and floating charges are, and what the implications are of the differences between them.

4 REGISTRATION OF CHARGES

The registration process

4.1 Certain types of charges created by a company should be registered within **21 days** with the registrar: s 395 (1) and s 399 (1). Charges securing a debenture issue and floating charges are specifically registrable: s 396 (1).

4.2 Other charges that are registrable include charges on:

- Uncalled share capital or calls made but not paid
- Land or any interest in land, but not rent or other periodic sums from the land
- Book debts
- Goodwill or any intellectual property
- Ships or aircraft or any share in a ship

4.3 The company is responsible for registering the charge but the charge may also be registered as a result of an application by another person interested in the charge.

4.4 The registrar should be sent **copies of the instrument** by which the charge is created or evidenced: s 395(1). The registrar also has to be sent **prescribed particulars of the charge**.

- The date when the charge was created
- The amount of the debt which it secures
- The property to which the charge applies
- The person entitled to it

4.5 The registrar files the particulars in the companies charges register which he maintains (s 401) and notes the date of delivery. He also issues a certificate which is conclusive evidence that the charge has been duly registered.

Delivery of further particulars

4.6 A mistake in registered particulars can only be ratified by **court order**, with the subsequent registration of a memorandum of satisfaction, if this:

(a) Involves a reduction in the amount secured, or

(b) The registration of a completely new charge, if the amount secured was increased or the property charged changed: s 404

Time period for delivery of particulars

4.7 The 21 day period for registration runs from the **creation** of the **charge**, or the acquisition of property charged, and not from the making of the loan for which the charge is security: s 395(1). Creation of a charge is usually effected by execution of a document. However, it may result from informal action.

The effect of non-delivery

4.8 We have seen that the duty to deliver particulars falls upon the company creating the charge and if no one delivers particulars within 21 days, the company is liable to a fine, as are its officers: s 399(3).

4.9 Non-delivery in the time period results in the **charge** being **void** against an administrator, liquidator or any creditor of a company.

4.10 Non-delivery of a charge means that the sum secured by it is payable by the company forthwith on demand: s 395(2).

Late delivery of particulars

4.11 The rules governing late delivery are the same as governing registration of further particulars, ie a **court order** is required for registration.

4.12 A charge can only be registered late if it is registered '**without prejudice to the rights of parties acquired prior to the time when the charge is actually registered**'. Therefore if a fixed charge is created but not presented for registration until nine months after it should have been, a fixed charge created and registered correctly during that nine month period will have priority over the earlier created charge.

Register of charges

4.13 Every company is under an obligation to keep a copy of documents creating charges, and a register of other charges, at its registered office: s 406(1) and 407(3).

4.14 Section summary

- Floating charges and charges creating a debenture are registerable, along with many other charges.
- The registrar should be sent a **copy** of the charge together with **particulars** of it.

- The registrar issues a certificate which is conclusive evidence of registration.
- Charges should be registered within **21 days** of creation.
- **Non-delivery renders** the **charge void.**
- A **court order** is required for **late registration** to be allowed, or **further particulars** to be accepted.

Question 3

A company creates a charge over a property in favour of Margaret on 1 May 20X0. It creates a further charge of the same type in favour of Chris over the same property on 13 May 20X0. The company has Chris's charge registered on 25 May 20X0, and Margaret's charge on 29 May 20X0. Whose charge ranks first, and why?

A Margaret's because her charge was created first and both charges were registered

B Chris's, because his charge was registered first

C Chris's because his charge was legitimately registered during a period where Margaret's charge was void because it had not been registered

D Margaret's because her charge was created first and Chris's charge was created at a time when Margaret's charge could have been legitimately registered

Answer

C. Margaret's charge would have taken precedence because it was created first had it been registered within the allowed period of 21 days, up to 22 May. However it was not registered until 29 May, and Chris's charge was legitimately registered in the period between 22 and 29 May when Margaret's charge was void. The court would probably have allowed late registration of Margaret's charge but not at the expense of Chris's rights, confirmed by *Re Monolithic Building Co Ltd 1915.*

5 DEBENTUREHOLDERS' REMEDIES

Rights of unsecured debentureholders

5.1 Any debentureholder is a creditor of the company with the normal remedies of an unsecured creditor. He could:

- **Sue** the company for debt and seize its property if his judgement for debt is unsatisfied
- Present a petition to the court for the **compulsory liquidation** of the company
- Present a petition to the court for an **administration order,** that is a temporary reprieve

Rights of secured debentureholders

5.2 A **secured** debentureholder (or the trustee of a debenture trust deed) may enforce the security. He may:

- Take **possession of the asset** subject to the charge if he has a legal charge (if he has an equitable charge he may only take possession if the contract allows)
- **Sell it** (provided the debenture is executed as a deed)
- Apply to the court for its **transfer** to his ownership by foreclosure order (rarely used and only available to a legal chargee)
- Appoint a **receiver** of it

5.3 The **appointment of a receiver** is the usual **first** step.

Receivers

KEY TERM

A **receiver** is a person appointed by secured creditors or by the court to take control of company property.

5.4 The debenture (or debenture trust deed) usually gives power to the debentureholders (or their trustee) to appoint a receiver in specified circumstances of default by the company. The debenture also generally provides that the receiver, when appointed:

(a) Shall have **suitable powers** of **management** and disposal of the assets under his charge

(b) Shall be an **agent** of the **company** and not of the debentureholders by whom he is appointed; the purpose of this stipulation is to safeguard the debentureholders against liability for any wrongful act of the receiver

5.5 Receivers are generally appointed under a floating charge. A creditor with a fixed charge alone normally sells the property.

Administrative receivers

KEY TERM

'An **administrative receiver**' is a receiver who is appointed under a floating charge extending over the whole or substantially the whole of the company's property.

5.6 He is in charge of the company's business, and he must be a qualified insolvency practitioner.

5.7 The secured creditor exercises a contractual power to appoint an administrative receiver when one of the specified 'trigger' events happen, such as failure to repay interest or profits falling below a certain level. However, he must first **demand repayment** in **writing** of the company's indebtedness and only on default can he appoint a receiver.

5.8 A receiver is appointed **in writing** and the appointment takes effect only if the person appointed accepts it not later than the next following day after the notice of appointment is delivered to him.

The effect of the administrative receiver's appointment

5.9 The immediate effect of any appointment of an administrative receiver is as follows.

(a) He **assumes control** of the **assets** subject to the charge and the directors' powers in respect of those assets are suspended during the receivership.

(b) Every **letter, order, invoice** etc issued by the company must state that a receiver has been appointed (eg 'In receivership' on the letterheads): s 39 IA.

(c) If he is appointed by the court or by the debentureholders as their agent, not the company's, his appointment operates to **dismiss employees** of the company automatically (though he may re-engage them if he wishes).

(d) Any **floating charge crystallises**.

(e) Publicity. Within **28 days** of being appointed he must send a **notice** of his appointment to all known **creditors** of the company: s 46 IA. The company must send the administrative receiver a statement of affairs within 28 days: s 47 IA. This will show its assets and liabilities and its creditors.

(f) The receiver within **three months** sends a copy of a **statement** and of his comments on it (or of a summary) **to the registrar**, the company and the debentureholders (and also to the court if he was appointed by the court): s 48 IA. This must cover:

- The **events** leading up to his appointment
- Any **disposal** or proposed disposal of **assets**
- The **carrying** on of the company's **business**
- The amounts expected to be available to other creditors

He must also send a **copy** to **unsecured creditors** and convene a meeting where they can consider it.

Powers of an administrative receiver

5.10 An administrative receiver is automatically given a long list of **statutory powers**, unless the debenture provides to the contrary (Schedule 1 and s 42 IA). These include powers to carry on business, borrow money and sell property.

5.11 Unless appointed by the court, the receiver is an agent of the company unless or until it goes into liquidation: s 44 IA. As agent:

- He is **personally liable** on contracts made in the course of his duties as receiver.
- He is **entitled** to an **indemnity** for that liability out of the company's assets.
- He can **bind** the **company** by his acts.

Functions of the administrative receiver

5.12 The function of a receiver is to manage or to realise the assets which are the security with a view to paying out of those assets what is due to the debentureholders whom he represents (plus the expenses including his own remuneration). If he is able to discharge these debts he vacates his office of receiver and the directors resume full control.

5.13 The **directors** remain in office and can exercise such of their powers as have not passed to the receiver; for example, they may convene a general meeting for the purpose of resolving to wind up the company. They may also take action to **safeguard** the **property** and **interests** of the company, if the receiver is unable or unwilling to do so.

5.14 The general responsibility of the receiver is to the **debentureholders** rather than to the company even if he is formally an agent of the company. The company as principal cannot instruct him on the exercise of his powers.

5.15 The essential distinction between a receiver and a liquidator is that the **receiver** merely **represents** the **secured debentureholders** with control of the assets which are their security - his task is to obtain payment of what is owed to them alone. A **liquidator** is appointed to **realise all the assets**, to pay all the debts of the company and to **distribute** any **surplus** remaining to the shareholders.

Priority of claims in receivership

5.16 The order of application of assets in the hands of the receiver is as follows.

(a) **Payment** of **expenses** of **selling property** or other realisation

(b) The **receiver's expenses** and his claims (if any) against the company under his indemnity; creditors to whom he is personally liable are subrogated to his rights against the company (if he becomes bankrupt), and so their claims come in at this point

(c) Any **expenses** of the **debenture trust deed** including the trustee's remuneration and the costs (if any) of an application to the court to appoint the receiver

(d) **Preferential debts** (if the charge was created as a floating one: s 40 IA)

(e) The **capital** and **interest** of the secured debt

Official receiver appointed by the court

5.17 If the debenture does not give adequate power to appoint a receiver (or to vest him with powers of management) the debentureholders (or their trustee) may apply to the court to appoint the official receiver with appropriate powers: s 32 IA. The court will only make the appointment if:

- **Principal** or **interest** on the **debenture** is in **arrears**
- The **company** has **begun** to be **wound up**
- The **security** is in **jeopardy**

5.18 The official receiver appointed by the court is **not** an agent of the debentureholders nor of the company. He is an **officer** of the **court** whose remuneration is fixed by the court (to be paid by the company). As an officer of the court he has its authority for what he does and it may be contempt of court to obstruct him.

6 TRANSACTIONS AT AN UNDERVALUE AND PREFERENCES 11/01

6.1 When a company goes into liquidation the court may avoid transactions at an undervalue and preferences.

6.2 A transaction '**at an undervalue**' is a gift or a transaction in the two years previous to liquidation (or administration), by which the company gives consideration of greater value than it receives, for instance a sale at less than full market price: s 238. However, such a transaction does not become void if the company enters into it:

- In **good faith**
- For the **purpose of carrying on its business**
- **Believing on reasonable grounds** that it will benefit the company

6.3 A company '**gives preference**' to a creditor or guarantor of its debts if it does anything by which his position will be benefited if the company goes into insolvent liquidation *and* the company does this with the intention of producing that result: s 239.

6.4 If at the time of the undervalue or preference the company was unable to pay its debts, or became so by reason of the transaction, and the company later goes into liquidation or administration, the liquidator or the administrator can apply to the court for an order to restore the position to what it would have been if no such transaction had taken place.

6.5 The relevant period which brings the avoidance powers into operation in relation to a transaction are as follows.

(a) **Undervalues two years** before the commencement of liquidation

(b) **Preferences**

(i) With a person **unconnected** with the company **six months** before the commencement of liquidation

(ii) With a person **connected** with the company **two years** prior to commencement

6.6 Unless the person in whose favour the undervalue or preference operates is connected with the company, the company must be **insolvent** at the time of entering into the disputed transaction, or must have become so in consequence of it, if it is to be disputed by the court.

6.7 If the court is satisfied that a preference has been given it can (under s 241):

- **Order return** of **property** or of the proceeds of its sale
- **Discharge any security** given
- **Order payment** in respect of benefit to the liquidator
- **Renew guarantee obligations** discharged by the preference
- **Charge property**

6.8 The term 'connected persons' appears in the law both in the context of preferences and transactions at an undervalue and also in relation to floating charges. A person is '**connected**' with the company if he is:

- A **director** or **shadow director** (see chapter on directors) of the company
- An **associate** of a director, shadow director or the company itself

6.9 These provisions are summarised below.

Transaction with		*Transactions at an undervalue*	*Preference*
Unconnected person	Time period before commencement	2 years	6 months
	Company insolvent at that time?	Yes	Yes
Connected person	Time period before commencement	2 years	2 years
	Company insolvent at that time?	Yes	No

Chapter roundup

- In this chapter we have discussed the formalities governing a company's borrowing. **Debentures** are important instruments of borrowing, and the security companies give in the form of **charges** supports debentures.
- A **debenture** is a document stating the terms on which a company has borrowed money. There are three main types.
  - A **single debenture**
  - **Debentures issued as a series** and usually registered
  - **Debenture stock** subsidised by a large number of lenders. Only this form requires a **debenture trust deed**, although the others may often incorporate one
- A charge over the assets of a company gives a creditor a **prior claim** over other creditors to payment of his debt out of these assets.
- Charges may be either **fixed**, which attach to the relevant asset on creation, or **floating**, which attach on 'crystallisation'. For this reason it is not possible to identify the assets to which a **floating** charge relates (until **crystallisation**).
- A **floating charge** has been defined as:
  - A charge on a **class** of assets, present and future
  - Which class **changes from time to time** in the **ordinary course of business**
  - Until the **charge** is enforced, the company can deal with the **charged assets**
- A **secured** debentureholder may enforce the security if the company defaults on payment of interest or repayment of capital.
  - He may take possession of the asset subject to the charge and sell it.
  - He may apply to the court for its transfer to his ownership by a foreclosure order.
  - He may appoint a receiver of it (which is the usual first step).
- On liquidation a **fixed charge** on assets has preference. Assets subject to a **floating charge** may be used to settle **preferential debts**.
- A **transaction at an undervalue** is a gift or a transaction in the two years before liquidation or administration, by which the company gives consideration of greater value than it received: s 238 IA. Such a transaction is **void** unless the company acted in good faith and for the purpose of carrying on its business, and believed on reasonable grounds that it would benefit the company.
- A company gives **preference** to a creditor or to a guarantor of its debts if it acts so as to benefit that person's position if the company goes into insolvent liquidation *and* does so with the intention of producing that result: s 239 IA. The transaction will be void if it was created within the 6 months before the commencement of liquidation.

Quick quiz

1 Which of the following are correct statements about the relationship between a company's ordinary shares and its debentures?

   A Debentures do not confer voting rights, whilst ordinary shares do.
   B The company's duty is to pay interest on debentures, and to pay dividends on ordinary shares.
   C Interest paid on debentures is deducted from pre-tax profits, share dividends are paid from net profits.
   D A debentureholder takes priority over a member in liquidation.

2 A fixed charge

   A Cannot be an informal mortgage
   B Can be a legal mortgage
   C Can only attach to land, shares or book debts
   D Cannot be invalid as a preference

3 What are the elements of the definition of a floating charge?

4 Company law requires a company to maintain a register of charges, but not a register of debentureholders.

☐ True

☐ False

5 In which of the following situations will crystallisation of a floating charge occur?

A Liquidation of the company
B Disposal by the company of the charged asset
C Cessation of the company's business
D After the giving of notice by the chargee if the contract so provides
E The appointment of an administrative receiver

6 A debenture trust deed is always required in connection with the issue of:

A A single debenture
B A series of debentures
C Debenture stock
D A secured overdraft facility

7 Certain types of charges need to be registered within 28 days of creation. True or false? (Max 30 words)

8 Certain transactions may be avoided if they occur within a certain time period of insolvency. Match the time period with the transaction.

(a) Floating charge in favour of an unconnected person	(i)	6 months
(b) Transaction at an undervalue	(ii)	1 year
(c) Preference in favour of an unconnected person	(iii)	2 years

9 What particulars of a charge must the Registrar be sent when the charge is registered?

10 What steps can a secured debentureholder take to enforce his security? (Max 30 words)

11 Fill in the blanks in the table.

FACTOR	SHAREHOLDER	DEBENTURE HOLDER
Role	Is a proprietor or .... of the company	Is a .... of the company
Voting rights	....at general meetings	....
Cost of investment	Shares .... be issued at a discount	Debentures .... be offered at a discount
Return	.... are only paid • Out of distributable profits • When directors declare them	Interest .... be paid when it is due
Redemption	.... on redeeming shares	....on redeeming debentures
Liquidation	Shareholders are the ...... people to be paid in a winding up	Debentures .... before shareholders are paid

Answers to quick quiz

1 A, C and D are correct. Whilst the company has a contractual duty to pay interest on debentures, there is no necessity for it to pay dividends on shares. B is therefore incorrect.

2 B

3 The charge is:

(a) A charge on a class of assets, present and future

(b) Which class is in the ordinary course of the company's business changing from time to time

(c) Until the holders enforce the charge, the company may carry on business and deal with the assets charged

4 True

5 A, C, D and E are true. As the charge does not attach to the asset until crystallisation, B is untrue.

6 C

7 False. Certain charges such as charges securing a debenture issue and floating charges need to be registered within 21 days.

8 Floating charge in favour of an unconnected person *1 year*

Transaction at an undervalue *2 years*

Preference in favour of an unconnected person *6 months*

9 A copy of the charge

The date that the charge was created

The amount of the debt which it secures

The property to which the charge applies

The person entitled to it

10 Take possession of the asset subject to the charge

Sell it

Apply to the court for a transfer to his ownership

Appoint a receiver of it

11

FACTOR	**SHAREHOLDER**	**DEBENTURE HOLDER**
Role	Is a proprietor or **owner** of the company	Is a **creditor** of the company
Voting rights	May vote at general meetings	May not vote
Cost of investment	Shares **may not** be issued at a discount	Debentures **may** be offered at a discount
Return	Dividends are only paid • Out of distributable profits • When directors declare them	Interest **must** be paid when it is due
Redemption	Statutory restrictions on redeeming shares	No restriction on redeeming debentures
Liquidation	Shareholders are the last people to be aid in a winding up	Debentures must be paid back before shareholders are paid

The following relevant questions are included in the Exam Question Banks

You can attempt these now. However, we would advise you to attempt these as mock exams at the end of your initial stage of study

Exam Question Bank	**Numbers**
Paper based format	27
Computer based assessment	24, 40

Exam question bank (paper based format)

This Exam Question Bank is in the format of a mock exam for the paper based format. It is the May 2002 exam. You have been directed to the relevant questions at the end of each chapter. Alternatively, you can attempt the whole Exam Question Bank as a Mock exam. If so, you should aim to complete the question bank in 2 hours.

Section A (all questions carry 2 marks)

1 Which ONE of the following statements is **correct**?

A The aim of the criminal law is to regulate behaviour within society by the threat of punishment.

B The aim of the criminal law is to punish offenders.

C The aim of the criminal law is to provide a means whereby injured persons may obtain compensation.

D The aim of the criminal law is to ensure that the will of the majority is imposed upon the minority.

---

2 Which ONE of the following is **correct**?

A The House of Lords is obliged to apply English Law, even if it contradicts European Law.

B The House of Lords must apply European Law even if it contradicts English Law.

C If European and English Law conflict, the House of Lords cannot apply either Law.

D The House of Lords must apply English Law unless it obtains government permission to apply European Law.

---

3 Which ONE of the following is **correct**?

A Professional advisers cannot be liable in respect of negligent advice in the tort of negligence, but may be liable for breach of contract.

B Professional advisers cannot be liable for breach of contact in respect of negligent advice but may be liable in the tort of negligence.

C Professional advisers may be liable in respect of negligent advice in either contract or tort.

D Professional advisers cannot be liable in respect of negligent advice in either contact or tort.

---

4 What is the legal effect of the following statement in a newspaper?

'**For sale. Computer, monitor and laser printer. Good condition. £500.**'

A The statement is an offer for sale.

B The statement is a 'mere puff or boast'

C The statement has no legal effect

D The statement is an invitation to treat

---

5 On 1 September, Seller Ltd wrote to Buyer Ltd offering to sell a machine at a price of £10,000, and stating that Buyer Ltd must accept by 10 September. On 3 September, Buyer Ltd wrote to Seller Ltd and stated 'I accept. Will you accept payment over three months?' On 5 September, Seller Ltd sold the machine to New Ltd, and on 6 September received a second letter from Buyer Ltd accepting the offer and offering to make immediate payment.

Which ONE of the following is **correct?**

A There is no contract between Seller Ltd and Buyer Ltd because the offer was withdrawn on 5 September when the machine was sold to New Ltd.

B There is no contract between Seller Ltd and Buyer Ltd because Buyer Ltd's letter of 3 September amounted to a counter-offer which destroyed Seller Ltd's original offer.

C Seller Ltd and Buyer Ltd contracted on 3 September.

D Seller Ltd and Buyer Ltd contracted on 6 September.

---

6 Which of the following examples of performance amounts to good consideration?

(i) The performance of an existing duty under the general law.
(ii) The performance of an existing contract in return for a promise by a third party.
(iii) The performance of an act, followed by a promise to pay for that act.

A (i) only

B (ii) only

C (i) and (ii) only

D (iii) only

---

7 Which ONE of the following is **incorrect**?

A A term may be implied into a contract by statute.

B A term may be implied into a contract by a court on the ground that the term is customary in the parties' trade.

C A term may be implied into a contract by a court on the ground that it would make the contract more equitable.

D A term may be implied into a contract by a court on the ground of business efficacy.

---

8 Which ONE of the following is **incorrect**?

A A condition is a term which the parties intended to be of fundamental importance.

B A warranty is a term which the parties did not intend to be of fundamental importance.

C If a condition is breached, then the contract must be terminated.

D If a warranty is breached, then the innocent party cannot terminate the contract.

---

9 Which ONE of the following contracts might be specifically enforceable?

A Alan had contacted to sell his house to Bob but has changed his mind and no longer wishes to sell it.

B Chris has contracted to buy a new Ford motor car but the garage is now refusing to honour the contract.

C Diane has contracted to purchase a number of tins of fruit for her business but the seller has now stated that he no longer wishes to proceed with the contract.

D Eduardo has contracted to sing at a concert organised by Fernando, but Eduardo has withdrawn as he has received a more lucrative offer from Giovanni.

---

10 In the event of a breach of contract, what is the purpose of damages?

(i) To punish the contract breaker.
(ii) To compensate the innocent party.
(iii) To put the innocent party in the same position as if the contract has been carried out correctly.

A (i) only

B (ii) and (iii) only

C (iii) only

D (i), (ii), and (iii)

---

11 Which of the following statements suggests that John is an independent contractor in relation to the work he carried out for Zed Ltd?

(i) He is required to provide his own tools.
(ii) He is required to carry out his work personally and is not free to send a substitute.
(iii) He is paid in full without any deduction of income tax

A (i) and (ii) only.

B (ii) and (iii) only

C (i) and (iii) only

D (i), (ii) and (iii)

---

12 Which ONE of the following is normally implied into a contract of employment?

A A duty to provide a reference.

B A duty to provide work.

C A duty to pay wages.

D An employee's duty to disclose his own misconduct.

---

13 A business has been registered under the name 'The Mark Jones Partnership Co Ltd'. What type of business organisation must this be?

A A partnership

B A private limited company

C A public limited company

D Any of the above as this is a business name.

---

14 Which ONE of the following statements is **incorrect** in relation to a public company limited by shares?

A The company must have at least one director.

B The company must have at least two shareholders.

C The company must have issued at least £50,000 of shares.

D The company must state in its Memorandum of Association that it is a public limited company.

---

15 Which of the following is **correct**?

(i) Purchasing a 'shelf company' enables business to commence more quickly

(ii) It is generally cheaper to purchase a 'shelf company' than to arrange for a solicitor or accountant to register a new company.

(iii) Incorporating a company by registration enables the company's documents to be drafted to the particular needs of the incorporators.

A (i) and (ii) only

B (ii) and (iii) only

C (i) and (iii) only

D (i), (ii) and (iii).

---

16 Which ONE of the following is **incorrect**?

A If a company's object is to carry on business as a 'general commercial company', the company may carry on any trade or business whatsoever.

B If a company acts outside its objects clause, it has acted *ultra vires* and the transaction is void.

C A company may ratify an *ultra vires* act by passing a special resolution.

D Any shareholder may apply for an injunction to prevent the directors from taking the company into an *ultra vires* transaction.

---

17 Which of the following statements is **correct**?

(i) The Memorandum of Association of a private company limited by shares may be altered by special resolution.

(ii) The Memorandum of Association of a private company limited by shares may be altered by a written resolution.

(iii) The Memorandum of Association of a private company limited by shares may be altered by an ordinary resolution.

A (i) only

B (ii) only

C (i) and (ii) only

D (ii) and (iii) only

---

18 Bee Ltd has an issued share capital of 1,000 ordinary shares of £1 each. Some of the shareholders would like to pass an elective resolution in order to dispense with the need to re-appoint the auditor annually.

What is the minimum number of votes which must be cast in order to pass the resolution?

A 500 B 501 C 750 D 1,000

---

19 Which ONE of the following is **correct**?

A A company intending to issue new shares for cash must first offer them to the directors.

B A company may dispense with the requirement to first offer new shares to the directors by passing a special resolution.

C A company issuing new shares for cash must first offer them to the existing members.

D A company issuing new shares for a non-cash consideration must first offer them to the existing members.

---

20 Which ONE of the following is **incorrect** in relation to an increase in a company's authorised share capital?

A The board must resolve to increase the authorised capital.

B The shareholders must pass a resolution to increase the authorised capital.

C The authorised capital clause is contained in a company's Memorandum of Association.

D The increase in authorised capital must be confirmed by the court.

---

21 Which ONE of the following is **correct**?

A The shareholders may dismiss a director irrespective of anything in the company's Articles of Association if they pass an ordinary resolution to do so, of which special notice has been given to the company.

B The shareholders may dismiss a director irrespective of anything in the company's Articles of Association if they pass an extraordinary resolution to do so, of which special notice has been given to the company.

C The shareholders may dismiss a director irrespective of anything in the company's Articles of Association if they pass a written resolution to do so, of which special notice has been given to the company.

D The shareholders may dismiss a director irrespective of anything in the company's Articles of Association if they pass an elective resolution to do so, of which special notice has been given to the company.

---

22 Which of the following is **correct**?

(i) Directors may vote themselves such salary payments as they think fit, irrespective of anything in the company's articles of association.

(ii) Directors are only entitled to be paid for their services if the constitution of the company so provides.

(iii) Directors must be paid a salary.

A (i) only

B (ii) only

C (i) and (ii) only

D (iii) only

---

23 Which of the following is **correct**?

(i) Individual shareholders cannot interfere with the management of the company unless authorised by the company's articles of association.

(ii) The majority shareholders can interfere with the management of the company unless prevented by the company's articles of association.

(iii) Irrespective of anything in the company's articles of association, the directors must act in accordance with the directions issued by the shareholders in the form of special resolutions.

A (i) only

B (ii) only

C (i) and (ii) only

D (iii) only

---

24 Which of the following can enforce the fiduciary duties owed by directors?

(i) The majority shareholders.
(ii) The company.
(iii) Individual directors.

A (i) and (ii) only

B (ii) only

C (ii) and (iii) only

D (iii) only

---

25 Which ONE of the following **correctly** describes the circumstances in which directors may be held liable to contribute to the assets of insolvent companies in respect of 'wrongful trading'?

A Where the directors have the intention of defrauding creditors.

B Whenever a company's liabilities exceed its assets

C Whenever a company become insolvent

D Where directors knew or ought to have known that insolvency was inevitable.

Section B

26 George Thompson has carried on a business for a number of years as a self-employed retailer of office furniture. He has now decided to incorporate his business, and to register GT Limited to acquire the business.

Required

(a) Complete this sentence:

'In order to register a private limited company, George will need to submit certain documents to the .... who will issue a certificate of incorporation if everything is in order (maximum of three words in the gap) (2 marks)

(b) Complete these sentences:

'One of the documents which George will need to submit contains the company's name, the situation of the company's registered office, a statement that the liability of the members is limited, and the authorised share capital and its division into shares. This document is called ....
.... and also contains the .... which sets out the business(es) which the company is authorised to carry on.'(maximum of three words in each gap) (4 marks)

(c) In no more than 30 words (in the shaded box below), explain how GT Limited's proposed Articles of association may be affected by the provisions of Table A. (4 marks)

....
....
....
....
....

(d) Complete this sentence:

'If, at a later date, George wishes to increase the authorised share capital of the company, he may do so by passing .... resolution.'

(Maximum of two words in the gap) (2 marks)

(e) In no more than 30 words (in the shaded area below), explain the liability of both the company and George in the event of the business becoming insolvent. (4 marks)

....

....

....

....

....

(26 marks)

---

27 During the sales of a motor car by S (Motor Dealers) Ltd to Anne, the company told her that the car had travelled only '5,000 miles since the installation of a new engine and gearbox'.

After purchasing the car, Anne paid £700 to have the car repainted, but later discovered that it had travelled more like 50,000 miles since the installation. She attempted to return the car and obtain a refund, but S (Motor Dealers) Ltd refused because it had honestly believed it statement to be correct.

As a result, Anne is considering taking legal action against the company for misrepresentation.

Required

(a) In no more than 30 words (in the shaded area below) define misrepresentation. (4 marks)

....

....

....

....

....

(b) State (in the shaded area below), the three types of misrepresentation. (6 marks)

....

....

....

(c) In no more than 30 words (in the shaded box below), identify the type(s) of misrepresentation S (Motor Dealers) Ltd has made and the remedy available to Anne. (4 marks)

....

....

....

....

....

(d) In no more than 30 words (in the shaded area below), explain whether the statement by S (Motor Dealers) Ltd to Anne is also a term of the contract. (4 marks)

....

....

....

....

....

(18 marks)

---

28 Greg, Harry and Ian are the sole shareholders of GHI Ltd. The company has an authorised share capital of £100,000 divided into 100,000 ordinary £1 shares. Greg is the sole director of the company and Harry is the company secretary. At present, the issued share capital is held as follows:

Greg	51,000 shares
Harry	29,000 shares
Ian	20,000 shares
Total	100,000 shares

The company, which has been valued at £300,000, has decided on the following transactions.

- To raise £60,000 in cash by issuing shares to Fiona.
- To borrow £40,000 from AB Bank plc

Required

Complete the following sentences

(a) 'In order to facilitate the issue of the new shares, the authorised capital must be increased by at least .... ordinary £1 shares.' (one figure in the shaded area) (2 marks)

(b) 'In order to issue the shares, Greg must be authorised by the shareholders or by the ....' (maximum of three words in the shaded area) (2 marks)

(c) 'Fiona will become a member of the company when she has been entered in the .... She must also be sent a .... within two months of allotment.' (maximum of three words in each of the shaded areas) (4 marks)

(d) In no more than 30 words (in the shaded area below), explain how Greg's voting power within GHI Ltd will be affected by the issue of shares to Fiona. (4 marks)

....

....

....

....

....

(e) 'If AB Bank plc requires security in the form of a debenture containing a .... charge, then the company will not be able to deal freely with the assets charged in the ordinary course of business. However, GHI ltd will be able to deal freely with assets which are secured by a .... charge.' (one word in each shaded area) (4 marks)

(16 marks)

Exam question bank (computer based assessment)

This Exam Question Bank is designed to reflect the format of a computer based assessment. You have been directed to the relevant questions at the end of each chapter. Alternatively, you can attempt the whole Exam Question Bank as a Mock exam. If so, you should aim to complete the question bank in 1 hour.

All questions, 2 marks each

1 Which of the following applies to a public company?

(i) It can commence business once it obtains a certificate of incorporation.

(ii) If it fails to obtain a s 117 certificate within 1 year of incorporation, a petition may be presented for its compulsory winding up.

(iii) If it commences business before obtaining a s 117 certificate, the transaction remains valid but the company and any officer in default is punishable by fine.

A (i) and (ii) only
B (i) and (iii) only
C (ii) and (iii) only
D (i), (ii) and (iii)

---

2 In which of the following circumstances is it **mandatory** for the DTI to investigate the affairs of the company?

A The company applies for it
B The court orders it
C Members holding at least 1/10 of the issued shares apply for it
D DTI considers that the company's affairs are being conducted in a fraudulent or unlawful manner

---

3 All the following statements relate to sources of law. Which one of the statements is **true**?

A Under the principle of judicial precedent, a judge must follow all previous decisions.
B The House of Lords is the main original source of legislation in the United Kingdom.
C The European Court of Human Rights is an important source of European Community law.
D A by-law made by a local government organisation is an example of delegated legislation.

---

4 In which of the following situations might the plaintiff still have the right to rescind?

A If the parties can no longer be restored to substantially the pre-contract position.
B If the rights of third parties, such as creditors or an insolvent company, would be prejudiced.
C If the party misled affirms the contract after discovering the true facts.
D If the contract has been performed.

---

5 In a case of negligent misstatement involving professional advice, which of the following is needed in order for a special relationship to arise between the person making the statement and the person to whom it is made?

A A contract must already exist between the two parties.
B The person making the statement must have done so in some professional or expert capacity.
C The statement must be made when the parties are face-to-face.
D The loss arising must not be too remote.

---

6 A wrote to B offering to sell surplus equipment for £15,000. B sent a written reply asking if payment could be made by instalments. What is the legal status of B's reply?

A B has made a counter offer.
B B has accepted A's offer.
C B has requested further information.
D B has rejected the offer.

---

7 Which of the following documents must be sent to the Registrar of Companies in order to register a company limited by shares?

(i) A Memorandum of Association
(ii) Articles of Association

A (i) only
B (ii) only
C Both (i) and (ii)
D Neither (i) nor (ii)

---

8 A private company may resolve to dispense with some of the administrative requirements of the Companies Act 1985 by passing an elective resolution. An elective resolution must be agreed to by

A A simple majority of those present and voting at the meeting.
B Seventy five per cent of those present and voting at the meeting.
C Seventy five per cent of all members of the company.
D All members of the company.

---

9 Which of the following does not, under table A, mean that a director must vacate office?

A He becomes bankrupt.
B He is convicted of a criminal offence.
C He becomes of unsound mind.
D He resigns by notice in writing.

---

10 Regarding the appointment of a company secretary, which of the following is true?

(i) A corporation may be a secretary to a company but if A has a sole director who is also a director of B, A may not be company secretary to B.

(ii) A single member private company must have a secretary who is not the sole director member of the company.

A (i) only
B (ii) only
C (i) and (ii)
D Neither (i) nor (ii)

---

11 Which of the following statements is **incorrect** in respect of the tort of negligence?

A No previous relationship need to have existed between the parties.
B To be recoverable the loss must not be too remote.
C The defendant must owe the claimant a duty of care.
D If '*res ipsa loquitur*' is claimed, the claimant must prove negligence.

---

12 Which of the following statements regarding exclusion clauses is incorrect?

A A clause which excludes or limits liability for breach of the implied condition as to title is void in consumer contracts but voidable in non-consumer contracts.

B A clause which excludes or limits liability for death or personal injury resulting from negligence is void.

C A consumer contract for the sale of goods may not exclude or omit liability for breach of the condition relating to quality.

D UCTA 1977 applies to contractual liability which arises in the course of a business.

13 What is the object of an award of basic damages for breach of contract?

A To ensure that the injured party receives payment for acts performed.

B To ensure that the injured party is in the same position as he would have been in had the contract been performed.

C To ensure that the defaulting party does not profit from his breach.

D To ensure that the defaulting party is penalised so that the breach will not recur.

---

14 What limits are laid down by s 320 in relation to substantial property transactions by the directors?

A Not less than £1,000 and exceeds £100,000 or 5% of the company's net asset value.
B Not less than £2,000 and exceeds £100,000 or 5% of the company's net asset value.
C Not less than £2,000 and exceeds £100,000 or 10% of the company's net asset value.
D Not less than £2,000 and exceeds £100,000 or 20% of the company's net asset value.

---

15 Which of the following is incorrect?

(i) The period of notice needed to convene a meeting of a board of directors must be at least 7 days.

(ii) If all the directors of a company are in the same place, no notice of the meeting need be given.

(iii) There is no legal requirement for a notice issued to convene a board meeting to specify the business which it is to transact.

A (i) and (ii) only
B (i) and (iii) only
C (ii) and (iii) only
D (i), (ii) and (iii)

---

16 Which of the following correctly defines an EU Regulation?

A A direction which is directly applicable without the need for national legislation.
B A direction which requires national legislation to give it direct effect.
C A direction which directly binds those to whom it is addressed.
D A clause in a UK statute which is subsequently endorsed by the EU.

---

17 John is employed by a company manufacturing cable. He is injured at work when a cable separates during manufacture and severs two of his fingers. He subsequently finds that his employer was not insured against such an eventuality and was in breach of the Health and Safety at Work Act 1974 at the time of the accident. John may

(i) Sue his employer at common law for failure to provide safe plant, machinery and premises.

(ii) Sue his employer in tort for breach of statutory duty.

(iii) Prosecute his employer for breach of the terms of the Health and Safety at Work Act 1974.

(iv) Prosecute his employer for breach of its duty to insure against the liability to employees for personal injury.

A (i) and (ii) only
B (iii) and (iv) only
C (i), (ii) and (iv) only
D (i), (ii), (iii) and (iv)

---

18 Which of the following statements is **incorrect**?

A A managing director is appointed by the board.
B The board is the agent of the shareholders.
C Individual directors cannot bind the company in contract unless authorised by the board.
D Directors owe duties of care and skill to the company.

---

19 Which of the following is *not* involved in a decision to prosecute for a criminal offence?

A The Director of Public Prosecutions
B The Crown Prosecution Service
C The victim
D The police

---

20 JRD Mechanics Ltd agree to service a fleet of trucks for SGB Enterprise Ltd for a total price of £20,000. Work is agreed to commence on 1 June and to be completed by 15 June. Owing to a strike and to problems with spare parts, the service of all the trucks is only completed on 30 June. JRD Mechanics Ltd admits to breach of contract but disputes the amount of damages claimed, being £10,000 for the loss of half a month's business profits (as certified by the auditors), £20,000 for the loss of certified profits on a new contract which was offered to the company on 20 June but which could not be taken up.

How much will JRD Mechanics Ltd have to pay?

A Nothing. The losses are too remote.

B £10,000. Only normal business profits are recoverable.

C £20,000. JRD Mechanics Ltd should have anticipated the special contract.

D £30,000. Normal business profits are recoverable and it is foreseeable that a severe delay will lost a customer profits which may become available.

---

21 Which of the following statements is **incorrect**?

A All the statutory rules on health and safety at work are set out in the consolidating Health and Safety at Work Act 1974.

B The Health and Safety commission oversees the working of the legislative system governing health and safety issues.

C Inspectors for the Health and Safety Executive have powers of entry and investigation and may issue improvement and prohibition notices.

D Breach of the various statutory duties results in criminal liability punishable by unlimited fine and/or imprisonment.

---

22 The law of contract is of special importance in providing a legal framework within which businesses can operate. In English law, a contract

A Can be entered into validly by all adult persons.
B Is always valid when both parties intend the argument to be legally binding.
C Comes under the remit of both criminal and civil law.
D Need not necessarily be in writing.

---

23 Which of the following is incorrect regarding a company's share premium account?

A Any cash or non-cash consideration received for shares in excess of their nominal value must be transferred to a share premium account.

B If an acquiring company secures 90% or more of the equity capital of another company as consideration for an allotment of its shares, any premium (from the excess of the other company's assets over the nominal value of its shares) need not be transferred to the share premium account.

C Share premium may not be used to pay up fully paid shares under a bonus issue.

D A company cannot distribute any part of its share premium account as dividend.

---

24 Which of the following statements is inaccurate?

A If a company gives a chargee rights over its assets while retaining freedom to deal with them in the ordinary course of business until the charge crystallises, that is a floating charge.

B A floating charge created within 12 months before liquidation may become void automatically on liquidation.

C If a floating charge is created before a fixed charge, it will take priority over the fixed charge.

D Fixed and floating charges should be registered within 21 days.

---

25 Which of the following could apply equally to a private company as to a public company?

(i) Its liability can be limited by guarantee.
(ii) It may offer its securities to the public.
(iii) The authorised share capital must be £50,000 or more.
(iv) It must have at least 2 members and 2 directors.

A (i) only
B (i) and (iv) only
C (iii) and (iv) only
D (ii) and (iv) only

---

26 Exe offers to sell a television for Wye for £100. Which of the following constitutes a valid acceptance of the offer?

A Wye replies: Would you accept £50 now and £50 next week.

B Wye replies: I'll give you £95 for it.

C Wye is happy with the offer so he doesn't reply expressly but waits for the television to be delivered.

D Wye's wife posts a letter confirming that Wye will pay £100 when the television is delivered.

---

27 A director has a common law duty of care to show reasonable competence (Re City Equitable & Co 1925). Which one of the following statements is not correct?

A A director is expected to show the degree of skill which may reasonably be expected from a person of his knowledge and experience.

B A director is required to attend board meetings when he is able.

C A director is entitled to leave the routine conduct of the business in the hands of its management.

D The duty does not apply to non-executive directors.

---

28 X Ltd, Y Ltd and Z Ltd have formed the XYZ unlimited partnership. If the partnership should become insolvent, which of the following statements is **correct**?

A The shareholders of each company are fully liable for the firm's debts.

B X Ltd, Y Ltd and Z Ltd are fully liable for the firm's debts.

C The directors of each company are fully liable for the firm's debts.

D The liability of X Ltd, Y Ltd and Z Ltd for the firm's debts is limited to the amount of their capital contributions.

---

29 Which of the following statements is inaccurate in the case of an action for breach of contract?

A The plaintiff is under a duty to mitigate his loss however he can.
B The plaintiff is under a duty to take reasonable steps to mitigate his loss.
C The defendant must show that the plaintiff has failed to mitigate his loss.
D The duty to mitigate loss is a common law duty.

---

30 Which of the following cannot be achieved by ordinary resolution?

A The dismissal of a director.
B An alteration of a company's Articles of Association.
C An increase in the authorised share capital of a company.
D A grant of authority to directors to enable them to issue shares.

---

31 Builder Ltd was under contract to build an extension for Land Ltd at a price of £40,000. Builder Limited completed three-quarters of the extension, stopped work, and was then placed in creditors' liquidation and failed to complete the extension. Which of the following is **correct**?

A Builder Ltd is entitled to nothing.

B Builder Ltd has substantially performed the contract and is entitled to a reasonable sum in respect of the work done.

C Builder Ltd has completed three-quarters of the work and is, therefore, entitled to £30,000.

D The contract between Builder Ltd and Land Ltd is frustrated.

---

32 An employer owes certain duties to his employees. Which of the following is the employer **not** obliged to do?

A To provide an itemised pay slip to any employee who works eight or more hours per week.
B To provide a reference when the employee seeks other employment.
C To provide adequate materials and a safe system of working.
D To reimburse to the employee all expenses properly incurred in the performance of his duties.

---

33 Which of the following statements regarding the law of misrepresentation is **incorrect**?

A Generally silence cannot amount to misrepresentation.
B All types of misrepresentation enable the innocent party to apply for rescission.
C All types of misrepresentation enable the innocent party to apply for damages.
D An honest statement of opinion by a layman cannot amount to misrepresentation.

---

34 Which of the following is **incorrect**?

A Directors may allot shares provided they are authorised to do so by the articles or by ordinary resolution.

B Authority to allot shares in a private company may be given by means of an elective resolution.

C Where directors allot shares wilfully in contravention of the rules, the allotment is void.

D Authority to allot can be given for a maximum of 5 years in the case of a public company.

---

35 Which of the following is inaccurate?

A A transaction entered into by a company shall not be invalidated because it exceeds the capacity of the company as stated in the memorandum.

B In favour of a third party dealing in good faith, a transaction entered into by a company shall not be invalidated because it exceeds the directors' powers to bind the company or authorise others to do so.

C A member can apply for an injunction to restrain the doing of an *ultra vires* act before it is done.

D The directors are not obliged by law to ensure that the company's assets are not used for *ultra vires* purposes.

---

36 Which of the following is not one of the criteria laid down as standards of behaviour which an employer should demonstrate in his redundancy selection procedures?

A He should offer alternative employment.

B He should give as much warning as possible.

C He should consult with the relevant trade union.

D He should make the selection fairly, having regard to attendance records, job efficiency and length of service.

---

37 In which of the following circumstances is a contract frustrated?

A It becomes impossible to perform the contract by the anticipated method, but an alternative method is available.

B It becomes substantially more expensive to perform the contract.

C The event which was the sole purpose of the contract does not occur.

D It becomes impossible to perform the contract, but one of the parties has accepted the risk of that impossibility arising.

---

38 Which of the following statements is **incorrect**?

A A public company limited by shares must have at least two directors.

B A private company limited by shares cannot invite the public to purchase its shares.

C A private company limited by shares may have one director who may also act as the company secretary.

D A public company limited by shares can invite the public to make loans to the company.

---

39 Which of the following statements relating to minority protection is **incorrect**?

A In order to bring an action for unfairly prejudicial conduct, member(s) holding at least 10% of issued shares must apply to the court.

B If the court finds that the company's affairs have been conducted in an unfairly prejudicial manner, it may make whatever order it deems fit.

C The courts may take the complaining member(s)' own actions into account when deciding whether affairs have been conducted in an unfairly prejudicial manner.

D An order to wind up the company on the just and equitable ground can only be made if no other remedy is available.

---

40 Which of these statements is **correct**?

(i) A public company limited by shares can issue both fixed and floating charges.
(ii) A private company limited by shares may issue only floating charges.

A (i) only
B (ii) only
C Both (i) and (ii)
D Neither (i) nor (ii)

Exam answer bank (paper based format)

1 A C is incorrect as it refers to civil law. D is a red herring. B might be seen as a subsidiary aim, but criminal law primarily acts as a deterrent to prevent certain behaviours in society.

2 B European law is superior to English law.

3 C Professional advisers can be liable in respect of negligent advice under the contract with their client, and may be liable in tort (as in Caparo).

4 D The statement in the newspaper is an **advertisement**, which is an invitation to treat.

5 D Buyer Ltd's statement on 3 September was a request for information. Seller Ltd appears to revoke the offer on 5 September when it sells the machine to New Ltd. However, as that revocation was **not communicated** to Seller, it is invalid, and Seller Ltd's acceptance creates a valid contract.

6 B Performance of an existing duty is not generally good consideration. In (ii), an existing duty under a contract can be consideration in a contract with a third party not related to the previous contract. (iii) is past consideration.

7 C The courts will not interfere to make 'better bargains' although they will sometimes imply terms that it is clear the parties probably intended to make them work (business efficacy).

8 C The innocent party may repudiate the contract, **or** he may affirm the contract. It is his choice. A, B and D are all correct statements.

9 A Specific performance is rarely ordered as damages are the primary remedy. It is never ordered in a contract for personal services, so D is incorrect. It is ordered where the item in question may have specific features which the buyer required. Hence, it might be ordered in the case of land (A). It would not be ordered in B or C, as in both cases (fruit and cars) the buyer would be able to get the same product elsewhere.

10 B You should have recognised the definition of damages here. (i) is incorrect as it is a criminal concept (punishment) and contract falls within civil law.

11 C (ii) would suggest that John is an employee.

12 C An employee is entitled to reasonable remuneration. (Statute imposes a minimum with the National Minimum Wages Act 1998.) There is no general duty to provide work (B), only in exceptional circumstances is this the case.

13 B The 'Ltd' in the title indicates this. D is incorrect as the **registered** name indicates the type of business it is.

14 A In C, the **issued** share capital must be £50,000. Only one quarter of the authorised share capital need be **paid up.** The minimum issued, paid up share capital is £12,500. A public company must have two directors.

15 D (i) and (iii) are clearly correct. (ii) is also likely to be correct, as the fact that it is quicker to purchase a company 'off the shelf' means that the solicitors'/accountants' fees will be lower, as they are the significant expense.

16 B The transactions is not void. The Companies Act 1989 gives commercial security to third parties contracting with the company in s 35, while preserving the rights of members to apply for an injunction against the contact (as option D states).

17 C The clauses of the memorandum which are alterable are only alterable by special resolution. A private limited company may do anything it would to by resolution of a general meeting by a written resolution.

18 D Note that it is an **elective** resolution.

19 C S 89 contains a provision for pre-emption rights when shares are being issued for cash. A private company may disapply pre-emption rights.

20 D The court is not involved in the increase in the authorised share capital of a company. A is correct, because as part of managing the company, the directors determine if an increase in share capital is required, although the shareholders must then authorise it.

21 A Only ordinary resolution is required. A written or elective resolution cannot be used to remove a director.

22 B Directors' pay is determined by the articles. (iii) would only be correct if the director was an employee, which is not necessarily the case.

23 A

24 B The duty is owed to the company and not individual shareholders.

25 D The phrase 'known or ought to have known' should have directed you here.

26 (a) Registrar of Companies

(b) Memorandum of association, objects clause.

(c) GT's own articles will override the Statutory Table A articles where they cover the same subjects. Table A applies to matters not covered in its own articles.

(d) An ordinary (resolution)

(e) GT Ltd would be liable without limit for its business debts. George would be liable for any amount outstanding on his shares for his original purchase.

27 (a)
- An untrue representation of fact
- Made by one party to the other before the contract
- Which is an inducement to the misled party to contract

(b)
- Innocent misrepresentation
- Negligent misrepresentation
- Fraudulent misrepresentation

(c) It appears to be a negligent misrepresentation. Anne may rescind the contract and claim damages. However, it could be constructed as innocent, leading to rescission (or damages in lieu).

(d) The statement is a term because:

- It was made by a trader
- It was made with special knowledge

28 (a) 20,000 (As the company's shares are currently worth £3 each.)

(b) Articles of association

(c) Register of members, share certificate

(d) Greg loses the ability to pass ordinary resolutions on his own, but his diluted holding will still allow him to block all other resolutions.

(e) Fixed, floating.

Exam answer bank (computer based assessment)

1 C A private company can commence business after the certificate of incorporation is issued but a public company must also apply for and obtain a trading certificate. This is the s 117 certificate referred to in (ii) and (iii).

2 B

3 D Option A is wrong because while there are criteria for following a previous decision, this does not mean all decisions are necessarily followed. Option B is wrong because the House of Commons is the main source of legislation. Option C is wrong because European law is made by the Council and the Commission.

4 D In the other three situations there would be no way to rescind.

5 B C and D are irrelevant and A is unnecessary as a liability could arise in tort.

6 C The facts in this scenario were similar to those in *Stevenson v McLean*. Options B and D should have been obviously wrong. Option A is not right because B has not suggested a different contract and seriously varied the terms of A's offer. He has merely asked for more information about the offer that he has been given.

7 A The memorandum of a company limited by shares may be endorsed 'registered without articles of association.' (The statutory Table A articles then become the company's articles in their entirety.)

8 A S 379A

9 B

10 B (i) would only apply if the sole directors of A was also the **sole** directors of B.

11 D In fact, the reverse is true. If ***res ipsa loquitur*** applies, it appears so strongly that negligence has occurred and the defendant must prove that it is not the case.

12 A The implied conditions as to title can never be excluded in a contract for the sale of goods.

13 B Options C and D are wrong as the object of damages is never to punish the defaulting party but to compensate the injured party. Option A is a description of quantum meruit, an equitable remedy.

14 C You should try and learn this rule.

15 A (i) The period of notice need be no longer than is reasonable to enable directors to attend.

(ii) A director may object to this.

16 A B describes a directive. D describes a decision.

17 A The employee has rights both in tort and contract. However, he cannot prosecute his employer. Prosecution is a criminal law action, and is undertaken by the state.

18 B

19 C

20 B Option C should be easily eliminated because if SBG could recover the £20,000, they should also be able to recover £10,000, making Option D the right answer. However, the special profits are too remote to have been in the contemplation of the parties. Option A is wrong because the loss of normal business profits from the use of the cars is reasonably foreseeable.

21 A There are several statutes on this subject, principally the HSWA 74. the Factories Act 1961 and the Offices, Shops and Railway Premises Act 1974. In addition, there are numerous sets of regulations including the Workplace (Health, Safety and Welfare) Regulations 1992, the Health and Safety (Display Screen Equipment) Regulations 1992 and the Management of Health and Safety at Work Regulations 1999.

22 D Option A is wrong because a person may not always have contractual capacity (particularly if he is not aware of what he was doing at the time of contracting). Option B is wrong because the contract may be invalidated by other factors, for example, misrepresentation. Option C is wrong because contract comes under the remit of civil law only.

23 C On the contrary, share premium can be used for this purpose since this merely converts one form of fixed capital into another. B: This is known as merger relief.

24 C The fixed charge ranks first since it attaches to the property at the time of creation whereas a floating charge attaches at the time of crystallisation (whereupon the floating charge becomes a fixed charge and a fixed charge created subsequently ranks after it).

25 A A public company which is limited by guarantee must also have a share capital.

26 D A illustrates a request for further information (Stevenson v McLean 1880). B illustrates a counter-offer where different terms are proposed (Hyde v Wrench 1840). C: Silence cannot constitute acceptance (Felthouse v Bindley 1862). D: Postal acceptance is effective from the time of posting (Adams v Lindsell 1818).

27 D

28 B As companies, they have unlimited liability for their own debts, including the debts incurred as partners.

29 A The plaintiff need not take any risky or discreditable measures.

30 B A special resolution is required to alter the articles.

31 C The doctrine of substantial performance states the party who has performed the work may claim the contract price less a deduction for the work outstanding. In other words, he can claim a reasonable sum.

32 B

33 C A misrepresentee can always rescind a contract, but he can only claim for damages if the misrepresentation was negligent or fraudulent. Option A is correct. Silence can only be a misrepresentation if it is a failure to correct a former representation that has now become misleading.

34 C The allotment is valid but allotting shares in deliberate disregard of the rules constitutes a criminal offence punishable by fine (s 80(9) CA85)

(D) The authority must also be given for a maximum amount of relevant securities. The period can be renewed for a fixed period of up to 5 years. A private company's authority can be given indefinitely or for a fixed period longer than 5 years under the elective resolution procedure (B).

35 D The directors do owe such a duty to the company. Breach of this duty can be ratified by the passing of a special resolution (s 35 (3)). A: s 35(1). B: s 35a(1). C: s 35(2).

36 A The employer is obliged to consider whether an offer of alternative employment can be made but is not obliged to make such an offer.

These criteria were set out by the EAT in Williams v Compare Maxam Ltd 1982.

37 C Extra expense does not represent frustration (B). If an alternative method exists that is not frustration (A). If a party has accepted the risk that performance may become impossible, the contract cannot be frustrated if the impossibility arises.

38 C A sole director cannot also be the company secretary: S 283 (2)

39 A Any member may apply; the limits given are those required for members who wish to request the Department of Trade and Industry to investigate the shares of a company. C is true, although it is not a requirement that the petitioner's conduct is blameless.

40 A A private company can issue both fixed and floating charges.

List of cases, key terms and index

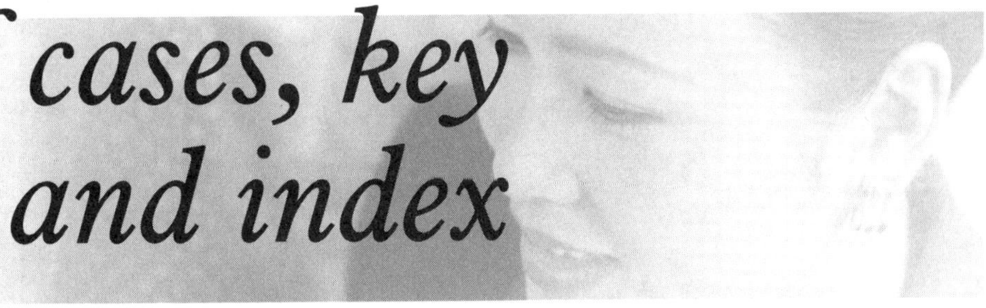

BPP
PUBLISHING

Glasgow Corporation v Taylor 1992, 29
Graham Oxley Tool Steels Ltd v Firth 1980, 138
Grant v Australian Knitting, 75
Greenhalgh v Arderne Cinemas Ltd 1950, 200
Griffin Hotel Co Ltd, Re 1941, 305

H and Others, Re 1996, 174
H Parsons (Livestock) v Uttley Ingham 1978, 102
H R Harmer Ltd, Re 1958, 263
Hadley v Baxendale, 100
Harris v Nickerson 1873, 46
Harvey v Facey 1893, 46
Hayward v Cammell Laird Shipbuilders 1986, 121
Hedley Byrne v Heller and Partners 1964, 31
Hendon v Adelman 1973, 173
Herne Bay Steamboat Co v Hutton 1903, 96
Hillas & Co Ltd v Arcos Ltd 1932, 70
Hivac Ltd v Park Royal Scientific Instruments Ltd 1946, 125
Hochster v De La Tour 1853, 99
Hoenig v Isaacs 1952, 92
Hogg v Cramphorn 1966, 246
Hollier v Rambler Motors 1972, 80
Honeywill & Stein v Larkin Bros 1934, 128
Hong Kong Fir Shipping Co Ltd v Kawasaki Kisa Kaisha Ltd 1962, 72
Howard Marine and Dredging Co Ltd v A Ogden & Sons (Excavations), 61
Howard Smith Ltd v Ampol Petroleum Ltd 1974, 246
Hyde v Wrench 1840, 50

J Spurling Ltd v Bradshaw 1956, 80
Jarvis v Swan Tours 1973, 103
JEB Fasteners Ltd v Marks, Bloom & Co 1982, 32
Jenice Ltd and Others v Dan 1993, 173

Kapadia v London Brought of Lambeth 2000, 135
Kelner v Baxter 1866, 183
Krell v Henry 1903, 96, 97

Laws v London Chronicle 1957, 141
Lee v Lee's Air Farming Ltd 1960, 163
L'Estrange v Graucob 1934, 79
Limpus v London General Omnibus Co 1862, 127
Lister v Romford Ice and Cold Storage Co 1957, 125, 128
Liverpool City Council v Irwin 1977, 77
Lloyd v Grace Smith & Co 1912, 128

MacNaughton (James) Papers Group Ltd v Hicks Anderson & Co 1991, 33
Mahon v Osborne 1939, 29
Malleson v National Insurance & Guarantee Corporation 1894, 198
McArdle, Re 1951, 54
Merritt v Merritt 1970, 52
Metropolitan Water Board v Dick, Kerr & Co 1918, 95
Morgan Crucible Co Plc v Hill Samuel Bank Ltd and others 1990, 33
Multinational Gas & Petrochemical Co v Multinational Gas and Petrochemical Services Ltd 1983, 253

NRG v Bacon And Woodrow And Ernst & Young 1996, 34
New British Iron Co, ex parte Beckwith 1898, 202
Neptune Vehicle Washing Equipment Ltd, Re 1995, 218

Olley v Marlborough Court 1949, 79
Overend Gurney & Co v Gibb 1872, 252

Panorama Developments (Guildford) Ltd v Fidelis Furnishing Fabrics Ltd 1971, 236
Payne v Cave 1789, 46, 48
Paris v Stepney Borough Council 1951, 28
Pavlides v Jensen 1956, 253
Payzu Ltd v Saunders 1919, 103
Pender v Lushington 1877, 268
Penrose v Martyr 1858, 173
Pepper v Webb 1969, 140
Pharmaceutical Society of Great Britain v Boots Cash Chemists (Southern) 1952, 47
Photo Productions v Securicor Transport 1980, 81
Pinnel's case 1602, 6, 57
Planché v Colburn 1831, 92, 105
Poussard v Spiers 1876, 71
Powell v Lee 1908, 49
Price v Civil Service Commission 1978, 134

Note: Key Terms and their references are given in **bold.**

BPP PUBLISHING

BPP
PUBLISHING

REVIEW FORM & FREE PRIZE DRAW

All original review forms from the entire BPP range, completed with genuine comments, will be entered into one of two draws on 31 January 2003 and 31 July 2003. The names on the first four forms picked out on each occasion will be sent a cheque for £50.

Name: ______________________ **Address:** ______________________

____

How have you used this Text?
(Tick one box only)

☐ Self study (book only)
☐ On a course: college (please state)__________
____
☐ With 'correspondence' package
☐ Other ______________________

Why did you decide to purchase this Text?
(Tick one box only)

☐ Have used BPP Texts in the past
☐ Recommendation by friend/colleague
☐ Recommendation by a lecturer at college
☐ Saw advertising
☐ Other ______________________

During the past six months do you recall seeing/receiving any of the following?
(Tick as many boxes as are relevant)

☐ Our advertisement in CIMA *Insider*
☐ Our advertisement in *Financial Management*
☐ Our advertisement in *Pass*
☐ Our brochure with a letter through the post
☐ Our website www.bpp.com

Which (if any) aspects of our advertising do you find useful?
(Tick as many boxes as are relevant)

☐ Prices and publication dates of new editions
☐ Information on product content
☐ Facility to order books off-the-page
☐ None of the above

Which BPP products have you used?

Text	☐	**MCQ cards**	☐	**i-Learn**	☐
Kit	☐	**Tape**	☐	**i-Pass**	☐
Passcard	☐	**Video**	☐	**Virtual Campus**	☐

How did you/will you take the exam for this paper? (Tick one box only)

Written exam ☐
Computer-based assessment ☐

Your ratings, comments and suggestions would be appreciated on the following areas.

	Very useful	*Useful*	*Not useful*
Introductory section (Key study steps, personal study)	☐	☐	☐
Chapter introductions	☐	☐	☐
Key terms	☐	☐	☐
Quality of explanations	☐	☐	☐
Case examples and other examples	☐	☐	☐
Questions and answers in each chapter	☐	☐	☐
Chapter roundups	☐	☐	☐
Quick quizzes	☐	☐	☐
Exam focus points	☐	☐	☐
Question bank	☐	☐	☐
MCQ bank	☐	☐	☐
Answer bank	☐	☐	☐
Index	☐	☐	☐
Icons	☐	☐	☐
Mind maps	☐	☐	☐

Overall opinion of this Study Text *Excellent* ☐ *Good* ☐ *Adequate* ☐ *Poor* ☐

Do you intend to continue using BPP products? Yes ☐ No ☐

On the reverse of this page are noted particular areas of the text about which we would welcome your feedback. Please note any further comments and suggestions/errors on the reverse of this page as well. The BPP author of this edition can be e-mailed at: catherinewatton@bpp.com

Please return this form to: Nick Weller, CIMA Range Manager, BPP Publishing Ltd, FREEPOST, London, W12 8BR

TELL US WHAT YOU THINK

Please note any comments and suggestions/errors below.

FREE PRIZE DRAW RULES

1 Closing date for 31 January 2003 draw is 31 December 2002. Closing date for 31 July 2003 draw is 30 June 2003.

2 Restricted to entries with UK and Eire addresses only. BPP employees, their families and business associates are excluded.

3 No purchase necessary. Entry forms are available upon request from BPP Publishing. No more than one entry per title, per person. Draw restricted to persons aged 16 and over.

4 Winners will be notified by post and receive their cheques not later than 6 weeks after the relevant draw date.

5 The decision of the promoter in all matters is final and binding. No correspondence will be entered into.

See overleaf for information on other
BPP products and how to order

CIMA Order

To BPP Publishing Ltd, Aldine Place, London W12 8AW
Tel: 020 8740 2211. Fax: 020 8740 1184
www.bpp.com Email publishing@bpp.com
Order online www.bpp.com

Mr/Mrs/Ms (Full name)

Daytime delivery address

Postcode

Daytime Tel | Email | Date of exam (month/year)

	7/02 Texts	1/02 Kits	1/02 Passcards	9/00 Tapes	7/00 Videos	Virtual Campus	7/02 i-Pass	7/02 i-Learn	7/02 MCQ cards
FOUNDATION									
1 Financial Accounting Fundamentals	£20.95	£10.95	£6.95	£12.95	£25.95	£50	£24.95		£5.95
2 Management Accounting Fundamentals	£20.95	£10.95	£6.95	£12.95	£25.95	£50	£24.95		£5.95
3A Economics for Business	£20.95	£10.95	£6.95	£12.95	£25.95	£50	£24.95		£5.95
3B Business Law	£20.95	£10.95	£6.95	£12.95	£25.95	£50	£24.95		£5.95
3C Business Mathematics	£20.95	£10.95	£6.95	£12.95	£25.95	£50	£24.95		£5.95
INTERMEDIATE									
4 Finance	£20.95	£10.95	£6.95	£12.95	£25.95	£80	£24.95	£34.95	£5.95
5 Business Tax (FA 2002)	£20.95 (10/02)	£10.95	£6.95	£12.95	£25.95	£80	£24.95	£34.95	£5.95
6 Financial Accounting	£20.95	£10.95	£6.95	£12.95	£25.95	£80	£24.95	£34.95	£5.95
6i Financial Accounting International	£20.95	£10.95							
7 Financial Reporting	£20.95	£10.95	£6.95	£12.95	£25.95	£80	£24.95	£34.95	£5.95
7i Financial Reporting International	£20.95	£10.95							
8 Management Accounting - Performance Management	£20.95 *	£10.95	£6.95	£12.95	£25.95	£80	£24.95	£34.95	£5.95 *
9 Management Accounting - Decision Making	£20.95 *	£10.95	£6.95	£12.95	£25.95	£80	£24.95	£34.95	£5.95 *
10 Systems and Project Management	£20.95	£10.95	£6.95	£12.95	£25.95	£80	£24.95	£34.95	£5.95
11 Organisational Management	£20.95	£10.95	£6.95	£12.95	£25.95	£80	£24.95	£34.95	£5.95
FINAL									
12 Management Accounting - Business Strategy	£20.95	£10.95	£6.95	£12.95	£25.95				
13 Management Accounting - Financial Strategy	£20.95	£10.95	£6.95	£12.95	£25.95				
14 Management Accounting - Information Strategy	£20.95	£10.95	£6.95	£12.95	£25.95		11/02	5/03	
15 Case Study				£12.95	£25.95		11/02	5/03	
(1) Workbook	£20.95								
(2) Toolkit		£19.95 (For 11/02: available 9/02. For 5/03: available 3/03)							
Learning to Learn (7/02)	£9.95								

* For paper 8 and 9, separate editions are available for the November 2002 and May 2003 exams. Please tick the exam you will be sitting.

Total

POSTAGE & PACKING

Study Texts

	First	Each extra	
UK	£3.00	£2.00	£
Europe***	£5.00	£4.00	£
Rest of world	£20.00	£10.00	£

Kits/Passcards/Success Tapes

	First	Each extra	
UK	£2.00	£1.00	£
Europe*	£2.50	£1.00	£
Rest of world	£15.00	£8.00	£

	First	Each extra	
MCQ cards	£1.00	£1.00	£

CDs each £

UK	£2.00	£
Europe*	£2.00	£
Rest of world	£10.00	

Breakthrough Videos

	First	Each extra	
UK	£2.00	£2.00	£
Europe*	£2.00	£2.00	£
Rest of world	£20.00	£10.00	£

Grand Total (Cheques to *BPP Publishing*) I enclose a cheque for (incl. Postage) £

Or charge to Access/Visa/Switch

Card Number

Expiry date Start Date

Issue Number (Switch Only)

Signature

We aim to deliver to all UK addresses inside 5 working days. A signature will be required. Orders to all EU addresses should be delivered within 6 working days. All other orders to overseas addresses should be delivered within 8 working days. *Europe includes the Republic of Ireland and the Channel Islands.